ULTRA AND MEDITERRANEAN STRATEGY

BY THE SAME AUTHOR

Ultra in the West

ULTRA AND MEDITERRANEAN STRATEGY

Ralph Bennett

William Morrow and Company, Inc.
New York

Library of Congress Cataloging-in-Publication Data

Bennett, Ralph Francis.
  Ultra and Mediterranean strategy / Ralph Bennett.
    p.   cm.
  Bibliography: p.
  Includes index.
  ISBN 0-688-08175-4
  1. World War, 1939–1945—Campaigns—Mediterranean Area. 2. World War,
1939–1945—Secret service—Great Britain. 3. World War, 1939–1945—Cryptography.
I. Title.
D766.B46 1988
940.54′23—dc 19   88-28626
                                                                              CIP

Printed in the United States of America

1 2 3 4 5 6 7 8 9 10

BOOK DESIGN BY NICOLA MAZZELLA

**TO MY SONS,
FRANCIS AND EDWARD**

PREFACE

Only the strange reverse-chronological order in which the material was released prevented this book—or something like it—from preceding *Ultra in the West* as the first to be based on the Ultra signals sent to commanders in the field between 1941 and 1945: it seemed natural to begin at the beginning rather than with the last twelve or eighteen months of the war, but this proved impossible.

Two unforeseen advantages have flowed from the compulsion to write in an unnatural order, however. The value of Ultra had long been recognized on all sides by D-day, and few then doubted the preponderant role it should play in intelligence and therefore in decisions based on an appreciation of the enemy's intentions and capabilities. In the second place, once the success of the FORTITUDE deceptions was assured, Ultra could say little of strategic significance (save in the Ardennes, where it went unheeded) though a great deal about operations large and small. On both counts, therefore, while many strands of detail had to be woven together in order to display the wide range of information provided by the source, the tale to be told was relatively plain and straightforward.

Things were very different during the previous four years. The supreme importance of Ultra had not yet been fully realized in 1941, and at a time of anxious defense in a war which was continually spreading into new theaters, strategy and the best use of scarce resources was a prime concern. It was in the Mediterranean that Ultra won its spurs, so to speak, and demonstrated that it was capable of rendering major assistance in strategic planning. The history of the war in the Mediterranean shows how this potential gradually came to be recognized, and thus offers scope for reflection on the developing relation of intelligence to military events. More may be learned from it than from an account of the war in the west.

Much has been written about these events in the last ten years, and many of the leading actors in them have published their memoirs; it has been an immense advantage to read their accounts during the composition of this book. In attempting to do justice to the riches and variety of my material, however, I have profited most from the verbal accounts of their experiences generously given me by some of those who served in the Middle East and Italy in senior positions. Among them I owe special gratitude to Field Marshal Lord Harding of Petherton and Sir David Hunt (both were directly concerned in almost every phase of the war in the Mediterranean), who have repeatedly allowed me to cross-question them about how they interpreted and used the intelligence provided by Ultra at particular junctures. Second only to them, I am deeply indebted to the late Lieutenant General Sir Terence Airey and Sir Edgar Williams, respectively chief intelligence officers of the Allied Armies in Italy and of the Eighth Army in the desert, for valuable information about the campaigns they helped to direct; and also to the late Elisabeth Barker and Sir William Deakin, who generously put their intimate knowledge of Yugoslav affairs at my disposal. I have profited greatly from conversation and correspondence with the late Patrick Beesly, Lord Freyberg, Mrs. Jean Howard, Mrs. Mary Noble, Sir Stuart Milner-Barry, Edward Thomas, and the late Gordon Welchman. I thank them all most warmly.

I am most grateful for the guidance of my British and American agents, Andrew Lownie and Michael Congdon, and for the care of my editors, Bruce Lee and Peter Straus. David Charles's clear and informative maps have more than fulfilled my request to him; he has my very warm thanks.

The British Academy made me a most generous grant for

the purchase of microfilms, and Magdalene College, Cambridge, and the History Faculty, Cambridge, made smaller grants for the same purpose. I acknowledge with grateful thanks their kindness in assisting and speeding up my work.

I thank also the staffs of the Public Record Office and the Imperial War Museum for the help they have regularly given me.

Every Ultra-based statement in the following pages is supported by one or more signals, but all references to the signals (like all other references) have been placed at the end of the book; when it was desirable to draw attention to the speed with which a particular piece of information was passed to commands abroad, the reference is given in the form 1630/10 JP 3955 1958/10. This means that signal number JP 3955 was derived from an Enigma message originating at 1630 hours on the tenth day of the month (the month is usually evident from the context) and was dispatched at 1958 hours on the same day—i.e., that only three hours and twenty-eight minutes separated the German and British times of origin; if no exact German time of origin was stated in the signal, the figures "1630/10" are replaced by a phrase like "early 10" or "10 September." Where no precise indication of time is given, it may usually be assumed that the relevant signal was passed within twelve hours of the German time of origin, but that it did not seem necessary to record the exact time of transmission. The vast majority of signals fell into this second category. There was also a small third category, where decrypt and hence signal were delayed for days or even weeks by cryptanalytic difficulties.

It has sometimes been necessary to refer to non-Ultra sources, whether contemporary or subsequent, to fill in a gap or reinforce an argument. I have endeavored always to frame my sentences to make the distinction immediately apparent, but I cannot hope that I have always succeeded. In order to avoid another unintentional ambiguity of language, I have always referred to communications between Germans in Enigma as "messages" and to Anglo-American derivatives from them as "signals."

Neither the nature of the Enigma machine nor the manner in which messages encrypted on it were rendered into intelligible German was widely understood in 1979. I therefore thought it wise to begin *Ultra in the West* with a chapter entitled "How It Was Done." Readers who would like to refresh their minds on these matters may do so by reading Appendix XIV, which is a shortened version of this chapter.

RALPH BENNETT

Cambridge and London

February 1988

CONTENTS

MAPS AND DIAGRAMS

1
BEGINNINGS—AND ROMMEL
February–June 1941

The breaking of the German Wehrmacht's Enigma cipher by the cryptanalysts of Bletchley Park in 1940 was an intellectual feat which was capable, as the few who knew about it quickly perceived, of giving Britain and her allies an immense advantage in the conduct of the war. For it promised, if the initial breach in the enemy's cryptographic defenses could be widened, to give access to the other side's military secrets on a scale never dreamed of by any previous belligerent.

The novelty of the situation did not consist only in the breaking of a supposedly invulnerable machine cipher, however. In combination with other cryptanalytic successes in similar fields over the next few years, it inaugurated a revolution which elevated intelligence to a more prominent position in military affairs than it had ever had before; the silicon chip and the computer have since then made the revolution permanent.

High-grade signals intelligence, it was found, could provide something no other source had been able to provide in the past—a reliable insight into the enemy's strategic thinking. Until the age of wireless, this had usually been unattainable. An agent could rarely gain access to records of discussions at the highest military or political level. Sending word of his discoveries out across hostile territory quickly enough for them to retain their value presented enormous difficulties; and, on receipt, every

15

piece of agent-derived information had to be assessed for reliability (had the agent been duped or persuaded by threat or
bribe to turn against his employer and "plant" misleading information?) before use could be made of it. The advent of radio,
and the mass use of it for military purposes, created an entirely
new situation. Radio enabled politicians at home, almost as
much as generals in far-off theaters of war, to control operations
from a distance; but if their communications could be intercepted and decrypted, a whole new field of hitherto inaccessible
knowledge was opened up to their enemies. As General Erich
Fellgiebel, head of the Heeresnachrichtenwesen, warned his
staff in 1939, *"Funken ist Landesverrat"* ("To use the radio is to
betray the country").

The first sign of the new intelligence situation was the British success in reading the German naval code during the
1914–18 war, but the significance of this feat was not widely understood. Thus the pre-radio state of affairs still prevailed in
1939. Military intelligence was not highly regarded by the fighting soldier, whose peacetime training attached a low value to it:
"Intelligence is rather a special kind of work and has a very
small place in the army in peace-time" was Haig's opinion after
World War I, for instance. Ultra—intelligence derived from
Enigma decrypts—brought about a complete reversal of this
position as soon as its range and depth were fully displayed in
the summer of 1942.

This book tells how Ultra influenced the war in the Mediterranean and how, from being at first only one among several
ingredients of military intelligence, none of them very highly regarded, it gradually became the chief constituent first of British,
then of Allied intelligence, carrying the whole concept of intelligence itself and of its part in military operations to a position of
far greater prominence than it had ever held before in the armed
forces of any country in the world. Since almost all the admirals,
generals, and air marshals who liberated Europe from the Nazis
in 1944–45 had learned the secret of Ultra and the immense
benefits of using it during their previous service in the Mediterranean, this is also in large part the story of how they and those

who served under them were prepared for the greatest campaign of their lives. For the intelligence officer and his commander, as for the fighting man, the Mediterranean was the training ground for the west. Experience gained, directly or indirectly, in Egypt, Tunisia, and Italy was applied to even greater purpose in France and Germany, and through Ultra, Mediterranean strategy brought direct influence to bear on subsequent events in the West.

The primary advantage of Ultra over all previous types of military intelligence was its reliability. Since it consisted entirely of private communications among Germans unaware that they were being overheard, it was completely trustworthy. This was in sharp contrast with the air of uncertainty inseparable from all agent-derived intelligence. It was impossible, of course, to be sure that everything relevant to a particular topic would be transmitted by radio and intercepted—whenever feasible, telephone, teleprinter, or courier were preferred to the laborious process of encryption, transmission by Morse, and subsequent decryption—but because both sender and receiver believed their communications to be secret, it was free from all suspicion of deceit. It did not necessarily follow that the eavesdropper had only to translate an intercepted message to comprehend its full meaning, however. All evidence, decrypted "hot" news from the field of battle as much as an obscure Latin phrase in Magna Carta, has to be considered in its context, principally the circumstances of its origin and the natural, unspoken assumptions of its author.

Until the summer of 1942, Ultra was somewhat deficient in both these respects. Incompleteness of coverage and incompleteness of context—these were the two principal barriers to the full acceptance of Ultra in its first twelve or eighteen months. Some of the many variants of Enigma were more difficult to solve than others, and the army keys were prominent among them. In consequence, there was almost no army context to Luftwaffe information (the air force keys were easier to break) for almost a year after the German intervention in the desert war, and (as will be seen) this caused some serious misjudgments. But all major difficulties had been overcome by the summer of 1942, and from that time onward Ultra played a leading part in the direction and prosecution of the war.

By that time, experience had also shown that decrypting German messages was not by itself enough to extract the promised advantage. Even translating the text could present quite formidable difficulties when unfamiliar technical terms were used, for instance, or when one message referred to another which had not been intercepted. Above all, a need was soon felt for specialists who possessed, or could develop, a feeling for the implications of sometimes obscure or cryptic messages and the patience to tease out the military intelligence hidden within them by drawing on their own gradually accumulating stock of relevant experience and the voluminous card indexes in which every scrap of information derived from Enigma was carefully recorded. These necessary remedies could not be applied at once, of course, and it was in fact some time before the cryptanalysts' achievement was matched by an equal ability on the part of others to convert the product of their skill into precise military intelligence, assess it correctly, and apply it effectively in the field—that is to say, before the potential advantage was fully realized in practice.

In retrospect, the length of time (twelve months or more) that passed before the information derived from Enigma was properly exploited is less surprising than the fact that the need to separate cryptanalysis from intelligence and to develop the peculiar skills the latter required was recognized at all. Very few possessed these skills in 1940, and fewer still could foresee that exploiting Enigma would call for them in a novel form and on an immense scale, for within a year or two Ultra became by far the largest and most reliable source of intelligence for all three services. Twenty-five years earlier, when the German naval code was broken, the desirability of such a separation had not been appreciated: cryptanalysis played the dominant role between 1914 and 1918, and no satisfactory system for disseminating the intelligence thus obtained was ever devised, with the result that full advantage of the decrypts was seldom taken. Had it been otherwise, Jutland would almost certainly have been a resounding victory.

It was of the greatest moment for the future, therefore, that it was realized during the winter of 1940–41 that there were three distinct stages in the exploitation of Enigma—decryption, translation, and the assessment of intelligence—and that it would be best to keep the three stages separate from each other as a matter of ordinary routine, but at the same time to encourage the closest cooperation among the three resultant working parties on the frequent occasions when the insights of one could help to solve the problems of another.

No steps to service Enigma on a twenty-four-hour, round-the-clock basis were needed or taken until the 1941 campaigns in North Africa and the Balkans greatly increased the daily output of decrypts. Ultra scarcely influenced the fighting in Norway and France in the spring of 1940. It affected the Battle of Britain and the countermeasures against the radio beams which guided the first German bombing raids much more directly, but the one was of short duration and the other of limited intelligence scope. Apart from what concerned the Blitz, Ultra slumbered during the winter of 1940–41. The Luftwaffe general key,[1] though already being broken every day, yielded very little, because in the absence of an active land front there was seldom much need to use radio, for most business could be better transacted by telephone or teleprinter, to which Bletchley had no access. Thus at the beginning of 1941 no one had enough evidence to do more than guess how illuminating the new source of intelligence might become once land fighting was widespread again, or how it could best be used. Nor had anyone much experience of weaving together separate items from it into a pattern intelligible to field commanders and capable of helping them to make their battle plans. Hut 3[2] was full of German scholars who could make quick and accurate translations of the decrypts, but as yet

---

[1] Known as Red, from the color of the crayon used to number the intercepts. It was first broken early in 1940, and before long was being decrypted every day. No naval Enigma was broken until the spring of 1941, and even then there were often serious gaps in decrypting one or another of its several variants. Army Enigma resisted all assaults until later in 1941, and much of it was only broken intermittently for several months thereafter.

[2] The department at Bletchley Park which dealt with all German army and air decrypts, the primary material on which this book is based.

it contained scarcely any trained intelligence officers; nor were there many more in London or Cairo.

This was the situation when the Mediterranean theater suddenly sprang into life in February and March 1941. Rommel landed in Tripoli on 12 February,[3] and German armies invaded Yugoslavia and Greece on 6 April. In all these areas, land lines were few or nonexistent, with the result that the air was soon filled with potentially decryptable Enigma messages. Almost at once it became clear that many of these messages could affect the fate of British troops in Cyrenaica, Greece, and, before long, Crete, and that speed in transmitting the essence of them could determine their value in action. Accordingly, it was decided to cut out the unavoidable delays of the existing method (translations forwarded from Bletchley to London, where the service ministries composed occasional signals for the field) by authorizing Hut 3 to draft and transmit Ultra signals direct as need arose,[4] and before long an exclusive radio link was established for the purpose. This enlightened decision had extremely important consequences. As a result of it, before long Hut 3 contained a small, self-trained, but highly professional body of intelligence officers who were rapidly becoming familiar with the peculiarities of Enigma intercepts and skillful at avoiding their hidden pitfalls (the inescapable consequence of the fact that many of the intercepts were random scraps of secret correspondence which had to be read without the background or context which would have explained their sometimes impenetrable allusions), but not afraid to suggest deductions which might prudently be drawn from incompletely understood facts. Rather more slowly, a corresponding body of officers familiar with Ultra grew up at the receiving ends in Cairo, Alexandria, the Western Desert, and Malta, and upon the mutual trust and

---

[3] To the best of my belief, it was on the same day that I first reported for duty in Hut 3. With the exception of the six-month period mentioned on pp. 104, 131n, I remained there until the end of the war.

[4] A note about the signals will be found in Appendix I. These signals embody the essence of such decrypts as were thought to be of operational value to the Middle East and later to the Italian and western theaters of war. They have now been released to the Public Record Office. The translations of the decrypts which underlay them, and the translations of decrypts dealing with other theaters of war, have not been released.

understanding of these two groups a great deal of the subsequent high reputation of Ultra was founded. The signals, it should be emphasized, were summary telegrams conveying the essence of the underlying decrypts in succinct form, together with such explanatory comment as previous experience or past Ultra information might suggest; they never included tactical or strategic conclusions or recommendations.

The first signal over the new radio link to the Middle East was sent on 13 March; this was little more than a fortnight after the first encounter between British and German troops in the desert, and the same length of time before Rommel's first offensive, while the invasion of Greece and Yugoslavia was only a month away. The few short weeks before these two emergencies, therefore, were all that the intelligence officers in Hut 3 (more of whom were now being recruited and trained) were granted in which to acquire preliminary experience in the art of composing precise and unambiguously informative signals—an art which, it was soon discovered, is much more difficult than it seems at first sight—and it was several months before trial and error taught us how to avoid the major pitfalls. Although comparison of some of the early signals with those composed later, when more experience had accumulated, strongly suggests that more skillful drafting could have made better use of the material, we were nevertheless able to send much potentially valuable intelligence to all three Mediterranean fronts in April and May 1941, when it was badly needed.

A misdirected scrupulosity on the part of those who laid down the security regulations placed the recipients under a handicap as great as that presented by our inexperience. Few if any of them were yet told the truth about the source of the new intelligence they were receiving, and most were asked to believe that an impossibly omniscient agent called Boniface or Agent OL was providing the information. In these circumstances, generals brought up to distrust all agents' reports and to rely on no intelligence save that gained through battle contact can hardly be blamed for paying little heed to Hut 3's signals, particularly after our first really prime strategic offerings proved unexpect-

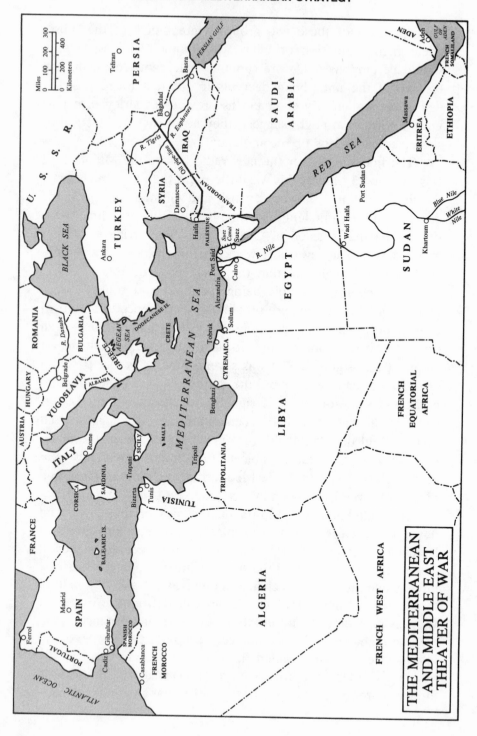

THE MEDITERRANEAN
AND MIDDLE EAST
THEATER OF WAR

edly misleading.[5] The relative value of any piece of intelligence depends on its provenance, and they were being deliberately denied knowledge of it. Moreover, the British army was still suffering in 1941 from shortages of all kinds (notably of specialists in armored warfare and intelligence work), was still using obsolete equipment over a range extending from tanks to petrol cans, and was still dominated by outmoded ways of military thought—so that its leaders could in any case hardly have made full use of the best possible intelligence even if the strategic situation had not compelled them to disperse their efforts in so many directions at once. The Royal Navy and the Royal Air Force were only slightly better off. It would be profitless to labor these well-known criticisms of Britain's unreadiness for war any further, but it is necessary to outline them again in order to explain one of the reasons why Ultra did not have a more direct and a more beneficial influence on events in 1941. However accurate it may be, information about the enemy can never alone be enough to win battles. It must first of all be properly understood and assessed, and then the force necessary to take advantage of it must be ready to hand. (This fundamental truth, which is too often overlooked, has recently been forcefully restated by General Sir David Fraser.) Ultra could not be fully effective until both conditions were met; neither was completely satisfied until the summer of 1942.

What was expected of Ultra in these early days, before it had proved its value and before its recipients had had a chance to discover its strong and weak points? Almost certainly, only the simplest and most direct tactical advantage and little else, it would appear from the first examples of its use in practice. It was only gradually realized that, on the contrary, the use of Ultra for tactical purposes faced two formidable obstacles. Time was one: a German message had to be intercepted, passed to Bletchley, decrypted, translated, assessed for intelligence value, and finally signaled to field commands, which then needed time

---

[5] Rommel remained aggressive, although there was apparently conclusive Ultra evidence that he would become quiescent, in the shape of instructions that he was to halt his advance. See p. 41, below.

to convert it into operational orders which could be used in battle. Even under exceptionally favorable conditions, it proved impossible to complete all these processes in less than two or two and a quarter hours—but meanwhile the bombing raid or the tank attack ordered by the original message might already have taken place. (There was also an inescapable interval—short or long, according to circumstances—between the receipt of the signal at the W/T station in Cairo or the desert and the moment when it was placed in the hands of the general or air marshal who could use it. In course of time, it was found that the Y Service could almost always beat Ultra for tactical purposes because it could be delivered sooner;[6] most tactical Ultra provided confirmation rather than new intelligence. Security was the other obstacle. Almost every day from the summer of 1941 until the fall of Tunis in May 1943, advance notice of the routes and sailing times of single tankers or convoys carrying reinforcements and supplies from Italy or Greece to Libya came off the decoding machines. To make direct use of them by attacking the ships, however, might arouse suspicions in German or Italian minds that their signals were being read, so the strictest orders were issued that a sighting by an aircraft on an apparently routine patrol over the area must always precede an air or surface strike, for the sinking of even the largest convoy could not compensate for the loss of the source which would probably follow an alarm and a precautionary change of cipher.

Two developments encouraged the shift in interest from tactics toward strategy. As time passed, more keys were broken, some of them used on radio links reserved for the high command. This traffic naturally carried strategic material, rather than the tactical material which was the business of the keys broken hitherto. Secondly, as intelligence officers at both ends became more accustomed to handling Enigma material, so attention focused increasingly on long-term matters like orders from Hitler or OKW, statistics of petrol and ammunition stocks and consumption rates, aircraft strength returns, tank losses and

---

[6]The Y Service decrypted lower-grade (i.e., less secure and more easily breakable) frontline communications. Interception and decryption were carried out only a short distance behind the front, and the results were made available at once.

new deliveries, and similar matters from which fluctuations in the offensive power of Rommel's and Kesselring's forces could be deduced and the time they would need to prepare for the next offensive forecast.

This process of evolution was slow, however, and the full benefits which flowed from it were long in coming. Although it sometimes seemed otherwise at the time, the results of disseminating Ultra intelligence in 1941 must now be judged on the whole disappointing. Churchill quickly appreciated Ultra's potential value, and so did its daily practitioners at Bletchley Park, but he was sometimes hasty in his attempted application of it and they had no authority to direct its use, their sole function being to inform field commanders, not to counsel them. As has already been pointed out, intelligence was then not highly regarded, and those who had the power to use it in battle often lacked the will to do so. "From 1939 to 1942 intelligence was the Cinderella of the Staff and information about the enemy was frequently treated as interesting rather than valuable," wrote Montgomery's Chief Intelligence Officer in 1945, emphasizing that "Ultra, and only Ultra, put intelligence on the map," and dating the process from June 1942 and its completion from Ultra's forecast of Alam Halfa about the middle of August. The forecast was, of course, the basis of Montgomery's successful battlefield countermeasures, but the chief significance of this advance knowledge of Rommel's last attempt to turn the Alamein line and break through to the Delta was strategic.

Almost as soon as Italy entered the war, Hitler offered Mussolini two armored divisions to help him in North Africa, but the Duce haughtily rejected the implication that he could not defend his empire himself. Since by the autumn of 1940 he was already issuing directives for the occupation of Greece and Russia, Hitler was content to leave it at that until the extraordinary success of Wavell's and O'Connor's winter offensive in Cyrenaica caused him to revive his offer and to send Fliegerkorps X to Sicily to protect Italian and harass British shipping in the Mediterranean. Well before O'Connor captured Tobruk (21 January 1941) and a month before he un-

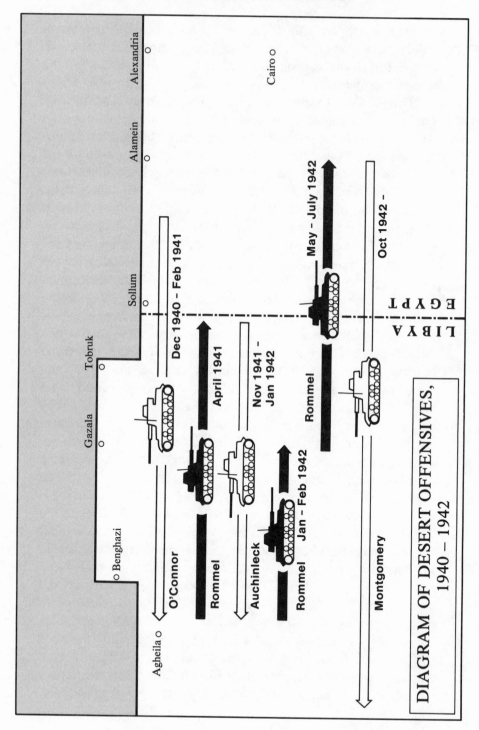

DIAGRAM OF DESERT OFFENSIVES, 1940 – 1942

ceremoniously bundled the Italians out of Cyrenaica, Hitler had decided that Italy could not be allowed to lose all her African territories and had proposed to send in mid-February a blocking force (it consisted at first of the hastily cobbled-together 5th Light Division) strong enough to stop the British and even to mount local counterattacks, but no more. This time Mussolini had no choice but to agree.

Churchill's immediate reaction to Wavell's success was to urge him to pursue the Italians and secure Tripoli as a supply port; if this called for more men and equipment, then "Ask, and it shall be given you," he cabled. But this, the mood in which he had risked sending tanks to the Middle East after Dunkirk, was soon replaced by the first of his many complaints about the disproportion between "teeth and tail" in the Army of the Nile and an order to comb out rearward services. Then on 10 January 1941—the same day that Hitler decided to send a blocking force to Libya—Fliegerkorps X attacked the aircraft carrier *Illustrious* (a heavy raid on Malta followed in the same week) and Ultra confirmed the existence of a Nazi threat to the Balkans. Churchill, who had long urged maximum help to Greece against opposition from the soldiers, at once laid it down that while nothing must stand in Wavell's way until he had captured Tobruk (it fell ten days later), "thereafter all operations in Libya are subordinated to aiding Greece."

By the time, two months after this, that Hut 3 sent its first signal to Cairo—nearly 100,000 more, addressed to fifty or more different field commands, were to follow by the end of the war—the resultant competition between Libya and Greece for the scanty British forces available had already reached a critical stage. The likelihood of German intervention in both countries had long been foreseen: one Axis partner might naturally feel bound to come to the aid of the other as he reeled back in shameful defeat, while there would be an even stronger moral obligation upon Great Britain to assist the intended victims if the latent German threat to the Balkans (the Italians were there already, having occupied Albania in 1939 and invaded Greece—with small success—in October 1940) should ever materialize. Symbolically, 8 February can be seen as the day on which the uncertainties of the winter resolved themselves and the pattern of the next three tumultuous months began to emerge—but only symbolically, for none of those whose duty it was to decide between competing claims seems yet to have grasped quite what was at stake or to have analyzed the issues clearly enough. Two events of that day cast long shadows into the future: the first contingent of the Afrika Korps left Germany for the south, and the Greek government asked for conversations about the strength and purpose of a British expeditionary force, should one be sent later on to help repel a second invader.

On receiving the Greek request, Churchill promptly halted Wavell, ordered him to hold the Cyrenaican frontier with minimum forces, and instructed him to prepare to move troops to Greece. Moral and political considerations were uppermost here: how could Britain aspire to lead Europe back to freedom and solicit American assistance in the task if she remained passive while the Nazis overran a country to which Chamberlain had pledged support as long ago as 1939? Long-term rather than short-term policy ruled, moreover, since possible present loss was discounted for the sake of honor and the future—for although the transfer of 30,000 men, 240 guns, and 140 tanks fatally weakened the defense of Cyrenaica, not even all the men and matériel in the whole Middle East could match the German armies now shown by secret intelligence to be assembling along the eastern frontier of the Reich for the invasion of Russia and the Balkans. Prudent military strategy was set aside in favor of a gesture—it could never have been more—in the service of a higher cause. Since all would be lost if the British base in Egypt was lost, however, one essential precondition to risk-taking ought to have been examined more carefully before the gesture was made: did the competent military authorities on the spot feel that the desert flank would still be safe if thus weakened in favor of Greece? At that moment Wavell (Commander-in-Chief in the Middle East), O'Connor (the general who had routed the Italians), and the staff in Cairo all believed that they could continue to advance and would be able to take Tripoli (without its port, the Germans could not even land in Libya) if left alone for a few more days,[7] and were confident that even with Tripoli, Rommel could not attack until May.

Both these conclusions were hasty and ill-founded, one of them disastrously so. The later experience of British and Germans alike suggests very strongly indeed that although it might have been possible to put together a mobile column strong enough to rout the remaining demoralized Italians and capture Tripoli before the Germans arrived (Rommel's successful adventuring in the coming April was along the same lines), it would have been extremely difficult to keep the column supplied on its way and quite impossible to maintain it in Tripoli for long. The thousand-mile land route was far too arduous, and the sea route impracticable against the assaults of Fliegerkorps X from the air. It is this which undermines any attempt to urge that a great opportunity was lost when O'Connor was forbidden to drive on for Tripoli.[8] The second conclusion (that Rommel could not attack until May), which was at least partly based on imperfectly understood Ultra, was equally mistaken.[9] But it was Wavell's grievous error in believing that he could denude the desert with impunity that underlay the disasters of the next few months, prevented the defense of Cyrenaica, and lost almost all that O'Connor had won. This, rather than an allegedly missed op-

---

[7]Many years later, it appeared that Rommel was of the same opinion at this time (Rommel, 95).

[8]Correlli Barnett overlooks this obstacle to the argument he puts forward in *The Desert Generals*. The excited assertion on pp. 67–68 of his second edition (1983) that Ultra confirms his 1960 arguments does not hold water. He castigates Churchill for preventing O'Connor from advancing to Tripoli and for thereby missing a great opportunity. O'Connor indeed saw a now-or-never tactical opening, but he did not pause to weigh up its logistical implications. Subsequent reflection can easily detect his oversight. Unweakened, he could have consolidated the frontier as a springboard for a later advance. But to go farther then would have risked losing all. (Rommel was equally inclined to "press on regardless"—that was his weakness as well as his strength—believing that supply could be compelled to conform to his tactical demands. Montgomery—admittedly with the bitter experience of his forerunners to warn him—took the opposite course, pausing at perhaps too frequent intervals to secure his supplies for the next advance.) Ultra had nothing to say about the chances of capturing Tripoli: there was no relevant Enigma when Churchill ordered Wavell to give Greece priority over Libya, nor even on the day of Beda Fomm (7 February), the battle which completed the annihilation of the Italians. It was not Ultra, though it gave a great deal of information about the German buildup in the Balkans, but politics supported by military misjudgment, which led to British intervention in Greece.

[9]See pp. 39–40, below.

portunity over Tripoli, is what so damagingly affected future strategy.

It was no doubt right in the peculiar circumstances of 1941 that the moral should ultimately prevail over the military and that the gesture to Greece should be made. But neither London nor Cairo seems to have realized that they knew less about Libya than about the Balkans (they remained so until Rommel's attack made Ultra more informative), and that this distorted their judgment; nor, unhappily, did they always draw the same conclusions from the same evidence. Wavell's appreciation was wrong when he made it, and it became more wrong with every day that passed, as Rommel sized up his opportunity. There is, moreover, reason to believe that he had already made up his mind on moral grounds before he was asked to consider intervention in Greece as a practical proposition, and this in spite of the fact that neither on a visit to Athens in mid-January nor during the longer stay he was now about to make was he allowed to inspect the Greeks' preparations for defense. At all levels, the question of aid to Greece was already so prejudged by early February, well before any final decisions were taken, that perhaps nothing could have put cold military calculation back into its rightful place in the forefront of discussion. An i ,superable obstacle prevented the unbiased appreciation of unwelcome intelligence—a situation which was to recur more than once during the war, but seldom with such far-reaching and disastrous strategic consequences.

Churchill's "halt" order to Wavell was accompanied by a decision to send Eden and Dill (respectively Foreign Secretary and Chief of the Imperial General Staff) to the Middle East to investigate and report. As the final decision approached, Churchill hesitated, cabling them, "Do not consider yourselves obligated to a Greek enterprise if you feel it will only be another Norwegian fiasco"; their prompt reply was strongly slanted in the opposite direction and recommended immediate aid. Until very recently, the CIGS had been vehemently opposed to the project: he had told the Cabinet so on 11 February, thereby provoking Churchill's wrath and an angry signal to Wavell specifically ordering aid to Greece and forbidding the attempt to reach Tripoli which he had hitherto urged. But now Dill changed his mind, and Wavell's was the dominant voice in his conversion. Yet Wavell too had originally been opposed to intervention, on the ground that it entailed too much risk; he seems to have come round to the opposite view, for reasons that are not clear, about the middle of February, and at once to have become an ardent supporter of the expedition. When all of them went to Athens on 22 February, Wavell confidently asserted that the troops he could spare from the desert stood every chance of stopping a German drive into Greece (Dill had already cabled London to the same effect), yet he had in front of him an appreciation drawn up by his own staff which expressed the contrary opinion! Furthermore, he knew that the RAF could not provide fighter cover.

It was at this meeting that the Greeks agreed,[10] reluctantly and under pressure, not to fight for Salonika and the north but to withdraw to the more defensible "Aliakhmon Line," the only position which the British believed offered any hope of successful defense. Next day the Cabinet in London accepted the advice of the men on the spot (Wavell's and Dill's recommendation overcame Churchill's previous hesitation), aware that the three commanders-in-chief were parties to it but unaware that these same commanders-in-chief could not justify their opinion in sound military terms because they had not seen the state of the Greek defenses or founded an appreciation on the evidence (or the lack of it) in their possession.[11] Furthermore, the Cabinet's decision was taken in the face of warnings from the Chiefs of Staff and the Director of Military Intelligence at the War Office to the effect that the expedition had little chance of success unless Turkey and Yugoslavia came in on the British side (which was then very unlikely), and that without them every man landed in Greece might be lost. Skepticism was not confined to the soldiers: Sir Alexander Cadogan, Permanent Under-Secre-

---

[10] Or did they? Carlton, 173–77, chronicles the subsequent disputes over exactly what was agreed on this point and blames Eden for blurring Wavell's clear call for an immediate withdrawal to the Aliakhmon Line.

[11] Sir Bernard Fergusson, who was Wavell's ADC at the time, said that Wavell was never asked for such an appreciation (Kennedy, xiii), but this is at best an incomplete excuse.

tary at the Foreign Office, recorded in his diary his belief that "we shall be alone with the Greeks to share their inevitable disaster."

Authorized now to reconnoiter the Greek defenses (though without seeing them for himself), Wavell seems to have begun at last to realize how poor the prospects of halting an invader really were. But neither this, nor the move of German troops into Bulgaria, nor the opinion of his DMI in Cairo, Brigadier Shearer, that the Germans could retake Cyrenaica unless it was reinforced instead of being stripped its defenses, nor even two disturbing items of news he received on 2 and 3 March—none of these sufficed to change his mind. The disturbing items were that the Greeks had not withdrawn to the Aliakhmon Line as arranged, and that Rommel would be ready to attack sooner than expected. The second came from the newly broken Light Blue Enigma key used by the GAF in the Mediterranean, which revealed the scale of the German buildup in Libya. Thus the British preparations for LUSTRE (the code name for the Greek expedition) went forward in what Alan Moorehead called "the hope that precedes adventure," rather than after sober military calculation.

Wavell's obstinacy is puzzling. At that moment there were no British troops in Greece (the first disembarked on 7 March), so that there was still just time for him to have second thoughts (his staff were already planning evacuation!) and to seek permission to reduce the scale of aid to Greece in order to safeguard his desert flank.[12] The very fact that he had scarcely enough men, guns, and tanks to meet all his existing commitments (he was responsible for East Africa as well as the Middle East) should surely have suggested that a smaller contingent might constitute a sufficient gesture toward the Greeks while also permitting the retention of a force large enough to defend Cyrenaica. It is particularly striking that he took almost all his serviceable tanks away from the desert, since his first visit there had shown that the few that were left were almost all worn out

---

[12]The first sign of this did not come until 3 April, when Rommel was already attacking: two divisions earmarked for Greece were diverted to face him.

by the mileage they had covered chasing the Italians. Admittedly, Wavell received very little accurate information about Rommel's strength and intentions during these weeks (though his later excuse that it was "so poor and vague that I largely discounted it" is unacceptable), but it is still hard to understand how the man who created the Long Range Desert Group to procure information from behind the enemy's lines and established "A" Force to deceive German intelligence gatherers could manage to disregard the warnings he was given. It was no excuse to say, in his official dispatch, that no definite information about German troops in Africa had been received "up to the middle of February." The Cabinet's final decision to aid Greece was not taken until 7 March, three weeks later, and although it may have been taken largely on moral and political grounds, it was Wavell's (and Dill's) unjustified confidence which entitled Eden to recommend it so strongly.[13]

During the 1930s, Wavell had acquired a reputation as a "thinking general," better equipped intellectually than his contemporaries to understand broad military concepts and the likely effects of new weapons and techniques. What he did—still more, what he did not do—in the spring of 1941 shows him to have been nearer the common run than many supposed. Perhaps he was already past his best by then, a general fated by the date of his birth (1883) to reach his peak during the militarily barren years of peace, as Eden eventually concluded. In 1937, aged fifty-four, he confessed to feeling stale and expected to be put on the retired list before long. Asked in 1939 for his opinion of several candidates for command of the British Expeditionary Force in France, the military historian and publicist Liddell Hart told Hore-Belisha (Secretary of State for War) that Wavell had "formerly been a man of marked originality of thought . . . but seemed to have gone off in the last year or two." As recently as 1934, Liddell Hart had thought him "a progressive soldier," although too "inclined to defer to superior rank," and recalled an

---

[13] Chur~~~~ ~~~~ newed hesitation, Eden's persuasion, and above all the reliance everyone
~~~~ ill-founded) optimism of the three Cairo commanders-in-chief are the
~~~~ of the account in Gilbert, vi. 1026–1030. Tedder laid the chief blame on
~~~~ *judice*, 32).

occasion when Wavell had immediately retracted unorthodox views on military training which he had just expressed in a lecture because the chairman, an officer senior to himself, took exception to them. Wavell had bowed to authority again, if with a somewhat ill grace, in August 1940 after a brush with Churchill (who told Eden that he did not find in him "that sense of mental vigour and resolve to overcome obstacles which is indispensable to successful men"). Eden's uncritical conviction that the Greek expedition was politically sound may have combined with a soldier's habit of obedience and his own sense of honorable obligations to make Wavell overlook his primary duty of calculating the balance of military advantage and disadvantage in cold blood. As Dill was to write in 1943, "Drive is not Archie's strong suit."

The major share of the blame must nevertheless rest on Eden's shoulders. The soldier is the servant of the politician in a democracy, and Churchill had taken the unusual course of investing Eden with plenipotentiary powers to decide about Greece. Eden did not, in fact, use these powers, but he knew that his advice would sway the Cabinet. It was therefore his responsibility to cross-examine Wavell until he either exposed the flimsy factual basis of his recommendations or satisfied himself that LUSTRE'S prospects were good enough to justify the manifest risks entailed. He plainly did neither; nor did he secure the "precise military appreciation" which Churchill demanded and which would have condemned the operation.[14] This is all the more strange because in November 1940 Eden had opposed the Greek expedition on the realistic ground that "Egypt is vital, Greece is not." Wavell's desert victories (but they were really O'Connor's) during the winter appear to have changed his mind; he and Dill had earlier been Wavell's champions, and events now seemed to justify their good opinion of him and prove Churchill's criticisms wrong. This is the view of Eden's latest biographer, who quotes Eden's recommendation to the Cabinet on 7 March: "Collapse of Greece without further effort on our part to save her by intervention on land, after the Libyan victo-

---

[14] See Appendix II, "The Mood of Early 1941."

ries had, as all the world knows, *made forces available,* would be the greatest calamity" (my italics). It was ironical that Europe was not much impressed by the moral gesture, and that the Greeks soon turned against the monarchy which the British action had been designed to support.

Only a small share can be assigned to Ultra of responsibility for failing to prevent the mistakes which led in April to the loss of all that had recently been won in the desert and in May to the disasters in Greece and Crete. By no means all of the comparatively little that was relevant seems to have been sent to the Middle East in any case, and the staffs in Cairo could not be expected to esteem it highly since they did not know what it was and so could not accord it the importance it deserved. By the time of the first direct signals in mid-March, the die had been cast in the sense that the desert was almost bare and that the British contingent had arrived in Greece; and none of the twenty or so signals between then and the start of Rommel's advance gave any hint of what was about to happen. A year or so later, when Ultra was more familiar to the generals and their intelligence officers, it is just possible that five orders for aerial reconnaissance of the British positions might have been hesitantly interpreted as indications of a coming attack. But they could equally well have been routine sorties—and it must not be forgotten that more than three years later a great deal of much more solid evidence of exactly the same kind before the German Ardennes offensive of December 1944 was completely misread.

There was not enough Ultra to have prevented the loss of Cyrenaica even if its every slightest hint had been heeded, and it is no prejudiced defense of the embryonic direct-signaling service to say so. Neither was the enforced British retreat to the Egyptian frontier simply the consequence of the departure of most of the army which had annihilated the Italians. It was also in great measure due to the defects of military tactics and foresight, which were themselves but one facet of that opaqueness of understanding, narrowness of outlook, and lack of professionalism which were to wreck so many of the desert army's plans for the next eighteen months and to prevent it from making the best use of equipment which, though in many respects woefully defective, would have been sufficient for the purpose if properly applied. The extent to which the pre-1939 British army fell short of what was required to fight Germans in the 1940s was realized far too slowly.[15]

Brooke, Dill's successor as CIGS, was more responsible than any other single individual for remedying these defects; he called the Greek expedition "a definite strategic blunder . . . a dangerous dispersal of forces." With hindsight, Churchill was of the same opinion: in September 1941 he said that LUSTRE was the only error the government had yet made. The blunder and its consequences could not be undone, but from them flowed still greater ills, for by seeming to explain the British retreat in Cyrenaica simply by LUSTRE, they helped to delay the necessary adaptation to German-style warfare. Errors of judgment, not lack of information about the enemy, were the primary cause of all this, but unfortunately they were soon compounded by the serious—though, in the circumstances, entirely pardonable—misinterpretation of several striking pieces of Ultra intelligence.

The directive in Rommel's pocket as he reviewed the first detachment of the Afrika Korps in front of Government House, Tripoli, on 14 February made it clear that his function was to stop the British from advancing further—and no more (or as Halder, the chief of the German Army General Staff, unkindly

---

[15]The defects and the rigid yet paradoxically "amateur" outlook of the British army between 1918 and 1939 have most recently been analyzed by Brian Bond, *British Military Policy Between Two World Wars* (esp. pp. 35–71), and their lamentable consequences underlined by General Sir David Fraser, *And We Shall Shock Them* (esp. pp. 2–23). Brooke's strictures are quoted in Fraser, *Alanbrooke,* passim.

Because it was less professional and less well trained than the German, the British army was the slower to adapt to desert conditions and to the demands of tank warfare (see, for instance, Lewin, *Afrika Korps,* 19; Westphal, 122; Carver, 255). British troops had been stationed in Egypt for many years past; but the 15th Panzer Division, which had fought through the 1940 campaign in France as infantry and had only been converted to tanks in November, was usually superior to its opponents from the moment it landed.

The repeated failures of British leadership in the early years and—most important for the proper use of a new, delicate, and potentially battle-winning type of intelligence—the prevalent lack of receptivity to new ideas are cruelly exposed and psychologically explained in Dixon, *On the Psychology of Military Incompetence* (esp. pp. 110–29, 288–301). See also Carver, *Dilemmas,* 16, 51, 121, 134, etc.

put it, "to see that Graziani does not go right back to Tripoli without fighting"). He was to establish a defensive front on the Gulf of Sirte but otherwise to act under the orders of the Italian High Command, subject to two conditions: his German troops were not to be split up, and he had the right of appeal to Berlin.[16] (Similar provisions applied to the Australian, New Zealand, and South African contingents under Wavell and his successors.) The corresponding Luftwaffe commander, General Geissler of Fliegerkorps X in Sicily, who controlled some 450 aircraft, was answerable not to the Italians but direct to Goering.

Within a week of landing, Rommel had pushed a reconnaissance screen as far as Nofilia, and Fliegerfuehrer Afrika (Generalmajor Froehlich), sent by Geissler to support him, had arrived with 50 Stuka dive-bombers and 20 fighters. Rommel was ready for anything by the time of his first clash with the British (curiously enough, it occurred on 22 February, the day of the decision to aid Greece), but GHQ Cairo was still convinced that he could not advance "for a considerable time." This was a rational estimate inasmuch as it reflected the difficulty the British had already found in supplying even a thinly held front seven hundred miles from base in Egypt, as well as anticipating the similar problem which soon faced the Afrika Korps. But it did not foresee that Rommel might improvise enough supplies for his tiny force and drive it across Cyrenaica as swiftly as he had driven the 7th Panzer Division across France in 1940, demoralizing a weakened opposition into headlong retreat. The most regrettable feature of British optimism was that it persisted for so long in the face of contrary evidence. Wavell still believed that there would be no advance "for a month or more," right up to the day Rommel opened his offensive on 30 March; the furthest he would go to meet Churchill's anxiety over the loss of the outpost at Agheila on the 24th was to "admit to having taken considerable risks in Cyrenaica."

A junior officer, returning from an official mission, reported to Halder on 7 March that Rommel's plans needed "clarification and a firmer grasp of what is possible." The High

---

[16] Formally, this arrangement continued in force throughout his stay in Africa.

Command, too, had not yet thought out its policy clearly. Halder, usually a skeptic about Rommel and Africa, was for a moment prepared to go far enough beyond the original "blocking force and counter-attack" scheme to approve an early assault on Tobruk, and even to contemplate Egypt as the objective for the following spring. When Rommel flew to Berlin on 19 March,[17] he prudently told Hitler only that he hoped to attack Tobruk in the autumn, but he was sternly ordered to confine himself to defense until the 15th Panzer Division arrived in May, and even then not to envisage anything more for the time being; an early attack on Tobruk was expressly ruled out. Removed far from all possibility of control by his return to Libya, however, Rommel saw that the capture of Agedabia on 2 April had opened the gateway into Cyrenaica and at once determined to disobey orders, coolly telling his Italian superiors that he had been given freedom of action. On the same day, Luftwaffe HQ Berlin declined to send more Ju-88s to Tripoli on the ground that "the centre of gravity of operations is elsewhere" (i.e., in Yugoslavia and Greece, which were invaded four days later); this was decrypted quickly and signaled in midafternoon. Before midnight, Churchill sent the complete text (in a slightly different translation; without the German, it is impossible to judge which was the more accurate) to Wavell, deducing from it that Rommel had no great force at his disposal and urging that every effort be made to drive him back.

This was the first of a number of similar interventions by Churchill, incautiously excited at the prospect of directing strategy in the light of Ultra and of using it to bend the generals to his will. The Prime Minister's authority naturally strengthened the existing tendency to believe that there was nothing much to fear from Rommel. The same conclusion seemed to follow from an OKW reminder to him that his advance was against orders (this apparently became known through Enigma, although there is no signal on the subject), and from the most striking of the scanty and intermittent Ultra signals of the next four weeks,

---

[17]Ultra revealed that he was going on the day the direct-signaling service began, but the news seems to have been sent to Cairo by another route (BI i.392).

which repeatedly drew attention to shortages of petrol and ammunition. Evidence in them that the Afrika Korps was heavily dependent on air supply helped to sustain the impression that it would soon grind to a halt, particularly when so much aircraft fuel was lost in one of the three ships the RAF sank on 4 May that flights had to be restricted.

Disobedience on a gigantic scale was not to be expected of any German general, particularly from one whose troops were few and not yet acclimatized, and the Ultra evidence reinforced this natural opinion. But in this the British were badly mistaken: despite his feats the previous May, they did not yet know their Rommel, his independence of mind and his speed of action. Cutting across the bulge of Cyrenaica and throwing his astonished enemy into confusion, he was outside Tobruk in a week and over the Egyptian frontier in a fortnight, boasting that he would soon be across the Nile and on the banks of the Suez Canal. Ruthlessly driving forward, he plunged straight into a hasty attack on the strongest sector in Tobruk's defenses because he was too impatient to wait for maps of the fortifications or to reconnoiter them properly, and was bloodily repulsed. Tobruk held out against all assaults and was a thorn in his side for another twelve months, but already he had scared Wavell into contemplating the possible loss of Egypt, the base on which the British position in Greece, Crete, and the whole Middle East depended. It was still only mid-April, just a few short weeks since Wavell had been planning to capture Tripoli.

So swift and so total a reversal of fortune was not only a grievous shock, contrary to what it had been natural to suppose was absolutely reliable evidence; unhappily, by this time Ultra was also preparing to make it still more difficult to understand what had happened and still harder to forecast the future. Persuaded by his recent behavior that Rommel had taken leave of his senses and that things were in a mess in Africa, Halder sent Generalleutnant Paulus (the same who was to surrender the Sixth Army at Stalingrad two years later) to restrain him. As a very senior member of Halder's staff and also an old friend of Rommel's, Paulus might be able to bring personal influence as well as formal authority to bear. Paulus reached Rommel's

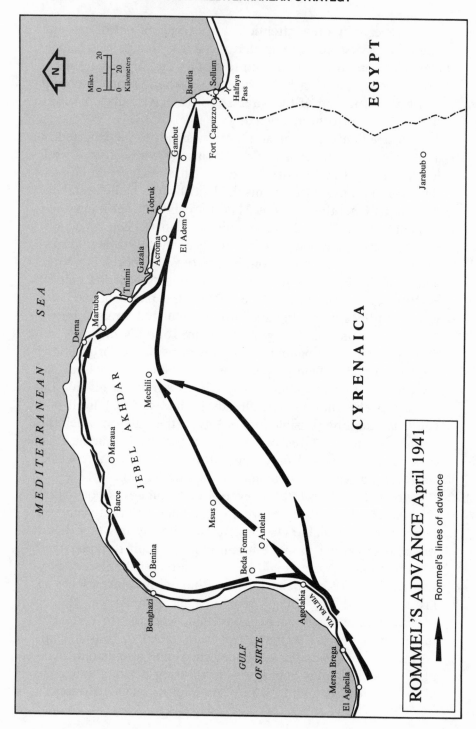

ROMMEL'S ADVANCE April 1941

→ Rommel's lines of advance

headquarters outside Tobruk on 27 April (Ultra revealed the visit of "Genlt Paulus, a specialist in armoured troops"), and a few days later reported to Halder the instructions he had given Rommel. Because he was many miles away from the terminal of the Tripoli-Rome cable, he sent them in Luftwaffe Enigma, with the result that a signal embodying their seven points went off to Cairo at dawn on 4 May. It said that Rommel was to hold what he had won but that, because his men were exhausted, he was not to advance further without orders, even after the arrival of the 15th Panzer Division,[18] for it was more important to retain Cyrenaica than to take Tobruk, Bardia, or Sollum. In addition, he was to prepare a reserve position at Gazala (halfway back across the "bulge"), and was given discretion to retire to it if he thought necessary. Nothing was, in fact, farther from Rommel's mind than retreat, as his actions soon showed.

The pattern of events which had followed the "centre of gravity" signal was now repeated. In the early hours of 5 May, Churchill sent Wavell a commentary on Paulus' instructions (the full text of which followed on the 7th),[19] emphasizing their "highly secret and authoritative character" and urging him to use his knowledge of them to launch his own attack as soon as possible, sharply reminding him that the necessary means were

---

[18]The 15th Panzer Division began its move to Africa in mid-April. Ultra tentatively reported it at Derna on 1 May (OL 203) and on 6 May listed several units belonging to it which had been sunk on passage (OL 235). Westphal, *Erinnerungen,* 117–20, uses this to show how British countermeasures hindered the German buildup.

[19]Connell, *Wavell,* i.427–29, adding that the information was derived from "a cipher which had lately been broken in London." Since Connell's book was published in 1964, this was an implicit revelation of the breaking of Enigma more than ten years before it was officially admitted.

Gilbert's reference (*Churchill,* vi.1080–81) to this wire of Churchill's is marred by a misleading footnote. Wavell, he says, "had been receiving Enigma decrypts direct from Bletchley Park," while Churchill "scrutinised . . . the original decrypts on which the messages to Wavell were based." In fact, neither saw *decrypts,* if that word be restricted to its proper meaning—the decrypted German text. Churchill saw teleprinted *translations* of the decrypts, and Wavell saw *summary telegrams* (OLs) *based on the translations.* Similarly, when Churchill "objected to the wording of a telegram . . . on the ground that it did not convey 'the atmosphere' of the original decrypt," the word "translation" should be understood in place of "decrypt." Churchill sometimes demanded a second translation and ordered this to be sent to Wavell verbatim, but without having seen the original in German (of which his knowledge was slender), so that his ability to judge "atmosphere" is open to question. There is an earlier example of this on p. 38.

on the way in the shape of the 200 or more tanks recently dispatched by the direct route in the "TIGER" convoy. The tanks ("Tiger cubs," Churchill playfully called them) reached Alexandria on 12 May, but without waiting for them Wavell sent all his reserves up to the front, where Brigadier Gott began an operation code-named BREVITY on the 15th. BREVITY was the first attempt at the operational use of Ultra in Africa, but, launched at Churchill's behest before adequate preparations could be made, it was a poor omen for the future. It ran into far more opposition than had been bargained for and soon came to an ignominious halt. British radio insecurity gave Rommel an accurate idea of his opponents' strength, and because no army Enigma key had yet been broken, Ultra had not yet begun the regular series of Afrika Korps tank returns which were so valuable later on. Very much the same is true of BATTLEAXE, the offensive which Wavell himself set in motion in mid-June, again at Churchill's insistence. British intelligence seriously underestimated the German armored strength a second time. Once more, intercepts gave Rommel plenty of warning, and although he had to save himself by "one of the greatest decisions of his career"— a well-timed tactical move of the 15th Panzer and 5th Light divisions—he was quickly able to blunt the axe and compel a British withdrawal.

Ultra had nothing to say about the ground situation either before or during BATTLEAXE (it had produced a little for BREVITY), yet this was only incidental to the failure. The "Tiger cubs" Churchill had trumpeted so loudly about had been shipped in such poor condition that most of them needed overhaul, and many were in the workshops so long that they took no part in BATTLEAXE. As soon as the fighting started, Rommel gained the upper hand by his skillful siting of 88mm antiaircraft guns for use against tanks; their shells could penetrate the thick armor of the British Matildas, off which smaller calibers bounced harmlessly. Rommel had used 88s against British tanks in France and again during BREVITY, but the British command was so far from understanding what he was about that for a long time to come German tank guns were blamed for destruction they had not caused. Although he had only a dozen 88s in June,

Rommel won the battle with them. There was nothing in Ultra up to that time about 88s, nor any hint of the use to which they were being put, save a single report on 18 May that 3,000 armor-piercing rounds were being sent to Africa along with 12,000 high-explosive shells for the 88s. It does not seem to have been noticed that this meant that one-fifth of the whole consignment was not intended for the 88s' normal antiaircraft role but for use against tanks in the land battle.

This incident is a reminder that a main obstacle to the successful use of Ultra in these early days was that whole categories of information were still completely missing from it. There were none of the directions about the use of 88s in ground or air combat, for instance, which were later common in the west. Again, Paulus' directive was exclusively concerned with ground strategy, but because army Enigma had not yet been broken, there was no infrastructure of military detail to give it depth and perspective. Army officers in Hut 3 were not likely to forget this, as they waited in vain for comparable employment while their RAF colleagues were busily composing signals about changes in the strength and location of Fliegerfuehrer's bomber and fighter Gruppen, which were now frequently reported. But at a higher level it may not have been so unmistakable. Over-anxious to turn Ultra to good account and to win victories in the desert to compensate for defeats elsewhere, Churchill had goaded Wavell without even pausing to wonder whether Paulus' words could bear the weight of interpretation he placed upon them without independent support. Neither he nor his advisers at home or abroad had the imagination to perceive the un-wisdom of basing strategy upon a single piece of uncorroborated evidence, no matter how unimpeachable its source. Unhappily, there was as yet nothing in Ultra like the later daily "Flivo" (air liaison officers') reports—which would have shown that Rommel was not acting in the spirit of Paulus' instructions—to warn Churchill that this single piece of evidence, though absolutely reliable in itself, was very far from giving the whole picture.

No war had ever yet been directed by men in possession of so copious a selection of other side's secrets as Ultra was beginning to provide. Everyone, therefore, had to learn from scratch the delicate interpretative touch required, and in these early days some found it difficult to bear constantly in mind that what they were reading was only a *random selection* of secrets, however remarkable a selection. Yet Churchill himself had in all likelihood already come nearer than anyone else to practicing this unfamiliar art. As First Lord of the Admiralty, in November 1914 he had established the famous Room 40 to decode German radio communications and had based action on its discoveries, while in the 1920s he had made a close study of the Secret Service's Russian decrypts. His experience might have been expected to prevent him from jumping too readily to conclusions from a single message in isolation, without background and without expert professional commentary. However—in 1941, at any rate—this was not his way. Years ago, as a young war correspondent in South Africa in 1900, he had decided that strategy and tactics were "just a matter of common sense. . . . Put all the elements of a problem before a civilian of first-rate ability and enough imagination and he would reach the right solution, and any soldier could afterwards put his solution into military terms." He was still acting according to the same belief forty years later, although on the larger stage of a world war this simplistic viewpoint could often put things badly out of focus. Wavell remarked later on that "Winston is always expecting rabbits to come out of empty hats," and Brooke, after working with him for four years, gloomily reflected that "he can never see a whole strategical problem at once . . . [but] settles on some definite part of the canvas and the rest of the picture is lost." Brooke had, in fact, hit the nail on the head after only a few weeks' experience of Churchill's ways: "Politicians still suffer from that little knowledge of military matters which gives them unwarranted confidence that they are born strategists."

Once his mind was made up and "Action this day" demanded, he was irresistible, because "his menacing power was overwhelming." Mrs. Churchill had to warn him of his overbearing ways almost as soon as he became Prime Minister, and his impatient manner was losing him friends a year later. Only

Brooke stood up to him regularly, and even he found the task of restraining his master's impetuousity exhausting. Churchill's interventions in the spring of 1941 unfortunately led to hasty, ill-prepared, and unsuccessful attacks which associated Ultra more closely than necessary with the misfortunes of BREVITY and BATTLEAXE, thereby helping to delay it in acquiring the reputation it was beginning to deserve.[20] For Wavell, the price of failure was dismissal.

There was another facet to what might almost be called the double deception accidentally practiced by Ultra on its avid but unskilled interpreters about this time. Just as Paulus' directive seemed to promise that Rommel would remain quiescent because he had been ordered not to advance, so mounting Ultra evidence about his supply difficulties suggested that he could scarcely do otherwise even if he wished. Four more ships were sunk by the RAF in Benghazi harbor on 8–9 May, with the loss of enough petrol to make the Afrika Korps' position "very serious" at a time when there were too few lorries for road transport and more were being sought from the French in Tunis. A great deal of aircraft fuel was destroyed in another raid a few days later, and more when a tanker blew up just before BATTLEAXE. Five reports of bomb and fuel stocks in forward dumps which were decrypted between mid-May and mid-June showed negligible increases with the passage of time, thus confirming the shortage of both lorries and coastal shipping. These were only small and random samples of the supply situation, and were no doubt understood to be such. Postwar investigation, however, has shown them to be not untypical of the whole, and it has even been persuasively argued that (as General von Rintelen, German liaison officer in Rome, hinted at the time) the Axis supply problem was insoluble by its very nature—for every advance so extended the supply line that the demand for transport space to keep stores moving over the long route from Tripoli to the front grew disproportionally fast (particularly if reinforcements were sent forward to exploit success), and might

---

[20] None of this, of course, is intended to belittle either the energy or the skill with which Churchill directed the war as no other could have done, or the invaluable support he gave to the whole Ultra enterprise from its earliest days.

even end by exceeding that of the whole Russian front. Yet Rommel remained aggressive, and was strong enough to bring the two Churchill-inspired attacks to a halt almost as soon as they started. To that extent, then, the evidence which suggested that he could not do so was misleading. How was this? Partly because British intelligence consistently underestimated his tank strength, about which Ultra said nothing; partly because the gloomy supply reports were allowed to obscure the fact that for every ton of cargo sunk en route or in African harbors, ten arrived safely in the hands of soldiers prepared to put up with a monotonous diet and to make every shot count; and partly because a purely statistical appraisal did not reckon with the damage a bold and resourceful leader could cause if he had determined followers armed with superior weapons. A year or so later, when current intelligence was available in greater volume over a more typical range and past records had accumulated in depth, it was usual to hold that better strategic guidance could be derived from an analysis of Ultra's logistical evidence than from anything it reported about the movement of troops on or toward the battlefield. This was very likely true by the end of the summer before Alamein, but not until then.

2
THE LIMITATIONS OF INTELLIGENCE: YUGOSLAVIA, GREECE, CRETE, IRAQ, AND SYRIA
April–June 1941

The strategy of the short campaigns in the lands bordering the eastern Mediterranean in the spring of 1941 was ordained before the advent of Ultra by considerations of politics, geography, and resources, not of military intelligence. However, Ultra provided enlightening information upon them all in turn, though in widely differing measure, and one of them, Crete, became in some respects a test case of what it could do.

Yugoslavia and Greece

The last ten days before the German invasion of Yugoslavia and Greece on 6 April 1941 saw several Ultra pointers to what was already known to be probable. On 27 March, for instance, Luftflotte 4 opened battle headquarters in the Balkans, the move of three divisions northward to Poland was immediately canceled on news of the change of government in Belgrade, and railway Enigma showed troop transports moving toward the Yugoslav frontier. To speed up the transmission of intelligence, signal links were established with British army and air headquarters in Greece and briefly also with the military attaché in Belgrade. The arrival of German aircraft in Romania, and orders for them to reconnoiter Belgrade and Athens, were re-

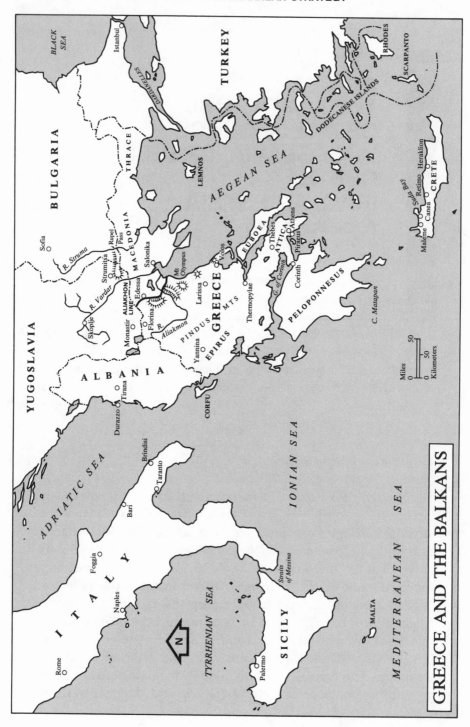

GREECE AND THE BALKANS

corded on 2 April. In the early hours of 5 April the exact moment at which the blow would fall became known: at first set for 0530 on the sixth, it was later changed to 0600 hours.

Operational messages began coming in as soon as hostilities started, and one of them established an early record for quick delivery: a report, issued at 1845 on 6 April, which gave the location of the German spearheads in Yugoslavia, was signaled in under four hours, and ten or a dozen accounts of the fighting, identifications of the units engaged, and statements of the positions they had reached, as well as of air or army intentions, were received next day. It was possible to send most of the resulting signals, and most of the 150 or so others transmitted during the brief fortnight the campaign lasted (British troops evacuated Greece between 24 and 29 April), within a few hours of the time of origin of the German messages on which they were based—a standard of punctuality which, because of cryptographic difficulties, it was not always possible to maintain in the years that followed, but which at the time gave an indication of what Ultra might be able to achieve in the future. The vast majority of these signals reflected the use of Enigma by the Luftwaffe to report urgent but of course ephemeral information about the positions of the forward troops or to order air attacks in front of them. Almost forty such situation reports were processed, at the rate of two or three a day. The most interesting of them to read now, and probably the most useful at the time, were those recording the advance on Belgrade on 4 April, the opening of the Rupel pass to supply traffic on the same day, the crossing of the Aliakhmon river on 15 April, and the intention to advance on Athens on 20 April but to pause briefly at Thermopylae first. (The gist of a decrypt explaining that the attack would be strengthened, but postponed until the 24th, was signaled at 0705 hours on the 23rd, thus giving notice that the defenses guarding the approach to the embarkation sites could be held for an additional twenty-four hours.) But contact with GHQ Greece— which was now on the move—had apparently been lost before confirmation that the attack would go ahead as planned could be signaled early next morning. Among warnings of air raids, it is worth recalling those issued at 0420/11 April for a raid on Volos harbor to take place later the same day, and at 2200/20 and 0105/21 for raids on the Piraeus at dawn and midday on the 21st respectively. (Volos and the Piraeus were the two main British supply ports.)

The intelligence value of all this information was extremely transient—once the troops had moved on or the raids had taken place, it became as much "dead" history as Wellington's dispositions at Waterloo—and therefore its usefulness depended entirely on the speed with which it could be made available to the appropriate commander in the field, on the restrictions placed upon its use to protect the security of the source (for to preserve Ultra, which careless use might imperil, was clearly more important than to win a campaign already beset with insuperable political, strategic, and logistical problems), and on the availability of the requisite force to convert it into action. The first condition was sufficiently met in Greece, as has already been seen; the second was an ever-present concern, emphasized by severe security regulations, of which GHQ was reminded in a signal of 22 April: "If moving HQ, please take greatest care to burn all deciphered material this series. Vital security our source." The third condition could scarcely be fulfilled at all, and this was crucial. An insufficient force (whose HQ staff was planning evacuation from the moment it landed), deprived of adequate opportunity to coordinate action with its ally before the campaign, was continually on the retreat once hostilities began. No general compelled to operate in these conditions could hope to have reserves handy in the right place to take advantage of the openings Ultra offered. With the possible exception of the Thermopylae signal, it is unlikely that Ultra assisted much in the defense of Greece, and certain that it could not have prevented defeat. But the many locations of the German spearheads which it provided undoubtedly enabled the retreat to be conducted tactically with a degree of confidence and composure which would otherwise have been impossible.

Since Greece could probably not in any case have been saved from German occupation, in one sense it did not matter that the new type of intelligence was little used. In another sense, however, it was extremely unfortunate. "Had the military dice not been weighted against the British, had there been enough men, tanks, and guns, Ultra would have paved the road to victory"—this after-battle reflection could not be contradicted from current knowledge or accumulated experience. Yet it was wrong. The future was to prove over and over again that advantage could seldom be taken of tactical information from Ultra: the nonfulfillment of one or more of the three conditions usually prevented it. Longer-term, strategic intelligence, it came gradually to be recognized, was Ultra's strong suit. Yet none of the intelligence provided in Greece was strategic; all of it was tactical. Thus the Greek campaign was a misleading advertisement for the value of the new and almost untried source in land operations. The coming months were to underline this.

Crete

It was the German assault on Crete which saw the first serious test of Ultra under operational conditions. When the island fell, it seemed that the test had been failed by a narrow margin, but in fact it was probably only Ultra's warning which enabled the defenders to come so near success and to inflict such heavy casualties on the German airborne troops that the reputation for invincibility they had acquired in the Low Countries the previous year was completely shattered. Because of these casualties,[1] the Wehrmacht attempted no more airborne operations for the rest of the war—notably refraining from what might have been a victorious descent on Malta—and this alone was worth far more than the £10 million at which Churchill is said to have valued the Ultra intelligence about Crete.

Whereas Hitler had been contemplating the invasion of Greece since the beginning of the year, it was not until late April, when the British were already leaving the country in haste, that he approved plans drawn up by General Student,

---

[1] In round figures, British, Australian, and New Zealander losses were 1,750 killed, 1,750 wounded, 12,000 prisoners. German losses were 2,000 killed, 2,000 wounded, 2,000 missing presumed killed. Excluding prisoners, German losses were therefore almost twice the British and allied (MME ii 147).

commander of Fliegerkorps XI's parachute and glider troops, for the capture of Crete and set 17 May as the starting date; his directive for Operation MERKUR ("Mercury") followed on 25 April. The British were just as slow, but even more hurried, in taking a decision to defend the island. Not until 18 April did Churchill and the Chiefs of Staff lay down Mediterranean priorities, and even when they did so they placed Crete below Libya and the evacuation of Greece, regarding it rather as a "receptacle"[2] for men withdrawn from Greece than as a strong outpost for the protection of Egypt, which was assigned first priority. No clear defense plan emerged until, after a large part of the expeditionary force had been evacuated from Greece to Crete at the end of April, the impossibility of ferrying everyone back to the mainland suddenly made it necessary to defend the island. A tiny garrison had been protecting the naval base at Suda Bay since November 1940, but none of its commanders had stayed long enough to work out a coherent plan of defense. Hence most of the men who fought so bravely in May were little more than weary refugees improvising defense at short notice— General Freyberg, appointed to command in Crete by Wavell on 30 April, was one of them—and it is astonishing that they so nearly repelled invaders who possessed the initiative, had complete superiority in the air, came fresh to their task, and had not been through the trauma of evacuation under fire. It was Ultra which so nearly gave them victory.

The threat of a landing in Crete was slow to emerge from a number of other possibilities. Fifty Ju-52 transport aircraft were flying to Romania and south Bulgaria for Fliegerkorps XI (which had controlled the 1940 air landings in the Low Countries) on 9 April, but there was no hint of the purpose for which they were being brought together. A parachute drop in front of the advancing German armies would conform to the pattern established in Belgium and Holland the previous year; Crete and Cyprus were other possible objectives. The projected move to Skoplje, in Yugoslavia, of a regiment of the 22nd (Air Landing)

---

[2] It was once more "a repository for evacuated troops" in the third volume of Churchill's *Second World War* in 1950 (Churchill iii.240).

Division, which became known on the same day, was open to the same variety of interpretations. Nor did the next intercept make the picture any clearer: General Suessmann (who was known to be connected with air landings, and who was in fact killed soon after he landed on Crete on 20 May) was interested in a reconnaissance of an unspecified area on 17 April; this did not point convincingly toward Crete, for the reconnaissance was to be carried out by Dornier 17 aircraft, whose range was believed to be too short to allow them more than a minute or two over Crete unless they took off from airfields farther south than any the Germans had yet occupied in Greece. Lastly, Fliegerkorps XI's intention to assemble at least six Gruppen (nominally 180 aircraft) of Ju-52s in Bulgaria on 21 April underlined the threat anew without indicating any particular target.

A fortnight's uncertainty was suddenly removed within the space of a few hours very shortly after this. Between midnight of 24–25 April and dawn on the 27th, the delivery of reports of an air reconnaissance of Crete to Fliegerkorps VIII and XI and to General Suessmann; OKL's intention to make ready large stocks of petrol for "the operational area of Fliegerkorps XI"; preparations for an attack on Crete involving bombers, fighters, and transport aircraft; the intended move of the 22nd (Air Landing) Division and the 7th Fliegerdivision (parachute troops) to Athens; the arrival of 51 Ju-52s in Bulgaria; and the receipt by Fliegerkorps VIII (which had supported the invasion of Yugoslavia and Greece) of photographs and maps of Crete, were all signaled with high priority.

In view of this sudden development, arrangements were hastily made on 28 April to send Ultra to the Air Officer Commanding in Crete, Group Captain Beamish (whose small force of obsolete aircraft deprived him of the means to make much use of it), and shortly also to General Freyberg personally. The combination of emergency, strict security, and novel signals procedure seems to have caused confusion which still obscures the intelligence picture and reached its peak in a plaintive inquiry on 6 May: "Please enquire of General Freyberg whether he is receiving OL information from Cairo. If not, please arrange to pass relevant OL information to him maintaining utmost security."

New information of the greatest moment emerged on 30 April in the shape of orders that until further notice, Suda Bay was not to be mined nor Cretan airfields bombed, in order not to hamper "the planned operation." An amphibious assault was evidently being prepared, not an attack from the air alone. Thereafter there was no news of any significance until 6 May, when a long signal transmitted to Crete and Cairo just before midnight imparted the fullest intelligence yet discovered.

This signal declared that preparations for an operation against Crete would probably be complete by 17 May.[3] The sequence of events was to be as follows:

First would come parachute landings by the 7th Fliegerdivision and the corps troops of Fliegerkorps XI to seize Maleme, Candia (Heraklion), and Retimo airfields, whereupon dive-bombers and fighters would occupy the two first named. Next would come an air landing to deliver the remainder of Fliegerkorps XI and its headquarters, which was to control the operation. Following this, Flak, three mountain regiments from the Twelfth Army in the Balkans, armored and antitank units, motorcyclists, and supplies would come by sea. The German Admiral Southeast would provide protection of the seaborne contingent with Italian motor torpedo boats and other naval forces, and sea transport would be in both Italian and German vessels. The operation would be preceded by a sharp air attack on RAF bases, army camps, and antiaircraft positions.

Next day, 7 May, the Director of Intelligence at the Air Ministry sent an estimate of the likely scale of effort and a forecast of the probable timetable. Its main points were: The "sharp air attack" might come on the day before the parachute landing and the arrival of the bombers and fighters, or on the same day. The air-landing troops and at any rate some light tanks would come on Day 1 or Day 2, the seaborne forces on Day 2. About 450 troop-carrying aircraft were in the area at the moment, and

---

[3] It was attributed to no particular source or sources, and reads like an undifferentiated compilation from several separate intercepts. The drafting customs of the time did not preclude such a thing, but there is nothing to prove the suggestion true.

the figures could without difficulty be raised to 600. Up to 12,000 parachutists could be dropped on Day 1 if two sorties were made, and 4,000 men and 400 tons of supplies might arrive on Day 2 in the air-landing operation. The maximum GAF effort for a single day was estimated at 150 bomber and 100 fighter sorties; about 60 Me-109s and 90 Ju-87s were available.

Six days later—the length of the interval is quite unexplained—a précis of these two signals, together with a little additional information, was sent to both Cairo and Crete as OL 302. It did not distinguish decrypted information from comment upon it, contrary to later standard practice, but since these two elements had been tolerably well differentiated in the two preceding signals, for once this did not matter much. It is, however, not clear whether the size of the force to be employed and the proportions into which it was to be divided between sea and air transport was decrypt or derivative comment. It will nevertheless be convenient to refer henceforth to OL 302 as the body of information available to General Freyberg, bearing in mind always that he had had almost all of it since 7 May, a week earlier than the date of OL 302, the text of which may be summarized as follows: Fliegerkorps XI, the 7th Fliegerdivision, and the 22nd Division,[4] supported by approximately 150 long-range bombers, 100 heavy fighters, and 600 transport aircraft, were under orders to capture Crete. Maleme, Herakleion, and Retimo airfields would be taken by paratroops on the first day, whereupon 100 dive-bombers and fighters would land on the two first-named. More infantry, motorcyclists, armor, and antitank guns would follow by sea in about twelve ships. An Italian tanker was due to dock at the Piraeus by 17 May with petrol for the takeoff airfields round Athens, and it would supply Crete later on. The total force to be employed would be between 30,000 and 35,000 men in roughly equal proportions of parachute, glider, and seaborne contingents.[5] Preparations were to be complete by 17 May.

---

[4] The 5th Mountain Division had in fact already been substituted for the 22nd Division because it would have a shorter distance to travel over the crowded and damaged Balkan railways.

[5] In the event, rather fewer men were employed, but considerably more aircraft.

Thus, a fortnight before the attack took place (Ultra gave notice of a short postponement on 16 May and suggested the 20th as the probable date on the 19th), Freyberg had a complete outline of Student's plan in his hands, and could arrange his countermeasures accordingly so far as security regulations and the poverty of his resources permitted.[6] So well did he do this that—although the events of 20 May showed that Maleme airfield, one of the targets designated in OL 302, had not been sufficiently protected—the attackers suffered far heavier casualties than they had anticipated and were compelled to revise their tactics. Even Ultra seldom gave so complete and accurate a forecast again—the disclosure of Rommel's plan before Alam Halfa in August 1942 and of Hitler's mad scheme which led to the carnage of the Falaise pocket just two years later are among the few comparable examples[7]—and it is difficult not to feel regret that prevailing conditions and his shortage of equipment prevented Freyberg from taking as much advantage of his foreknowledge as Montgomery, Eisenhower, and Bradley could.

Freyberg has sometimes been blamed for mistaking the Germans' objectives, for believing that the main assault would come by sea, and for weakening the all-important defense of Maleme in order to be ready to repel a seaborne attack which, it is said, was never central to the enemy's plans and which in fact was disposed of by the navy before it reached the coast.[8] This criticism overlooks, among many other things, Wavell's orders

---

[6]In his forthcoming biography of his father, Lord Freyberg has convincingly shown that General Freyberg would have strengthened the defenses of Maleme had he not been expressly forbidden to do so. Security regulations forbade the taking of action on uncorroborated Ultra evidence. Since an attack from the air was an obvious possibility on general grounds and without Ultra evidence, however, and since ordinary prudence therefore suggested strong airfield defense, the prohibition would in this case appear to have been unnecessary, for strengthening the defense could hardly betray the breaking of Enigma. The novelty of Ultra, its foreseeable future importance, and the sudden nature of the emergency make it nevertheless easy to understand why what now seem excessive precautions were then thought desirable.

[7]See pp. 140–145, below, and Bennett, 112–24.

[8]For instance, A. Clark, *The Fall of Crete* (Blond, 1962), 34–36, 102–5; I.McD. G. Stewart, *The Struggle for Crete* (Oxford, 1966), 108, 482; and R. Lewin, *Ultra Goes to War* (1978), 158–59. All appear to depend directly or indirectly on the account, heavily prejudiced against Freyberg and often factually inaccurate, which one of Freyberg's brigade commanders gave to Churchill on 13 June (PRO.PREM 3/109). It should also be noted that all three books were published before the 1941 signals reached the Public Record Office in 1981.

to Freyberg when he appointed him on 30 April—to expect an airborne attack by five or six thousand men and a follow-up landing from the sea—and the intelligence report which Freyberg circulated down to battalion level on 16 May,[9] which stressed airborne attacks on the three airfields (heavy raids on them had already started by then), but included a seaborne contingent consisting of antiaircraft batteries and troops as part of the first day's operations. Above all, it disregards the Luftwaffe's domination of the sea round Crete, which meant that the Royal Navy could not maintain a presence there continuous enough to guarantee the island immunity from invasion by sea.

Freyberg's first assessment, telegraphed to London on 5 May, had been that he could cope with an air attack on its own but doubted his ability to repel air and sea assaults in combination unless he was reinforced beforehand. A moment's reflection on the peculiar conditions in Crete, on the general outlook prevailing in early 1941, and in particular on the training and experience of senior commanders down to that time serves to explain why Freyberg should be anxious about a seaborne attack, although Ultra laid more stress on landings from the air. To begin with, he was more isolated and alone than any subsequent general. Ultra was being sent to him personally and exclusively, and he was forbidden to show it to anyone or to discuss it with his intelligence staff. He had known nothing at all about Ultra until Wavell appointed him to command in Crete, and so was quite without experience in interpreting it. Yet almost at once he was compelled by events to make operational decisions in the light of it, without the benefit of a second opinion or any advice whatever. Secondly, in the whole course of history no island had ever

---

[9]The text is in Davin, 77; it reads alarmingly like a close paraphrase of OL 302.

Security regulations forbade both the direct use of Ultra in operations, unless it was corroborated from another source, and (because of the danger that compromising papers or men "in the know" might be captured) the publication, except in heavily disguised form, of intelligence derived from it outside the narrow circle of those who had been formally indoctrinated and warned about the sensitivity of the source. In order to prevent the dangerously wide dissemination of signals and their possible capture in battle, Ultra was not normally distributed below the level of an army headquarters or the equivalent in the other services. Freyberg's was not an army command, and Ultra signals were sent to him personally; but it seems doubtful whether even this would have been permitted under later regulations, given the extreme vulnerability of Crete. No Ultra was sent to Arnhem in September 1944, for instance.

been captured except from the sea. The only evidence that the new airborne arm could overpower ground defenses consisted of the seizure of two lightly held airfields in Norway in April 1940 and the capture of the Belgian fortress of Eben Emael and two bridges over the Albert Canal on 10 May—daring enterprises which Goebbels' propaganda and British lack of reliable information still shrouded in wild and improbable rumor even a year later. The first parachute battalions in the British army would not be formed for another six months. Finally, the fact that the Royal Navy's command of the Mediterranean was being seriously challenged for the first time since Nelson's victory over the French in Aboukir Bay in 1798 was in itself enough to reinforce fears of attack by the traditional means. In all these circumstances, it was natural that Freyberg's plans should follow the well-established pattern, in spite of Ultra; his apprehension of danger from the sea can only be faulted by an abuse of hindsight.

Ultra itself, however, goes a long way toward refuting the charge that his appreciation of enemy intentions was wrong. Admittedly, all the information he had received put a parachute landing in the forefront, but the sea landing was clearly an integral part of the same operation and was scheduled to take place at an early stage in it. This was something Freyberg could not lightly disregard. Several later signals pointed in the same direction. On 11 May, twelve ships, totaling 27,000 tons, were being readied for the expedition in Naples and in Sicilian ports, some to carry troops and some supplies. Eight of them were to proceed to the Piraeus on the 16th and 17th and to leave again on the 19th. This last item was signaled at 0130 hours on 18 May, and there was nothing thereafter—except the difficulty the enemy would obviously have in keeping to so tight a schedule—to suggest that the seaborne arm of the invasion would be later than expected or any weaker than already indicated (i.e., about 10,000 men strong). Right down to the hour, whatever it may have been, on 18 May at which this signal was delivered to him, therefore, Freyberg was certainly right to prepare the best defense he could against a landing from the sea, and this signal would have confirmed him in his decision to do so.

Nor did he receive the slightest hint from any source during the next three days to suggest that the enemy had changed plans, save that no sea landing was in fact attempted on the 20th. Fliegerkorps XI's intentions for 21 May, signaled early the same morning, showed that the enemy had still not done so, for they were that Canea would be attacked from the sea during the day. One of the many breakdowns in communications with Crete delayed the receipt of this signal, but it was received normally at Royal Navy headquarters at Alexandria and contributed to the successful naval actions in which the troopships and troop-carrying caiques composing the expedition were sunk at sea. Next day, advance warning was given of large-scale air attacks on naval formations, but unfortunately this could not prevent the sinking of the destroyers *Kelly* and *Kashmir*.

German headquarters in Greece could only communicate with the takeoff airfields and with the landing parties by using radio, and this ensured that the number and quality of the intercepts remained very high throughout the operation—the first day's targets were confirmed twenty-four hours in advance, for example—and the speed with which messages were decrypted and signaled was greater then ever: the record was lowered on the first afternoon when OL 385, announcing that Maleme was in German hands and that General Suessman, of the 7th Fliegerdivision, had been killed in action, went off only three hours and twenty-five minutes after the German message which underlay it. This same signal, however, also vividly illustrates Freyberg's command problems and shows how little use Ultra can have been to him once battle was joined. The German original, composed just after midday, clearly exaggerated the parachutists' success, for the British withdrawal from the airfield did not begin until evening. Out of contact with his own men, Freyberg signaled Wavell at midnight that, so far as he knew, the defense of Maleme still held. It is impossible to be sure whether or not he had received OL 385 by then, but he would scarcely have told Wavell that all was well at Maleme if he had seen it, and he would hardly have omitted to plug the gap in his lines which the loss of Maleme represented if he had known that the gap existed. Maleme did not finally fall until the afternoon of 21 May.

The scale of the attack on Maleme (where the runways had not been destroyed, although the last British planes had left the previous morning) and the determination with which it was pressed home in spite of casualties severe enough to lower the fighting spirit of some units proved the key to the whole operation when the defenders were forced off the airfield. Ultra warnings that Maleme was now the principal objective began just after midnight on 21–22 May and were regularly repeated, together with evidence that it was becoming the main entry point for the reinforcements which Student hastily poured in to secure his hold on the island, but they cannot have arrived until after the situation had become too critical for them to be of much practical value. Returns of the number of sorties made by Fliegerkorps VIII on 26 and 27 May and of the number of aircraft serviceable were by now of merely historical interest. Crete was evacuated on 31 May.

The completeness of Ultra's forecast of the course of events and the slender margin which separated victory from defeat for either side invite a moment's reflection on the advantage this intelligence gave the defense and on the way it was utilized. Here, it seems, was a chance to inflict the first defeat on the Nazis, and perhaps to change the direction of the war by denying Hitler an island base in the eastern Mediterranean. Could the opportunity offered by Ultra really have been turned to such a good account as this, given the limitations of time, space, and available resources? Or were these limitations so severe that Crete was doomed from the start in any case? Writing from the vantage point of one who had helped to plan the operation, de Guingand had "a feeling that we might have defeated the first Axis attempt at capture," although he doubted whether Crete could have been held for long, and sharply criticized the inadequate preparations for defense. It is at any rate tempting to suppose, with Roskill, that Freyberg would have prevailed if even a few of the men, guns, and tanks lost in Greece had been sent instead to garrison Crete in good time, and that his victory would have brought strategic benefit to Britain. In this case, and if in addition the prohibition on the direct use of Ultra had been raised, Freyberg could have deployed enough additional anti-aircraft guns round Maleme to wipe out most of his assailants before they reached the ground. This would have prevented Student from gaining control of his chosen portal of entry for the reinforcements without which he could not engage the defenders on equal terms. A few Matildas (Student had no tanks at first) would have broken up any other landing parties before they could concentrate, a few more motor vehicles and radio sets could have maintained better contact between the scattered defense groups, and so on. Had some of this been foreseen by a commander-in-chief with a broader vision than Wavell's and a firmer grasp of the best disposition of the meager British forces in the Middle East,[10] then—but only then—might the intelligence provided by Ultra have swayed the balance in favor of the defense. As things stood in reality, the advantage was bound to lie with the other side, although Freyberg knew what it planned to do. Crete is a prime example of the truth that force as well as foreknowledge is needed to win battles.

Would a different result in Crete have changed the course of the war and so have provided a compelling illustration of Ultra's supreme value? It seems unlikely, but no answer can be more than a guess. Speculation at the first remove from actuality, as in the last paragraph, is a worthwhile historical exercise if it sheds enough new light on the events to induce a better understanding of them. Anything more must be shunned as mere fantasy, because it tampers with too many of reality's features and leads at once to still wider and more fanciful speculation. To ask what would have been the consequence of victory in Crete is first to ask, like Sir David Hunt in *A Don at War,* whether Rommel could ever have been beaten without the division or more it would have been necessary to take from the desert to garrison Crete, and next to wonder whether both Malta and Crete could have been held at the same time. The tribulations of Malta and the Eighth Army in 1942 suggest the answer "No" in both cases, and it then seems natural to pass on, by way

---

[10]"The P.M. laments very strongly that the tanks which he asked Wavell to send to Crete were not sent. They might have made the whole difference to the battle" (Colville, 390, entry for 23 May 1940).

of the reflection that Malta was on all counts incomparably the more important of the two islands, to the conclusion that the loss of Crete was either the lesser of two evils, inasmuch as the cost of winning it deterred Hitler from an airborne attack on Malta, or a blessing in disguise, because it would have been so expensive to garrison.[11] But here the barrenness of unbridled speculation stands revealed: this conclusion, whether true or not, is totally divorced from reality, because at no time was the defense of Crete considered in either of these ways. There seems simply to have been an abrupt and sudden switch (evidently in consequence of the Ultra signals of 24–27 April already quoted) from the "receptacle for refugees" of 18 April to the attitude summed up in Churchill's cable to Wavell only ten days later: "It ought to be a fine opportunity for killing the parachute troops. The island must be stubbornly defended." There had been no time to think further ahead.

Iraq

Just as British troops were hurriedly leaving Greece and Enigma was foreshadowing an assault on Crete from the air, Wavell's cup of troubles was filled to overflowing by the transfer to him (against his will) of responsibility for Iraq, where the situation had been growing steadily more threatening all through April. At the beginning of the month the pro-Axis Rashid Ali seized power and appealed for help to Berlin and Rome. His main requirement was arms, to enable him to evict the British from the two bases (one near Baghdad, the other near Basra) which they occupied under treaty. Both Hitler and Mussolini reacted slowly to Rashid Ali's appeals, with the immediate consequence that he could not press home his attack on the RAF base at Habbaniya outside Baghdad and soon had to call it off in face of a spirited and resourceful defense.

---

[11] Although they still held their air bases in Greece, the Germans were to find supplying Crete something of a headache, and had to fly its garrison, the 164th Division, over to Egypt hurriedly in July 1942 in an effort to keep up the momentum of Rommel's advance.

It was only at this point—the end of the first week in May—that Enigma was able to assist the hard-pressed British Commander-in-Chief in any way; decrypted Axis diplomatic messages were already doing so, and they remained the chief secret intelligence source throughout the Iraq operation. Ultra signals produced little beyond a few useful but hardly first-rank items. Military equipment was being collected on an Athens airfield on 8 May, and the men about to use it were ordered to remove all badges from their uniforms—a pointer to a destination in either Iraq or Syria, where the Vichy French were known to be assisting the passage of supplies to Iraq. Transport aircraft were assembling at Rhodes next day for what appeared to be the same purpose, and a couple of days later Iraqi markings were to be painted on German aircraft on the same two airfields. By the middle of May, mine-laying aircraft were allotted to Iraq (evidently to block the rivers); during the first week of June, 45 fighters were to be delivered; and large consignments of petrol and ammunition were being flown in by the same route. While these arrangements strongly suggested German intervention on an increasing scale, they still anticipated a definite decision by Hitler (his Directive 30 was dated 23 May; Ultra discovered one paragraph of it), whose six-week delay had in fact by now combined with resolute action by the small British forces to make Rashid Ali's position untenable. Baghdad fell on 31 May, and Iraq remained beyond German reach for the duration of the war.

Operations began in Iraq at much the same time as in Greece and ended on the same day as the evacuation of Crete. The coincidence in time divided the attention of the British and German commands alike, although it is plain that both were more concerned to control the Mediterranean than the Tigris-Euphrates valley. Each side hesitated so long before committing more than token forces that the outcome was decided by the mere handful of men the British scraped together. Each suffered a defeat and gained a victory. Crete attracted more attention at the time, and still does, but the strategic value of Iraq was the greater. The expulsion of the Germans from Iraq strengthened the British hold on the Middle East, which, when reinforced by control of Syria in July and Persia in August, interposed a barrier (if as yet only a flimsy one) in the way of Hitler's project of dominating the whole area from the Caspian Sea to the Persian Gulf after his expected quick victory in Russia.

Syria

Syria opted for the Vichy government when France fell in 1940, so that its pro-German sympathies as well as its geographical position made it a potential threat to British power in the Middle East. A British declaration of July 1940 took account of this: Great Britain, it stated, would not permit Syria and Lebanon to be used as a base for attacks on any country with which Britain was on friendly terms. When it became known in mid-May 1941 that German aircraft were using Syria as a staging post on the way to Iraq, it was necessary for the British government, hard pressed though it was on all hands, to try to forestall the German occupation which seemed the likely next step. British troops crossed the Palestine-Syria frontier on 8 June, assisted by a small Free French contingent.

Ultra's main service at this time was to reveal the scale and regularity of Franco-German cooperation. The personnel of a French fighter unit, some 75 strong, were reported flying to Syria via German-held Greek airfields on 21 May, and 30 or 40 French aircraft flew from Tunis to Beirut via Brindisi two days later; several similar reports followed during the next fortnight. Until the end of May, there could be no certainty whether the pilots and aircraft would stay in Syria or move on to Iraq, or, indeed, whether success in Crete would lead Hitler to attempt to consolidate his hold on the eastern Mediterranean by adding Cyprus to his conquests. This source of alarm is reflected in two signals, dated 21 and 28 May, which the Air Ministry sent to Cairo over the Hut 3 route (presumably because they were based on Ultra intelligence); they forecast another airborne operation after Crete and estimated that at least 300 Ju-52 transport planes could take part in it.

Soon after hostilities began in Syria, on 8 June, signs of

German irresolution and doubt quickly appeared in Enigma, giving very welcome encouragement to the British command, whose advance became bogged down almost as soon as it started. By 13 June, Fliegerkorps X had been told not to attack Syrian targets without express orders from Berlin, a French admiral had used an Enigma link to tell Berlin that French resistance was bound to collapse in a few days if Luftwaffe raids were put off much longer, Berlin had replied by forbidding German aircraft to land in Syria even if they were assisting the French, and the Italians in Beirut had voiced their belief that there was no way in which a British advance on the city could be prevented. Only Goering differed, angrily ordering the strongest possible attack on British ships off the Syrian coast.

During the second half of the short campaign, frequent reports continued to note the arrival of French reinforcements in Syria. But the only signal of much strategic significance before the French surrendered on 11 July was one of 3 July which showed that German arms and ammunition were being ferried through Greece, but that the dispatch of troops was still only under consideration. Rather late in the day, this to some extent compensated for the absence, until now, of any indication whatever whether or not German ground forces were going to Syria—a reflection, of course, of the fact that army Enigma was not yet being broken.

Retrospect

Four anxious and turbulent months in the spring and early summer of 1941 seemed to have brought little more than a string of disasters to the British and a series of triumphs to the Axis, the invasion of Russia on 22 June chief among them. From the standpoint of strategy, hindsight sees this as too gloomy a picture and can discern gains as well as losses. German attempts to infiltrate the Arab world had been frustrated for the time being at any rate; the Iraqi oil wells and the pipeline to the Mediterranean which they fed were now better protected, and so was the western approach to the Persian Gulf, with the Abadan refineries and the flank of the supply route to Russia (this was finally made secure when Russian and British troops occupied Persia in August). The naval and air base in Malta was still relatively safe, and Egypt too, the defeats in Crete and the desert not having proved lethal.

Ultra was not yet in a position to play a major role in great matters like this: neither of the only two keys being broken regularly was normally used to convey information at this level. One of Ultra's two biggest scoops, the Paulus report, proved in the end to be more of a hindrance than a help, it is evident, mainly because Rommel disregarded it—which Ultra could, of course, not foresee—but partly also because too much reliance was put in high places on its bare text alone. The other, the revelation of Student's plan for the assault on Crete, nearly turned a tactical tide but had in the end very little bearing on strategy. Nevertheless, the outstandingly high quality of the information supplied on these two occasions had drawn attention, in England if not yet in Cairo, to the potentialities of the source. Unfortunately, a summer of comparative inaction in the desert afforded little opportunity of demonstrating them further.

The capacity of those who handled the raw decrypts to turn them into operationally useful intelligence swiftly and accurately improved greatly during these same months, and in retrospect this may in the end have proved more important for the eventual reputation of Ultra than anything else; as they approached the end of their apprenticeship, they were gradually developing into a reliable channel for conveying information which was coming to bear more and more directly on the conduct of the war. Plunged with little warning and no training into the tricky business of drafting extremely urgent operational signals barely three weeks after the direct service to the Middle East opened, the intelligence officers in Hut 3 had to learn their trade the hard way. A look back at our signals shows that over the first three or four hundred, we gained enough experience to improve our drafting technique very considerably—and by good fortune, many of the lessons were learned in time for Crete. The style of the signals in late May is already much clearer and more concise than before, unintentional ambiguities of phraseology are disappearing, and there is usually a proper distinction between priorities. Three defects mar many of them, however, limiting their intelligence value, and unfortunately these defects persisted for some time to come. Few state the time at which the underlying German message originated, although this was nearly always approximately clear from external signals data (which, of course, included by routine the time at which an operator began transmitting), if not from any direct statement. Similarly, few named the originating German authority and the arm of the service to which he belonged or gave any indication of his status in the hierarchy of command; yet the source of a piece of information and its approximate age at the time of receipt are vital ingredients in assessing its value. Thirdly, too little care was taken to distinguish factual statements made in the German original from comments upon them. This occasionally makes the precise meaning and bearing of the resultant text hard to measure even today, and it must sometimes have baffled recipients as they strove under battle pressure to use our signals to guide them toward appropriate action; some examples have been given in the account of the assault on Crete. A possibly excessive security consciousness may have been a contributory cause of a looseness and imprecision of structure which seems amateurish now, but this was probably a fault on the right side at a time when recipients were still inexpert in the use of Ultra and the danger of losing the source altogether was ever-present.

3
RESTLESS INTERLUDE
June–November 1941

Auchinleck replaced Wavell as Commander-in-Chief Middle East at the beginning of July, and at once Churchill began urging him on to the attack, just as he had his predecessor. This time there was a certain justification for the Prime Minister's attitude. Reinforcements were beginning to arrive in sufficient numbers to make success seem likely, and it was still expected that the Russians might collapse in August or September,[1] thus releasing ample German troops to invade Egypt either by the eastward approach through Libya or from the north through Syria and Iraq. The best way to dispose of both threats, it seemed, was to bring the Syrian campaign to a quick and successful conclusion (General Dentz and the Vichy forces in fact surrendered on 11 July), and to drive Rommel out of Africa by a preemptive strike before he became too strong to shift. Like Wavell before him, however, Auchinleck took a cautious and more realistic view. Instead of attacking at once, he proposed to delay while he gathered strength. He must have two or three fresh divisions and time to train them, he said, before he could safely move forward, as well as adequate air cover and naval support, and he refused to entertain the possibility of an offensive before the beginning of November. To this position Auchinleck held with the utmost tenacity, even under fierce

---

[1] This view continued to prevail for some time after Ultra began revealing in mid-July that all was not well with the German offensive.

cross-examination when he and Tedder were summoned to London for consultations at the end of July.[2] Because the enemy now held all the airfields from Sicily right round the coast to Greece and the Aegean, it was no longer safe to risk the direct route through the Mediterranean to Alexandria or Port Said for ships bringing supplies and reinforcements; the most that could be done from the west was occasional heavily escorted convoys from Gibraltar to nourish Malta, the base from which Axis shipping could best be harassed. The only alternative route to Egypt involved the long haul round the Cape, which lengthened the journey by two months and many thousands of miles and increased the time lag between a decision in Whitehall and action in the desert almost intolerably.

The same dilemma—desire for an early offensive so as to make the first strike, but anxiety over the resources to make it effective—was troubling the Axis as well. Both sides were acutely aware of the fragility of their logistical situation and of the obstacles in the way of improving it. No sooner had Rommel halted BATTLEAXE than he began demanding four panzer divisions so that he could take Tobruk and thereby solve his forward supply problem. (He does not seem to have realized that Tobruk harbor could not handle cargoes in anything like the volume so large a force would require.) Hitler momentarily agreed in a directive of 14 July, which spoke of equipping four fresh panzer divisions for service in the tropics (this was the exact size of the force which General von Thoma had recommended sending to help the Italians after his mission of inquiry in October 1940). The demands of the Russian front soon killed this proposal, but it would in any case have been quite impossible to maintain so large a force in Libya without a really radical transformation of the whole supply system. All through July, OKH was anxiously balancing the disappointing tonnage delivered over the precarious transport routes against the likelihood of a British attack; if this came in the near future, it was doubtful

---

[2] Tedder replaced Longmore as AOC-in-C Middle East on 1 June. Together with Coningham, who took over command of the Desert Air Force in July, and with the encouragement of Auchinleck, Tedder established the system of army-air cooperation which played a vital part in all subsequent fighting in the Mediterranean.

whether it could be beaten off, concluded Halder on the sixth, for the outcome even of BATTLEAXE had hung by a thread. It was because of this that Rommel flew back to Germany at the end of the month to discuss the bearing of supplies on strategy with Hitler and Halder (it was a reflection of the similarity of both sides' problems, rather than mere coincidence, that his visit took place at the same time as that of Auchinleck and Tedder to London for the same purpose), but words alone could not alter facts as unpleasant as British naval and air superiority or the inevitability of burning up 10 percent of every cargo of petrol unloaded at Tripoli in order to transport the remainder to the front by road. General Bayerlein (Chief of Staff, Afrika Korps) later insisted that by the end of September only a third of the promised number of men and a seventh of their supplies had been delivered, with the result that Rommel was compelled to postpone his planned offensive.

Both sides, then, were struggling with the same intractable problem throughout the summer and early autumn. Fortunately, it was a problem which Ultra was by now well fitted to illuminate, since decrypts of Italian naval traffic could be combined with the regular flow of those reporting Fliegerkorps X's reconnaissance and convoy-protection activities. At least two-thirds of the 1,400 signals sent to the Middle East between BATTLEAXE in June and CRUSADER in November came from these two sources. Though both were highly informative about intended ship movements, as a rule neither made mention of the cargoes the ships carried, and this remained a serious gap in our information until one of the army keys (known as Chaffinch) used in Africa was read for a few weeks in the autumn and more regularly from the following spring.

Many of these signals betray an atmosphere of strain—on occasion, of near panic—which reflects the British naval and air domination of the Mediterranean during the second half of 1941. Fliegerkorps X was so starved of aircraft for the benefit of the Russian front that the balance of advantage swung back in favor of the British only a week or two after the loss of Greece and Crete had seemed to deny it to them indefinitely. Between the beginning of July and the end of October 40 Axis vessels, with a total tonnage of 180,000 tons, were sunk on passage across the Mediterranean, with the result that a fifth of the cargoes loaded in European ports failed to reach North Africa; fuel and general military stores suffered in about equal proportions. The advantage the Axis derived from possession of the Cyrenaican airfields was to some extent offset at this time by an increase in the striking power of the RAF in Malta (50 Hurricanes were flown in during September, for instance), so that it was found safe to base a squadron (known as Force K) of two cruisers and two destroyers in the Grand Harbor to prey on Axis shipping. From late October, Force K so dominated the central Mediterranean that the flow of supplies to Rommel was more severely restricted than ever, although the assertion by Westphal and others that "not a single ship" got through during this period is incorrect. Faced with a crisis, Hitler yielded to the pressure of Raeder and Rommel shortly after Force K reached Malta, ordered 21 more U-boats into the Mediterranean to join the 6 he had already sent (Ultra soon identified most of them),[3] strengthened the Luftwaffe, and appointed Kesselring to the new post of Commander-in-Chief South to coordinate and direct air strategy. Within a week or two, U-boats had torpedoed an aircraft carrier and a battleship, *Ark Royal* and *Barham*. Force K had to withdraw before Christmas, and the air-sea balance tilted once more against the British by the end of the year. It was not to change back again until Alamein.

During that summer and autumn, both sides resolved their dilemma in the same way, refraining from serious military operations (unless the mysterious German thrust on 14 September be counted an exception) while they tried to accumulate enough reserves to sustain a major offensive. Both were forced into postponements, and both were eventually ready in the same week: Auchinleck's CRUSADER of 18 November only anticipated Rommel's intended attack on Tobruk by a day or two. The absence of large-scale military activity was no doubt the un-

---

[3] This mean that a third of all operational U-boats (and about a sixth of the total operating and coming into service) were in the Mediterranean. (Roskill i.614).

derlying reason why Ultra provided so little operational intelligence during the summer, but another was the continued invulnerability of the army keys. By contrast, the copious flow of naval material from Italian sources made for an imbalance which was not redressed until the end of September.

A consistent pattern in shipping and supply information was established in June and prevailed until the early autumn. At least five or six times a month, the sailing from a Greek or Italian port of a convoy of supply ships or troop transports could be signaled to naval and air headquarters in Egypt (to Malta as well, when a direct link was opened in mid-September) sufficiently far in advance for the convoy to be intercepted somewhere along a route which was usually set out in considerable detail (points at which ships regularly altered course were often disguised under code names, but the disguise was soon penetrated and the points identified). Routine reconnaissance flights by the RAF 201st Group, based on Alexandria, could then be adjusted to ensure that planes were in the right places to spot convoys apparently by chance, after which bombers, submarines, or surface craft, as appropriate, could attack without compromising the source.

Even if attack was impossible or ineffective, the sight of a reconnaissance plane overhead might be enough to scare the convoy into a hasty return to port, thus at any rate delaying the supply program. On 27 June, for example, air reconnaissance forced a convoy carrying 5,000 men back to Taranto, and the same thing happened again a month later. A series of messages during August and September revealed the tribulations of the tanker *Bellona,* which was too slow to avoid the aircraft and destroyers which relentlessly harried her and was unable to reach Bardia and deliver petrol which was said to be "of the highest importance" to the Afrika Korps; she had instead to take refuge in Suda Bay before returning to the Piraeus, where she was eventually replaced by a faster vessel.

Among the many cases where it is not now possible to be quite sure that the sinking of a particular Axis transport can be directly ascribed to Ultra, a few stand out as absolute certainties. On the afternoon of 17 August it was learned that a convoy of four large liners escorted by six destroyers would leave Naples at midnight the next day bound for Tripoli, where it was due to arrive early on the 20th; only three of the liners reached their destination, the fourth being sunk on the way by the Malta-based submarine *Unique*. Next month these three were to sail for Tripoli from Taranto, and again we had more than twenty-four hours' notice of their route and timings; this time two more, each of 20,000 tons, were torpedoed and sunk on 18 September by *Unique*'s sister ship, *Upholder,* on the basis of "special intelligence." A day or two before this, a cargo of fuel, part consigned to Fliegerfuehrer and part to the Afrika Korps, was sent to the bottom off Trapani four days after its route was signaled to Alexandria and Malta.

Ironically enough, these last events came just after Hitler had ordered Fliegerkorps X to concentrate on convoy protection because of the serious shipping losses which were being suffered! Ultra did not report his decision in so many words but was quick to note action which evidently flowed from it—the planned development of two Sicilian airfields, presumably to house the bomber and fighter Gruppen which it had been proposed to transfer there from Greece in September. The deduction that Fliegerkorps X's move to Greece in June was now being slowed down or reversed was plain.

Force K's first and greatest successes in early and mid-November admirably illustrate the value of Ultra in the logistical war of attrition. CRUSADER began on 18 November between the first and second of them, and their effect on the land campaign can be amply documented from the same source. The mere presence of Force K contributed, within a few days of its arrival in Malta, to the suspension of supply traffic on 1 November, but there was some uncertainty about how long the ban would last because on a previous occasion it had been lifted in twenty-four hours. Thus a signal dispatched on the afternoon of 8 November spoke only hesitantly of there being "some evidence" that in spite of it a convoy had sailed the previous night. The convoy's indubitable existence and its probable ports of departure and destination (Naples and Tripoli) were confirmed the same evening, and the signal was the means of directing first a reconnaissance aircraft and then Force K to the target. In the early hours of 9 November, all seven merchant ships in the convoy, and two out of the four escorting destroyers, were sunk by the gunfire of Force K.[4] Part of the cargo thus denied to the Germans became known while the action was going on: it included 600 tons of GAF stores and 20,000 rounds of 88mm Flak ammunition. (Rommel, it is now known, immediately reported that all sea transport had been stopped because of this disaster, adding that to date he had received only 8,000 of the 60,000 men he had been promised through Benghazi.) Another and more heavily escorted convoy, first forecast on 15 November, was attacked on the 22nd and driven back to Taranto, where it stayed for a fortnight. Two ships from a third, which Fliegerkorps X had been calling for urgently since the beginning of the month (because threatening British troop concentrations and a serious decline in African fuel stocks made it imperative to accumulate 3,000 tons of aircraft fuel in Cyrenaica at once), was sunk en route to Benghazi on 24 November, by which time a week of the CRUSADER battles had made such inroads into Flieger-fuehrer's stocks that his operations were seriously endangered. Air transport, an extravagant way to move petrol from place to place, had to be hastily improvised.

Even when all proper precautions like preliminary air reconnaissance were taken, such "close marking" of convoys could hardly fail to arouse suspicions, particularly when it so often proved lethal. Count Ciano, Mussolini's son-in-law and the Italian Foreign Minister, found the annihilation of the seven-ship convoy on 9 November "inexplicable," for example. Some risk was inseparable from the operational use of Ultra, but it was essential to keep it to the absolute minimum. To preserve the security of the source by restricting the number of those who had access to it (even the commander of Force K was not among them) and to discourage rash actions which might sacrifice it for good in the pursuit of transient advantage were therefore ever-present anxieties. No really serious breach of security seems to have occurred, but Whitehall sent several sharp rebukes to Mid-

---

[4] Santoni, 120, mistakenly denies Ultra the credit.

dle East authorities for carelessly imperiling it.[5] Constant watch-
fullness was particularly necessary after Ultra showed that the
Italians were breaking some British codes and knew, for instance, that Malta had signaled to an aircraft in flight the estimated position of a convoy which Ultra had identified.

A dozen or more returns of aircraft fuel stocks, rendered at
various dates during the summer and early autumn, showed the
effects of the British near-blockade in dramatic form. Stocks in
Tripolitania—that is to say, reserves already landed and awaiting forwarding to the operational area—stood at 4,000 tons in
May but sank to 3,000 in June and to 1,400 at the end of July.
By the beginning of September they were down to a little over
400—just a tenth of the May figure—and remained near that
level, with one brief exception, for the next two months. Moreover, the decline in stocks in the rear was not accounted for by a
corresponding increase farther forward; on the contrary, figures
for the forward area followed the same pattern as those at base.
From 2,800 tons in early September, they dropped steadily
(again, with one brief exception) to 2,350 tons in October and to
only 1,460 tons on 8 November. On the basis of two sets of
consumption figures for October, this meant that just before
heavy fighting began there was about a month's supply of aircraft fuel near the front and rather less at Tripoli—provided always that the current rate of and consumption was unchanged;
in fact, of course, it was bound to rise sharply when mobile warfare began again.

As the petrol shortage grew worse with the approach of autumn, so evidence of the anxiety it was causing became more
and more striking. As early as July, Fliegerkorps X was being
asked to step up its antisubmarine patrols because "future operations will be imperilled by further shipping losses." The
Fliegerkorps passed this request on to the Italians, referring particularly to British submarine activity off Benghazi, but could do
little itself because there was not enough petrol in Africa for it

---

[5] Jealous for the safety of a source which he regarded as peculiarly his own, Churchill
himself sent at least two personal reminders about Ultra security that autumn (Gilbert
vi.1233, 1242).

to transfer units even for a short time, since Fliegerfuehrer had
only sufficient for two or three days' fighting at the level entailed
by the recent battles round Sollum. (It was at this time that
Halder contemptuously wrote in his diary, "Safeguarding transports is an Italian affair. In the present situation ['of aircraft
shortage on the Russian front' is presumably to be understood]
it would be criminal to allot German aircraft for the purpose,"
even though he had recently been told that the 5th Light Division was so short of petrol that it would hardly be able even to
get to the battlefield if ordered to attack Sollum.) Fliegerfuehrer
was not content that his plight should be known only to his immediate superiors but dispatched his complaint direct to Berlin
as well. It was because the Afrika Korps was so short of fuel
that the tanker *Bellona* was to sail from Italy to Benghazi, with
the consequences already noted, and this news was considered
so important in Whitehall that the Chief of Air Staff sent a special signal urging that every possible step be taken to sink the
Bellona. "All available means" were to be used to move fuel
forward from Tripoli at the end of August (the same phrase recurred two months later, this time in relation to the use of transport aircraft—which were also in short supply!—to ferry petrol
to Benghazi); road transport was exclusively reserved for it, but
there were not enough lorries, the Italians were threatening to
recall those they had lent, and the 400 bought from the French
would take several weeks to make the journey from Tunis.
Shortly before heavy fighting began, Fliegerfuehrer urgently demanded new radar equipment to cope with British air superiority, presumably because he was burning up fuel as fast as he
got it and wanted to economize by better fighter control. OKH
became seriously worried when the sinking rate rose to 50 percent in September, and called for convoys carrying artillery to
Africa to be specially protected (by chance General Boettcher,
who was coming to take charge of Rommel's artillery, and
whose gunnery did so much damage at Sidi Rezegh in November, was awaiting embarkation at Naples the same day); a note
appended to this signal says that it was sent "at the special request of the Prime Minister."

Ammunition too was becoming a cause for concern: 88mm

shells were urgently required to enable the Flak batteries to combat British aircraft. A ship loaded with 16,000 of them was torpedoed and damaged off Tripoli, and there was still a shortage at Benghazi in late November. Finally, two very welcome intercepts of 7 November delivered into our hands comprehensive surveys of the Luftwaffe's petrol and ammunition resources on the eve of battle, together with estimates of the amounts of each which could be brought over to Africa by the end of the month.

By autumn, the navy and the RAF were making the convoy routes to Tripoli too dangerous, and in any case stores landed there had to be shifted several hundred miles nearer the front before they were of much use to Rommel or Froehlich. Various ways of overcoming these problems were tried, but none proved very efficacious. Coastal shipping was short—there were said to be only four German ships engaged in coastal traffic, with no more than 2,300 tons capacity among them—and there were Italo-German wrangles about sharing it. A few tankers were sailed direct to Benghazi, and the dividing line between the two areas of responsibility was altered so that the duty of protecting Benghazi fell to Fliegerkorps X instead of to the Italian air command, which was less well equipped and less effective in operations. But the lack of storage tanks there meant that anything over 1,500 tons had to be in barrels until a 5,000-ton tank was constructed in December, and again there were disagreements with the Italians over amounts and transport arrangements. As a last, desperate resort, petrol was several times sent in by U-boat, and troops by destroyer and Ju-52s.

It is not easy to judge what effect this prolonged catalogue of German woe may have had on the direction of British strategy. Certainly Churchill, whose bold imagination was always finding new lines for it—"conjectural schemes," he admitted some of them were—was thinking in terms far wider than Mediterranean logistics when he chided Auchinleck for delay ("It is impossible to explain to Parliament and the nation how it is our Middle East armies have had to stand for 4½ months without engaging the enemy while all the time Russia is being battered to pieces"), and when for a few weeks in the autumn he strove to get agreement to his plan (WHIPCORD) for the invasion of Sicily in the spring of 1942, as soon as Auchinleck should follow his expected victory by occupying Tripolitania. This, he claimed, was the only way then possible to open up a second front in Europe. It was the temporary weakness of Rommel and of the GAF in the Mediterranean (caused by Germany's heavy investment in the invasion of Russia) which persuaded him that the "fleeting opportunity" should be seized before a Russian collapse freed enough German troops and aircraft to rule it out forever. For throughout the autumn and winter, Churchill was preoccupied by fear for the northern flank of the British position in the Middle East if Germany gained a quick victory over Russia. "Any day now," he telegraphed to Cripps (Ambassador in Moscow) on 28 October, "Hitler may call a halt in the east and turn his forces against us." Yet Turkey was still deaf to offers of alliance, and the defenses of Iraq and Persia were alarmingly feeble. The same preoccupation with "danger to my northern flank" recurs again and again in Auchinleck's *Despatch*. On the other hand, that Ultra evidence for the poor performance of the German supply system played some part in shaping Churchill's thoughts is proved by his "special request" that the attention of the Middle East should be drawn to OKH's concern over the safety of military convoys.[6] But neither Cairo—more troubled by the potential threat to Egypt and Persia from an enemy who might soon have reached the Caucasus—nor the Chiefs of Staff in London were convinced that the fragility of Rommel's supply lines invited a lengthy British advance westward even if CRUSADER proved a resounding victory, and WHIPCORD was quietly dropped at the end of October.

Nevertheless, the abundant signs in Ultra of German supply difficulties undoubtedly helped to encourage the small circle of Ultra readers to share the mood of buoyancy and confidence (founded on the certainty of matériel preponderance over the enemy, especially in the air—according to Westphal, the Via Balbia was only safe to use at the RAF's mealtimes!) which pre-

---

[6] See p. 76 above.

vailed on the British side in the weeks before CRUSADER. Exactly how the evidence was interpreted, however, and what the effect on Rommel was judged to be cannot now be known—whether, for instance, any attempt was made to set the number of sinkings known from Ultra or claimed by the RN and RAF against the number of ships known or believed to have reached their Libyan destinations safely; whether the clamor of complaint was taken at face value (as it was by Churchill when he urged Auchinleck to attack quickly because Rommel's army "was having the greatest difficulty in so much as existing"); whether allowance was made for the natural exaggeration of soldiers eager to conjure what they deemed essential from superiors reluctant or unable to grant it; whether the conclusions drawn from Ultra signals were suitably cautious and objective or whether emphasis was given only to those items which confirmed the mood of optimism. We know now, it must be remembered, that despite all the evidence cited above, by the autumn of 1941 Ultra had not yet "enabled the British to put the screw on Axis supply traffic in the Mediterranean" with anything like decisive effect, although the opposition was relatively weaker than it became in 1942, because we also now know that the sinking rate averaged only 20 percent over the whole five months between BATTLEAXE and CRUSADER, and only rose to a really dangerous level during Force K's brief reign.

On the other hand, the same Ultra evidence does show very clearly that even this 20 percent was enough to do grievous harm by preventing the stockpiling of fuel, weapons, and explosives in the forward area, and that this delayed the start of the Axis offensive. The delay enabled Auchinleck to strike first and thus to reap the intended benefit of his policy of deliberately holding back his blow until he had accumulated sufficient stocks to make it (as he hoped) decisive. The 20 percent sinking rate, low as it seems when compared with the hundreds of opportunities presented by signal after Ultra signal about future shipping movements, was therefore enough to deprive Rommel of the initiative. How much of the 20 percent was entirely due to Ultra, and how many ships would anyhow have been seen and sunk even if Ultra had not been there to guide the spotter planes, cruisers, destroyers, and submarines to their targets, it is impossible to tell, but there can be no doubt that Ultra's share of the intelligence which led to the sinkings was a large one. But this is not all. Although the Eighth army began CRUSADER at a moment of its own choosing and with more tanks and guns in the field and far more in reserve than the enemy, it was only just strong enough to win the battle of attrition which followed. In spite of his supply problems, Rommel very nearly gained the day. There is consequently a second point to score up to Ultra's credit. Since Rommel did so well with so little, it may reasonably be argued that with a little more he would have won. Ultra's share of the meager 20 percent was, then, very probably strategically decisive. Tactically, Rommel was more than a match for Cunningham and Ritchie, against whom he fought in CRUSADER. With more resources at his command, he might well have trounced them, captured Tobruk, and driven the Eighth Army back to the Nile instead of himself retreating to the Gulf of Sirte. If anything like the debacle of June and July 1942 had occurred at Christmas 1941, the consequences would have been infinitely more damaging than they were six months later, for Russia was still teetering on the brink of defeat, and the Americans, reeling under the shock of Pearl Harbor, were nowhere near ready to intervene in the Mediterranean. It is not too farfetched to suggest that Ultra's share in the 20 percent just tipped the scales against Rommel, and that its influence on the course of events was therefore enormous.

What few in the desert realized, and what perhaps only Brooke, Montgomery, and a few others could foresee, was that the optimism which prevailed throughout the Eighth Army in November 1941 because of its preponderance in weapons concealed shortcomings in generalship, equipment, and tactics which would prove nearly fatal. The campaign in France had shown Brooke how physically soft the army had become since 1918, how amateurish and conservative its outlook; as GOC, he was busy correcting these shortcomings in Southern Command, but no comparable remedy was applied in the Middle East until—six months before Montgomery arrived—Auchinleck created the post of Director of Military Training in February 1942 and appointed one of the Eighth Army's most experienced and farsighted officers to it. In the army as a whole, the malady was too widespread for rapid cure, and soon after he became CIGS, in December 1941, Brooke wrote in his diary, "Half our Corps and Divisional Commanders are totally unfit for their appointments, and yet if I were to sack them, I could find no better." In the final analysis, these shortcomings had more to do with the outcome of CRUSADER than any military intelligence before or during the battle.

Looked at from the opposite point of view, the Ultra evidence about Axis supplies raises a profound but unanswerable question. If the comparatively low rate of sinkings actually achieved was such a serious embarrassment, does it not seem to follow that even a modest increase in it would have so starved Panzergruppe Afrika that it would have been unable to fight a major battle, so that neither Rommel's skill nor British shortcomings could have saved it? Why was a higher rate not attained? Was it because Ultra was not exploited to the full? After the severe losses in surface vessels which had been incurred off Crete, the Admiralty is rather to be praised for the boldness which (at Churchill's prompting) risked Force K in the Mediterranean than blamed for insufficient effort. But in spite of the shortage of modern aircraft of all types and the overriding need for caution in using a source which it would be fatal to compromise, it does now look as if the RAF could have done more, and this is not to forget the great improvement in its effectiveness (notably in army-air cooperation) brought about by Tedder and Coningham.[7] Damaging as they were, British naval and air attacks on Axis transports were not decisive, and in retrospect at least it can be seen that this had wide strategic repercussions. So good a chance to cut Rommel's lifeline was not to come again for a long time: Kesselring and Luftflotte 2 saw to that almost at once by paralyzing Malta. If that lifeline had been cut before CRUSADER, however, Rommel's army would have withered

---

[7] Respectively, AOC-in-C Middle East and AOC Desert Air Force since June and July (MME ii.277–78; Terraine, 337–57).

and died,[8] WHIPCORD would no longer have been mere fantasy, and the humiliating defeats and laborious recovery of 1942 would not have been necessary before the Axis could be cleared from the northern shores of Africa. Yet no one seems to have thought at the time that the sinking rate could be appreciably improved, and this has to be borne prominently in mind today. Cunningham's attack plan for CRUSADER included the sentence "It is understood that the enemy supply situation cannot be interfered with to a much greater degree than at present." No later historian has suggested otherwise, and there does not seem to be any surviving record or discoverable recollection of complaints that Rommel's supplies were getting through too easily. No doubt the maximum effort was made which the available ships and aircraft permitted. With hindsight, however, it seems clear that in autumn 1941, Ultra brought within reach a fleeting chance to starve Panzergruppe Afrika of essential supplies so completely that it might have been brought to a dead stop.[9]

With the exception of scraps which, when put together, enabled the Air Ministry to send Cairo the complete GAF order of battle in the Mediterranean, virtually no operational intelligence other than naval was derived from Ultra in July and August. The mists suddenly cleared about the middle of September, and the outlook remained far brighter from then on. Two different factors brought about the change, but their influence cannot be separated, because German inactivity during the summer began to give way to active preparations for an offensive at much the same time as our first direct access to the doings of Rommel's army came with the breaking of the Chaffinch key which it used. Henceforward, Hut 3 was almost always working at high pressure until the end of the war.

The first signs of change were a few items which were evi-

---

[8] As it very nearly did on 7 December (see p. 92, below). The pressure which forced Rommel to retreat then reinforces the suggestion advanced herein, as do Raedor's views reported on p. 94.

[9] Rommel's force had been upgraded to an armored group on 1 August, but this had only recently been reported by Ultra. In conformity with his increased responsibilities, Rommel was promoted full general.

dently the preliminaries of the strange and apparently purposeless operation which Rommel code-named SOMMERNACHTSTRAUM ("Midsummer Night's Dream"), a one-day raid into Egypt on 14 September. It accomplished nothing save to confirm Rommel in his mistaken belief that no British attack was in the offing, and it came to an ignominious end when the tanks ran out of petrol and the halted column was heavily bombed from the air. Ultra may fairly claim to have given warning of SOMMERNACHTSTRAUM, since a request from Panzergruppe Afrika for regular air reconnaissance of Sidi Barrani, Mersa Matruh, and El Daba during a "special undertaking" due to take place on 14 September was signaled to Cairo and Western Desert (with which there was now a direct link) at dawn on the 11th, following news that the 21st Panzer Division (recently formed out of a reinforced 5th Light) was at Derna.[10] The move of 100 aircraft, some of them a new and faster type of Messerschmitt fighter, to forward airfields on 13 September to support SOMMERNACHTSTRAUM could not be signaled until the next morning, and so arrived too late to reinforce the warning. It was on the eve of this raid, too, that the first *Tagesmeldung* ("Day Report") from Fliegerkorps X was signaled—the forerunner of thousands of similar reports and forecasts from the same and other air and ground commands.

For the next six weeks, incoming messages were scanned for hints either that Rommel was about to launch a major offensive or that he expected Auchinleck to do so. At first, the signs were few and ambiguous, and it was not until early in November that clear indications of a forthcoming German attack on Tobruk were apparent. Thus, although a plan to bomb or sabotage the desert railway which carried British supplies (it was even then being extended westward in preparation for CRUSADER)

---

[10] BI ii.294 denies that Ultra gave advance notice of SOMMERNACHTSTRAUM. This is only true in the most literal sense, for mention of a special operation by Panzergruppe on a stated date in a stated area was a warning which could scarcely be misunderstood. If indeed it was the British withdrawal in face of the 21st Panzer's advance which confirmed Rommel in his belief that they were not preparing to attack, then the Ultra warning (which presumably suggested the withdrawal) was of considerable importance, for it enabled Auchinleck and Cunningham (GOC Eighth Army since August) to practice a profitable deception.

and put it out of action for a month, references to guns and ammunition bought from the French as being "of vital importance to Panzergruppe's future plans," and the location in the forward area of the newly identified Division z.b.V. Afrika (soon to be converted into the renowned 90th Light Division) and the 15th Panzer (under its new commander, General Neumann-Silkow) all suggested that preparations for attack were well advanced, this inference was nevertheless ruled out at the end of September by a message from the German Liaison Staff in Rome which informed Panzergruppe that it did not anticipate being able to clear the bottleneck in personnel transport for two or three more weeks. Appended to the signal conveying the last item to Cairo is the note "Minister of Defence directs that General Auchinleck shall see," plainly in order that he might be encouraged to mount his own offensive before Rommel could be ready.

Shortages of guns and shells, particularly antitank guns and antiaircraft shells, were Panzergruppe's main preoccupation. The urgency of these and similar demands was evidently the result of fears that the British might attack before its own preparations were complete, but no indication of Rommel's expected readiness date was received until the first week in November. Vague mention of Panzergruppe's "projects" and of "operations" which might be jeopardized by the lack of 88mm Flak ammunition first acquired precision of meaning when they were seen alongside the need to ensure that at least 3,000 tons of aircraft fuel reached Cyrenaica by 20 November. This news was signaled on 5 November, in ample time to show that Auchinleck's plan (made in mid-October) to attack on or about 15 November would give him first strike. Further evidence tending to confirm this was soon available: emergency plans were being made on 9 November for the training of junior commanders before the "impending attack," all army leave was stopped on the 10th, and new forward fuel dumps were established. Little room was left for doubt by orders, signaled before midday on 17 November, for two detachments of fighters to transfer "shortly" to Africa to operate in support of Panzergruppe for three or four days, and none after the discovery that Rommel, who was planning to fly to Rome at the beginning of the month, would be returning via Athens at dawn on the 18th, just as the Eighth Army would be moving up to the attack. Here was conclusive proof that CRUSADER would take the enemy by surprise.

Rommel's timing was therefore well enough known through the medium of Ultra. What of his objective and the direction of his intended thrust? To capture Tobruk, which had escaped him in April, had by this time become a fixation with Rommel, but there was no hint of this in Ultra until 8 November, when Panzergruppe called for sixty copies of a photo-mosaic of Tobruk to be ready by the fifteenth, and 11 November, when it wanted thirty enlargements of a particular sector of the defenses. Both signals left Hut 3 for Cairo within a few hours of their German times of origin, but for some now quite incomprehensible reason they were given only low priority; they may therefore not have arrived until the next day, but this was still well before Rommel planned to begin his assault. The methods to be used were soon revealed: inflatable landing boats and engineer equipment for crossing minefields were being assembled at Derna.

Lastly, two very informative intercepts in the week before CRUSADER gave welcome confirmation to British calculations of the scale of opposition to be met on the ground and in the air. The first of what was to become a long series of tank strength-returns showed that on 11 November the Afrika Korps had 35 Mark IVs, 139 IIIs, and 70 IIs ready for battle. The Mark II was now obsolescent, so that the British total of nearly 500 seemed to compare very favorably with the remaining 174 (to which rather more than 100 tanks of doubtful fighting value in the Italian XX Corps should be added). In fact, the Eighth Army had less of an advantage than this suggested, because it did not know that face-hardened armor or extra plates bolted over the most exposed parts of the main structure of many German tanks had rendered them impenetrable by most British antitank guns except at dangerously close range. Nor did Ultra reveal that Panzergruppe could deploy 140 heavy antitank guns, 35 of them 88s.

Less than a week later, a comprehensive strength return for Fliegerkorps X showed 254 serviceable aircraft out of a total of

423, including 127 (out of 207) in the subordinate detachment under Fliegerfuehrer Afrika. This return was so detailed—it listed the number of serviceable machines in every unit—that it produced one of the longest signals yet. It came a month too late to prevent the fierce disagreement about serviceability rates which (in spite of Ultra's regular interception of periodical returns from both German authorities) had broken out in October between the Air Ministry and Tedder's headquarters in Cairo, but it settled the argument finally and proved that (as was also the case with tanks) few reinforcements had reached the Germans since they first intervened in Africa. The low serviceability rate[11] (it had long been a source of disquiet; Fliegerfuehrer had no aircraft available for reconnaissance in mid-November, and only dive-bombers for escort duty), which was in marked contrast to German skill in recovering and repairing battle-damaged tanks, emphasized British superiority in the air: the RAF expected to have 528 aircraft ready for CRUSADER.

---

[11]Low though it was, the serviceability rate in the Mediterranean was considerably higher than in the GAF as a whole: under the rigors of the Russian winter it fell from 64 percent to only 44 percent between June and October, out of an aircraft total which remained almost static, between 3,300 and 3,500 (OKW/KTB i.110E).

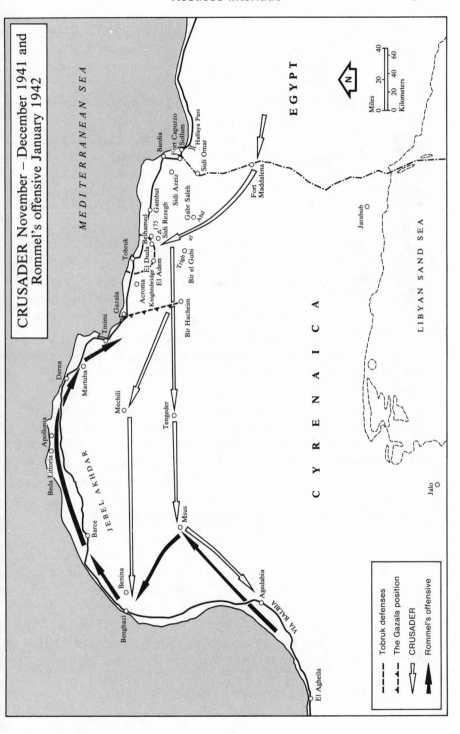

CRUSADER November – December 1941 and Rommel's offensive January 1942

MEDITERRANEAN SEA

EGYPT

Miles
Kilometers

N

LIBYAN SAND SEA

CYRENAICA

Bardia
Fort Capuzzo
Sollum
Halfaya Pass
Sidi Omar
Fort Maddalena

Sidi Azeiz
Gambut
Gabr Saleh
△175
Sidi Rezegh
Abd
El Duda Belhamed
Acroma
Knightsbridge
El Adem
Trigh
Bir el Gubi
el

Tobruk
Gazala
Tmimi

Jarabub

Derna
Martuba
Mechili
Tengeder
Bir Hacheim

Apollonia
Beda Littoria

JEBEL AKHDAR

Barce
Benina
Msus

Jalo

Benghazi

Agedabia
VIA BALBIA

El Agheila

Tobruk defenses
The Gazala position
CRUSADER
Rommel's offensive

4
CRUSADER:
VICTORY INTO DEFEAT
November 1941–February 1942

The sometimes foolhardy bravery which too often took the place of rational military action in 1941 was tragically illustrated by the daring raid which cost Lieutenant Colonel Geoffrey Keyes his life on the night of 17–18 November. The object of the raid was to kill or capture Rommel at what was thought to be his headquarters at Beda Littoria (the Italians had foreseen a landing on the nearby coast on the 14th), and thereby to throw the German command into confusion just as the British offensive opened. Unfortunately, no one stopped to wonder whether Beda Littoria—two hundred miles behind the front—was the sort of place the hard-driving leader Rommel had shown himself to be would choose for a headquarters (in fact, it was an administrative base). Moreover, Ultra had shown Rommel intending to fly to Italy on 1 November, and there had been no sign of his return. Proper liaison between intelligence and operations could have produced a hint that he was unlikely to be found at Beda Littoria on the night chosen for the raid, but in 1941 the two were still too often segregated.[1] As it turned out, Rommel flew back from Athens on the morning of 18 November, but his intention to do so was not known through Ultra until too late; the raid was already in progress while the high-priority signal (the German text was only decrypted shortly be-

---

[1] For further discussion of this segregation and its remedy, see pp. 100–103.

fore midnight) conveying the news of his journey was on its way to Cairo.

Rommel's absence also showed the success of the deception which "A" Force under Colonel Dudley Clarke was now practicing with extraordinary skill. Deception was, of course, not a new military art, but in its desert form it was invented—or reinvented—in 1941 with astonishing results. It is a strange reflection that only in the two fields where an originally quite amateur approach had to develop highly professional rules for its own peculiar game—deception and desert reconnaissance—did the British outdo the Germans until late in 1942.

The official history of deception is still unpublished, and such partial accounts as are now in print do not always carry conviction and are often in conflict with one another. While the means that were employed remain for the present obscure, therefore, their success is broadly plain. Misleading information was somehow passed to Rommel which suggested that far from planning a major offensive in the western desert, Auchinleck was even preparing to transfer troops northward to help the Russians defend the Caucasus. Rommel was thereby induced to think that he could choose his own time without reference to British intentions; his leisurely program, revealed through Ultra, made it possible for CRUSADER to precede his attack on Tobruk in spite of Auchinleck's insistence on delay. Only one aspect, relatively unimportant, of the British cover plan made an appearance in Ultra. The possibility of a "left hook," an outflanking move via the oases of Siwa and Jarabub, had at one time been briefly examined before being discarded because it entailed insuperable problems of supply. Thereafter, rumors of it were sedulously disseminated, and some of the fake supporting evidence provided was detected by German reconnaissance and reported in Enigma.

For the first day or two of the offensive, an unjustified optimism prevailed at Eighth Army HQ and in Cairo, but once Rommel had sized the situation up he got the better of it for a time, and CRUSADER only became a short-lived victory—but a victory on points, not the expected knockout—when the British preponderance in matériel enabled them to win the battle of attrition after three weeks of wildly confused fighting and maneuvering.

Lieutenant General Sir Andrew Cunningham, the conqueror of Ethiopia, had been commanding the Eighth Army since September, but he had no experience of armored warfare on the scale which the desert was now to see, and he could not match Rommel for originality or speed of thought. His plan for CRUSADER betrayed this: to push his tanks forward, wait for the Germans to react, and then hope to destroy their armor in the subsequent collision. But this was to surrender the initiative voluntarily, to invite the enemy to choose his time and method of attack, and in any case a column of tanks is free to roam the desert and could not be treated as an objective; his plan was "like penning a savage bull in a hencoop." Moreover, almost at once Cunningham dispersed his own armor (he had far more tanks than Rommel), instead of keeping it massed to crush the Afrika Korps, so that Rommel was able to destroy it piecemeal. In the fighting round Sidi Rezegh on 20 November and later, Cunningham "picked up the bill for twenty years of military decadence" and lost the armored battle he had designed CRUSADER to provoke. His nerve was shaken by Sidi Rezegh. Auchinleck ordered him to continue the advance nevertheless, but replaced him on the 26th with Major General Neil Ritchie, his own Deputy Chief of Staff. Ritchie, unhappily, was to be Auchinleck's second bad choice of army commander.

On the other hand, by behaving quite out of character for several days, Rommel gave the Eighth Army more opportunities than it deserved. For forty-eight hours he did not believe that he was facing a major offensive, he suffered heavier losses in tanks than he could afford, and he did not take full advantage of the initiative which Cunningham had presented to him by his weak opening gambit. Then, on 24 November, he made his famous but foolish "dash to the wire" (the wire fence that marked the frontier between Cyrenaica and Egypt), which took him right away from the main battlefield outside Tobruk for three days, and in the course of which he missed two supply dumps the British had prepared for CRUSADER, although each was six miles square. By the end of the month, the Eighth Army had just managed to open a corridor into beleaguered Tobruk, but neither side had shown much sound military sense; the commander of the 21st Panzer Division, taken prisoner on 29 November, declared that many were dissatisfied with Rommel's leadership, thus echoing Auchinleck's and many others' opinion of Cunningham.

Both sides were becoming exhausted, but Panzergruppe was near the end of its tether. The Afrika Korps was down to 40 tanks, like Fliegerfuehrer it was critically short of fuel, and enough of the precious 88mm guns had been lost to make the replacement of only four of them the subject of a special plea for urgent delivery on 26 November.[2] Toward the end of November, "at last reality caught up with Rommel" as he girded himself for the retreat which he could not now avoid. On 7 December, the day the Japanese bombed Pearl Harbor, he decided to withdraw to the fallback position at Gazala which Paulus had recommended six months earlier, and Panzergruppe was digging in there on the 11th as Hitler sealed his own doom by declaring war on the United States, thus ensuring that its vast industrial resources and reserves of manpower would eventually be turned against the Third Reich.

This first phase of CRUSADER, it can now be plainly seen, was almost an object lesson in the principle that Ultra was seldom at its best on tactical intelligence. Apart from a hint of Rommel's intention to make his dash for the wire, it cast few rays of light through the fog of war of which Auchinleck complained and which so often blinded both sides to what was happening. No echo was heard in Ultra, for instance, of the seventy frantic signals which Rommel's operations officer, Oberstleutnant Siegfried Westphal, sent to his errant commander from the headquarters he had so abruptly deserted, and this in spite of the cryptanalysts' success in breaking several days of the two army keys about this time. GAF Enigma, on the other hand, betrayed the long-term deterioration of German resources through the records of fuel stocks which were intercepted almost

---

[2]Rommel had fewer than a dozen 88s by the end of December, and was driven to use dummies (Irving, 140).

every day. After only the first forty-eight hours' fighting, the reserves of aircraft petrol in Cyrenaica had already dropped to a third of what they had been on 8 November, and with only small fluctuations stocks continued to diminish steadily. The position was said to be "catastrophic" by 26 November, and a calculation based on the return for that day and on known average rates of consumption forecast optimistically that there would be no petrol at all in Cyrenaica by 1 December unless new supplies were received. Fliegerfuehrer's operations were several times reported as jeopardized by the shortage, and emergency transport of comparatively small quantities by U-boat and Ju-52 was laid on. Fliegerfuehrer's aircraft strength was being eroded in combat at the same time, in spite of the arrival of a Gruppe of fighters from Germany—54 fewer fighters were serviceable on 26 November than at the beginning of the British offensive.

Ultra itself can claim to have been in large measure the cause of the "catastrophic" situation in Cyrenaica. On 22 November it showed that two ships, *Procida* and *Maritza,* were to transport badly needed petrol from the Piraeus to Benghazi the next day. Churchill urged that they be destroyed at once, and the Royal Navy sank them both on the 24th. Between them they had been carrying more than three times the amount of petrol in all the dumps in Cyrenaica that day, and news of their loss meant that replacement supplies were immediately declared to be "of the utmost urgency." It was just after this that Auchinleck issued an Order of the Day:—"Attack and pursue. All out, everyone"—and turned the tide which had been running against the Eighth Army for a fortnight. The bearing of Ultra on his action is evident: if the sinking of *Procida* and *Maritza* grounded Froehlich's aircraft, Rommel's tanks would at once become sitting ducks for the RAF.

It was the cumulative effect of British pressure on the Axis supply lines throughout the autumn which won CRUSADER, not generalship—the generals had failed to prevent the "maddening muddles" which were already beginning to generate the inferiority complex that infected the Eighth Army for the next six or eight months. But Rommel continued to retreat—he was back at Agheila on the Tripolitanian border by the end of the year—and both London and Cairo still expected the British advance to go on. A paper Churchill wrote at sea on the way to the "Arcadia" conference in Washington in mid-December imagined a victorious Auchinleck reaching the Tunisian frontier before long (the Chiefs of Staff watered his enthusiasm down, however), and an Air Ministry estimate of future GAF strength in the Mediterranean, based on Ultra and dated 28 December, took "the eventual capture of Tripolitania" for granted. But although Fliegerfuehrer had only enough petrol for a single day's sorties on 10 December, and none at all on the 23rd, and although two Italian cruisers carrying petrol were sunk in an Ultra-based operation on 12 December, the means to continue the pressure and drive the Axis out of North Africa were slipping from the British grasp on the eve of apparent triumph.

The first signs were at sea. A little before the affair of the *Procida* and *Maritza,* the carrier *Ark Royal* was torpedoed off Gibraltar while operating with Force K, and just after it the battleship *Barham* was sunk in the western Mediterranean. In the context of CRUSADER, however, the disastrous failure of an Ultra-based attempt at another convoy interception was even more ominous. It became known on 10 December that the Italian battleship *Littorio* would shortly be concerned in "an operation" of some kind, and two days later that the cargo vessel *Ankara* was about to leave Taranto for Benghazi via Navarino, in Greece, sailing from Navarino at 0200 hours on 14 December escorted by the battleship *Doria* and two cruisers. *Ankara*'s intended route was given in detail. After one false start, *Ankara* and a Tripoli-bound convoy of three ships sailed on 16 December. A British squadron set out from Alexandria to intercept, and was joined by Force K from Malta about dawn on the 17th. *Ankara* reached Benghazi safely next day, and the combined British fleet was in hot pursuit of the others when a cruiser and a destroyer were mined and sunk off Tripoli, and two more cruisers damaged. The same morning, 19 December, a daring Italian human-torpedo attack in Alexandria harbor put the battleships *Valiant* and *Queen Elizabeth* out of action for several months. The whole balance of naval power in the Mediterranean was altered at a stroke. Force K's reign was over, but Rommel had not yet retreated beyond Gazala.

The second sign of an altered power balance was a major restructuring of the Axis command. It was slower in making its full impact than events at sea, but it had still more far-reaching strategic repercussions. By mid-September 1941, as pressure on the supply routes to Africa was becoming acute, Admiral Raeder, Commander-in-Chief of the Navy (who had long been urging that England was the chief enemy, not Russia, and that combating England demanded a positive Mediterranean policy), lent his powerful support to loud complaints from the German military staff in Rome to the effect that shortage of supplies was about to lose North Africa and close the Mediterranean to the Axis. The only remedy, they pointed out, was strong naval and air reinforcement, including "the return of the Luftwaffe to Sicily."[3] For once, Hitler listened to advice. He ordered U-boats to the Mediterranean immediately, and even before Force K's depredations began in earnest he transferred Luftflotte 2, one of his six air fleet headquarters, and Fliegerkorps II (a powerful mixture of bombers and fighters) from Russia to Sicily with instructions to neutralize Malta, the base from which British pressure on Axis supplies was chiefly being exercised. Field Marshal Albert Kesselring, a former soldier who had changed uniforms in the 1930s to become one of the founders of the Luftwaffe and had recently been a leading exponent of army-air cooperation with von Bock's army group on the Russian front, was to take command as Oberbefehlshaber Sued ("Commander-in-Chief South").[4] While placing him nominally under the Duce, this title gave Kesselring authority over German and Italian naval forces as well as the two German Fliegerkorps (II in Sicily and X in Greece), but not over Rommel, who remained formally subordinate to General Bastico and the Italian army command (but, of course, inevitably open to the influence of a German superior in rank who also controlled his supply lines). Kesselring's rela-

---

[3] Fliegerkorps X had begun moving from Sicily to Greece in June (OLs 527, 532, 549. See p. 173), but that the move was soon being reconsidered was apparent from OLs 809, 990, and 1141 in August and September.
[4] Hereafter OB South.

tions with his allies were always better than Rommel's, and from now on his stature grew steadily in the estimation of friend and foe alike. By the autumn of 1943 he could persuade Hitler not to abandon Italy as Rommel recommended—thereby in effect condemning the British and Americans to the long and costly slog north astride the Apennines, but his own side to steady and still more debilitating losses comparable to the "running ulcer" of Spain which so weakened Napoleon—and it was to him that Hitler turned to save Germany when the Allies crossed the Rhine in March 1945.

Not for the first nor the last time, major command changes on both sides happened to coincide. Churchill appointed General Sir Alan Brooke (later Viscount Alanbrooke) to succeed Dill as CIGS just before CRUSADER (with the incidental result that there was no effective professional military guidance from London during the battle), and Brooke assumed office on 1 December, a week before Pearl Harbor. Brooke and Kesselring were two of the dominating figures in strategy for the remainder of the war.

Ultra got wind of Luftflotte 2's move—the first positive sign that the British in the Mediterranean could bring some relief to the Russians—about the end of October. A long summary of air operations in Russia dated 2 November appears to treat its imminent departure as a matter of common knowledge, but adds the cautious comment "No indication of destination of Luftflotte 2." Kesselring was first reported in the Mediterranean on 5 December (a fortnight after his arrival), just as Fliegerkorps II was settling into its new Sicilian bases (Ultra was still not quite sure it had arrived in mid-December), and was already developing strategic views at variance with Rommel's a week later. Two signals, dispatched within an hour of each other on the evening of 13 December, alerted Cairo to the conflict of opinion as soon as it occurred. Rommel felt that the military situation might compel him to withdraw to Derna that night, while Kesselring urged that the supply lines could best be safeguarded if Panzergruppe held a position forward of the town. A signal over the Ultra route from Air Ministry to Air Intelligence, Cairo, on 8 December had already explained the new command setup correctly, and although the implied disagreement between them about Derna naturally raised the question whether Kesselring had authority over Rommel or not, the right answer was implicit in the conclusion that there was no evidence to suggest it. As soon as Rommel retreated from Derna (Ultra gave notice on 16 December that he intended to do so almost at once), the disagreement became apparent, of course. Their relations did, in fact, get off to a thoroughly bad start, since Rommel could legitimately complain of a lack of air support and of the careless bombing of the Afrika Korps' tanks by the Luftwaffe. Ultra knew only that both men were increasingly anxious about fuel supplies, and gave the (falsely, as it turned out) encouraging news on Boxing Day that in Kesselring's opinion the transport of reinforcements to Africa by air was out of the question for a considerable time to come.

The presence of a supreme commander in the Mediterranean theater and the arrival there of several hundred more aircraft was bound to raise both the volume and the potential importance of Enigma traffic there. On the first day of 1942, major key changes threatened to make much of it unreadable, but the cryptanalysts rose to the occasion and scored a series of remarkably swift successes. The Light Blue, which had revealed so much about German activity in the Mediterranean, went out of use on 31 December; in future, each Fliegerkorps had its own key, and so did the GAF ground administration, Luftgaustab Afrika. Fliegerkorps X's new key, Gadfly, was broken the day it came into force, and the other two by the middle of January. Although it could not be read with the regularity of Light Blue, Locust disclosed enough about Fliegerkorps II's plans to alleviate in some degree the agony which Malta suffered in the New Year when Kesselring began the raids which were the prime reason for his appointment (e.g., by warning Malta at dawn on 6 January that raids were planned for later that day). In Libya, Primrose enabled a close watch still to be kept on Fliegerfuehrer's fuel and bomb stocks. The only fly in the ointment was that Rommel's army keys became recalcitrant again for the next few months; Ultra was thereby denied the chance of forecasting the offensive of 21 January 1942.

The strategic significance of Kesselring's appointment was great, but it must not be exaggerated. Until Hitler got cold feet and refused to sanction Operation HERKULES against Malta in May, it showed that OKW was attaching more importance to the southern front than hitherto by transferring men and machines to it from Russia, and to this extent it released the brake which Halder and Paulus had tried to put on Rommel's impetuosity. But except in Hitler's mind,[5] it was never intended to activate one arm of a huge strategic enveloping movement—the other arm to hinge on the Caucasus when the Germans eventually occupied it—designed to loosen forever the British hold on the Middle East, fear of which haunted London and Cairo for the next few months. Not until General von Thoma, captured at Alamein in November, admitted that the threat of envelopment was accidental rather than planned was this apparent, but by then the danger was past in any case.

Neither of these two pointers to the future had been properly appreciated by the time Rommel struck again on 21 January, gaining a surprise as great as he had secured the previous spring but this time with more serious consequences. Enough of his supply ships were still being sunk at the turn of the year to obscure the conclusions about a shift in the balance of sea power to which hindsight now makes it possible to assign an earlier date, and the sole object of Kesselring's appointment was still believed to be the reduction of Malta. Thus there was nothing to prevent Rommel's retreat from reviving the facile optimism of November, and nothing—unhappily—to stop Middle East intelligence assessments from illustrating the dismal truth that the human mind tends to see only what its preconceptions condition it to see, and too often blinds itself to evidence which might lead to contrary conclusions.

There was no doubt that shortage of petrol for tanks and aircraft had been the main cause of the German withdrawal, and although Ultra was beginning to show that there were occasional days (i.e., 4 December and 5 January) when supply momentarily

---

[5]Directive 32 of 11 June 1941 (Trevor-Roper, 78–82). See pp. 110–111, below.

overtook demand, the general trend was still downward, in spite of the shortening of the supply lines consequent upon the evacuation of Cyrenaica. By early January, Panzergruppe and the Eighth Army were tentatively probing each other's positions at Agheila: the one tired and dispirited by the long retreat, the other overextended and thin on the ground because of the long advance and the difficulty of bringing up supplies from a railhead the other side of Tobruk, four or five hundred miles away, and weakened also by the departure of two good Australian divisions to the Far East and their replacement by less battle-hardened formations. At a conference on 12 January, Rommel's senior intelligence officer, Major von Mellenthin, suggested that current relative strengths were crucial, and that for the next ten days or so (but not longer) the Afrika Korps and the Italian Motor Corps would have more tanks in the forward area than the Eighth Army. Now, therefore, was the moment to strike. Von Mellenthin's calculations proved correct, and his prescience was the foundation of Rommel's next victory. For estimates of the number of German tanks in the desert were at this critical moment the Achilles' heel of intelligence at Eighth Army and GHQ Cairo alike. Just before Panzergruppe abandoned Derna, *Ankara* and *Monginevro,* two of the ships which had escaped on 17 and 18 December, had unloaded 22 and 23 tanks at Benghazi and Tripoli respectively, but Eighth Army and GHQ both refused to believe that heavy cargo could have been discharged from *Ankara* (whose movements into and out of Benghazi again were exactly traceable in Ultra) because the docks were found to have been systematically destroyed when the Eighth Army entered the town shortly afterward. Nor does an Ultra mention of 17 Mark III tanks being on board one of the ships (unnamed) in this convoy seem to have caused them even to contemplate the possibility that the Afrika Korps was being reinforced as it retreated. Evidently unmoved by Ultra reports of the arrival of an unspecified number of tanks at Benina for the 15th Panzer Division on 17 December (the dating proved them not to have been the same as those carried by *Ankara*) and by several references to the projected airlift of a panzer company to Tripoli, indifferent also to the forward troops' insistence that they had captured new tanks on 27 December and that the Afrika Korps was fielding substantially more tanks than current intelligence estimates allowed, GHQ continued to hold that Rommel was still in difficulties. "I suppose there is a possibility that Rommel may stage a counter-offensive," wrote Auchinleck to Ritchie on 4 January, clearly scouting the idea, and to Churchill on 12 January he signaled, "I am convinced that the enemy is hard pressed." His official *Despatch* (written, of course, long after the event) is no less sanguine—"The enemy seemed too weak to stage a counter-offensive," and "It seemed highly unlikely" that Rommel could attack before February.[6]

Opinions like this were based in large measure on GHQ Cairo's repeated underestimates of German tank strength. How far was Ultra to blame for this, and how far the intelligence staffs in the Middle East? Since the army key, Chaffinch, had become unreadable again in early December, Ultra was back to where it had been for most of 1941: such scraps of information about the army as came our way were only incidental to traffic in a GAF cipher between GAF authorities. Ultra recipients who knew nothing about the complexities of Enigma, and could be told nothing, could not be expected to realize this and to make allowance for it—indeed, it is doubtful whether it was sufficiently remarked on in either Hut 3 or the War Office. An unprecedented amount of convoy information was being decrypted in January, but cargo manifests were as scarce as ever and, of course, only dealt with GAF cargoes when they did appear. If tanks or antitank guns were not listed, this did not mean that there were none on board the ship in question, only that the GAF was not concerned with them. Several references to the freight carried by *Ankara* and *Monginevro* were decrypted, but none mentioned tanks. If Middle East construed this to mean that neither carried tanks (in fact, as already noted, they carried nearly 50 between them), then they were forgetting the signal

---

[6]It is true that although Auchinleck's Operation Instruction No. 110 (*London Gazette*, 15 January 1948, 377–78) to Ritchie on 19 January begins, "My present intention is to continue the offensive in Libya and the objective remains Tripoli," the rest of it is concerned with detailing what is to be done if the Eighth Army is forced to withdraw. But the instruction was confessedly governed by "the fluidity of the general strategic situation" (i.e., Russia and the Far East), not by any apprehension of an attack by Rommel.

stating that there were 17 Mark IIIs on board one of the vessels. This should surely have been a warning against hasty and comfortable conclusions, and might even have led to the deduction that for some reason the manifests were incomplete. Ultra did not give much help, plainly, but this can hardly serve as an excuse for loose reasoning. Still less defensible is Middle East's apparent failure even to envisage the possibility that two new convoys announced on 3 January might be carrying tanks (in actual fact they brought 54 and "a large number" of antitank guns), particularly in view of an inquiry, addressed to the naval authorities in Tripoli and quickly answered in the affirmative, whether 25-ton armored fighting vehicles could be unloaded by lighter from ships expected to dock shortly.[7]

Several contradictory statements are in print about the number of tanks under Rommel's command at the moment he attacked on 21 January, and about the difference between this and the British estimate. The OKW War Diary credits the Afrika Korps with 97 on 19 January, probably rising to 111 on the 20th, with 28 more on the way up to the front, plus 89 in the Italian Motor Corps; Auchinleck's dispatch estimates Rommel to have 70 medium tanks all told, including about 25 German, with another 20 available at short notice. On this basis, there were three times more tanks ranged against them than Eighth Army believed; on another basis of calculation, the discrepancy was only 100 percent—42 estimated, 84 actually sent into battle. Either way, the error is culpably large. Had the error (whatever precisely its size) not been made, Auchinleck would not have had to write, "On 21 January the improbable occurred and without warning the Axis forces began to advance."

The new CIGS, Brooke, was almost alone in refusing to wear rose-tinted spectacles, and in sensing that the sweets of victory might soon turn sour. In mid-January he warned Auchinleck about his intelligence staff's highly colored reports, and after the event he made very plain his belief that "overoptimistic intelligence played a large part in accounting for your

---

[7] All the variants of Mark III and Mark IV tanks weighed between 20 and 25 tons.

troubles," putting the blame squarely on the shoulders of the Chief Intelligence Officer, Brigadier Shearer, whom he eventually persuaded Auchinleck to dismiss at the end of February. But good came out of it. Auchinleck replaced Shearer with a member of his own planning staff, Lieutenant Colonel (later Major General Sir) Francis de Guingand, who pleaded total ignorance of intelligence but quickly became adept at it, injected alertness and accuracy into his subordinates, and encouraged more rational methods of work in what had perhaps been too impressionistic an organization. De Guingand soon recruited two junior officers who, with one who was already serving under Shearer, were to play dominant roles in British intelligence for the remainder of the war: Brigadier Sir Edgar Williams, Brigadier Enoch Powell, and Colonel Joe Ewart, to give them their final ranks (Williams and Ewart were responsible for operational intelligence, Powell for supply). All had been professional academics before the war, and there is little doubt that the similarity of their mental outlook to that of the predominantly academic staff in Hut 3 gradually promoted a mutual trust and understanding between two bodies of men engaged upon complementary aspects of the same task two thousand miles apart, and led in time to a much closer relationship in the elucidation of common problems than had hitherto been the case.[8]

We and our Middle Eastern clients had in recent months been unwillingly conducting a "dialogue of the deaf," which seriously hampered the proper use of Ultra intelligence. The nui-

---

[8]In the course of that same February, Auchinleck created the new post of Director of Military Training and appointed to it Major General John Harding, who, having been Chief of Staff to O'Connor and his successors, had more experience of desert fighting and its requirements than most and knew what was lacking in the training and cooperation of infantry and tanks. During March, Brooke, deeply concerned about the mishandling of the armor, sent out Major General Richard McCreery, one of his best tank officers, to advise Auchinleck.

Within the space of the same few weeks in the spring of 1942, therefore, significant steps were being taken in three different fields to rectify past shortcomings and to give fresh purpose and new direction to Middle East Command. No single mind originated them all (but Brooke was closely concerned in two of them), and there appears to have been no deliberate and coordinated policy linking them together. The historian's retrospective glance, however, cannot but notice the distinctive pattern made by these three separate but contemporary events. Some of the tools with which Montgomery later finished the job were already being forged four or five months before he appeared on the scene.

sance continued for some time yet—indeed, it was temporarily aggravated by the heightened tensions and shortened tempers which followed the disasters of the next few months—and the easier relations referred to above did not become the accepted norm until the late summer of 1942. This dialogue of the deaf was the product of distance combined with a baffled frustration consequent upon the continual reverses on every front, and, unhappily, it made itself felt even at the highest levels. "Long distance arguments," wrote Desmond Young apropos this very period, "like long-distance telephone calls in India, leave the exasperated participants with the impression that there is a half-wit at the other end of the line." Half a century later, when no one composes telegrams anymore and anyone can dial a number on the other side of the world and take it for granted that each party will hear the other clearly, it is hard to remember that even the most carefully worded telegraphese never conveys quite the same meaning to the receiver as to the sender, and that in those days answers to requests for clarification could take infuriatingly long to arrive, particularly when cables and W/T channels became clogged with traffic in consequence of the war in the Far East.

Examples of the impediments to the intelligent exchange of views are numberless. The failure of someone in Cairo to give London a simple piece of information about tank axles led to grievous misunderstanding and many wasted months of effort in the autumn of 1941. The serious disagreements about the number of Axis tanks which reverberated throughout the spring showed "how misleading figures—especially telegraphese figures—can be," until they were summarily ended by a series of Ultra tank returns which put the figures beyond argument.[9] Auchinleck wrote out a signal to the CIGS on 28 December 1941 which Brooke could not answer until 21 January, and his answer was not received in Cairo for another three weeks. Misunderstandings were rife as tempers snapped in the long-running debate over Malta and a renewed desert offensive in the spring and culminated a week before Rommel attacked in May, with

---

[9] See page 118, below.

Auchinleck so far failing to grasp the central argument of Churchill's latest attempt to goad him into action that he was driven to reply, "I *am assuming* that your telegram was meant to *imply*" not a diversion to help Malta but a full-blown offensive (my italics).

The near-impossibility of personal contact compounded the problem. Distance and the scarcity of air transport precluded travel between London and Cairo for all but those who would now be called VIPs, with the result that in both places men became progressively less able to perceive each other's meaning through the telegraphese, and therefore felt increasingly isolated from each other. On the rare occasions when personal contact was possible, disagreements could be quickly resolved, as in the case of sharp differences of opinion between Tedder in Cairo and Air Ministry in London about GAF strength and reinforcement rates on the eve of CRUSADER. Auchinleck himself was the chief victim of this feeling of isolation. Pleading that he could not be spared from his post, he refused to come home in March for the thorough discussion which might have brought his and Churchill's points of view closer together (he was not in fact as averse to an offensive as his signals suggested). Instead, Churchill sent Cripps and Nye (Lord Privy Seal and Vice-Chief of the Imperial General Staff respectively) to Cairo; they agreed with Auchinleck, which maddened Churchill but did not advance the discussion. The "offensive note" which Brooke had to stop the Prime Minister from sending later the same month was another product of the strain Churchill was under.

At this distance of time, and without benefit of the interrogatory signals exchanged between the service ministries and Hut 3 on the one hand and GHQ Cairo on Eighth Army on the other,[10] it is impossible to assign exact dates to the Ultra manifestations of these phenomena or to quote specific examples. Memory, however, clearly recalls continual frustration between autumn 1941 and the following spring; Middle East did not seem to understand simple English and asked what appeared to be a

---

[10] Outward signals were prefixed AWL and inward GAD; neither series is yet in the Public Record Office.

string of silly questions; no doubt they felt the same about us. Once the hurdle of distance could be leaped, of course, misunderstandings evaporated like mist before the morning sun. The first few visits by Hut 3 personnel to Cairo, which took place during the summer of 1942, resolved many problems, and complete harmony reigned well before I myself flew out at the end of October.

A major internal reorganization—it amounted in the end to a complete revolution—in the spring of 1942 contributed a great deal toward improving the quality of our intelligence service and ensuring that the needs of our clients were properly understood and met. The steadily growing volume of more complicated material and a hastily enlarged staff had placed increased responsibility upon willing but inexperienced shoulders, but had also increased the need for firmer control and a clearer chain of command. At Bletchley, as in Cairo and the desert, the amateur had to become more professional if he was to do his job properly. Here, too, no written records can be consulted, so all dating is hazardous. Government by committee (perhaps not wholly unlike the "decision by discussion" which plagued the Eighth Army under Ritchie) worked badly during the winter of 1941–42 and was replaced in the spring, much to the relief of all concerned, by the enlightened despotism of Wing Commander (later Group Captain Sir Eric) Jones, under whose strong but skillful management our affairs prospered for the next three years. Calm returned, discipline was restored, and the language of signals was further standardized to prevent ambiguity and doubt at the other end.[11]

Meanwhile, de Guingand's influence was helping to secure more respect for intelligence in Cairo, so that it gradually came to be regarded as a regular ingredient in planning instead of something only loosely related to the desert battles. His task was made easier by improvements in the service. During the spring, the cryptanalysts regained—and this time never lost—their hold

[11] For instance, three different degrees of uncertainty in words or phrases (arising from a garbled text or from the use of radio intelligence to conjecture the identity of a sender or addressee missing from the original) were now regularly represented by "strong," "fair," or "slight" indications.

over Panzer Army's two main keys (Chaffinch and Phoenix),[12] and began to break early every day an army-air cooperation key (Scorpion) which carried up-to-the-minute news from the battle-field. Soon we were providing information about Rommel and his army in larger measure and in greater depth than ever before, and the credit of Ultra—and with it that of intelligence generally—rose in proportion. "Ultra and only Ultra put Intelligence on the map," wrote Brigadier Williams in October 1945, reflecting on his experience over the last five years. "From 1939 to 1942 Intelligence was the Cinderella of the Staff and information about the enemy was frequently treated as interesting rather than valuable." The full benefits of what amounted to a revolution in generalship were not enjoyed until the battles of Alam Halfa and Alamein, in September and October, but the trend was already in the right direction several months earlier.

The first six months of 1942, which thus saw the handling of intelligence in both England and the Middle East gradually acquiring new purpose and new momentum, happened also to be the period during which Rommel received the best service of intelligence that ever came his way in the desert. Decrypts of the well-informed signals sent to Washington by the American military attaché in Cairo gave him an insight into British strategy and intentions, and an efficient Y Service provided up-to-the-minute tactical information. Between them, these two sources inspired many of his best strokes between January and June, but both suddenly dried up about the time his exhausted army reached its point of greatest and most dangerous extension in front of the Alamein defenses. Suspecting that their code was compromised, the Americans changed it at the end of June; Hauptmann Seebohm's W/T Listening Company was destroyed, and its telltale files captured, when the 9th Australian Division overran Tell el Eisa early in July. Thus Rommel was blinded just as Ultra was at last beginning to endow the British with second sight. The coincidence of the two events in time was the product of chance, but the consequences were momentous.

---

[12] Panzergruppe was upgraded to Panzer Army on 22 January; Ultra discovered this a week later (MK 2174). At the same time, Rommel was promoted Generaloberst, "Colonel General"; the rank does not exist in the British and American armies.

*   *   *

To return, however, to the beginning of the year and the first of the several disasters which were to precede this happy state. Only three or four Ultra signals can possibly be construed as offering any warning of Rommel's advance on 21 January, and none of them fills the bill at all convincingly—a tribute, presumably, to the great secrecy with which Rommel veiled his intentions from both OKW and the Italian Commando Supremo, lest he be forbidden to move at all. On 17 January, Fliegerfuehrer needed more bombs "in view of the operations of the next few days," and on the 19th his intentions for the following day were to bomb British airfields and positions on the southern flank. The first of these signals was given the highest priority, but that it was understood to imply nothing more than air operations is evident from the lower priority accorded to the second when it was transmitted on the evening of the 20th—that is, after the raids could be presumed to have taken place. In fact, there were still some twelve hours to go before Rommel set his tanks in motion. Further proof is provided by two signals of the 21st. Fliegerfuehrer's intentions for the day (to bomb British camps, airfields, and supply traffic in Cyrenaica) were signaled at 1215 hours. Exactly six hours later they were followed by a comment to the effect that there were "indications that this may be connected with intended ground operations." Rommel had advanced at first light, but those who composed these signals later in the day were evidently quite unaware either of the advance or of any likelihood of it.

That night Fliegerfuehrer claimed that complete surprise had been secured. He was quite right, and this was the first of several reasons why everything now began to go wrong for the British, just as it had done in April 1941. As General Sir David Fraser acidly but aptly puts it, "The *dramatis personae* had changed . . . only the illusions remained." Once more the headmaster came to the rescue of his pupil, but with less success than when he, rather than Ritchie, had commanded the Eighth Army at the beginning of December. The 1st Armoured Division disintegrated as the 2nd Armoured had done in April 1941, and this, combined with Rommel's deliberately misleading feint toward Mechili, led to confusion, contradictory orders, and hasty retreat.

News that the RAF was preparing to leave Benghazi in a hurry reached the Germans very quickly, for Ultra revealed it in a signal timed 1445 hours on 25 January. So too did knowledge of the dissensions within the British command. The source in the first case was probably, and in the second certainly, the radio reports to Washington of Colonel Fellers, the American military attaché in Cairo. Ultra quickly produced three more extremely suspicious-looking items of the same kind (one of them was expressly based on "a source in Egypt"), but they appear not to have attracted the attention of the signals security branch.

There was not much Ultra news of the ground fighting in late January and early February, and (most unusually) what little there was came from Italian sources, not German. This turned out to be unfortunate. Although the first of the resultant signals quite explicitly attributed its information about Rommel's future plans to the Italian V Air Corps, and although the next two made it clear that they contained what V Air Corps believed Rommel had told General Gambara (commanding the Italian Motor Corps)—i.e., that they were all second- or third-hand reports from an ally Rommel was known to despise and frequently to mislead—Churchill immediately seized upon the first and based advice to Auchinleck upon it, just as he had done in the case of Paulus. "You have no doubt seen most secret stuff about Rommel's presumed intentions, namely clearing up triangle Benghazi-Msus-Mechili and then withdrawing to waiting lines about Agheila," he wired to Auchinleck on 28 January, repeating verbatim the words of MK 2118, which had been sent the previous day. But V Air Corps' version of Rommel's intentions was completely wrong. Disregarding Mussolini's insistence that his primary task was to protect Tripolitania, at that very moment he was boldly pushing deeper into Cyrenaica, hoping to repeat the sensational thrust to Tobruk and the frontier which he had made in 1941. It was not to Hut 3's credit, on the other hand, that we did not give the source (it appears to have been German) for a situation report of 30 January which foresaw no serious resistance being offered to the Axis advance before Mechili and Derna, or that the first express Ultra evidence that the advance had petered out halfway across Cyrenaica had to be completely redrafted before it conveyed the correct shade of meaning. The two armies had in fact come to rest on the Gazala line about 6 February; Rommel's decision to go no further for the time being could not have been deduced from Ultra until a signal of the 9th, which showed the Afrika Korps being moved back toward Benghazi and the Italian Motor Corps replacing it at the front. This came from an unimpeachable source, a Panzer Army situation report, but it did not explain that the advance had stopped only because it had completely outrun the supply services.

5
DESCENT TO DISASTER: FROM GAZALA TO ALAMEIN
February–August 1942

Throughout 1942, and particularly during the first six months of the year, Axis and Allies alike were faced with a series of strategic options between which they were compelled to choose. Some of the choices they made proved even more crucial than could have been foreseen at the time.

On the Axis side, Hitler alone decided. His criteria were irrational and impressionistic, and his decisions were in the end fatal to his cause. During 1942 he plunged the German armies deeper and deeper into Russia, yet paradoxically the prospect of a Russian collapse receded almost as fast, until the obstinate defense of Stalingrad on the Volga paved the way for the ignominious German surrender there in February 1943. Although he had already allowed the Mediterranean some preference over the Atlantic and the attempt to throttle Britain's lifeline by diverting a substantial proportion of his U-boat fleet thither, he failed either to capitalize on Rommel's victories or to capture Malta, because he hesitated too long between the two; he listened to Goering's fears of another Cretan bloodbath if a parachute assault was mounted against Malta, and to Kesselring's bland assurance that his bombers had so weakened the island by the end of April that its submission would be a formality, instead of heeding the insistence of Raeder and the German navy that to drive the British out of the Mediterranean would fatally weaken their grip on the whole Middle East and mark the first step in the annihilation of Germany's chief enemy. Both his courses of action brought some immediate advantage but proved ultimately disastrous.

Russia had become her ally in June 1941 and the United States in the following December, but Britain was still effectively alone at the beginning of 1942. There could be no real cooperation with a Soviet leader who divulged none of his thoughts or intentions. The U.S. Chiefs of Staff, having accepted the principle of "Germany first," initially looked upon all Mediterranean enterprises as distractions from the main task, designed merely to prop up the crumbling British Empire, and were only with difficulty persuaded in July to agree to the TORCH landings in French North Africa. Anglo-American decisions were taken far more rationally than those of the Axis, but far more slowly because of the need for prolonged discussions; they paid no dividends until the second half of the year, but proved in the end exceedingly sound investments.

Whenever they tried to foresee their enemy's next moves in the first half of 1942, the British were almost mesmerized by persistent fears of a German plan to crush Britain between the arms of a gigantic pincers[1]—an eastward thrust from Cyrenaica meeting another coming south from the Ukraine, either through Anatolia and Syria to Cairo or through the Caucasus to the Persian Gulf and the oil wells upon which the British armies in the Middle East depended. In the early spring, both London and Cairo expected a Russian collapse to start the pincers closing in April or May (the date was repeatedly revised with the passage of time until forecasts of this kind became superfluous in the autumn). Unknown to them, Hitler had issued a directive in just this sense in June 1941, even before he launched BARBAROSSA, but the Russian winter and unforeseen delays in the advance of his armies were already removing the concept of a two-pronged envelopment of the Middle East into the realms of fantasy by the time the Libyan front came to rest at Gazala in

---

[1] See p. 78, 97, above.

February 1942, although the fall of Rostov in late July kept the fear of a thrust through the Caucasus alive in some minds. Too little was known of reviving Russian military plans and power for this to be apparent, however. (The Minister of State in Cairo, R. G. Casey, wrote in June, "We know nothing of Russian intentions. We do not know whether they intend to fight for the Caucasus at all.") In addition, the rapid progress of the Japanese, who took Singapore in February and began a relentless drive through Burma toward the frontiers of India, made the nightmare still more terrifying by compelling the diversion of reinforcements intended for the Middle East and the removal of ships, divisions, and aircraft from the old theater of war to the new, thus weakening still further the opposition which could be put up against either of the two conjectural German thrusts.

As a former Commander-in-Chief in India, Auchinleck was peculiarly sensitive to the Japanese danger. All through the spring he fended off Churchill's increasingly sharp reminders that he was expected to attack Rommel by insisting that to do so before he was ready would only expose Egypt to unnecessary peril and uncover his northern flank. Toward the end of March, for instance, he wrote, "We must not become involved in operations in Libya which cannot be broken off at short notice . . . to release forces to meet the enemy elsewhere," and he rejected the Prime Minister's demand that he return home for consultations on the ground that he could not be spared from the post of danger. In early May, as the British evacuated Mandalay and the Japanese occupied Lashio on the Burma Road, he even proposed to send three divisions from the desert to India and to postpone his own offensive until the middle of June or even to abandon it altogether. This brought a direct War Cabinet order in reply: either attack at latest by the time of the Malta convoy planned for June, or resign. Auchinleck complied, but his lasting preoccupation with his northern flank was shown when on 19 May he nevertheless issued his third (in a series extending back to February) precautionary instruction on action to be taken if a German attack through the Caucasus developed during the coming desert battle.

It is usual to criticize Auchinleck's attitude in these ex-

changes for the way in which he appeared to ignore the plight of
Malta, then more serious than ever, and to hold Churchill's rebukes justified on that ground. At least as remarkable, however,
is the small amount of heed apparently paid by both men to the
Ultra evidence currently available, which had by now made it
tolerably clear that Rommel would attack at the end of May or
in the first days of June,[2] and that therefore any further postponement of the British offensive would certainly hand the initiative to Rommel. Nor is this all. An important ingredient in
Auchinleck's wish to delay attacking at Gazala was his overestimate of German tank strength. Yet Ultra had begun providing
periodical tank-strenth returns in March and produced the latest
of them early in the morning of 7 May, at the most heated moment in the London-Cairo correspondence.[3] As already noted,
appointments previously made were improving the way in which
intelligence was assessed at GHQ Middle East and in the desert
at much the same time as the quality of the signals containing it
was rising.[4] What was still lacking, unfortunately, was a proper
appreciation by the Commander-in-Chief and his subordinates
of the value of Ultra, which was therefore denied the chance of
playing as large a part in directing plans and operations as its
quality and handling now deserved. Hamilton quotes Sir Edgar
Williams, whom de Guingand had brought from Cairo to liven
up Eighth Army intelligence during the Gazala battle, for the
opinion that under Auchinleck, Ultra "never seemed to get put
to any purpose." There were to be some signs of a change for
the better during the summer, but Ultra only came into its own
with Montgomery.

The war of movement stopped at Gazala in early February,
and for the next three months the combatants "lay motionless in
the desert," in Churchill's impatient phrase. Both sides were
temporarily exhausted by the winter battles and by the weary
trek across Cyrenaica and back again. But if the front was quiet,
behind the lines there was frenzied activity as the two armies

---

[2] See pp. 115–117, below.
[3] MK 5059. See p. 118–119, below.
[4] See pp. 104–105, above.

sought to rebuild their fighting strength for another effort and to accumulate the stocks of petrol, food, and ammunition without which neither could launch an offensive. The compulsion to do so was the greater because of the unsatisfactory nature of the Gazala Line. Unlike the positions at Agheila, where the front had by now come to rest twice in twelve months, or at El Alamein, where it settled later that summer, it had an open flank which could be turned by a southward enveloping movement—the tactic Rommel adopted with success at the end of May.

A shortened supply line was the only advantage Eighth Army derived from its retreat to Gazala—apart, of course, from the satisfaction of having halted the enemy farther west than in 1941. At Agheila in January, XIII Corps had needed 1,400 tons of supplies of all kinds every day, but the most that could be managed by sea transport from Egyptian ports to Tobruk (over three hundred miles from Agheila: Benghazi was still blocked by German demolitions) and the long lorry-haul thence, or from railheads still farther east, was only 1,150 tons. The amounts were smaller, but the proportionate shortfall and its predictably dire consequences were similar to those previously suffered by Rommel and to those which recurred in his complaints to Rome and Berlin, which Ultra was to make so familiar in the months to come.

In this renewed battle of supply, the Axis now had some notable advantages. The U-boats which Raeder had persuaded Hitler to send to the Mediterranean magnified the danger to British naval vessels from beneath the waves at the same time as Fliegerkorps II's 300-odd aircraft in Sicily were increasing it from the skies. Another victim was Malta, which now entered upon its most agonizing months—bombed daily, reduced almost to starvation, and no longer usable as a naval or air base against Axis trans-Mediterranean shipping. Already in January 1942, 66,000 tons of cargo reached Libyan ports safely, and in April Ultra showed that 60,000 tons of ammunition, food, and rations for all three branches of the Wehrmacht had been unloaded there, plus 1,800 lorries and guns, while over 10,000 men had been flown in by air—substantially more than a recent estimate in the hands of Panzer Army. By now very few of the ships that

plied between Naples, Taranto, or the Piraeus and Tripoli or
Benghazi were being sunk on the way,[5] and less than 1 percent
of what they carried was lost. A main contributing factor to this
abrupt shift in the logistical balance was the change in ownership
of the Cyrenaican airfields when the Eighth Army fell back to
Gazala. Henceforth, the RAF was based farther away from
Tripoli, the chief Axis port; this prevented it from succoring
Malta and made attacks on Axis convoys more difficult. Conversely, the Axis could attack Malta and protect Tripoli and the
convoys. The main purpose of the offensive to which Churchill
repeatedly urged Auchinleck was to regain these airfields and
save the beleaguered island.

So long as the front remained static, the most valuable service intelligence could render was to discover the rate at which
the enemy was replenishing his supplies of fuel and weapons and
the date and direction of the offensive he was certain to resume.
Hampered as it was by the temporary loss of the army keys
(they were retrieved in April), Ultra was not at first well placed
to meet these requirements, and in some respects the first three
months of 1942 were a disappointing and frustrating period—the
last Hut 3 was to endure. Italian naval and German air decrypts
continued to give plenty of information about shipping movements (although for the reasons just given, less advantage could
be taken of any targets they presented), but cargo manifests
were once again conspicuous by their absence; the news that 71
tanks and 3,000 tons of aircraft fuel had reached Tripoli on 23
February was one of the few exceptions that proved this general
rule.

By way of compensation, analysis of a dozen aircraft fuel
stock returns decrypted between late February and the middle
of May gave useful pointers to German strategy. In this three-
month period, total stocks gradually crept up from just under
5,000 tons to a peak of 6,000 tons in May. Even this 20 percent
increase (due, it would seem, almost entirely to the one big ship-

---

[5] An exception, traceable to Ultra, was the *Victoria* (at 13,000 tons very much larger
than most of the transports on the route), torpedoed and sunk on 23 January with 1,000
troops on board (MKs 1938, 1956, 2007, 2045).

ment already noted) was less remarkable than a shift, first visible on 7 May, in the proportion of stocks held in each of the three geographical areas under which the returns were habitually listed. For some weeks, stocks on the operational airfields in Cyrenaica remained steady at six or seven hundred tons. An overpowering desire to move petrol in bulk to the forward airfields, irrespective of plans for an offensive, became apparent in mid-March, when RAF raids on them were causing such serious concern that Kesselring called for more attacks on the British bases to stop the bombers from taking off, and was forced to order all other tasks "to be subordinated to that of regaining air supremacy." By 7 April, Kesselring, at his HQ in Sicily, had convinced himself that Fliegerfuhrer had "enough petrol to meet all demands," but those on the spot were evidently less sanguine. On 14 April it was ordered that four out of every five lorries on the Tripoli-Benghazi run were to be loaded with aircraft fuel until further notice. On the 16th, Luftgaustab Afrika nevertheless lodged a formal complaint about the inadequacy of road transport to the forward airfields: every available lorry was being used, and so was the scanty coastal shipping, but still too little petrol was being delivered; the only solution was more air transport. Ten days after this, Luftgaustab made its case another way: deliveries at the current rate, it pointed out, did little more than keep up with daily consumption (some 50 or 60 tons) at the front, and asked that the tanker *Saturno,* then at sea, should be diverted to Benghazi. These representations appear to have borne fruit. Within a week, three forward airfields held over 800 tons between them (a 30 percent improvement), and the next comprehensive fuel return showed the total in Africa reaching 6,000 tons for the first time, with Cyrenaica now accounting for a quarter of it instead of a sixth as hitherto.

A comment to the 16 April signal drew attention to "considerable efforts since 14 April to increase GAF fuel transport forward." Vague though it might be as to date, here was the first direct hint that large-scale operations were in the offing.

As decrypts of army Enigma began to become available currently in the second half of April, an approximate forecast of date became possible. Commenting on information from "a particular reliable source" (presumably an intercept of one of Colonel Fellers' signals) on the 24th, Kesselring remarked that the attack the British were planning would come "too late," since the source showed that it could not begin before 1 June. The context left it uncertain whether Kesselring meant that the Axis would have captured Malta by then, or would have resumed the drive toward Egypt. The same inference about date followed from an assurance given to Panzer Army by the German General attached to Italian Headquarters in Rome on the same day, to the effect that reinforcements sufficient to bring it up to strength (Panzer Army claimed to be 12,000 below establishment) would arrive by the middle of May, but this time the ground offensive was plainly meant. Other evidence suggested a slightly later date. OKW issued a warning that reinforcements for Africa would have to be cut down because of the demands of the Russian front, and that only a few small items among the many which Panzer Army had asked for could be delivered, and even these not before June. To sweeten the pill, OKW added that 36 tanks were awaiting onward shipment in Germany and that 21 more would be supplied in May. Panzer Army thereupon submitted a shorter shopping list which included lorries and tractors urgently needed in view of "coming projected operations," begged that all the promised 57 tanks might be delivered in May, and spoke of increasing the standard issue of petrol from 1 June—which seemed to imply that large-scale operations would begin about that date. (In actual fact, no date for the offensive had been fixed by the time of this correspondence in late April. OKW and Mussolini did not issue the necessary directives until 4 and 5 May; directly after this, Rommel outlined his plans to his corps commanders.) By mid-May, an earlier date momentarily seemed more likely again—Panzer Army wanted 80 assault boats urgently (for a seaborne landing near Tobruk?—no purpose was stated), but they proved too large for either German or Italian transport aircraft, and OKH could only promise to send them by sea "if they arrive in time"—but this was only a transient impression. Pointing out on 15 May that reinforcements landed at Tripoli would come too late for "the known projected operation" because of the time required to move them up to Gazala, Panzer Army asked that all sailings after 20 May should be routed to Benghazi.[6] On the 22nd, General Cruewell, who had commanded the Afrika Korps in the winter battles and had lately been in Berlin, urging Panzer Army's pressing need for tanks and tractors on OKW, was expected to return to Africa during the next two or three days, and Panzer Army received from OKH the text of a British report (neither provenance nor date were given) which included the words "there are indications that a German attack on the British positions is imminent." In view of these accumulated signs, it should have been easy to guess the meaning of the news that a most secret communication was to reach Fliegerkorps X from Kesselring's headquarters in Taormina during the early evening of 25 May (by coincidence, the Ultra signal recording the fact was transmitted at the same time): evidently the code word for the start of operations was about to be passed.[7] The opening of OB South's battle headquarters at Derna at 0800 on 26 May merely confirmed the importance of the operation.

That GHQ Middle East had correctly forecast the date of Rommel's offensive has been common knowledge since the publication of *Operation Victory* in 1947 by the late Sir Francis de Guingand, who, as DMI, paid a special visit to the desert to ensure that the Eighth Army was on the alert. It is now plain that it was Ultra which made the forecast so accurate.

Indications of the point at which the blow would fall were far less enlightening, and this was soon to prove a serious drawback. Tobruk, the prize Rommel had lost the previous spring through his own impetuosity and the quick thinking of Brigadier Harding, who took charge at the critical moment, and which is now known to have haunted him ever since, first appeared in a

---

[6] Yet there had already been suggestions that more ships were being routed to Benghazi than the port could handle. Ultra reported the harbor congested on 21 May (MK 5625), but the RAF does not seem to have accepted the implied invitation to bomb it more vigorously than usual.

[7] The code word was VENEZIA. It did not appear in Ultra at all (compare the single reference to HERKULES, p. 121 below). This is evidence of good German security; it must be remembered that the wide distribution of Enigma machines meant that large numbers of cipher operators necessarily had knowledge of the contents of the secret documents they enciphered, and had to be prevented from knowing or guessing too much.

suggestive context as early as 9 March, when Fliegerfuehrer asked for the latest photographs of the fortifications. It occurred again on 25 April, after a six-week interval during which there was no hint of an objective, with the announcement that Panzer Army intended to attack the town by the end of May. Thereafter the shots were very scattered. Aerial photographs were wanted of the defenses of Bir Hacheim, at the southern end of the British line, on 29 April; of the area west and southwest of it three days later; and of Bir Hacheim again on 23 May. Tobruk and Gazala rated several mentions each in May, and Sidi Barrani and the Egyptian coastline as far east as Alexandria one or two. Nothing very solid could be deduced from all this: a frontal attack would have to strike somewhere near Gazala, an enveloping movement would have to go round Bir Hacheim, a thrust into Egypt would be the natural way to exploit the success of either. The reiterated references pointed clearly to Tobruk as at any rate the first objective, but left the route toward it, the most desirable knowledge of all, open to speculation.

Inaccurate estimates of German tank strength had been the Achilles' heel of British intelligence in BATTLEAXE and CRUSADER, bringing the first to a sudden stop and paving the way for the offensive which wiped out most of what had been gained by the second. Now, the series of tank returns which began in the spring of 1942, and continued (irregularly but without prolonged intermission) to come from Ultra until the end of the war, for the first time provided trustworthy information about the enemy armor. It was soon clear that the Afrika Korps' striking power was growing fast in March and April, as the British grip on Mediterranean shipping slackened. A total of 159 German and 87 Italian tanks on 11 March had become 264 and 151 six weeks later. The main increase was in Mark IIIs, for which the Eighth Army's new Grants were more than a match, but there were a few of the new Mark III "Specials" and Mark IVs with their more powerful guns (but, according to Rommel, no ammunition for the latter!). These figures had crept up to 270 and 165 by 6 May, the last return before the start of the German offensive. At last there was firm ground on which to base future calculations, and a known recent rate of growth as a guide to what could be accomplished in the new conditions of sea transport. This was a highly significant advance in the provision of intelligence in a vital field. It put an end—though not immediately—to the speculative estimates of the past, which had sometimes been badly wrong and had recently caused friction between London and Cairo.[8] On 4 February, for instance, GHQ Middle East had believed that Panzer Army could deploy 42 German and 185 Italian tanks, when the true figures were 102 and 80; Cairo went almost to the opposite extreme a little later, estimating that there would be 168 and 276 on 1 March, whereas Ultra soon showed that even ten days after this there were in fact only 159 and 87. A Cairo estimate of 21 March, though presumably drawn up after taking these figures into account, was still pitched too high, for it predicted 350 German tanks by 15 May (that is to say, it expected an additional 200 to arrive during the next seven weeks—a far greater rate of reinforcement than had yet been achieved), but there were only 270 in the Ultra return of 6 May. However, the absence of any more Ultra on the subject before the offensive may have obscured a sudden rapid increase in the reinforcement rate that almost justified the estimate—unless the Long Range Desert Group's road watch on the Via Balbia near Agheila made up the deficiency; 332 German (and 228 Italian) tanks took the field on 25 May. Against them were ranged nearly 800 British tanks, almost the three-to-two superiority which Cairo regarded as the minimum necessary to ensure success.

By contrast with the desert, Malta was Ultra's blind spot. To follow up Fliegerkorps II's bombing, the Axis began in January to consider a Crete-style invasion by air and sea, and when they flew to Hitler's East Prussian command post in February, Rommel and his operations officer, Westphal, urged on a reluctant Fuehrer the desirability of removing this thorn from Panzer Army's side. In April, Rommel renewed his plea, and OKW appointed a planning staff. The British feared what the Germans were in fact busy planning. As it became progressively more dif-

---

[8] See p. 112, above.

ficult to run fuel, food, and ammunition convoys into Grand Harbor, so the prospect that Malta might be starved out and invaded grew nearer; by the end of April, the Defence Committee in London doubted whether the island could hold out beyond the end of June. Only a few days later, the two dictators agreed (unwisely, as it proved) to let Rommel have his head— he had now changed his mind and preferred an immediate offensive in the desert to the freeing of his maritime supply lines— and to defer HERKULES, as the attack on Malta was codenamed, until after he had captured Tobruk.

Ultra was unable to offer more than minimal assistance in these critical weeks. Good telephone and teleprinter links between OB South's Sicilian base and Rome, Berlin, and the Fuehrerhauptquartier behind the Russian front kept all important business off the air, nor was it possible, as on many other occasions, to reconstruct high-level decisions from their derivatives at lower levels. Occasional Fliegerkorps II serviceability returns and records of the number of sorties flown against Malta gave some indication of the weight of assault that could be mounted, but offered no basis for deductions about Axis strategy. Several items about the arrival in Africa of supplies for a detachment of parachutists were more likely to herald a descent on Tobruk than on Malta (for which the appropriate takeoff airfields would be in Sicily); in any case, the detachment soon returned to Germany, leaving its equipment behind, and at the end of March the War Office thought that an invasion of Malta was unlikely in the immediate future. Only two signals can have been of any real assistance in elucidating the enemy's plans. An order that several unspecified units from both Fliegerkorps were to move secretly to new bases on 28 April could be regarded as a strong indication that HERKULES had been at any rate postponed[9]—as was, in fact, the case after the Salzburg-Berchtesgaden meeting between Hitler and Mussolini at the end of the month. Postponement did not mean cancellation, and some preparatory exercises continued. HERKULES was the

---

[9] In fact, some went to Russia and some to reinforce Fliegerfuehrer for the coming battle in the desert.

"special operation" for which Cavallero, the Italian Chief of Staff, wanted two lighters sent back to Italy on 9 May, but the low priority given to the signal shows that the code name (omitted from the Ultra signal under current security rules) meant nothing to its originators.[10] No further enlightenment came from Ultra in May, but the slackening of air attacks on Malta (with the result that its power to strike at Axis seaborne traffic speedily recovered) and the depletion of Fliegerkorps II's strength led nevertheless to the right conclusion—that the invasion had been postponed. In point of fact, things were already moving beyond mere postponement. Before the end of May, Hitler foreshadowed the fatal decision he was to take next month: to cancel HERKULES altogether if Rommel was victorious. Yet, as the events of the next six months were to show, unless Malta was permanently neutralized by capture, Rommel's supply lines were so vulnerable that his army, small though it was, could scarcely be maintained at Alamein, let alone reinforced for the advance into the Delta which would make it the southern arm of the pincers movement of which Hitler had once dreamed.[11]

During the night of 26–27 May, the Italian infantry, with a stiffening of Germans, made a great show of attacking in the north and center behind a heavy artillery barrage; somewhat later, British reconnaissance detected the armor sweeping southwest from Rotonda Segnali toward and round Bir Hacheim, but it was not until after dawn that the first was recognized as no more than a demonstration to distract attention from the second, which was the main thrust. On 20 May, Auchinleck had pointed out the obvious to Ritchie—that Rommel would either try to drive straight for Tobruk through the center of the British line, or approach it from the south round Bir Hacheim, feinting at one while concentrating on the other. He chose the first of

---

[10]This was the only mention of HERKULES in Ultra: BI ii.346. It is doubtful whether the code name would have conveyed any meaning in Cairo or Malta either, had it been signaled in accordance with later practice.
[11]The inevitably disastrous consequences of the cancellation of HERKULES, because thereby the German supply problem became insoluble and the British regained the initiative, are well brought out in Lewin, *Hitler's Mistakes*, 114–15.

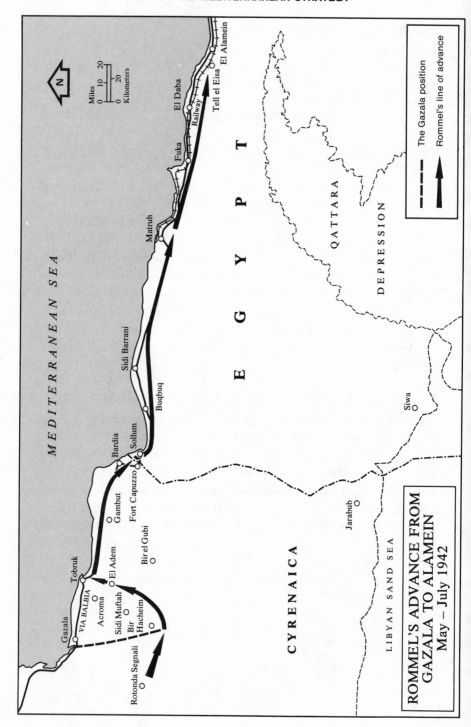

ROMMEL'S ADVANCE FROM
GAZALA TO ALAMEIN
May – July 1942

these alternatives as the more likely, and repeated his erroneous forecast on the 25th. It was a strange choice, for the sweep round the unprotected south of the Bir Hacheim outpost was, in spite of the unavoidable consumption of scarce petrol and the wear and tear on tank tracks, a much more enticing course than a head-on collision with the most strongly fortified sector of the British defenses. Auchinleck's was a serious mistake, which Ultra had not helped him to avoid, and it was soon compounded by Ritchie's reluctance to concentrate his armor (a repetition of Cunningham's mistake in CRUSADER) in spite of his fore-knowledge of Rommel's intentions, and by his corps command-ers' slowness to realize that the southern thrust was the genuine one. A copy of Rommel's battle orders, captured on 28 May, revealed the truth; but meanwhile two British armored brigades were overwhelmed piecemeal by a force which in combination they could have defeated. But the Afrika Korps had suffered heavily too, and Rommel withdrew it into what came to be known as the Cauldron (south of Sidi Muftah) until a passage for supplies could be cleared through the minefields; his position was for a time desperate.

Ultra was rather erratic at this juncture. Panzer Army's in-tentions, announced on 29 May, to go over to the defensive on the 30th were signaled that evening and were closely followed by the admission that the British were now fighting better and that German losses in matériel had been "considerable." But it was disappointing that there were delays of a week or more in de-crypting returns of serviceable tanks at the beginning of June, because Ritchie might have seized the initiative determinedly if he had known how weak the opposition had momentarily be-come. The Africa Korps had only 135 battle-worthy tanks on 1 and 2 June, compared with 270 on 6 May, but the information was already out of date by the time it became known at Eighth Army. By then, extra recovery vehicles and tractors were being sent to prevent the permanent loss of tanks damaged in battle, the 15th Panzer had acquired three each of the new long-bar-reled Mark IIIs and IVs to add to the ten the 21st Panzer listed on 1 June, and Panzer Army was predicting that its tank strength would rise by 20 percent in the course of the next few days.

On the credit side, and not restricted by reference to a particular moment in time, were two signals about German tactical methods. On 31 May, Panzer Army intended to remain stationary in the Cauldron and to lure to destruction on its antitank gun screen the British armor which was blocking its supply route, as a preliminary to counterattacking the shattered enemy. A week later, Rommel promulgated a three-point directive for the conduct of the tank battle: (1) tank-to-tank fighting was so costly that it was only to be engaged in as a last resort; (2) long-range artillery bombardment was to be avoided because it was a waste of shells "at a time when the ammunition situation is strained"; and (3) British tanks were to be allowed to approach close enough to the German gun line to ensure their destruction by antitank-gun fire. These two signals were transmitted between the anniversaries of BREVITY and BATTLEAXE, where just such tactics had left their victims mystified as well as beaten in 1941. Now the trick was given away by its inventor himself: there could no longer be any doubt how Rommel won his victories.

Ritchie was amazingly optimistic for the first few days of June and even contemplated being able to advance as far as Benghazi, but his grasp of the initiative was so loose and so hesitant that three times in six days Panzer Army recorded the impression that the British were playing a waiting game. Although defective maintenance was depriving him of some air support, by 5 June Rommel felt confident enough about the future to order three thousand maps of the coast from Sidi Barrani to Alexandria in preparation for an advance into Egypt, and to plan the elimination of Bir Hacheim as a first step even before he had finished wiping out the British forces surrounded in the Cauldron. Messages dated 4 and 5 June to this effect could not, however, be signaled until the 8th, by which time his immediate intentions were already apparent. The failure of Ritchie's attack on 5 June (the preliminary bombardment was so ill-directed that the shells fell in empty desert) in fact marked a turning point, after which Axis fortunes always prospered and British continually declined. Having first discussed plans with Rommel, Kesselring went to Rome on 8 June to negotiate with OKW about future operations, and visited Rommel to tell him the results of his mission as soon as he got back. Meanwhile, Rommel had boasted on the 9th that he could capture Bir Hacheim next day, and was as good as his word. (Kesselring thought he should have been even quicker, and sent him a sharp rebuke in Enigma.)

Only a day or two after the fall of Bir Hacheim, Ultra began to develop into a much more powerful intelligence-gathering instrument than it had been hitherto. The cryptanalysts had already regained their hold over the army keys, which had provided unique logistical information when temporarily mastered in the autumn, and now added a new facility in reading them currently, which of course greatly increased their value in use. Not content with this, they broke a new army-air cooperation key (christened Scorpion), which proved its worth at once and was to be invaluable before and during the battle of Alamein. The folly of those in control of German signals security magnified this crytographic success beyond all our expectation: a whole month's daily settings of Scorpion could be predicted in advance once the first day was broken, for it was found that a series of settings, already used once and therefore familiar to the cryptanalysts, was being repeated (though in a random order), with the result that each new day's break could be made with much less than the usual expenditure of bombe time. (The machine used to solve Enigma messages was called the bombe.) Thus from shortly after midnight each day, Scorpion transmissions could usually be read soon after they were intercepted, and maximum value extracted from the reports of air liaison officers (Fliegerverbindungsoffiziere—"Flivos" for short) attached to army formations. Before long, the Flivos were among Hut 3's most regular providers of frontline information—not only by announcing when a Flivo (and therefore his division) was about to move from one part of the line to another, or from reserve up to the front, for instance, but by indicating the route to be followed and the speed with which the move was actually being carried out. Orders for tank attacks and requests for air support were also common, but it was seldom possible to go through all the stages (interception, decryption, translation, signal drafting, transmission) in time for these to be tactically useful to commanders in the field.[12] On the other hand, such messages could on occasion prove early indications of a coming shift of the enemy's strategic balance (from one flank to the other, for instance), and in this way they possessed an importance which far exceeded any tactical value they might have. Panzer Army's morning and evening reports, which were often carried on Scorpion wavelengths, conveniently summarized the events of the day, and they too sometimes included items with strategic rather than merely tactical significance.

It followed from all this that a far more complete and accurate picture of Panzer Army's intentions, order of battle, and state of deployment and supply could be painted than had been the case hitherto, when only keys belonging to ancillary arms were being decrypted. Now Panzer Army itself was open to constant inspection. As already described, a small but highly qualified body of men capable of turning this new opportunity to good account was already in post at Eighth Army and GHQ Middle East; from now on, these men had high-quality material to analyze and could rely on daily deliveries instead of only sporadic offerings. Like could now regularly be compared with like, as Flivo reports and Panzer Army appreciations accumulated day after day; deeper insights could be gained into Rommel's mind and actions and into the state of his army. Henceforth there was always a context or background against which a novel or startling item could be set for comparative interpretation: wide-ranging orders like those that Paulus had issued the previous year were less likely to mislead because it was now possible to detect whether they were being implemented or not, and serious miscalculations of the enemy's armored strength were less likely to occur. From being an occasional blinding flash of light in darkness, Ultra became a standard ingredient of military intelligence. This was a tremendous gain, although for the mo-

---

[12] See, however, note 16 on p. 131.

ment it was obscured by the remorseless march of events which began when the British made mistakes round Tobruk and Rommel was quick to profit from them. By mid-August, the immediate crisis in the desert was past, and in the less anxious weeks which followed the new range of information could be more profitably exploited in what was in some respects Ultra's best period of the whole war. By the early spring of 1943, however, these new qualities had begun to generate a kind of antibody; Ultra's very bulk, reliability, and regularity were beginning to lull the critical faculties of less experienced intelligence officers in the Tunisian theater to sleep, tempting them to regard Ultra as omniscient and as freeing them from the need to consider whether it might not occasionally leave something unsaid.

So many highly informative signals were sent in such good time during the ten days between the fall of Bir Hacheim and the loss of Tobruk that it is easy (but almost certainly wrong) to imagine that a more responsive mind and a firmer hand than Ritchie's might have turned them to the Eighth Army's immediate tactical advantage, seized the chance to profit from Rommel's early mistakes, and perhaps saved Tobruk. Fliegerfuehrer's orders to bomb the Acroma-Tobruk road at dawn on 13 June and Panzer Army's to advance north and northwest were known very early on the same day, well before the first, at any rate, could be obeyed—and therefore in time for it to be thwarted—and just twenty-four hours later Panzer Army's purpose was stated plainly: to isolate the Gazala sector and bar the way to a British retreat eastward. Everything still pointed to Tobruk as Rommel's next objective (divisional movements and intentions on 15 and 16 June, for instance), but the first explicit confirmation did not come until the afternoon of 18 June, thirty-six hours after Auchinleck, varying his earlier determination not to let the place be invested, gave Ritchie a peremptory order to hold Tobruk. Several signals sent on the 19th invited the deduction that the attack would reach its climax on the 20th. It did, and the fortress which had held out so long the previous year now fell in a single day. Churchill has recorded his shock at hearing the news while conferring with Roosevelt in Washington: "If this was typical of the morale of the Desert Army," he reflected, "no measure could be put upon the disasters which impended in North-East Africa." Roosevelt at once heartened him by offering the first 300 Sherman tanks (at the cost of robbing the U.S. armored divisions to which they had just been issued) and dispatching them by fast convoy to Egypt, where they helped very materially to turn the tide at Alamein four months later.

For the next fortnight, Rommel drove his army forward at breakneck speed, with the object of getting to the Nile before the British could recover from the shock of losing Tobruk and from the ensuing chaos. During the whole of this period, signals could be drafted from decrypts containing frontline information only a few hours old. Most showed where Panzer Army's formations and Fliegerfuehrer's squadrons were, and what they intended to do next; a minority progressively chronicled the Germans' appreciation, from their Y Service (which was replacing the now silenced Fellers as their main source), of the disposition and movements of British troops. The two combined to draw a constantly changing panorama of the fighting which was seldom more than a few hours behind the clock, and in some respects even occasionally ahead of it. Against this background, Auchinleck (who relieved Ritchie and took over direct command of Eighth Army himself on 25 June) could study Rommel's and Kesselring's plans almost as soon as they were formulated, and endeavor to frustrate them.

The Axis infantry was ordered to assemble by 24 June to make a feint attack on the Halfaya-Sollum sector of the frontier while the armor attempted an outflanking movement in the south by night. The purpose was to annihilate what remained after "the core of 8 Army" (claimed to be 45,000 men, 1,000 tanks, and 400 guns) had been taken in Tobruk.[13] Even when Rommel decided to bring the operation forward by a day, advance warning could still be given. By thus penetrating beyond the Egyptian frontier, Rommel was contravening Mussolini's in-

---

[13] Only about 32,000 men were in fact taken prisoner in Tobruk. The tanks and guns were less of a prize from the German point of view than the 1,400 tons of petrol, 5,000 tons of provisions (enough for several weeks, and a major relief to their hard-pressed supply lines), and 2,000 vehicles (MME iii.274).

structions (and Kesselring's vehemently expressed advice) to halt there by 20 June so that as many aircraft as possible could be concentrated for the final assault on Malta. As soon as he had secured Tobruk as a forward supply port, however, Rommel appealed to Hitler to release him from the obligation to obey this order, and was granted permission to continue his victorious progress. Hitler's "final decision" to prefer Cairo to Malta— "the goddess of battles comes to a warrior only once"—gave Rommel freedom to run his head fruitlessly against the slowly consolidating defenses of Alamein and has been described as having "destroyed the Axis' last chance of retaining a position in Africa."

Although British resistance was stiffer than expected and Kesselring's intelligence staff was crediting the RAF with 2,471 aircraft, of which 761 were believed serviceable,[14] Rommel determined to launch a major attack on the Alamein position at 1500 hours on 30 June; the signal which betrayed his intention seventeen hours in advance also gave the complete line-up of Panzer Army in preparation for it. After a postponement until 0100/1 July, the revised plan anticipated a quick breakthrough. For a moment, Rommel believed that he had isolated and surrounded the British position, but he had already appreciated that Auchinleck intended to stand his ground, and 1 July—the crucial day for both commanders[15]—passed without the victory he craved. On 2 July, progress was reported difficult and resistance stubborn in face of continuous pressure. Next day, Rommel and Kesselring were back at their old game of blaming each other: Rommel wanted more air support because of "the condition of the troops." Fliegerfuehrer explained that his fighter pilots were strained to their limit and that it was beyond their power to manage more than four sorties a day. He demanded two more fighter Gruppen (officially, 60 aircraft) to

---

[14] At the end of May the true figure had been 929, only 190 of which were with the Desert Air Force. Fliegerfuehrer could muster 110 serviceable out of 210 on 22 June (MK 7296). The German total in the Mediterranean theater as a whole had been something over 400 at the end of May; in addition, there were some 1,200 Italian planes in the Mediterranean (MME iii.220–21).

[15] Sandstorms in the desert and exceptionally high temperatures added to their own and their tired troops' discomfort.

ease their burden, but Kesselring's rejoinder claimed that since the army had not kept its promise to lend enough lorries, it was impossible to move men and machines to new landing grounds.

That evening Rommel called a halt, justifying his action by the low fighting strength of the army (only 1,200–1,500 men per division) after its recent exertions, the strained supply position, and the hardening British resistance,[16] suspended his attack "temporarily," and ordered Panzer Army over to the defensive. Auchinleck knew of Rommel's decision soon after midnight, and when the next evening's situation report gave notice that the German armor was being disengaged and Italian infantry being brought up to take its place in the front line, he could be certain that, at least for the time being, the German advance had come to a halt.

Evidence to support Rommel's claims about supply and reinforcement problems had been accumulating ever since the fall of Tobruk. Four Italian aircraft were ordered to ferry 70 replacements a day from Lecce, in southern Italy, to Benghazi from 23 June onward, but within a week Panzer Army needed ten times as many every day for a fortnight, and a special transport Gruppe of 43 Ju-52s was commissioned to lift 500 of them; as many as 70 JU-52s were employed on 5 July. More men were flown from Greece via Crete—1,500 on 3 July—but this drained Crete of petrol, and arrangements were hastily made to send men by sea until petrol became available again. After this, a remark appended to Berlin's notification of his July quota must have sounded ominous to Kesselring: if there were "more urgent tactical needs" (the Stalingrad offensive and the drive into the Caucasus had just begun), the amount might have to be reduced. Petrol for the panzer divisions was so urgently needed by 24 June that Hitler himself ordered the tanker *Avionia* from the Piraeus to Tobruk with all speed; its route appeared in Ultra next day, and an exceptionally large number of intercepts en-

---

[16] Faithful to old habits, Churchill had a fresh translation of this signal sent "Personal for General Auchinleck by order of the Prime Minister" (MK 8264). Rommel used exactly the same words when he came to write up the story of the campaign later (Rommel, 248–49); he had only 55 tanks and 65 antitank guns left (OKW/KTB ii. 107).

abled its voyage to be followed closely. The ship was set on fire in Heraklion harbor, in Crete, and became a total loss. Hitler also intervened personally to speed up the dispatch of 40 tanks, 49 antitank guns, and 30 howitzers on 26 June (20 of them were about to be delivered at Mersa Matruh on 5 July). A list of its requirements put out by Panzer Army four days later appears to take account of them but asks for 40 more tanks in July as well as additional antitank guns. A statement by the German quartermaster in Italy on 9 July suggests that not all of them had arrived by then, but shows that he had recently received 60 new tanks from Germany for shipment to Libya.

By the time Rommel halted at Alamein, then, Ultra had taken the measure of the logistical problems his headlong rush had generated for both him and Kesselring, and had sketched the outline of the proposed solution.

The first few days of July confirmed the great leap forward in the amount of Enigma traffic which could now be processed. Existing sources became more productive than ever, and the new breaks into Scorpion and (in mid-July) into an army supply key known as Thrush added to what now became a daily flood of material.[17] Probably no time, except the early weeks of the Normandy landing two years later, saw so much Ultra so densely concentrated upon so short a front as the forty miles from the sea to the Qattara Depression along which the fighting now raged. To the customary daily strength, serviceability, and activity returns of Fliegerfuehrer and Fliegerkorps X were now

---

[17] As explained on p. 125, unwise German encryption procedures greatly simplified the decryption of this army-air cooperation key for the next six months. To cut out the delay (capable of entirely destroying the operational value of ephemeral tactical intelligence) inseparable from the retransmission to England of traffic intercepted in Egypt, from 12 July onward each day's setting was wirelessed to Cairo, and one or two Hut 3 officers went out to GHQ to translate and signal the decrypts. I myself flew out for this purpose in October and remained until early in the New Year. Signals based on Scorpion were of great value in making known the "thrust lines" along which Rommel's tanks sought to continue their advance in the confused fighting of late July, for instance, and in locating his armor during the battles of Alam Halfa and Alamein. As Panzer Army retreated westward in November and December, distance made interception more and more difficult, traffic diminished almost to vanishing point, and the service was withdrawn. Records of the signals sent from GHQ Cairo have not survived; few are likely to have been duplicated in signals from Hut 3.

regularly added Panzer Army's morning and evening situation reports, which commented on current events and gave the position and intentions of every Axis division engaged in the fighting. As they accumulated, these reports gradually built up an intimate description of the workings of Panzer Army which proved invaluable, and they gave a number of first-rate strategical pointers as well as a large amount of tactical intelligence.

With the Axis army nearing exhaustion and the British shaken and disorganized by their hasty retreat, small successes or failures could have disproportionally wide repercussions. It must have been a considerable bonus for Auchinleck to know, for instance, that his plan to lure Rommel's main body southward (where it attacked an empty "box" and momentarily claimed a breakthrough), while he himself attacked in the north, had pulled the wool briefly over Rommel's eyes. The 9th Australian Division captured the important Tell el Eisa salient before Rommel could react, and a hastily organized defense only just saved Panzer Army HQ but could not prevent Hauptmann Seebohm's Horchkompanie (W/T Listening Company) from being overrun, thus depriving Rommel of valuable insights into British moves which he was never able to replace.[18] Moreover, the Afrika Korps' rush back north after its abortive southern sally consumed quantities of petrol, which, as Ultra showed, was already dangerously scarce.

The Axis never managed to advance beyond the position it had reached in early July, and it has been debated whether this was because Auchinleck regained the initiative by a series of well-timed blows or whether Rommel lost it because he could not keep up his momentum—whether at what is sometimes erroneously termed "First Alamein" Auchinleck gave "the winning pull" in a tug-of-war, as Barnett proposed in *The Desert Generals,* or whether, in the words of Lord Harding (who, as Deputy Chief of Staff to Auchinleck, was intimately concerned in the momentous events of these days), Rommel had simply "run out of steam."

---

[18] See Westphal, *Erinnerungen,* 130, and Behrendt for the great value of Seebohm to Rommel.

Intelligence about the enemy cannot show positively whether Auchinleck did or did not seize the initiative, because it knew nothing of his thoughts and motives. Admittedly, Ultra shows Rommel halting because of stiffer British resistance as well as because of his own waning strength, and in early July several signals of potentially great tactical value were transmitted far enough ahead to have influenced Auchinleck's moves. But this is not enough to prove that Auchinleck seized the initiative.[19] Nor does Auchinleck's own much-disputed attitude toward a possible withdrawal to the Delta and even up the Nile square with the claim that by the middle of July he had "won the defensive battle and saved Egypt."[20] On the contrary, a large body of evidence, pointing with growing clarity to the conclusion that, while not abandoning hope of a further advance, Rommel rapidly became convinced that he could not make such an advance without first "getting up a fresh head of steam," so to speak, began to accumulate in Ultra from the very moment he called a halt on 3 July.

Defects of execution rather than defects of generalship bedeviled every one of the successive stabs Auchinleck delivered at the Axis line during July: some of his commanders were incompetent, and the armor was often irresolute (the mutual distrust of armor and infantry was at its height). Ultra enabled him to plan these stabs, however, in the secure knowledge that behind all Rommel's tactical aggressiveness lay a desperate shortage of men and matériel and an apparently irremediable logistical weakness—a situation which Rommel himself repeatedly described as a "crisis" at the time and later as the cause of "the abandonment of our offensive plans which conditions had

---

[19] Barnett's recent attempt (*Desert Generals*, 2nd ed., 242–44) to read the account in BI ii.395–97 as buttressing his original claims for Auchinleck must be held to fail. Because a given piece of information was available in time, it does not therefore necessarily follow that it governed action. Direct causation has to be demonstrated if a rigorous argument is to be founded upon a particular case—and it is precisely this direct causation which can so seldom be demonstrated in the whole history of the effect of intelligence on operations. Historians must always remember that *post hoc* is not the same as *propter hoc*. Moreover, (1) given the prevailing uncertain (though improving) relationship between the intelligence and operations branches in Cairo and the desert in the summer of 1942, causation would have to be absolutely certain, and (2) there is far *more* Ultra evidence to support the "run out of steam" line of reasoning, as will shortly be seen.
[20] See Appendix III, "Auchinleck, Montgomery, and Rommel."

forced upon us." Recording the restoration of the line after the 23rd Armoured Brigade's "Balaclava charge" on 3 July, for instance, Fliegerfuehrer described the situation as nevertheless still very tense, and drew attention to the "critical" state of his fuel supplies and to the "deterioration" in fighter aircraft serviceability.

Pressing demands for reinforcement, particularly for the replacement of casualties, began as the advance came to a halt. "Continuation of the present very strenuous fighting" urgently required 500 officer replacements for Panzer Army on 3 July, and Kesselring backed this up next day with a promise to keep air transport moving. An exchange of telegrams between OKW and Panzer Army on 8 July was very revealing: in reply to Berlin's reminder of its April warning that only single units could be sent in the way of reinforcements, and that even these would take time to assemble, Panzer Army insisted that if even current operations were to continue, the Afrika Korps and the 90th Light Division would have to be brought up to establishment (after all the men and matériel received during the next four weeks, this would still have entailed something like 13,000 men and 400 tanks), and that, in addition, the staff of an army corps and two garrison divisions would be needed for the occupation of Egypt. Within a week, Hitler accepted the first recommendation in full, stressing particularly the need to keep deliveries of tanks and antitank guns at a high enough level to maintain establishment standards, and before long he was demanding and receiving a statement of casualties (Panzer Army attributed its heavy losses to the RAF's continuous bombing and to artillery barrages reminiscent of World War I) and sending General Warlimont, of OKW Operations Staff, to make a personal investigation on the spot. Warlimont flew to Africa on 23 July and at once called for substantial improvements in the arrangements for troop transport from Greece. On his return, he assured Rommel that after "exhaustive conversations" in Rome on his way back, he had seen the Fuehrer, who had "received his report and suggestions and agreed to them." All this evidently weaned Rommel away from a half-formed decision to retire to the Libyan frontier and, coming on top of his intervention over petrol and tanks in June, is likely to have convinced Rommel and Auchinleck alike that for the first time Hitler was investing heavily in the African campaign. But Hitler did not explain how the huge logistical problem which was bound to follow from large-scale reinforcement was to be solved. In a single day (3 August), for instance, Kesselring wanted air transport from Crete for the army reduced so as to save petrol for tactical operations at the front, and the head of the German Transport Staff in Rome twice bluntly pointed out the unavoidable conflict of interests—the more troops, the less supplies—instancing the fact that every ship capable of carrying badly needed lorries was already committed to ferrying the 164th and Pistoia Divisions and the Ramcke Brigade over. The intractability of the logistical problem, of which both sides had had bitter experience in the past, was here again starkly confirmed.

The list of reinforcements actually reaching Africa—most of them from the area of Generaloberst Loehr, OB Southeast— soon reached such formidable proportions that it amply confirmed the risks the Axis command was running. The 1,500 men flown in from Crete on 3 July were to be followed by as many more over the same route in the next two days. Between 500 and 1,000 were flown from Crete or Athens on most days in the middle of the month, but men were still "very urgently" needed on 23 July. A total of almost 20,000 for Panzer Army and 5,000 for the GAF reached Africa during July, among them elements of a parachute formation (the Ramcke Brigade) from Germany and most of Fortress Division Crete, which was renamed the 164th Division as its three regiments arrived in Africa. Rommel soon decided that "to avoid heavy losses against superior British armoured forces," the 164th Division's antitank-gun allocation should be reorganized along the same lines as that of the 15th and 21st Panzer Divisions, and there ensued a long wrangle over the nonarrival of the 196 guns required for the purpose. Rommel ordered absolute priority for them, but they had still not even got as far as Greece by 9 August, when the 164th Division was holding a front of twenty-five kilometers with only three or four antitank guns per battalion.

Information of this and every other kind concerning Panzer

Army's supply and transport arrangements was now being systematically analyzed by the specialist staff de Guingand had set up to exploit the far greater volume of such material which Ultra was now regularly providing. Gone were the days when an occasional scrap could give a momentary and perhaps misleading glimpse of this vast field; now even occasional cargo manifests (for so long beyond Ultra's power to provide) could from time to time crown the regular statistical surveys of Rommel's and Kesselring's quartermaster services which were maintained in Cairo. From them, well-founded deductions could be drawn for the guidance of the Commander-in-Chief. On 10 July, for example, the Italians doubted whether they could manage a discharge rate of more than 1,000 tons of cargo a day in the Tobruk docks, and returns over the next fortnight showed the correctness of their judgment—an average of 1,500 tons a day was not attained until the end of July, nor 2,000 until early August. A heavy RAF raid on 6 August reduced the rate to 600 tons for a time, and it recovered to only 1,000 tons a day. The old demand for supplies to be routed to the most forward port—now Tobruk, in preference to Benghazi—because of the otherwise excessively long haul to the front was heard again: there were not enough lorries, and many were wearing out after months of continuous use; coastal shipping was too slow, and anyway the last coastal sailing vessel was sunk in Tobruk harbor with a cargo of ammunition on 31 July. The German navy thought Tobruk too risky to use, particularly for an urgently needed tanker like the *Rondine* on 20 July, but so pressing was the fuel shortage in both the other services that *Rondine* nevertheless docked in Tobruk a few days later. The 6 July raid was no doubt in response to the news that the port was so congested that some ships were having to postpone their sailing dates by up to a week in order to be sure of getting a berth—the policy of using Tobruk to the maximum was clearly self-defeating—but it is again permissible to wonder why the sinking rate was not higher (*Rondine*'s route was known well in advance), as also why more of the Ju-52s plying daily between Crete and the forward airfields were not shot down.

Bitter complaints from both Panzer Army and Luftgaustab

Afrika about acute fuel shortages recurred over and over again during the weeks that followed the stabilization of the front, but without noticeable effect on the stocks held by either. These fell from an average of around 3,000 tons (in forward and rear areas taken together) of aircraft fuel at the beginning of June to a mere few hundred between mid-July and mid-August, and, in the case of the army, from upward of 5,000 tons in mid-June to 3,000 by early July and between 1,000 and 2,000 thereafter.

In sum, therefore, Ultra showed that the German land and air forces were living a hand-to-mouth existence at Alamein in August, and that their most strenuous efforts were bringing no noticeable improvement in what was to them a very alarming situation. It followed that British strategic planning could safely reckon that any resumption of the offensive by the Axis in the immediate future would rest on an extremely fragile logistical foundation.

In one important respect—tank replacements and rein-forcements—Ultra's performance left something to be desired in July. No Afrika Korps tank returns were intercepted between 2 June and 31 July. Two, believed to be from the 21st Panzer, showed low serviceability figures on 12 and 23 July (22 and 23 respectively, with 36 more under repair on the latter date), and shipping intelligence indicated only a steady trickle of new machines arriving after the 60 which were awaiting shipment to Africa on 9 July—half a dozen or so at a time, but no large consignments. On the other hand, OKH asserted that a total of 110 tanks had left Germany for Panzer Army between 27 June and 23 July, and promised as many more in August. The Ultra background was therefore hardly adequate preparation—but the Y Service intercepts may have compensated—for a group of three returns in the four days from 31 July to 3 August which gave figures of 128, 149, and 133 respectively for the Afrika Korps, and also showed 89 and 96 Italian tanks. An even steeper rise was apparent ten days later—185 German and 173 Italian tanks—and it was very noticeable that the number armed with the new long-barreled 75mm gun was rising fast: to 55 on

31 July, and 64 on 2 August.[21] The 3 August return also compared the battle and establishment strengths of all the German divisions in men, guns, and motor vehicles, adding that 25 to 30 percent of the vehicles were continuously under repair but that spares were in short supply, and stated that 244 German tanks had been written off as total losses in the recent fighting.

Finally, three signals in mid-July admitted the success of Auchinleck's deliberate policy of concentrating his blows against the Italians and revealed that Rommel intended to counter it by a process which became known to British intelligence as "corsetting." On 11, 12, and 15 July, Rommel told Berlin and Rome, Italian divisions had broken and fled, leaving many prisoners in British hands—a sign of lowered morale which made it necessary to include a backbone of German troops in each Italian formation, a step which in turn called for still more German reinforcements. The Italian response was to dispatch the high-quality (because German-trained) Folgore Parachute Division to Africa at once, but the German reinforcement program does not appear to have been further modified to meet the new need.

---

[21] MME iii.436 has similar but not identical figures for similar but not identical dates.

6
THE EIGHTH ARMY'S FIRST VICTORIES: ALAM HALFA AND ALAMEIN
August–December 1942

Progressively more disturbed by the Eighth Army's plight since the shattering loss of Tobruk, and profoundly distrustful of Auchinleck's leadership, Churchill determined to see the situation for himself: "Now for a short spell I became 'the man on the spot.' Instead of sitting at home waiting for news from the front, I could send it myself. This was exhilarating." He and Brooke flew to Cairo on 4 August. Decisions followed swiftly. Alexander was to succeed Auchinleck as Commander-in-Chief Middle East, and Montgomery would replace him at the head of the Eighth Army. (Gott, then commanding XIII Corps in the south, their first choice for the Eighth Army, was shot down and killed on 7 August while flying back to Cairo, without knowing of his appointment.) Montgomery reached Cairo on the 12th and went up to the front next morning. Misliking what he found there, from the headquarters mess enclosure ("a wire-netted cube, full of flies and important military personages," Churchill called it. "What's that? A meat-safe?" asked Montgomery. "Take it down at once and let the poor flies out") to the layout and plans of the army, Montgomery assumed command at 1400 hours, nearly two full days before the arranged time. He was moved to this unauthorized action by his discovery that there was complete uncertainty about what was to be done if Rommel attacked again; this, he felt, made the situation "impossible, and in fact dangerous." He stressed the imminence of attack and his own confidence that he could repel it in his famous address to senior officers the same evening: "I understand that Rommel is expected to attack at any moment. Excellent. Let him attack." "We will hit Rommel and his army for six right out of Africa," he went on, but he wanted a fortnight to make his preparations.

Alam Halfa

Lucidly as he had already been briefed by de Guingand (whom he shortly made Chief of Staff, and whom he retained in that post until the end of the war), it is scarcely to be supposed that Montgomery had yet had time to assimilate what Ultra had to say on the matter. Yet he spoke not a moment too soon. Only three hours after his address ended on the evening of 13 August, an order from Mussolini was signaled to his desert headquarters: "rapid preparations for a renewal of the offensive" were to be put in hand, the Duce reserving to himself the right to decide when to launch it. This gave more immediate significance to Panzer Army's request on 8 August for photo reconnaissance of the Nile valley from Cairo to Wadi Halfa, and even to an agreement between the two dictators in mid-July that Rommel should command the Army of Occupation in Egypt. Thirty-six hours after Mussolini's order came the first indication of date: Panzer Army asked the quartermaster's office in Rome how much petrol, ammunition, and food it could expect to receive by 25 August.

More exact information did not lag far behind. Between them, two signals sent within half an hour of each other on the evening of 17 August—just four days after Montgomery took over—gave a very full picture of Rommel's intentions. In the first, Panzer Army forbade ground reconnaissance near the Qattara Depression "in order not to arouse enemy suspicions in this area"—a prohibition which was to prove the Afrika Korps' undoing at the end of the month when it stumbled into an unsuspected minefield which fatally delayed

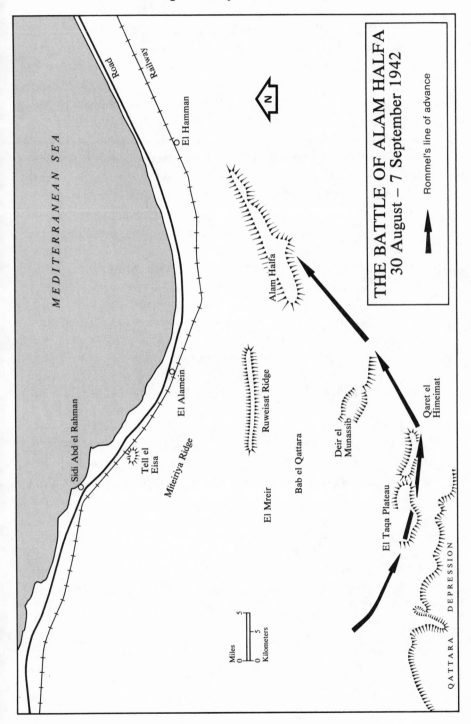

THE BATTLE OF ALAM HALFA
30 August – 7 September 1942

→ Rommel's line of advance

MEDITERRANEAN SEA

Road
Railway
El Hamman

N

Sidi Abd el Rahman
Tell el Eisa
El Alamein
Miteiriya Ridge

Alam Halfa

Ruweisat Ridge

El Mreir

Bab el Qattara

Deir el Munassib

Qaret el Himeimat

El Taqa Plateau

QATTARA   DEPRESSION

Miles
0   5
0   5
Kilometers

the first stage of its advance. The second, an appreciation drawn up by Rommel on the 15th and decrypted on the 17th, was one of the most outstanding cases where Ultra disclosed the complete enemy plan well ahead of the event: Student's for the assault on Crete and Hitler's for the ill-starred Mortain offensive in August 1944 are perhaps the only true parallels in the field of ground operations. Until early in August—so began Rommel's appreciation for OKH and OKW—Panzer Army's situation had been critical, but now the men were more rested and supplies would soon be adequate for an offensive, provided continuous shipments of petrol and ammunition were maintained. A British convoy bearing one armored and one infantry division had just reached Suez, and there would be another in a fortnight's time; this would enable the Eighth Army to mount a strong offensive in mid-September. Until the end of August, therefore, the Axis would have a slight superiority in tanks, and equality or better in other arms, but then the balance of advantage would begin to swing the other way. It should be possible to break through in the south, where there were as yet no fixed defenses and only weak forces, but the British would begin to construct fortifications in September. The enemy's superiority in the air made it imperative for the Axis to attack on a moonlight night; there would be a full moon on 26 August. Kesselring agreed with this choice of approximate date; no other offered equally good prospects, and any postponement (necessarily of four weeks, because of the moon) would make success very unlikely.

The defensive battle of Alam Halfa,[1] which Montgomery fought and won at the end of August, from the positions in which he found Eighth Army when he took over command, was the first unequivocal victory of a British general over Rommel; CRUSADER had turned to dust and ashes in a few weeks, and

---

[1] As GSO 1 (Plans), Lieutenant Colonel (now General Sir Charles) Richardson drew up the plan for Alam Halfa under Montgomery's direction. His account in *Flashback* (111–13) follows a line very similar to that taken here. General Richardson's severe criticism of Auchinleck and of his "extra" DCGS, Dorman-Smith, is illuminating (*Flashback*, 102–11).

the mere fact that Rommel could attack again on 30 August is proof enough that "First Alamein" in mid-July was no more than a temporary check. Right from the moment on 6 September when the Axis armor turned back with nothing to show for its efforts but burned-out tanks, Alam Halfa was recognized as an event of great significance, and before Christmas 1942 it could already be seen as the turning point in the African campaign and the foundation upon which Montgomery was building a fame greater than that accorded to any British commander since the outbreak of war. Was the victory the creation of his own unaided genius, as Montgomery himself claimed, or did he silently appropriate a plan devised by others and then, "wearing a second-hand coat of glory, set out for the top"?

Both suppositions are wide of the mark: the one because it selfishly claims too much for a single man, the other because it completely misrepresents what happened. The dispute over them has gone on too long, and it should now be laid to rest. Real life seldom admits of such rigid categories as black and white, nor is historical truth often illuminated by the search for heroes and villains. The flash of a general's genius does not win a battle unless his soldiers are resolute and have shells for their guns; conversely, all the available evidence suggests that Montgomery did not even read the existing plan, let alone adopt it, though there is never likely to be absolute proof of this.

The Ultra evidence cannot settle the matter conclusively either way, but in combination with a strict attention to chronology it can make clear much which would otherwise be obscure and confusing. On 27 July, Major General Dorman-Smith, Auchinleck's Deputy Chief of Staff, wrote an "Appreciation of the situation in the Western Desert," which Auchinleck accepted and later printed in his official *Despatch*. It came to the same conclusion as Rommel did three weeks later: that the British would not be strong enough to attack until mid-September, but that the Axis could do so at the end of August. It proposed a defensive battle "in the area El Alamein—Hammam" but did not name the Alam Halfa ridge, nor specify that it was the key to the defense. Auchinleck himself did name it, but only as one among other features. Both emphasized a mobile defense

in the south, where the troops were to be "well trained in harassing defensive technique." In many respects there is plainly a
general resemblance between the Dorman-Smith–Auchinleck
assessment and Montgomery's actions, but the mobile defense in the south was the exact opposite of the static role
Montgomery imposed on armor and infantry in that area when
battle was joined. There is a second essential difference too.
The 27 July plan did not suggest a strong garrison for Alam
Halfa, nor did Auchinleck provide one in the few days of
authority that remained to him, although he did take some steps
to fortify it and to mine its approaches. Montgomery, on
the other hand, "appreciated at once that the Alam Halfa ridge
was of vital importance, but was virtually undefended," and at
2200 hours on the evening of that fateful 13 August he asked for
and got the 44th Division from Alexander for the express purpose of garrisoning it, although the division had only recently
landed and had not yet completed its desert training in the
Delta.

The summons to the 44th Division went out only some
twelve hours after Montgomery first sighted Eighth Army headquarters. He cannot possibly have been able, on top of everything else he did that day, to study the Dorman-Smith plan in
detail before asking for the 44th Division. Indeed, de Guingand,
setting out "to put the record straight and settle once and for all
the Alam Halfa who dunnit story," gave an assurance that "to
the best of my knowledge Montgomery never examined any
plans or appreciations that existed at this time," although he
implied that he outlined them to Montgomery verbally himself.
It is therefore far more likely that Montgomery recognized the
supreme importance of the Alam Halfa ridge of his own volition
than that he simply adopted the 27 July plan lock, stock, and
barrel. But it is idle to speculate further or to erect theories
upon either hypothesis; we cannot know the springs of his action
with absolute certainty.

On the other hand, the topography of the area invites the
deduction which Montgomery was not alone in making. An
army which, facing opposition on the Alamein line, wishes to
reach the Delta must either batter down the front door round

the Ruweisat feature or force an entrance through the side door by sweeping round to the south. The Alam Halfa ridge bars the southabout sweep before it can cut communications between Alamein and Alexandria; the ridge must therefore be captured, otherwise the attacker has no choice except retreat or annihilation. Montgomery sensed the importance of garrisoning Alam Halfa strongly as soon as he reconnoitered the ground. This realization, simple in itself and with hindsight obvious enough (Montgomery's plan "devised itself by its obviousness," thought Alexander), was vital. Others thought the same, but they had no authority to garrison the ridge; Auchinleck, who had the authority, did not make it a key defensive position. Rommel had spotted this; he wrote afterward that "the Alam Halfa ridge was the key to the whole El Alamein position," and in the outline plan which he sent to Berlin on 15 August he noted that there were as yet no fixed defenses in the whole south, and that he intended to attack before the British began to construct them. Montgomery had already divined this on 13 August, as soon as he saw the ground. His military instinct—there was little time for reason and reflection on that crowded day—told him what Rommel would do and how to counter it. "All great commanders have acted on instinct," wrote Clausewitz, "and the fact that their instinct was always sound is partly the measure of their innate greatness and genius." Although Montgomery was without desert experience, instinct showed him how he could at one and the same time halt Rommel in his tracks, show the old desert hands the folly of exposing their tanks by charging about in the open (the tanks are not to stir from their hull-down positions, and "you are not to let yourself be mauled," he instructed Horrocks when appointing him to command XIII Corps), turn Rommel's antitank gun tactics against their author, and by these means restore the Eighth Army's self-respect enough to guarantee victory in the hard-fought battles to come.

Ultra's priceless gift to Montgomery was the confirmation, a fortnight before battle was joined, that his instinct was right, and that victory was certain if his orders were carried out strictly. From this sprang the confidence which enabled him to turn a modest tactical success into a strategic triumph of the first order.[2] Unfortunately, it also encouraged him in the mistaken belief that because he had done so once he could always read Rommel's mind.

During the bare fortnight which elapsed between the decrypting of Rommel's intentions on 17 August and the start of the battle, Ultra piled up so many confirmatory indications that its ultimate inability to discover the precise moment of the "off" probably mattered very little. For instance, three senior officers, all of whom had been wounded during the summer, returned from leave on almost the same day—Rommel's Chief of Staff and his operations officer, and the commander of the 15th Panzer Division; Kesselring ordered every available lorry out for "the short-term supply" of petrol to forward airfields; Italian tanks moved forward by night in conditions of great secrecy and were to be camouflaged; Mussolini approved Rommel's suggested date for "the offensive" (but did not reveal what it was); two hundred copies of sketches of the Alamein defenses and the "fortifications" of Alexandria were to be flown from Berlin to Tobruk by 27 or 28 August; there would be two conferences on the 25th, one at which Flivos would discuss signals arrangements and another for which Kesselring and five senior GAF officers required maps showing the British defenses and the disposition of both air forces; army vehicles were to fetch petrol and ammunition from Benghazi "for the last time" on 25 August; and, last and most informative of all, Panzer Army told OKH on the 27th that since ships due that day with petrol and ammunition were not now expected for another twenty-four hours, Rommel could not decide about "the known operation" until 29 August. This signal went out thirty-six hours before the Afrika Korps attacked: all the others had preceded it.

---

[2]By stating that "no basic change was made in 8 Army's plans following the change of commanders—nor was any required by the intelligence given in the signal of 17 August," BI ii.409 equivocates—it would seem deliberately—over the disputed question and mischievously mishandles evidence. It avoids explicitly asserting that Montgomery took over Auchinleck's plan but uses phrases ("No basic change" and, a few lines farther on, "Auchinleck's successors retained his general plan") which clearly imply that he did; and it makes no reference to the crucial fact that Montgomery made a deliberate redisposition of forces before he knew of the Dorman-Smith proposal or the Ultra signal. See also Appendix III, "Auchinleck, Montgomery, and Rommel."

Evidence bearing on Rommel's claim that his strength would grow faster than the Eighth Army's throughout August was inconclusive and contradictory. Three tank returns supported the claim. From 133, on 3 August, the German figure climbed to 185 on 12 August, 216 on the 21st, and 234 on the 28th, and in the last two cases the "Specials" numbered 90 and 97 respectively, almost half the total. The Italian count was 151, 210, and 243 on the same three dates, and all but a couple of dozen were mediums. Clearly, Panzer Army was being reequipped with more powerful tanks at a faster rate than ever before, whereas the Eighth Army, far weaker now than at Gazala, could count among its 478 tanks only 71 Grants, which alone were a match for the "Specials."

Under several other heads, however, there was more encouraging news for the Eighth Army. First, Rommel was revealed as in scarcely good enough health to command the offensive he had planned. A medical report which he forwarded to Berlin on 21 August (it was decrypted three days later) explained that low blood pressure and stomach trouble, aggravated by the strain of recent weeks, meant that only "fairly long" specialist treatment in Germany could restore him to duty fully fit. He therefore requested the earliest possible appointment of a successor, and suggested Guderian, the originator of Blitzkrieg tactics. Alleging that there was no suitably qualified panzer general fit for tropical service (Guderian had been dismissed from the command of the Second Panzer Army in front of Moscow in December 1941, after a quarrel with von Kluge, and was now in disgrace), Berlin authorized the temporary promotion of General Nehring from the Afrika Korps to Panzer Army, but under the supreme command of Kesselring, who had never had authority over Rommel. Thereupon Rommel made a sudden recovery, and on 26 August he was declared fit enough to direct the offensive, provided that a doctor was in constant attendance.

Secondly, right up to the end of August, Ultra gave good reason for believing that none of the Eighth Army's preparations to give the attackers a hot reception had been detected, and that British camouflage and deception had fooled the Germans into supposing that no special steps had been taken to strengthen the fixed defenses in the south. Neither Flieger-fuehrer's daily air reconnaissance reports nor the frequent Ultra summaries of German Y Service results suggested that anything out of the ordinary had been noticed. A Panzer Army situation report, signaled only a few hours before the tanks moved forward, was almost conclusive proof that the 44th Division had not been spotted manning the Alam Halfa ridge, and that a tentative suggestion on 20 August that "a new division had arrived" had been discounted (the 44th Division does not seem, in fact, to have been confidently identified until about 8 September), while another showed that no special opposition was expected there.

Only a couple of months earlier, things would have been very different. But now the Fellers decrypts were gone for good, and Seebohm's successor lacked Seebohm's skill. Instead of knowing all about British preparations—perhaps even enough to suspect why they were so remarkably appropriate—Rommel had no inkling of the reception that awaited the Afrika Korps. His unawareness magnified Montgomery's advantage.

What the official Italian naval history calls "the hecatomb of the tankers," which began now and lasted until after Alamein, was the chief consequence of the unprecedented amount of logistical intelligence supplied by Ultra during this period. Although Malta could not yet be relieved, pressure on the island diminished sufficiently after the cancellation of HERKULES to give it "a new lease of life" (to quote the German quartermaster in Rome), and allowed it to resume its former role of harrying Axis trans-Mediterranean traffic, thus significantly assisting the work of the Royal Navy and the RAF from their Egyptian bases.[3] A Panzer Army appreciation of 18 August underlines the proviso about fuel deliveries with which Rommel had qualified his statement of intentions by pointing out that at the current rate of consumption, petrol stocks would be exhausted

---

[3] Too late, the Italians began to regret their part in the abandonment of the plan to invade Malta. "Unless we neutralize Malta, all is lost," said Cavallero on 6 September (OKW/KTB ii.108; GS iv.64).

by 26 August—the very day Rommel had chosen for his offensive. Taken together, these two signals put Alexander, Montgomery, Harwood (Naval C-in-C), and Tedder in at least as good a position to estimate the strength of the thread by which Rommel's chances of success hung as the staff at OKW to whom Rommel had addressed his 15 August appreciation, and enabled them to do their utmost to cut that thread. The conclusion was inescapable: unless tankers reached Tobruk regularly (petrol landed at Benghazi could not be brought forward in time), the offensive would wither for lack of nourishment. A comprehensive supply survey which Panzer Army issued on 20 August went even further than that of the 18th by demonstrating that consumption had exceeded receipts by 4,600 tons since the beginning of August, and that only 3,000 tons (equivalent to ten days' supply at the current relatively low rates) had been received in the same twenty-day period. Inside information of this kind led to a deliberate policy of assaulting Rommel's supply lines on a scale which had not been seen since the previous autumn, and Ultra was at once able to demonstrate the success of a policy which it had itself prompted.[4]

A few examples must suffice. The torpedoing and subsequent beaching of the tanker *Pozarica* on 23 August reduced all three Italian army corps to such serious straits that they were compelled to borrow petrol from their allies—who were soon heard complaining that the Italians had had an unfairly large share of fuel deliveries in June, July, and August, although the Germans had done most of the fighting—and forced the German supply officer in Rome to publish a revised sailing program next day. The new program provided for nearly 5,500 tons of fuel to be delivered by 4 September, but cautiously added that while "every effort will be made to adhere to this programme, no guarantee can be given." Rome's caution was soon justified.

---

[4]The total tonnage of ships sunk in the last three months of 1941 was actually 7,000 tons more than in the first *seven* months of 1942. June and July 1942 saw only 22,000 tons of Italian shipping lost, but in August the total rose to some 60,000 tons and remained at that monthly level, or higher, until the surrender in May 1943. German and Italian losses together totaled almost 320,000 tons in the period August–December 1942. (Figures are from Roskill i.537, ii.76, 344, 432. BI ii.728–38 gives details of ships sunk between June and October 1942 as a result of Ultra information.)

The route and sailing date of the tanker *Giorgio* (carrying nearly half the 5,500 tons) and orders for it to make all possible haste to Tobruk had already been signaled, together with much information concerning other ships, including the tankers *Picci Fassio* and *San Andrea* and several cargo ships carrying petrol in barrels. *Giorgio* reached Tobruk (where half its load was found to be contaminated), but *San Andrea* (with 3,000 tons of German army petrol), *Picci Fassio* (with 1,150 tons of Italian army petrol), *Istria, Dielpi,* and *Camperio* were soon at the bottom. The loss of the three last-named, complained Panzer Army, meant that of 2,400 tons of petrol promised for 28 August, only 100 tons had actually arrived. In consequence of all this, the already much-revised sailing schedule was thrown into complete disarray and the opening of the planned offensive delayed. Complaints flew thick and fast: Panzer Army ended a powerful plea for a special delivery of 3,000 tons of fuel and 2,000 tons of ammunition with the bleak comment that because of the recent poor performance of the supply services, it had now no fuel reserves; Rome countered with a long review which included the unconvincing claim that nearly 4,500 tons of army petrol had crossed the Mediterranean safely in August, and only 550 tons had been lost in transit. The 15th Panzer had to refuel its tanks with aircraft petrol on the first day of the offensive, although Kesselring was complaining at the same time of a severe shortage of aircraft fuel. (Berlin became so confused by events that it first refused Kesselring's plea for special treatment and then withdrew its refusal a couple of days too late to affect the fighting.) Convincing proof of the effect of the fuel interdiction policy came with Rommel's explanation that he was forced to halt the attack on 1 September and go over to the defensive in an exposed position under the Alam Halfa ridge because petrol expected on *San Andrea* (sunk; see above) and *Abruzzi* (bombed and set on fire) had not arrived.[5]

---

[5] The safe arrival of *Picci Fassio* and *Abruzzi* had been declared "of decisive importance for the fighting in Africa" on 31 August (QT 505). Neither reached its destination. Visiting the Afrika Korps next morning, Rommel was bombed six times in two hours, and was nearly hit himself. Fliegerfuehrer's aircraft were outnumbered and outfought by the RAF's new tactics (Rommel, 279–80; Terraine, 378–83).

*   *   *

Emphatically as these and other signals underlined the Axis' supply problems, and close as they suggest that the Afrika Korps' tanks came to lasting immobility and Fliegerfuehrer's aircraft to being grounded, it is necessary to repeat the warning already given—that on their own they do not give a true picture of the situation. Improvisation had enabled Rommel to overcome apparently insuperable difficulties in the past, and would do so again. Increasing experience of Ultra was beginning to force the reflection that German quartermasters were no more immune than those of other armies from the temptation to exaggerate their shortages in order to obtain a larger share of the next allocation,[6] so that statements like "all reserves used up" were not to be taken literally. Postwar analysis has shown that a great deal more petrol and ammunition reached Libya than was sunk on the way. Even in August (the worst month so far from the Axis point of view), only 41 percent of fuel loaded in Italy or Greece was lost at sea. Ultra could now usually discover that a given tanker had been carrying such-and-such a tonnage of petrol for the German or Italian army or air force, and thus offer precision in place of what would otherwise have been no more than guesswork, but it ought not to have led (and as far as can be seen did not lead—no doubt because of the new care and minuteness with which its much-enlarged logistical component was now studied in Cairo) to over-optimistic conclusions of the kind Sir John Kennedy expressed to Churchill during a conversation on 26 August—that Rommel would not be able to attack because he was too short of supplies.

Apart from revealing, in fairly good time, that it was shortage of petrol which made the Afrika Korps halt "temporarily" on the morning of 1 September, and from confirming on the 5th that it was returning to its starting line (except that Montgomery controversially allowed Rommel to retain possession of the Himeimat plateau in the south), Ultra contributed nothing of

---

[6]Rommel discovered the prevalence of this habit as Panzer Army retreated through Cyrenaica after Alamein. He demanded accuracy in future, and threatened offenders with severe penalties (QT 7058, of 25 November).

importance to the "Six Days Race," as the Germans called the
battle of Alam Halfa. It had performed a tremendous service by
disclosing Rommel's intended strategy in advance and had little
to add on the tactics of a battle where all the movement was by
one side. As soon as it was over, however, Panzer Army
usefully summarized its after-action conclusions: just over 3,000
casualties (including 369 German and 167 Italians killed)—due
mainly, it had already reported, to continuous day and night attacks by the RAF, the decisive effect of which Rommel later
stressed; 36 German tanks destroyed; a present strength of
42,000 Germans and 82,000 Italians (yet the German contingent
had received only 8,500 tons of supplies in August and the Italians three times as much); the imminence of a serious supply
crisis—only eight days' fuel and fourteen days' ammunition in
stock (Panzer Army forbore to remark that this was a great deal
better than a week earlier), so that more air transport was essential to make up for the "uncertainty" of the sea route; and, because the British were reinforcing, the urgent need to transfer
the 22nd Division from Greece and Crete[7] (here Panzer Army
forgot that the more men there were to feed and equip, the
worse the logistical problem would become, as Rome had explicitly pointed out on 29 August).

An Ultra signal transmitted on 15 September momentarily
took some of the gilt off the gingerbread of the Eighth Army's
success by suggesting that the enemy might suspect that Enigma
was being broken. British prisoners taken during the recent
fighting had said that an Italian officer captured by the British
had given away Rommel's plan of attack, its place, and its date,
so that the British had been ready to meet it. This sounded so
alarmingly like a thin and unconvincing disguise for the Ultra
signal of 17 August that it awoke doubts about security at
Eighth Army headquarters. Whatever the precise origin of the
story, the Germans made no damaging inquiries and made no
change in Enigma, but measures were at once taken to prevent a
recurrence of this sort of anxiety: Signals containing particularly

---

[7]It never arrived, but was retained to garrison Crete against an imagined threat. An
infantry regiment was sent instead.

sensitive "hot" news or "gossipy" items about individuals were henceforth to be given a specially restricted circulation. The system was cumbersome to operate, but at least it had the merit of appearing to prevent one type of dangerous leak.

His first three weeks with the Eighth Army, even his first few days, were possibly the most influential of Montgomery's whole period of military command; during this short time, the seeds of his reputation for invincibility were sown, not least in his own mind. After thirty years of waiting, his chance had come. The prospect inspired him. He was like a coiled spring when he landed in Cairo: touchdown and the "meat-safe" released the power compressed in the spring. Before him lay the opportunity to demonstrate his superiority over his predecessors by pulling their chestnuts out of the fire, while all the world watched an almost unknown general take on the world-famous Rommel who had always carried everything before him. He came, he saw, and at once he made the plan for victory which his military training and experience, tempered by the physical geography of the battlefield, dictated to him. This was rational and soldierly. Yet it was done so fast—in no more than twelve hours—that it was almost intuitive.[8] Only four days later, an intelligence source of which he had no previous experience showed him that his enemy was about to act exactly as he had foreseen. Even the dullest would be lifted by such a discovery; an easily inflatable self-confidence like Montgomery's took it as a sign that the God of battles was with him and that he was destined to triumph. Here was certain proof that he was not like others, but a better, more professional, soldier than they, and that the words he had used in his 13 August address were not only much-needed morale boosting but the very truth. When Rommel's tanks retired defeated a month later, all the world shared his conviction. "The morale emerging from the promise [made in the address] so positively fulfilled formed the psychological background conditioning the victory which was to follow.

---

[8] Such speed was uncharacteristic. He was usually much more deliberate—ponderous, his critics said. Only at El Hamma, in all probability, was he as quick and as right in a crucial decision (see p. 214, below).

Thereafter intelligence came into its own," wrote Sir Edgar Williams, reflecting on the source of an army's morale in the nature of a man and the fact of a victory: a man with a peculiar and highly individual psychological makeup, and a victory which proved one of the turning points of a war. If, as Sir Edgar insists, intelligence and the attention Montgomery paid to it were the basis of that victory, then may it not be that the strategic confidence—or intolerable arrogance—which sustained Montgomery when he forced through radical revisions of the plans for invading Sicily and Normandy (revisions without which both landings might well have failed) owed much of its strength to Ultra's earlier demonstration that his intuition was correct? The Montgomery legend was born at Alam Halfa; it fed upon itself, and upon the largely Ultra-based successes its hero continued to win, and even its most distasteful aspects cannot hide the immense contribution it made to the eventual Allied victory.

Alamein

Strategy temporarily receded into the background after Alam Halfa, save in the sense that everything hung upon the issue of the decisive battle for which both sides were now preparing. In it, for the first time, the superior weight of British and American matériel, firmly controlled by a newly resolute leadership, would be pitted against the professionalism, the mature experience, and the sheer determination of the German soldier. Rommel called it a battle without hope, but no one in London, Cairo, or the Western Desert took the same view or regarded victory as a foregone conclusion. Unable or unwilling to comprehend either why an offensive could not follow hard on the heels of Alam Halfa or why Montgomery had forecast that Alamein would begin with a ten-day "dogfight," Churchill kept pressing for an earlier date than Alexander and Montgomery proposed, and right up to the last stages of the battle Brooke had to restrain him from sending critical telegrams to the Middle East. Again, because the old desert hands doubted the capacity of their new equipment to beat down the opposition, Montgomery was compelled to modify his original bold plan and to note how the ingrained mutual mistrust of infantry and armor blunted their vigor in action. An earnest faith in victory prevailed everywhere, but no certainty. Alamein can only be understood if this is kept in mind. Could Montgomery stop the swing of the Libyan pendulum at last, or would Eisenhower get to Tripoli first?[9] This was Churchill's constant worry. If neither moved fast enough, "God knows how we shall keep Malta alive" when her supplies ran out in October.

The narrow cone of rock and desert in the neck of which the Eighth Army was blocking the Axis advance toward the Delta does not widen out at its western end until sixty or seventy miles farther from Egypt than Alamein, too far away to influence Montgomery's conduct of the battle until its very last stage. Only tactical maneuvers and tactical surprise (achieved in the event, remarkably enough) were open to him. The very great number of Ultra signals sent in September and October admirably set out the tactical background to his plans, but only in the field of logistics could anything of wider strategical import be discerned. The Ultra intelligence provided between Alam Halfa and Alamein (that is, between 6 September and 23 October) can therefore be summarized briefly under a few familiar headings.

Rommel's immediate personal future, upon which doubt had suddenly been cast at the end of August, became clear as soon as Berlin decided to appoint a temporary successor. General der Panzertruppe Georg Stumme, who had commanded the 7th Panzer Division before Rommel took it to France in 1940 and had since fought with success in Poland and Russia, was to leave Berlin for Africa on 15 September, it was discovered on the 10th. Ultra followed Stumme to Africa via Rome, and noted that he took over Panzer Army on 22 September and that Rommel immediately flew to Europe. There followed complete silence about his return, but only a few hours before the artillery barrage which ushered in the battle of Alamein began, it became known that he had still been in Austria on the 17th.

---

[9]The landings in North Africa were to take place at the end of the first week in November.

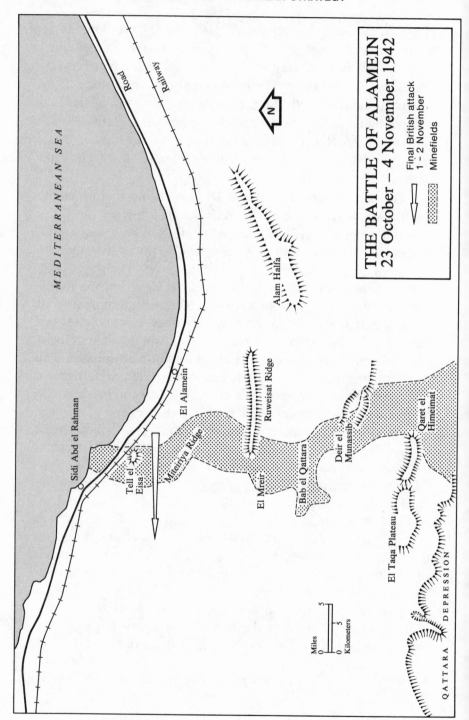

THE BATTLE OF ALAMEIN
23 October – 4 November 1942

Final British attack
1 – 2 November

Minefields

Four tank returns (conveniently enough, all of them fell in the three weeks before Alamein) showed the number of German tanks quickly restored to its pre–Alam Halfa level, but the proportion of the powerful "Specials" increasing by some 20 percent; Italian numbers rose a little further. The last of the four returns, issued on the morning of Alamein and signaled next day, showed 80 IIIs and 86 III "Specials," and 8 IVs and 30 IV "Specials" in the Afrika Korps.[10] Against them, the Eighth Army could muster 170 Grants, 252 Shermans, 76 Crusaders with 6-pounder guns, and more than 500 tanks of older types— over 1,000 tanks all told.

Other varieties of strength return were plentiful. Two, separated by an interval of a month, showed the rate at which Panzer Army was being reinforced. On 21 September it numbered 59,000 fighting troops and 15,000 ancillary personnel; with sick and wounded, this made 76,000 Germans in all (GAF and Flak added another 19,000). Just four weeks later, the total had risen to 91,000—a reinforcement rate of 4,000 a week (too few tank crews among them, Panzer Army complained). There were also 146,000 Italians in Africa, some of whom were under independent Italian control and did not form part of Panzer Army.[11]

Side by side with figures like these appeared the first signs of a German manpower shortage. Toward the end of September, the GAF as a whole was ordered to give up 50,000 men to the army, and in mid-October fifteen-year-old boys were to be recruited as auxiliaries in order to release soldiers for combat duties.[12] The local influence of the manpower shortage could at

---

[10] An intention to ship an unspecified number of the new and untried "Tiger" tanks (Mark VIs) was announced on 23 September (QT 2004). The Tiger's weight in fighting trim was stated as 57 tons (more than twice the weight of a IV "Special"). An inquiry whether 50-ton tanks could be unloaded at Tobruk went unanswered. OKH planned to send 10 Tigers to Cyrenaica in November and 10 more in December (QTs 3413, 3639), but TORCH resulted in their diversion to Tunisia (QTs 6291, 6452, 6528, 6866, 7537, 7998).

[11] The opposing fighting strengths at Alamein are stated by the official British history to have been 195,000 British and 104,000 Axis—50,000 Germans and 54,000 Italians (GS iv.62).

[12] Thus Ultra produced significant evidence of a German manpower shortage shortly before the general crisis caused by the opening of a third front in Tunisia was made apparent at the highest German command level (see the letter from Fromm, Commander of the Home Army, to Keitel in GS iv.337).

the same time be detected in the various GAF returns, which continued to come to hand with their accustomed regularity. The number of Fliegerfuehrer's serviceable aircraft was known almost every day, Fliegerkorps II's and X's rather less often, together with the base airfields and temporary locations of most units. Thus in the week before Alamein, Fliegerfuehrer's serviceability rate could be observed fluctuating between 30 and 50 fighters, 10 and 20 ground-attack aircraft, and 40 and 50 dive-bombers—less than a quarter of the total in the Desert Air Force, which supported Eighth Army. This discrepancy in air power was now leading to fatigue and sickness among German bomber crews as they tried to compensate for it by flying extra sorties, as well as to low serviceability rates and serious wastage. For example, Fliegerfuehrer lost 81 aircraft, including 54 fighters, in the first three weeks of October, and attributed it mainly to the pilots' lack of skill and experience. Kesselring bluntly refused to accept this excuse: fighter losses on that scale, he said, could not be replaced, and ways (he did not explain what) must be found to reduce them. The shortage of thirty or more bomber crews in the two Fliegerkorps, he had already ruled, was to be made good by raiding the transport Gruppe—which was itself soon under heavy pressure to fly in reinforcements for Panzer Army to make up for the unreliability of sea transport!

More striking than any of this, and of greater significance both immediately and in the longer term, were repeated indications of the chaos into which the Axis supply system was falling in the weeks before Alamein. So far as petrol for its tanks and lorried infantry was concerned, Panzer Army could scarcely be described even as living from hand to mouth by the third week in October, so erratic and so subject to last-minute interruptions had the supply become. If British action could create such an extraordinary state of affairs now, what might it not accomplish if, following a victory by the Eighth Army, the RAF could reoccupy the Martuba airfields, which would give its aircraft the range necessary to protect Malta, and then, in company with the navy, make the island once more a base from which both could prey at will upon the Axis supply lines?

For the first week or two after Alam Halfa, a cautiously optimistic tone prevailed in German reviews of the supply situation. Panzer Army[13] thought that things had improved a little on 12 September, for there was now sufficient petrol for sixteen days at current rates of consumption; a week later, it believed that with strict economy it could manage on the 9,000 cubic meters of fuel it expected to receive each month, in spite of a calculation which showed that consumption had never dropped below 9,500 cubic meters in any of the last four months, and had almost touched 15,000 in June, when the capture of Tobruk and the great advance had consumed vast quantities. Perhaps further reflection brought second thoughts; by 24 September, a monthly intake of 8,000 tons (considerably more than 9,000 cubic meters) was felt to be barely sufficient, and no real improvement was expected until coastal shipping and the railway linking Tobruk with Alamein could eliminate the need for road haulage eastward from Benghazi and concentrate supply traffic on Tobruk, the alleged underuse of which had lately been the cause of several complaints. Another survey the next day still foresaw all needs being satisfied except fuel, of which there was a universal shortage, but the special allocation of 10,000 cubic meters of petrol announced on 29 September would have provided some alleviation had there been any sign of its delivery.

The number of ships sunk on the way to Africa showed no sign of diminishing, however—there would be none at all left in another six months, commented Ciano—and Panzer Army began to sound a sourer and more apprehensive note in the first few days of October. Only 54 percent of its requirements had been met in September, it declared, and 8,000 of the 11,000 tons of petrol received had been used up on unavoidable supply journeys and current needs; at this rate, stocks would be exhausted in three weeks' time even if the British remained quiescent. The comparable figures for rations were far worse: only 1,800 tons were received but almost three times as much was consumed; fresh fruit and vegetables, flour, and soft drinks were particularly short; and severe cuts in daily rations had been necessary.

---

[13] Officially renamed German-Italian Panzer Army on 24 September (QT 2112).

The food shortage was emphasized again in the same week, and was blamed for the prevalence of undernourishment, lessened efficiency, and the high sickness rate. Now that all the British provisions captured in June and July had been eaten up, the situation was intolerable because of consistently inadequate deliveries, ran another complaint from the same source. As soon as he had settled himself into Rommel's seat, Stumme described rations as having reached "an almost unsurpassably low level" in a forthright statement to Kesselring in which he demanded 30,000 tons of supplies a month as "an imperative necessity to maintain the African theatre of war," and pointed to the urgent need to reinforce an army whose numbers were "daily decreasing through illness"[14] Kesselring's answer was to make promises which he probably knew he could not keep. Stumme may now have gone over his head, for Hitler soon took a hand, urging Cavallero to do everything in his power to improve the transport of German supplies, particularly ammunition and food.

The last week before the British offensive saw two important decrypts complete this picture of disarray and unpreparedness. One was the complete tanker program for 21–29 October, the critical period, which was signaled on the 17th. Only four days later, the devastating consequences of the action taken on this signal were made plain when Panzer Army reported a serious fuel shortage because the tanker *Panuco* (listed in the program as due to arrive in Tobruk on the 21st with 4,500 tons of petrol) had been torpedoed. Stocks in hand (less than four-fifths of the cargo of *Panuco* alone) would now last eleven days at current rates if all went well; but by 25 October there would only be four days' worth east of Tobruk, with the result that the mobility of the German troops would be seriously impaired if the British attacked. Another signal confirmed, leaving aside new deliveries, that unavoidable current consumption would use up all the petrol in the forward area by 29 October.

In just three weeks, then, air and sea attacks had halved the potential endurance of Panzer Army's tanks and motor trans-

---

[14] Other evidence showed that this was little or no exaggeration. In two successive ten-day periods, 1,500 men reported sick, and in the first of them the men flown in were barely numerous enough to make good the wastage (QTs 3059, 3638).

port—from twenty-one days on 1 October to eleven on the 20th—and left its commander to ponder the unpleasant fact that unless fresh supplies of petrol arrived almost daily and were instantly brought up to the front, he would be compelled to stop fighting before the end of the month even if he did not move his tanks from their present positions to meet the needs of battle. It was well for what remained of his peace of mind that he was unaware that his British opposite number knew as much about his difficulties as he did himself.

The grim situation thus displayed presented Alexander and Montgomery with an incomparable opportunity. Nemesis was at long last about to overtake the enemy in retribution for past errors of judgment: Hitler's and Halder's, in not realizing that an African commitment could prove as much of a running sore for Nazi Germany as Spain for Napoleonic France, unless designed on a scale large enough to guarantee quick and total victory, and unless an efficient transport system capable of maintaining the large army this made necessary was placed under exclusive German control; Rommel's, in repeatedly insisting that it was the duty of the quartermaster's branch to meet his every operational demand no matter what the practical difficulties. By October, all that was required to set Nemesis to work was a blow heavy enough to make a breach in the strong defenses behind which Panzer Army was sheltering, a breach wide enough for the tanks to pour through into the rear areas and, by creating immediate chaos there, prevent an orderly retreat by the fighting troops and expose the shortcomings of a maintenance organization so starved of resources that it could neither recover from a severe setback nor find the means to establish a second line of defense.

The whole Axis army could then have been wiped out in, or even before, the same Egyptian-Cyrenaican frontier area where long ago O'Connor had discomfited the Italians under Graziani. Montgomery might in that case have reached Tripoli quickly enough to distract the attention of the scratch force hastily assembled against TORCH sufficiently to enable Eisenhower to capture Tunis in December 1942 instead of May 1943,[15] thus perhaps shortening the war by six months.[16] None of this was achieved. By the middle of October, Ultra was showing the British commanders a vision, but they let it vanish before their eyes like mist in the sun.

A few aspects of Ultra's contribution to victory in the battle deserve mention before this point is pursued further.

An elaborate deception plan was devised to mislead the enemy about the time and place of the coming attack. The Long Range Desert Group raided Benghazi, Barce, and other Cyrenaican airfields in mid-September, using an approach route through the oases of Siwa, Kufra, and Jalo. Success was only moderate, but the aftermath of the raids was more profitable than the raids themselves. As had been intended, they drew German and Italian attention to the southern end of the front and encouraged just those fears of a southabout "left hook" by the Eighth Army which "A" Force was endeavoring to implant in their minds. Documents captured from the LRDG at Jalo showed, according to OKW on 18 September, that the British intended to hold the oasis for three weeks in conjunction with their offensive, which anyhow was expected to open in about that time. Kesselring called for aerial reconnaissance of Kufra, the British garrison which the Italians planned to overwhelm, and from late September until Alamein intercepts steadily showed that the deep margin of the Sahara was being kept under regular surveillance from the air or, in the case of Siwa, on the ground.

Evidence about the success of the rest of the deception plan was mixed. British order of battle and locations were known fairly accurately, but in spite of what has just been said, as well as of sightings of fresh tracks (mostly faked, no doubt) and of tanks and armored cars on the edge of the Qattara Depression, the likely point of attack was not placed quite as far south as the deception planners hoped. Instead, the main British concentra-

[15]Even as things were, the Axis command was anxiously preoccupied with threats to the Gafsa-Gabès sector linking Libya and Tunisia in November. See pp. 179, 193, 198, below.
[16]See Appendix IV, "A Shortened War?"

tions were thought to be near the Ruweisat Ridge—some ten miles south of the Miteiriya Ridge, where the blow actually fell—and the attack was expected there and possibly on both sides of the coast road as well. Platitudinous warnings that the attack would come "soon" were common, but even in the third week in October, Fliegerfuehrer's reconnaissance pilots regularly reported "quiet day" or "nothing special"—that is to say, that the various camouflage devices (covers that hid tanks, ammunition dumps disguised as parked lorries, etc.) were deceiving both eye and camera. The evening reconnaissance report for 22 October ran, "quiet; slight increase in British forces in south" (perhaps a reflection of the MELTINGPOT plan, which sought to suggest that the 10th Armored Division had moved south), and this was signaled twelve hours before the attack began. Even at last light on the 23rd, just before the guns opened fire, it was still "Quiet day. No change." This regular negative evidence put it beyond doubt that Eighth Army was about to secure complete tactical surprise, in spite of the flatness of the ground, the absence of cover, and the familiarity of the tactical options open to it.

Stumme having died of a heart attack while reconnoitering the battlefield on the first morning, Rommel flew back from Austria to resume command of Panzer Army on the evening of 25 October. The news that greeted him was grim. Two tankers, carrying 4,000 tons of petrol between them, had been sunk that afternoon; others followed them to the bottom in the next day or two. ("Now we really are up against it," he remarked as a third went down.) This precipitated an immediate crisis. With the main attack still to come, it was believed, only two or three days' reserves of petrol were within reach of Panzer Army, as Kesselring ordered planes to operate continuously day and night to fly in emergency supplies from Crete while a hundred or more transport aircraft and gliders, most of them hastily brought in from south Russia, resupplied Crete from Greece. Coming on top of the existing fuel shortage, the tanker disasters meant that a situation which had become "grave in the extreme" by the evening of the 28th was the more threatening because adequate petrol for the Afrika Korps' remaining 81 tanks was not to be relied on. The same reasoning also made it virtually certain that when Rommel followed his instinct and concentrated the Afrika Korps once again by shifting the 21st Panzer northward from its position opposite the British center (where it was "corsetted" with the Italian Ariete armored division) to join the 15th Panzer in confronting the British spearhead, he would not be able to move it back again if Montgomery later chose to switch his main assault elsewhere—an uncomfortable truth which Rommel himself was being forced to recognize. The destruction of the tankers could be signaled almost at once, the move of the 21st Panzer only with a delay which did not in the end matter, since it had been picked up in good time by the Y Service. The same was true when the 90th Light was ordered into battle alongside the Afrika Korps on the afternoon of 29 October: decrypting difficulties held the signal up until early on the 31st. The knowledge that the main German strength was now concentrated within eight or ten miles of the coast was instrumental in leading Montgomery to choose—though after more hesitation than hindsight now finds it easy to understand—a more southerly line for the decisive thrust (Ultra located the 21st Panzer well to the north of it on 31 October), which made the final breakthrough on the night of 2–3 November.

Hitler now did his best to destroy the army whose victorious commander he had in triumph promoted Feldmarschall a mere four months ago. By the end of the summer it had become evident that the grandiose campaign to wipe out the Russian armies in the bend of the river Don, reach the Caspian, and occupy the Caucasus, which he had planned as Commander-in-Chief of the Army (a post he had assumed in December 1941), was flagging badly. Possessed by a new madness as reality refused to dance to the tune played by his fantasies, he became morose and ill-tempered, shunning the company even of sycophants and flatterers. In September he dismissed Halder, the Chief of Staff of the Army, for daring to criticize his amateur strategy, and announced his intention to educate the General Staff in his own brand of fanaticism and bend the whole army to his will. Halder noted in his diary that already "the correct choice of words was more and more disregarded when orders were given. High-sounding words like 'annihilate' or 'destroy,' phrases like 'prevent them from escaping' were used, even when the action they described was impossible, instead of soberer and more precisely calculated instructions."

Thus Hitler was in no mood to comprehend what was happening at Alamein or to react rationally to two radio messages which Rommel sent him on the evening of 2 November and which Ultra enabled Alexander and Montgomery to read soon after dawn next day. The first reported that the army was exhausted, that a breakthrough could not be prevented, that there was not enough petrol to move more than a short distance, and that "the possibility of the annihilation of the army must be faced," the second that orders had been issued for a fighting withdrawal to begin at once.[17] Hitler's reply was the first in a series which was soon to become familiar as the fortune of war turned against him: ". . . hold on, do not yield a step . . . victory or death." "This order demanded the impossible," Rommel wrote later, but for twenty-four hours he loyally tried to carry out his Fuehrer's command. But the situation was already out of control, and putting the withdrawal order into reverse added to the confusion among the broken divisions. On the morning of 4 November he asked permission to retire to a nominally prepared position at Fuka, and in the evening Hitler and Mussolini gave their reluctant consent. But there was no stopping at Fuka or anywhere near it: the long retreat and the lumbering pursuit had begun.

Ultra had discovered in good time the first—and from the intelligence point of view by far the most important—of these telegrams[18] (signs of withdrawal were not observed from the air until later the same morning), and the acceleration of events thereafter would have reduced the operational value of the oth-

---

[17]The duty officer at the Fuehrerhauptquartier who received the teleprinted copy of the second message in the middle of the night failed to realize that it differed significantly from its predecessor by announcing that the retreat had started, and therefore did not bring it to Hitler's notice immediately. As soon as he discovered this, Hitler reduced him to the ranks and dismissed General Warlimont, the head of his section at OKW. Some time later, he was persuaded to restore them both to their former positions (OKW/KTB ii.894–98).

[18]The texts are printed in full in MME iv.475–77.

ers considerably even if they had been decrypted sooner. In any case, however, it was not tactical details, even when they were as important as these, but the revelation of Panzer Army's threadbare logistical state which was Ultra's chief contribution to the battle, as it had been to the preparation for it.

7
THE SLOW PURSUIT ACROSS LIBYA: ALAMEIN TO TRIPOLI
November 1942–January 1943

By the time the order to withdraw was given, Panzer Army was already doubtful whether it would be able to make a stand at Fuka, and within twenty-four hours Rommel had decided that with only eight tanks left in the 15th Panzer and losses so high that only battle groups remained of all his divisions, it would be impossible. The Halfaya pass was briefly considered as a halting place, but by the evening of 7 November the evacuation of Tobruk was contemplated, Benghazi harbor was overcrowded, and "surplus" aircraft petrol was being dumped behind the Agheila position. The scale of the retreat and the reasons for it were thus abundantly clear. Still more conclusive evidence of the weak state to which a lost battle and the helter-skelter which followed had reduced Panzer Army came in during 10 November: the 15th Panzer had now no tanks and less than 1,200 men, the 21st Panzer only 11 tanks and barely 1,000 men, the 90th Light just 1,000 men, and the Ramcke Brigade 700 men. The four of them had managed to carry away only 29 antitank guns all told, and 50 88s had been lost. There was only enough petrol for the army to move 150 kilometers at most, and stocks at Benghazi could not be brought forward in time. Confirmation that only rearguard delaying actions were to be expected for some time to come and a first hint of the impact of the TORCH landings were apparent when Hitler and Mussolini jointly warned Rommel on 10 November

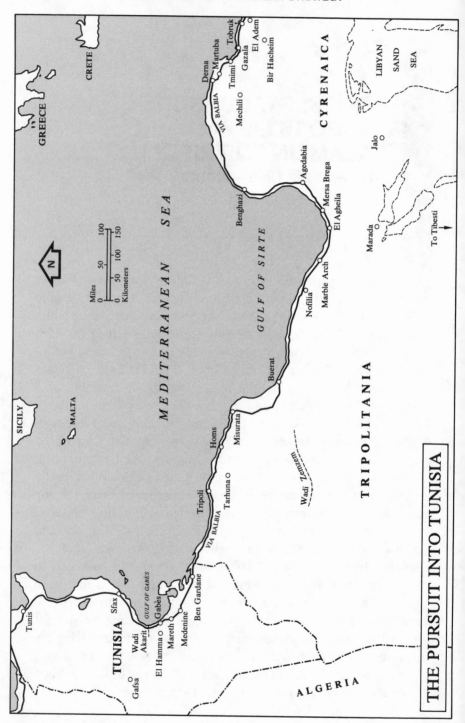

THE PURSUIT INTO TUNISIA

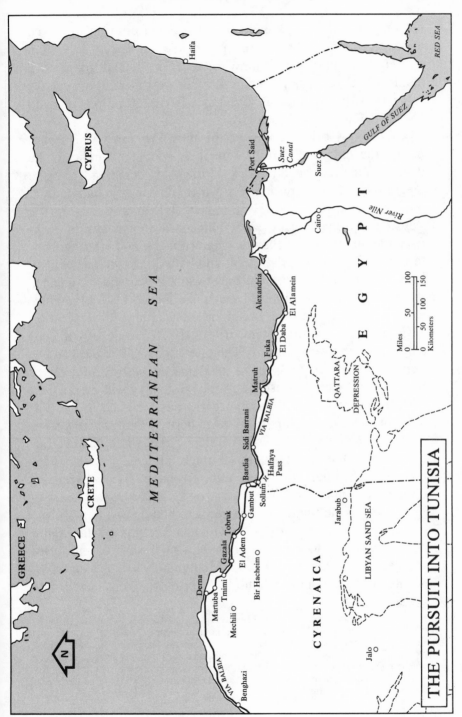

THE PURSUIT INTO TUNISIA

not only that the preparation of the Agheila position would be endangered unless he offered protracted resistance at Sollum and Halfaya (both places were in fact about to fall into British hands) but that the new landings farther west made it imperative to prevent the situation in Cyrenaica from getting out of hand and to defend Tripoli properly.

Even this brief sample of the most striking Ultra signals during the first week after Alamein is enough to indicate the degree of despair at all levels of the Axis command and the magnitude of the opportunity which its victory had laid at the Eighth Army's feet. By the same token, it shows up the slowness and inadequacy of the immediate steps taken to profit from the opportunity.[1] Plainly, there could be no better moment to cut off Panzer Army's retreat and by a quick encirclement to give it the deathblow than at once, while it was still off balance and reeling back in confusion. Such had indeed been Montgomery's intention when he issued his first orders for Operation LIGHTFOOT in mid-September: "OBJECT. To destroy the enemy forces opposing 8 Army. The operations will be designed to *trap the enemy in his present area and to destroy him there.* Should small elements escape to the west, they will be pursued and dealt with later." This object was not achieved in the moment of victory, and opportunities to destroy Panzer Army were missed repeatedly all the way to Tripoli. The whole Allied strategy in the Mediterranean was lastingly affected by what happened—or, rather, by what did not happen—in Cyrenaica during November 1942.

Loyal to the ungrateful master who had denied him a place in the victory parade, in 1947 de Guingand attributed the Eighth Army's slowness to the heavy rain which fell on 5, 6, and 7 November, not to any oversight of Montgomery's. The next year, Montgomery committed himself in print to the same excuse

---

[1] One of the objects of the battle had been to capture the Martuba group of airfields by mid-November in order that they might be used by fighters providing cover for the STONEAGE convoy on the last stage of its passage to Malta with urgently needed supplies. This was achieved only just in the nick of time. From this delay stemmed the decline in army-air cooperation which reached serious proportions a month later (Terraine, 387), and the coolness between Tedder and Montgomery which was often to mar their relations in the future.

("only the rain saved them from complete annihilation"), and went on using it all his life. "Rain was not to blame for everything, but it did wash away an opportunity which had not been fully grasped," concluded the official history in 1966, proposing congestion behind the front, petrol supply problems, weak RAF support on 5 November, and the absence of a fresh pursuit force waiting for its leash to be slipped, but otherwise developing no serious criticism of Montgomery's generalship. Most recent writing has preferred the opinion several senior Eighth Army generals expressed at the time—that Montgomery was overcautious and missed the chance of a quick kill because he tried to move forward on too broad a front, and because he had not sufficiently worked out in advance how he would exploit the victory he intended to win. (On 4 November "I felt frustrated. I reckoned I could have gone ahead alone," said Major General Harding, commander of the 7th Armoured Division.) Thus Barnett, Liddell Hart, Carver, Lewin (all without benefit of Ultra), Jackson, Irving, Hamilton, and even (up to a point) the official British intelligence history criticize Montgomery in varying degree, particularly for not pressing the pursuit more vigorously in the first few days, though they recognize that much of the blame for this attaches not to him but to Lumsden, the commander of X Corps, the so-called *corps de chasse*.

While it must not be forgotten that many of his troops were tired after twelve days' continuous fighting and that Montgomery knew he had not yet had time to train a still largely amateur army into an instrument which could be relied on to obey his every command with confidence and alacrity, close examination of the Ultra evidence powerfully supports these criticisms. If they had been brought forward quickly, only a fraction of X Corps' 270 tanks—perhaps the 7th Armoured Division's 52 Grants and Shermans, in accordance with Harding's wish—would have sufficed to overrun the meager 11 tanks, which were all the Afrika Korps had on the 9th, without taking the slightest risk, and the figures already quoted show that Montgomery was carrying caution to absurd lengths if he really feared later on, as he repeatedly said, that Rommel might mount a counterattack strong enough to bring about another "Benghazi handicap" and renew his threat to Egypt. (Rather surprisingly, this suggestion has lately been restated by General Fraser.) At no stage in the slow advance across Cyrenaica is his very proper desire to keep casualties to a minimum a sufficient excuse for Montgomery's hesitation. Given Ultra's continuing assurance of Rommel's weakness, the casualties incurred in a single encircling movement somewhere in Cyrenaica would probably have been fewer than those likely to be incurred in a three-month-long slog all the way to Tripoli. The number of fighting men who could be maintained at the end of a lengthening supply line was, of course, bound to shrink until a sizable port was captured, but at least they were not subject to continual harassment from the air (petrol shortage restricted Fliegerfuehrer's activities, and his strength fell from 113 to 63 aircraft between 10 and 20 November). On the other hand, British air activity severely hampered the retreat of Panzer Army, which continually complained of supply difficulties—its quartermaster did not expect its position to improve until the 22nd, when it would have reached Agheila.

News on the evening of 13 November that Agheila was the immediate goal was quickly followed by Kesselring's assumption that a stand would be made there, and Luftgaustab's contrary belief that Misurata (three hundred miles farther west, and only a hundred miles from Tripoli) was more likely on supply grounds. Four days later, Rommel's opinion that Agheila was only defensible if petrol, tanks, guns, ample ammunition, and reinforcements for Fliegerfuehrer were forthcoming at once (an obviously impossible condition) made it plain that he would only fight a rearguard action there, and soon his quartermaster hinted at the next bound by ordering Buerat (a hundred miles closer than Misurata) to be stocked up with fuel and rations. Rommel's intention was evidently to retreat as fast as he could. Quick British action—which, he knew, was not yet being taken—was therefore required if he was to be caught, and the opportunity for it was the greater because his progress was still being seriously delayed by petrol shortage. Partly because of a muddle about the rerouting of a tanker (which was anyhow shortly sunk), his situation worsened by the hour throughout 15 November until by evening he called it so "catastrophic" that his army was "almost immobilised." The same word occurs next day in Panzer Army's evening report, which revealed that the Afrika Korps had not been able to move south from Benghazi as intended, and Rommel used it again on the 17th. Emergency air transport provided enough petrol (some of it aircraft petrol) to shift the Africa Korps and the 90th Light a short distance on 18 November, but at midnight Kesselring had to tell Rommel that he was now out of range and that air supply of fuel was no longer possible. In view of all this, it cannot be maintained that "Rommel had been crying 'Wolf' in order to ensure increased petrol supplies."[2] His need was genuine; the situation was far too acute for him to indulge in bureaucratic word-games.

Here, surely, in the proof of Rommel's desperate state, was a clear invitation to Montgomery to slacken his methodical pursuit for a moment and repeat O'Connor's tactics of 1941 by a lightning stroke across the desert from Mechili to cut Panzer Army off as it crawled painfully the long way round the Cyrenaican "bulge" by the coast road, no matter that the blow would not now be as heavy as a week earlier—the 7th Armoured Division could only muster half as many fit tanks as on 4 November. Hitler, alert to reality for once, foresaw the danger as soon as the Eighth Army crossed the Egyptian frontier on the 12th, and called on Fliegerfuehrer to prevent it: twenty British armored cars had been spotted at Antelat earlier the same day. Thus the presence of even a tiny reconnaissance party was enough to arouse fears of another Beda Fomm at the highest level, and Montgomery knew this by some time on 14 November. Nevertheless, vital time was wasted. Montgomery is said not to have seen Rommel's "catastrophic" message until some eighteen hours after the signal conveying it was transmitted, and it was not for another two days after this that a force of any strength took the shortcut along the chord of the Cyrenaican arc to intercept Panzer Army between Benghazi and Agheila. It came too late; Rommel was already behind the Agheila defenses. Rommel's subsequent account bears witness to his relief at reaching Agheila safely (having lost scarcely a man since To-

---

[2]He was soon to rebuke his own subordinates for just this offense (QT 7058).

bruk) and to the anxiety about petrol and its effect on his army's mobility which had continually racked him since Alamein.

Montgomery later claimed that he bluffed Rommel out of Agheila by persuading him that he might lose his whole army if he stood and fought, and implied that he did this quickly. The opposite would be nearer the truth—that Rommel bluffed him into putting off his assault until mid-December, just as he (Rommel) had predicted. A correspondence with Mussolini and Hitler between 17 and 23 November showed Rommel forecasting that Eighth Army would not attack for two or three weeks, but that when it did he would not have enough men, tanks, or guns to resist with any prospect of success, so that "the probability of the annihilation of the remaining elements of Panzer Army must be faced." There is no question of Rommel needing to be "persuaded" of his own weakness; he was only too well aware of it, and Ultra had told Montgomery so.

Similarly, it is difficult to discern any sound basis for Montgomery's estimate that Rommel had 100 tanks and "considerable numbers" of antitank guns about the end of November. Successive returns showed the Afrika Korps' miserable 11 tanks of 9 November rising to 35 (or 43: Rommel and his quartermaster gave different figures on the same day) on the 23rd, 49 on 1 December, and 54 on 2 December.[3] Toward the end of November, moreover, a long technical appreciation by Panzer Army's tank specialists showed them admitting the superiority of the Eighth Army's new equipment. According to this document, Sherman tanks chose to fight at a range of 2,000 or 3,000 meters, a distance at which even 88s could not engage them effectively, while the new British 17-pounder antitank gun was knocking out German tanks with relative ease. Guns of greater penetrative power, and tanks with thicker armor, were urgently needed.[4] True, there were plans to send 24 new tanks over to

---

[3] Forty-two Italian tanks were also mentioned in the last two returns, but they were of low fighting value.

[4] The new Mark VI Tigers possessed both these advantages—but a consignment intended for Rommel had already been diverted to Tunisia (see p. 157, n. 10), and by 2 December, ten days after the appreciation just quoted, Tigers were low on Panzer Army's priority list: antitank and other types of gun occupied the first five places, Tigers only the twelfth (QT 7841).

Panzer Army, and huge tonnages of petrol, ammunition, and food (the bread ration had been low or nonexistent for some time) were airily promised, as so often in the past—"all fine talk for the future" was the sour comment of General von Rintelen in Rome—but in fact only 12 new tanks were issued before the end of the month, and only 22 in all were actually delivered between 25 October and 14 December. Worst of all, from Rommel's point of view, the Stalingrad crisis and the Tunisian emergency were reducing his status, which only four or five months ago had been so exalted, to that of the commander of a second-class army; his promised reinforcements and precious shipping space had been filched for von Arnim; and his supply route had been switched to run through Tunis and Bizerta (where it was at the mercy of Kesselring and others) instead of Tripoli, in spite of his protests and of the four hundred extra miles of road and rail haulage this imposed, and although the land route was still far from secure. (A compromise, suggested by Panzer Army on 4 December, to route tankers to Sousse, their cargoes to go thence overland to Sfax and onward partly by landing craft and partly by lorry, ran into immediate trouble over inadequate unloading gear and almost came to grief when the RAF severely damaged Sousse harbor, put the railway to Sfax out of action, and scared French and Arab labor away.)

What more did Montgomery need to convince him that it would be safe simply to mask the Agheila defenses and make a quick dash to surround Panzer Army and destroy it utterly?

Three things at least can be pleaded in extenuation of his three-week delay (23 November–14 December) in front of the Marsa el Brega–Agheila position: the psychological block which made those who had been there before feel there was almost a law of nature which forbade them to advance further—i.e., a matter of army morale; his desire not to incur avoidable casualties (the Brega defenses were exceptionally thickly mined, and the 51st Division's eventual assault was very costly); and the difficulty of bringing up sufficient supplies to sustain a force large enough to tackle even the enfeebled Afrika Korps. But Ultra is not among them. The first three are impossible to evaluate precisely at this distance in time, but the Ultra signals can be read now exactly as they were then.

The most recently published account of the events of November and December 1942 is that given by Sir Edgar Williams to Montgomery's biographer. Memory has once again played an unkind trick; the facts are not quite as Sir Edgar remembers them, and the conclusions to be drawn are therefore different. On this occasion Rommel was not two-faced, reassuring Hitler by radio that he would hold on as long as he could while really intending to false-front Montgomery by withdrawing the moment he was attacked; he had done this sort of thing several times before, but not now. On the contrary, he went to great lengths to make certain that Hitler knew the unpleasant truth, and Ultra revealed that he had done so. Thus it misrepresents the facts to say that "we were sometimes hindered by Ultra, because Rommel was too good a soldier" to do what the decrypts said he intended to do, or that "the source material was too good" because it would have been easier to reach the right conclusion without it. The plentiful Ultra of these weeks gave a true picture of Panzer Army's plight, one which corresponds with what became known subsequently and with what Rommel wrote in his memoirs; it omitted only to indicate how skillfully a German army could conduct a fighting retreat.

Rommel's grim forecast, already quoted, was in fact his emphatic way of pointing out the consequences of the "Stand fast" order (the only one Ultra reported at this time) issued by Hitler and Mussolini jointly on 22 November. Here was no tongue-in-cheek obeisance to a Fuehrer he intended to deceive, but a sincere, if foredoomed, effort to make him face reality. A few days later, Rommel felt "in duty bound" to explain in person his conviction that Africa was lost, and he flew off to Rastenburg without first seeking permission. It was in vain; he met a frosty reception from a Hitler distracted by Stalingrad and Tunisia and came back "a broken man," according to Westphal, empty-handed save for an airy promise of 60 tanks and 100 antitank guns a month (December deliveries turned out to be only 21 and 34 respectively, and as usual it was soon plain that the promise would never be kept). On 2 December, while Rommel was still on his way back to Libya, another decrypt showed that Kesselring now shared Rommel's pessimism, and realized that Panzer Army would not make a stand at Agheila but would fight its way back to "the known rearward defensive zone" (evidently Buerat, in view of previous hints). At least as early as 2 December, therefore, Montgomery knew for certain that Rommel intended to escape from a position which both generals knew could be outflanked, but he had been receiving strong hints to this effect for the past fortnight.

Action to prevent the escape now became more urgent than ever, as Ultra proceeded to demonstrate. The Italians wanted to withdraw during the night of 5–6 December, but Rommel was too short of petrol and transport to do the same, and on the 6th he appealed for help to Kesselring, pointing out that he had so little fuel that he could neither disturb the British deployment nor counter any outflanking move they might make. Here, surely, was yet another clear invitation to deliver a quick "left hook" and surround Panzer Army while it was unable to move, a course which would have the added advantage that it would make a costly frontal assault unnecessary. Churchill evidently thought so. On 11 December he invited Alexander to drop Montgomery a "friendly hint" to this effect. "Will he not seem foolish," he wrote, "if, as is possible, there is no battle at Agheila and Rommel slips away?"

Daily (sometimes twice-daily) reports from Panzer Army about this time showed the petrol shortage growing if anything more acute (Rommel said there was only enough for fifty kilometers on 14 December, and next day feared that it would run out altogether at Nofilia) and increasing signs of the British turning movement, which eventually began on the night of 11–12 December—i.e., that the moment of escape had come but that it would be a very hazardous moment for Panzer Army. Fliegerfuehrer meanwhile was in similar straits: he had only enough fuel to get back to Buerat and could promise no support at all to the ground forces on the 15th.

With two unimportant exceptions, both after the British advance had at last begun, all the Ultra signals quoted in the last two paragraphs were dispatched to Montgomery within twenty-four hours of their German time or origin, some much more quickly.

It is plain, then, that Montgomery knew more than enough about Rommel's predicament to be sure that he could not possibly make a surprise counterstroke like that of the previous January and that he himself could safely take the risk of an enveloping movement to surround and capture Panzer Army without any compulsion to mount a formal frontal attack on the Marsa el Brega defenses. He deliberately chose to disregard the invitation implied by the Ultra intelligence, in spite of a further attempt by Churchill to hurry his advance along at the end of December.

Broadly speaking, the pattern thus established was repeated at every succeeding stage of Rommel's retreat: despite his difficulties, which were amply documented by Ultra—deteriorating health and increasing friction with the Italians were now added to the familiar list—he managed to extricate his army from every outflanking movement and to preserve it intact for an eventual junction with the Axis forces in Tunisia. There were occasional variations in the pattern, notably between Agheila and Tripoli, when Montgomery's own logistical problems forced him to move with unwonted speed, but the outlines remained constant.

As attention shifted to Buerat on the evacuation of Agheila, Rommel's strategic thinking was once again made clear in an exchange of signals between him and his nominal superior, Bastico, Italian Commander-in-Chief in Libya, which may be summarized thus:

ROMMEL: What shall I do if the British bypass the Buerat position?

BASTICO: Hold the position to the last.

ROMMEL: That is no answer. They could strike at Tripoli by swinging far to the south first, and only screen the Buerat defenses without attacking them. What shall I do if they do this? Remember that I am very short of petrol. Please reply urgently.

Bastico's reply was not intercepted (according to Rommel, it was evasive), but Rommel's dilemma was plain enough, and his inability to interfere with a "left hook" was several times repeated. Even supply lorries were stranded with empty fuel tanks for days on end, while nearly 150 Ju-52 transport planes, which had so often relieved a fuel crisis in the past, were suddenly whisked away to southern Russia to succor the beleaguered Sixth Army at Stalingrad, where the emergency became acute in late November. Cargo manifests, frequent at this period, appeared to consist largely of trivia so often as to prompt the reflection that the incompetence of the supply staffs in Italy was as much to blame for Panzer Army's difficulties as the continuous Ultra-based air and sea assault on Axis shipping.

Rommel's plans for Buerat were further revealed at the turn of the year. First, he would move the nonmotorized Italians to the rear; this would take about ten days, but if he waited for the British to attack, as the Italian command was urging, most of them would not get away at all. The motorized German divisions, with their 60 surviving tanks, would then move back by bounds, at a speed determined by the severity of the British pressure, to the Tarhuna-Homs line (which Bastico warned him was hardly prepared for defense at all). By this time, he hoped, the sting would have been taken out of the British advance. However, his own preference was to withdraw to Tunis at once, because he feared that a deadly thrust by Eisenhower might cut him off from his supply base by severing communications with it between Gafsa and Gabès (not to speak of the menace of Leclercq and the Free French coming up from Tibesti), thus "closing the Tripolitanian mousetrap."

Several very rewarding breaks of army Enigma now gave an abnormally complete confirmation of the intractable strategic problem facing the Axis command. His appreciation that the British were indeed preparing a formidable "left hook" led Rommel to tell Bastico on 2 January that withdrawal from Buerat was now "imperative" and to warn him that if this developed in strength, he might not be able to hold the Eighth Army off for as long as the Italians wanted. Mussolini, now completely lost in a fantasy world, had been instructing Rommel to move slowly enough to spend three weeks on the way from Buerat to Homs and another three from Homs to Tripoli, and there had been a furious quarrel when Rommel and Kesselring met Bastico on 30 December.[5] Following this, an immensely long signal of 5 January set out Panzer Army's supply situation in great detail: up to 33,000 tons a month were needed, yet only 5,871 tons had been delivered in December; there was just enough petrol for the retreat, but none for offensive operations by the armor; ammunition was inadequate for the major battle which was expected shortly; 576 antitank guns and 340 tanks were urgently needed,[6] but subsequent correspondence with Kesselring produced nothing but a protest that Rommel's figures were wrong and that he had received more than he admitted, together with another empty promise that 60 or 70 antitank guns were on the way and would be delivered as soon as possible.

The lengthening British supply line was by now posing a very serious problem, which was accentuated by a gale at Benghazi which delayed the discharge of cargo. Montgomery concluded that the only solution was to make a single rapid thrust to capture Tripoli within ten days and secure the port, which alone could bring permanent relief.[7] The advance began on 15 January against an enemy who had admitted that he would not be able to stand up against it and was pushed ahead with enough vigor to achieve its object with two days to spare. Indeed, had the 7th Armoured Division not been forced to check its advance momentarily when its commander was wounded at a critical moment outside Tarhuna, it might have been able to take full advantage of Rommel's predicament. But aerial reconnaissance (Fliegerfuehrer's daily strength returns showed that he could put more machines into the air now than

---

[5]Ultra did not pick up Mussolini's instructions but discovered that Hitler concurred with them. The signal (VM 539) conveying this contains an interesting attempt—as successful as permitted by the evidence, which was inadequate for the purpose—to reconstruct them. This was the only significant gap in Ultra about this time, and it is worth noting that every major point in the account given in MME iv.229–30 can be documented from Ultra signals, most of which were dispatched within twenty-four hours of the German originals.

[6]Panzer Army claimed that the retreat cost it only 17 antitank guns and 14 tanks—hardly a tribute to the vigor of Eighth Army's pursuit; 20 and 14 respectively had been lost at sea.

[7]In so doing, Montgomery "showed real stature and had obviously overcome his urge for exaggerated caution," wrote Rommel, unwontedly appreciative of his opponent's generalship (Rommel, 395).

in the recent past) gave Rommel sufficient warning for him to take a sudden decision on 19 January to begin the withdrawal to Mareth at once.

Tripoli fell on the twenty-third, but Panzer Army escaped envelopment once more and was soon across the Tunisian frontier. Mussolini's six weeks had shrunk to only three, but what remained of Panzer Army was one stage nearer Tunis and safety. Montgomery had laid the desert bogey and driven the Axis from Libya. He had turned the Eighth Army into a body of professional soldiers with pride in their achievements. He had made himself the best-known British soldier since Haig and Allenby. But he had not fulfilled his promise to "hit Rommel for six out of Africa," although Ultra had offered him repeated opportunities to do so.

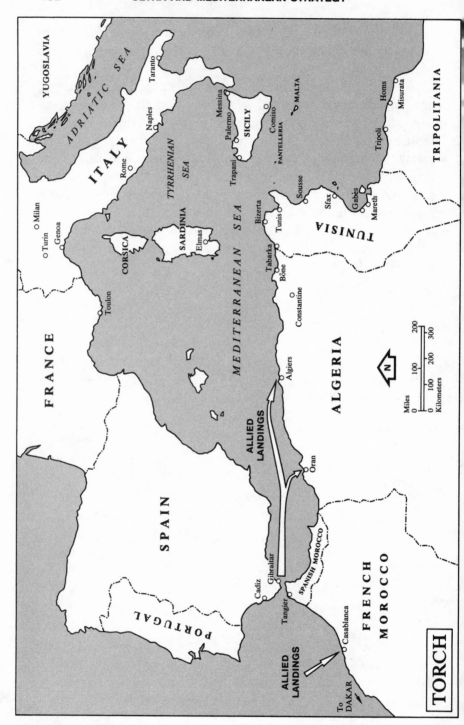

8
TORCH: THE TUNISIAN CAMPAIGN
November 1942–May 1943

The First Two Months
The expedition to French North Africa was born of a compromise which, when the occupation of Tunis led almost inevitably to the invasion of Sicily and then of Italy, had a major influence on the whole conduct of the war. Once it had been agreed that the war against Germany should take precedence over the war against Japan, American urgency for action pointed to the narrow escape of the Russians from defeat in December 1941 as a compelling reason for an invasion of Europe in 1942 (ROUNDUP). British caution—justified in the event, when experience showed how hard put to it both citizen armies were to match German professionalism, even in 1944—warned that a small force (all that could yet be managed) was certain to be annihilated by an unweakened enemy. Churchill, who had long wanted the occupation of the French territories and had hoped that a successful CRUSADER would lead Auchinleck to them (GYMNAST) as soon as he had secured Tripoli, found an ally in Roosevelt, and the two political leaders went over the heads of their military advisers (who were locked in sometimes bitter disagreements during the spring and early summer of 1942) to impose a solution which guaranteed early action but did not imperil an eventual landing in strength on the Channel coast. GYMNAST, now rechristened TORCH and reoriented to face east, not west, was agreed between them at the

end of July. "This is the true Second Front in 1942," said Churchill, but it was Roosevelt's veto which silenced the objections of his Chiefs of Staff, who thought the British irresolute about ROUNDUP and suspected them of selfish national aims in the Mediterranean.

General Eisenhower, hitherto based in London to command the U.S. army detachments in the European Theater of Operations, was appointed Commander-in-Chief on 6 August; after initial changes, when first Alexander and then Montgomery were transferred to Egypt, the British contingent was to be led by Lieutenant General Anderson. Eisenhower's plan, issued in its final form only on 10 October, provided for landings at Casablanca, Oran, and Algiers (one outside the Mediterranean, two inside). The easternmost, Algiers, was still some four hundred miles from Bizerta and Tunis, the ultimate objectives, but it was thought unwise to risk a more easterly landing place in view of the possibility of prolonged French resistance. In retrospect, the risk could have been taken and the campaign shortened, but this could not have been foreseen at the time. The date of the landings was set for 8 November, after anything earlier had been found impracticable.

What little Ultra there was about the western basin of the Mediterranean and its approaches during the autumn of 1942 pointed reassuringly to the conclusion that neither of the Axis partners foresaw a landing in French North Africa. Only one intercept (curiously, it was the first of them all) pointed disturbingly in the opposite direction. On 25 September, the German General attached to Italian Headquarters in Rome forwarded without comment to Panzer Army an agent's report to the effect that it was believed in Vatican circles that between the middle of October and the middle of November, U.S. troops would land at Dakar and British troops in North Africa. This was never signaled to Cairo, though presumably it was made known to Eisenhower's headquarters, then still in London. Dakar was one of the many false destinations being put about under the TORCH cover plan. Another of these "notional" destinations surfaced in Ultra soon after this, with the announcement on 10

October of plans to reinforce Crete by 17,000 men, plus motor transport and 350 guns; since 17,000 was the establishment strength of a first-line division, and since it echoed that mentioned in a slightly earlier program for the reinforcement of Panzer Army, it was possible to read into it the diversion of resources away from both of the Axis' real danger points, Egypt and Tunisia, and to chalk up another success for the deception staff.

By the end of October, unusual activity at Gibraltar could no longer be concealed. Kesselring nevertheless retained a cool enough head as the battle of Alamein approached its climax to tell Rommel, who had demanded extra air support for Panzer Army, that he would provide some at once, but that more depended on the development of "the Gibraltar situation." But the move of a Gruppe of fighters from Sicily to the Aegean on 29 October implied that he did not expect much trouble from the new quarter. The aircraft—some from the south Russian front, some from as far afield as Norway—sent to strengthen Luftflotte 2 on the 2nd, 3rd, and 4th of November were almost certainly the "important air reinforcements" promised in Hitler's "Victory or death" signal to Rommel, not preparations to attack the approaching Allied convoys (the first of which was not reported in Ultra until 5 November, and even then by an agent in Algeciras who had not been able to discover its destination) or their supposed landing place. Not until midday on 4 November were bombers of Fliegerkorps II, temporarily detached to Fliegerkorps X in the eastern Mediterranean to escort vessels carrying supplies to Rommel, warned to be ready to return to their home bases on receipt of orders connected with Gibraltar, and late that evening fighters were still being transferred from west to east, this time from Comiso, in Sicily, to Tobruk. Several intercepts of the 5th and 6th about attacks on an Allied convoy showed a hasty decision by Fliegerkorps II to use Elmas in Sardinia as base airfield for this purpose, but also a continuing bafflement about the direction in which the convoy was heading. A reference to "the destruction of the Axis African front" could only mean that the convoy was presumed to be carrying reinforcements for the Eighth Army to be landed in

Egypt, although none had taken the direct route for well over a year; a seaborne assault on Benghazi, Sardinia, or Sicily and the resupplying of Malta were other possibilities canvassed by different German authorities.

Postwar investigation showed that the Italians made the best guess about Allied intentions and that the Germans fell for almost all the "notional" objectives at one time or another, favoring in particular the interpretation that the convoys they had observed from the air were carrying reinforcements to Malta. (The assault on Malta had in fact recently been called off because the RAF was shooting down too many German aircraft.) Jodl was even rash enough on 7 November (like Canaris a year later, on the eve of Anzio) to declare his belief that French North Africa was the *least* likely place for an Allied landing, because it might drive the French into the Germans' arms.

Thus, when none of the Ultra evidence right up to the moment of the Allied landings suggested German suspicions that French North Africa was the destination of the ships they had observed passing through the Straits of Gibraltar and continuing on an easterly course, it was fairly representing Axis opinion, although of course it was far from solid enough to serve as the basis for a firm conclusion at the time. It may, however, have brought some relief to minds which had become obsessed with the prospect of attacks by U-boats and by the Luftwaffe, either from its existing bases or from Spanish airfields, as well as of resistance by the French.

Complete strategic surprise—seldom achieved, because it is so difficult to attain—was in fact gained on this occasion, and this has rightly been described as a triumph for security. The full measure of Allied success which should have followed was denied by two unfortunate errors, however. Preparation to exploit surprise—without which the surprise itself would be a mere empty illusion—was far less thorough than preparation for securing that surprise. In view of the lack of battle experience on the part of almost all those about to be engaged in ground operations, this would anyhow have been difficult to avoid. The second error was less forgivable. The planners paid too little attention to the possible speed and volume of Axis build-up once the alarm had been given—that is to say, the enemy was not expected to react on anything like the scale which he in fact attained right from the start. In view not only of the way Rommel had improvised his way to victory in Libya but also of everything the Germans had accomplished in the Middle East since infantry, armor, and aircraft were suddenly diverted from the planned invasion of Russia to the unplanned invasion of southeast Europe in 1941, this is far less easy to understand. Early estimates that Axis reaction would be hesitant and slow were never significantly revised. Ultra was able to remedy this to some extent by giving immediate warning that right from the first few hours the reaction was swift and powerful.

That this valuable information was secured and made available to Eisenhower and his lieutenants was the result of a happy innovation which carried one stage further the improved relationship between intelligence and operations which has been mentioned already.[1] For the first time—but the precedent now set was always followed thereafter—Bletchley was permitted advance knowledge of a forthcoming operation and urged to lay plans to assist it. This gave the cryptanalysts time to regain regular contact with Locust, the key belonging to Fliegerkorps II in Sicily, which had been broken almost as soon as it appeared in January but had since fallen low in the priority list while all efforts were concentrated on mastering keys which could throw light on the desert battles. One of Locust's first fruits was now a useful count of the aircraft serviceable at Elmas on 7 November, which was in the hands of Allied commanders the same evening; the news that there was only one day's aircraft fuel there followed within a few hours. Declaring that the struggle in the Mediterranean had reached a climax, Kesselring demanded maximum effort from the Elmas detachments, rather curiously calling on the crews to ensure that their exertions were "not surpassed by our Japanese comrades of the air." Next day, Goering took a similar line when he denounced a lack of aggression among fighter pilots, but he was probably referring to those

---

[1]pp. 101–105.

operating against the Desert Air Force over Panzergruppe Afrika's retreat through Cyrenaica, since he linked his complaint with the recent death of the famous ace Hauptmann Marseille, who had fought under Fliegerfuehrer Afrika.

Early on 9 November, less than twenty-four hours after the TORCH landings, came the first moves of German aircraft to Tunis, and these were signaled soon after nightfall. Fliegerkorps II established an advanced headquarters in Tunis during the day, taking up station at El Aouina airfield, and a Sea Transport Office was shown to have been operating in the docks since the previous evening, although the fact could not be reported until the 10th. The German decisions to move into Unoccupied France and to establish a bridgehead round Tunis were known less than three hours after they were put into effect at dawn on 11 November. Almost from the moment the first Allied troops disembarked, therefore, Ultra was giving broad hints that the German reaction would be quick and probably powerful, thus providing a valuable corrective to the more sanguine expectations prevalent in many quarters.

Because of initial difficulties with the French—Darlan did not order a cease-fire until 10 November—and for a number of other reasons, the British First Army did not move forward until 14 November, and the delay was long enough to frustrate all hopes of a quick success. But the prospects of an early victory— "Tunis by Christmas" had been the hope—were in reality never bright. This was a first attempt at the unified control of an Allied force, and the command structure proved in practice too clumsy to fulfill its function effectively. Very few of the ground troops of both Allies had any experience of combat (the British only in Norway and France more than two years before), and, not surprisingly, they made the same sort of mistakes that the Eighth Army had only recently learned to avoid. The Axis build-up was much quicker and more powerful than had been predicted, but the Allied reaction to it was culpably slow. (It has been persuasively argued, for instance, that more vigorous air and surface action could and should have been taken against Axis trans-Mediterranean transports, and that this might have prevented the arrival of the men and tanks which just managed to

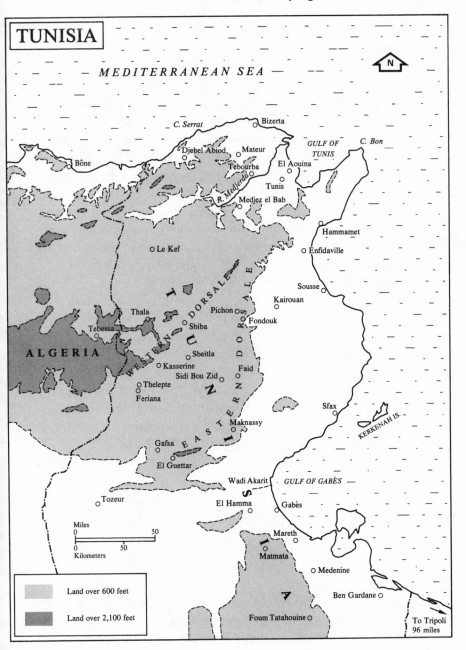

TUNISIA

— MEDITERRANEAN SEA —

N

C. Serrat

Bizerta

Bône

Djebel Abiod

Mateur

GULF OF
TUNIS

C. Bon

Tebourba

El Aouina

R. Medjerda

Tunis

Medjez el Bab

Hammamet

Le Kef

Enfidaville

Sousse

Kairouan

Thala

Pichon

Sbiba

Fondouk

Tebessa

ALGERIA

Sbeitla

Kasserine

Faid

Sidi Bou Zid

Thelepte

Feriana

Sfax

Maknassy

KERKENAH IS.

Gafsa

El Guettar

Wadi Akarit

GULF OF GABÈS

WESTERN DORSALE

EASTERN DORSALE

TUNIZ

Tozeur

El Hamma

Gabès

Miles
0   50

0   50
Kilometers

Mareth

Matmata

Medenine

Land over 600 feet

Ben Gardane

Land over 2,100 feet

Foum Tatahouine

To Tripoli
96 miles

halt the Allied army's advance fifteen miles from Tunis on 28 November—by which time the German Naval Operations Staff had found supplying Tunis "easy," and Goering was boasting that Tunis was only "a panther's leap" across the water from Sicily.) The charge of slow and inadequate action strikes home still more forcibly in the light of OKW's order of 14 November that for the time being Tunis might poach Rommel's supplies. Finally, the unusually heavy December rainfall prevented all movement off the roads both at the front and over the Allies' long and fragile lines of communication. But by that time, the chance—such as it was—had already been missed long ago. The December rains in Tunisia were no more responsible for the length of the campaign than the November rain at Fuka was for the escape of Panzer Army from Montgomery's pursuit.

During the week before the First Army's advance, Ultra continued to monitor the Axis build-up in considerable detail, revealing its unexpected speed and weight. To the enemy, however, his position seemed extremely precarious for some time yet, and opinions in Tunis and Bizerta were sharply divided over whether or not the defense that was being improvised would hold. We know now, for instance, that the High Command did not at first react with the urgency and decisiveness which Kesselring and others showed locally. It was not until 10 November that OKW gave Kesselring a general instruction to "beat the Americans to it and establish a bridgehead," and Warlimont subsequently criticized the slowness of a "grotesque" command structure and annotated the OKW War Diary with ridicule of Hitler for leaving his East Prussian headquarters for Munich in order to address his old comrades on the anniversary of the 1923 "Beer Hall Putsch" instead of attending at once to the perilous situation which TORCH was creating for the Axis in North Africa.

Ultra knew none of this, but it reported that a "Kampfgruppe T" (it included a company of Panzergrenadiers and a dozen armored cars) was being formed in Tunis on the 10th, that Flak was being flown to El Aouina next day, and that an extension of the bridgehead to Bizerta was under consideration on 12 November because a convoy of two steamships (one of them carrying tanks and motor transport) was already on its way there. Air transport brought in over 500 men of all three services[2] as well as 74 tons of stores on the 12th, and 600 more men, from Parachute Regiment Goering, on the next day, when the 3rd Motor Torpedo Boat Flotilla had also arrived. By the 13th, Kesselring was expecting to use Gabès and Sfax airfields, 150 miles south of Tunis, and had defined his new subordinates' responsibilities. A former GOC Afrika Korps, General Nehring, was to command a corps (it was not identified as XC Corps for another four days) with "Division Lederer" and, soon, others under him; Lederer was to reconnoiter in a wide arc from the north coast at Bône round to Gafsa. There were already 3,000 men at Bizerta by 14 November (many details of their transport and equipment were known), and OKW had ordered that "as a provisional measure," arms and supplies destined for Rommel should be redirected to Tunisia—170 tons of petrol was being sent to Tunis on 15 November, although Rommel had asked for it to be unloaded at Benghazi, and two Panzer Abteilungen were promised. A Gruppe of fighters which was known to be equipped with the new Fw 190s, faster and more powerful than anything hitherto seen in Africa; and several individual Staffeln were moving to Bizerta on the 15th, and a Panzer Abteilung and 26 tanks were due shortly.

Thus by the time Anderson moved forward, both he and Eisenhower knew that an embryonic German occupation force had been improvised, and that it would no longer be anything like so easy to rush the defenses of Tunis and Bizerta as it would have been even a few days earlier. The Allied failure to take Tunisia in November, and the consequent protraction of the campaign far into 1943, can undoubtedly be traced to this delay, but how far the delay was due to avoidable miscalculation, including a failure to make proper use of Ultra-derived intelli-

---

[2] Two or three times that daily rate had not sufficed for Panzer Army recently, as a series of complaints throughout October and early November showed (QTs 3059, 3102, 3117, 6155, and many others). Extra transport aircraft were drafted in to meet the emergency—the 40 Ju-52s on the Crete-Tobruk run on 2 October had doubled or tripled by the 29th, and there were 15 large Gotha gliders as well (QTs 2844, 4756, 4767). As Panzer Army retreated, all these and others were diverted to support the Tunisian bridgehead.

gence, and whether much could in fact have been changed, given the obstacles already mentioned, is far harder to determine. Experience of using a delicate source like Ultra in battle was as lacking in the Allied force as experience of battle itself. None of the army and RAF officers who were to handle it had been taught their job beforehand through temporary attachments to SLUs in the desert—unlike the Americans later assigned to army and air commands in Normandy, who were sent on highly educational tours of Mediterranean headquarters in 1943. Because he had to be so continuously on the move, and because communications were at first so bad, it is uncertain how much Ultra Anderson was able to see in the early days, and army Y Service was almost nonexistent until well into the New Year. In almost all fields, both the Allied command as a whole and its British component fell far below the standard recently attained in Cairo and the desert, most notably in intelligence and in the close cooperation of army and air commanders which had been the foundation of the victories Tedder and Montgomery had won.[3] If the early warning that Locust would be needed was a welcome sign that the new alertness was not confined to the Middle East, the intelligence arrangements for TORCH suffered for many weeks yet from the ineffectiveness which had once prevailed in Cairo and the desert.

In the light of all that has been said, it is not surprising that things seemed to Kesselring to have moved so fast and so favorably for the Axis in the first week that by the evening of 16 November he could feel cautiously satisfied with the situation, believing that he had managed to halt the Allied advance along the coast road through Tabarka and Djebel Abiod by air attacks. (He had, in fact, gained superiority in the air almost at once, and was to retain it until after Christmas.) His opinion,

---

[3] When Sir David Hunt, then a comparatively junior intelligence officer at GHQ Cairo, was sent on a liaison mission to Eisenhower's headquarters at Algiers in December, he found that the intelligence staff there "did not know what they ought to be doing and had learned a whole lot of wrong things which they ought not to be doing," though a somewhat better state of affairs prevailed at the First Army. These shortcomings were remedied on the establishment of the 18th Army Group in mid-February, as the intelligence summaries from that time onward show (Hunt, 147–51; PRO.WO 208/3581).

together with the rather less sanguine views of the German Naval Staff in Tunis (who were apprehensive about the attitude of the French), was signaled before dawn next morning.

Just over a week later, Nehring composed a very gloomy appreciation which must rank as the single most strategically valuable intercept of the campaign so far. Axis troops were blocking all the approaches to Tunis, but he doubted their capacity to hold either port or airfield for long if attacks continued in superior strength, as at present. His forces were too thin on the ground to link Tunis and Bizerta into a single bridgehead and hold it securely; this could only be achieved if reinforcements were sent "on a scale quite different from hitherto," which seemed very unlikely. Although he soon ensured the supersession of Nehring as land commander, Kesselring's earlier satisfaction with developments does not seem to have long outlasted the receipt of this pessimistic forecast. On the very next day he told Rommel of his fear that the Americans might join up with the Eighth Army through Gabès and Sfax (his own XC Corps, supported by a contingent from the Italian Superga Division, with 35 tanks, had for some time been under orders to close the southern flank by occupying the same towns to counter an American thrust which was reported to have cut the Sfax-Gabès road on 17 November), and he promised to send a score of anti-tank guns to increase the firepower of an ad hoc force which was being hurriedly put together in Tripoli to prevent this link-up, passing on Mussolini's order that the Gabès defile (where Montgomery was soon to outflank the Mareth Line in spectacular fashion) was to be defended at all costs. This early example of the Axis treating the two fronts as parts of a single whole was soon followed by another: on 28 November, the Afrika Korps was about to send 12 Mark IV tanks to join the scratch defense force. Thus both arms of the Allied advance were causing the Axis serious misgivings, just as the Allied attempt to capture Tunis before proper defense could be organized was reaching its climax. The Ultra evidence of these misgivings shows more clearly than ever how very near the attempt came to success, and underlines the shortcomings of Eisenhower's force and their consequences.

Kesselring was evidently still in a mood of anxiety when he demanded that the 10th Panzer Division (the imminent dispatch of which had been reported on 23 November) should disembark as quickly as possible and when he ordered it to attack at dawn on 1 December near Tebourba, in the Medjerda valley, where the threat to Tunis was most acute. The attack was successful in halting the Allies. A signal sent shortly afterward showed that XC Corps had 2 Tigers and 64 other tanks available for this action, although twenty-four hours earlier OB South had reported no more than 25 tanks, 3 Tigers, and 7 armored cars fit for battle in the whole of Tunisia. The 10th Panzer Division seems to have arrived in the nick of time and gone into action straight from the quayside.

Throughout the period during which the Allies advanced almost to the gates of Tunis but failed to force an entry, Ultra coverage of Axis sea transport expanded until it became almost complete. Unfortunately, however, it suffered at first from the defect familiar in the early months of the desert war: neither the Italian naval nor the German air cipher carried much information about cargoes. An extremely detailed account of the routes and timings of the ships which accomplished the rapid occupation of Tunisia could be compiled from Ultra signals, but only a few tantalizing hints of what they carried. Daily returns of tonnages unloaded in Tunis and Bizerta (and, before long, in Sousse and Sfax as well) gave a good indication of scale, but they usually provided only bare totals without breakdown into categories. Shipping movements showed how heavy the traffic was, and by late November Bizerta harbor was so crowded that there were fears that the RAF would find it a tempting target. Heavy disembarkation losses were anticipated unless more antiaircraft guns could be sent at once, but this did not prevent Kesselring from sharply admonishing the local Flak commander for not shooting down more Allied aircraft with what he had, nor from complaining that Axis losses were "intolerable." The fears proved justified, and the Flak remained inadequate. "If the present violent air attacks continue," complained the Sea Transport Office on 13 December, "Tunis harbour will shortly become unuseable," and went on to demand more fighter protection and the suppression of Malta, the suspected source of the raids. Many ships never reached harbor at all; Ultra reported half a dozen sinkings at sea in the first week of December, for instance, several of them plainly the consequence of signals conveying early warning of routes and timings.

Nevertheless, reinforcements and supplies were by now coming in so satisfactorily that, exactly a month after the day the Germans had first set foot on French territory, Kesselring was ordering Luftwaffe supplies for Libya to be routed through Tunis, not Tripoli, to take advantage of the shorter sea crossing. Regular traffic began at once, and in another week Rommel's supplies followed suit (though more than one Tunisian port was used), even when bombing cut the Tunis-Gabès railway for ten days and army lorries had to be diverted from their normal tasks to bridge the gap and succor Panzer Army.

After pausing for a week or more, Eisenhower made a second effort to capture Tunis, on 22 December. It foundered in rain and German resistance on Longstop Hill, a prominent feature which commanded the way forward down the Medjerda valley, and by Christmas Day he concluded that the Axis had won the race for the build-up, and that he would not be able to renew the offensive for another two months. Ultra information about German reinforcements was doubtless not the least of the many influences that led him to this conclusion. As early as 6 December he had known that Kesselring felt strong enough to extend his bridgehead; a week later, Kesselring believed that the initiative was passing to the Axis all along the front, and the regular interception of situation reports from the newly created Fifth Panzer Army showed this being put into immediate effect.[4] (To keep the Luftwaffe on its toes for the Longstop Hill Battle, however, Kesselring wrote on the 20th that it would "still be difficult in the extreme" to repulse an Allied attack unless the ground troops received massive air support.) Eisenhower's intelligence officers no doubt drew his attention to Ultra proof of the steady inflow of German soldiers—sometimes at the rate of 1,000 a day—and to the imminent arrival of the newly formed

---

[4]The Fifth Panzer Army was established on 5 December under Generaloberst von Arnim.

334th Division in late December (the first hint of the move was signaled within a week of Hitler ordering it). Tank shipments were now recorded with such frequency that it is probable that if due allowance is made for fluctuating numbers under repair and for the 34 tanks lost at sea when the *Menes* went down at the beginning of December, Ultra had accounted for most of the 146 tanks plus Tigers which, according to the OKW War Diary, were ready for action on Christmas Eve.

Kasserine

The temporary setback—it proved to be no more, though the first American defeat was a very great shock at the time— occasioned by the action in the Kasserine pass in mid-February, came about for one very simple reason: inexperienced Allied commanders and troops were suddenly confronted by one of the most experienced (and certainly one of the quickest-thinking) German generals of the day. The result was predictable. Seen in retrospect, the complexity of the intelligence problem—would the imminent attack come from the northeast, the east, or the south?—is almost as great now as it evidently was in 1943; and the difficulty an inexperienced intelligence staff found in unraveling it then is matched today by the difficulty, even with the benefit of hindsight, of seizing on clues which were missed at the time and using them as guides through the labyrinth. Solving an intelligence problem has often been likened to fitting together the pieces of a complicated jigsaw puzzle; in the case of Kasserine, some of the most vital pieces were missing, and some of the remainder could be fitted together in alternative ways with equal plausibility. It is hardly surprising that mistakes were made.

By the beginning of 1943, Eisenhower and Montgomery had advanced far enough toward each other for the narrowing gap between their respective adversaries to attract increasing attention. As soon as it became clear that Tunis and Bizerta were not to be captured quickly, it began to seem that by landing in French North Africa the Allies had not so much caught the Axis between the arms of an inexorably closing vise as presented them with interior lines and the means of keeping the First and Eighth armies apart. But to begin with, the two Axis armies were also far away from each other—Tunis is more than 450 miles from Tripoli—and there was a weak link in the long line of communications which joined them. Local geography dictated that these communications must pass through the narrow "Gabès gap" between the salt marshes and the sea where the coast turns northward at the western end of the Gulf of Sirte. The French and the U.S. II Corps had established a front—if a rather fragile one—along the crest of the Eastern Dorsale (thus overlooking the coastal plain and potentially threatening movement along it from Tunis to Gabès), and II Corps was soon edging southeast toward the Gabès narrows.

As has been remarked already,[5] Axis sensitivity to pressure at this danger spot had been manifested early on, when the occupation of Sfax and Gabès was ordered as a counter to an American thrust which was reported to have cut the coast road, and an emergency force was hastily put together to defend it against a renewal of the thrust in December. Concern about the insecurity of his supply line (which was also his escape route) led Rommel to repeat to Bastico at the beginning of January his long-held conviction that the only wise strategy was for him not to prolong the defense of each position in turn as he retired, but to withdraw into Tunisia as quickly as feasible.[6] Renewed attention was drawn to Axis dissensions over strategy and to the vulnerability of the link between Rommel and von Arnim by another Rommel-Bastico exchange on 11 January. To the question "Can you release 164 Division to protect Sfax and yet still fulfil orders to gain as much time as possible—at least two months to Mareth?" Rommel (who was still east of Tripoli and three hundred miles away from the old French defense lines at Mareth) replied with one of his most lucid appreciations; but the very lucidity required to compel the Italians to face facts was even more informative to British and American eyes when a de-

[5]P. 193.
[6]See p. 179.

crypt became available next day. "Any reduction in my forces now," ran Rommel's reply, "reduces both my chances of gaining time and my defensive strength at Mareth, which is the final defensive position. But the cutting of my vital supply artery would be still worse. So if the danger already exists, and if 5 Panzer Army cannot deal with it, then I must. But my retreat will be quicker in consequence." He went on to explain that the 164th Division was hardly suitable for the purpose, since it was only 3,500 strong and almost completely without transport, and to suggest that the 21st Panzer would be preferable: "The loss of it would weaken me more, but Sfax would be better protected. In any case, 21 Panzer is already earmarked as strategic reserve behind the Mareth position. But I must have a special allocation of 600 cbm of petrol if I am to send 21 Panzer." Next day Mussolini accepted the offer of the 21st Panzer, but he still repeated, parrot-fashion, that the two months' interval was essential if the Mareth defenses were to be adequately prepared. To keep his options open, Rommel immediately reiterated his doubts whether both objects could be achieved at one and the same time. During the next fortnight, a series of signals describing the 21st Panzer's slow and laborious progress provided a case study in the effect of petrol shortage on mobility; even though it left its tanks behind to help Rommel defend Tripoli, the 21st Panzer was repeatedly brought to a halt on its way via Medenine to Sfax, where it at last arrived on 26 January.

All through January, Ultra continued to show how deep was Axis concern about the vulnerability of the Gabès defile but how little was in fact being done to protect it. Thus Kesselring ordered the occupation of El Guettar on 1 January, stressing its "vital importance"—doubtless because it covered the last stage of the route from Tebessa, in central Tunisia, southeastward through Gafsa, the direction from which Rommel feared the Allies would menace Gabès from the rear—but his orders had still not been carried out ten days later, by which time a small American detachment was in possession. Italian GHQ Tripolitania, which had just taken over responsibility for Gabès (although there was still some disagreement about its exact boundary with Rommel's command), had "no definite information" about Allied strength round Tebessa and Gafsa on 3 January, and this was still the case on the 5th, in default of aerial reconnaissance. But by that time Bastico and Rommel were planning to take Gafsa before the Allied advance predicted by an American prisoner; this was said to be "essential if Rommel is to survive." By the 11th, an American force with tanks was known to be concentrated "southeast of Tebessa (SE Kasserine)"—the first mention of that fateful name—and part of it had been spotted from the air in Gafsa itself a few days later. The Sbeitla-Kasserine-Feriana road (the other main approach route from central Tunisia) was to be specially watched on 22 January; more tanks were seen at Sbeitla, and the conclusion was drawn on the 26th that a large-scale attack would soon be launched from that direction. The future battlefield was here identified well in advance. But Kasserine was only the first of four battles (Medenine, Mareth, and the Wadi Akarit were the others) fought in February and March for control of the slender communications link between the two fronts.

With the 21st Panzer's move north into the Tunisian theater at the end of January, then—the first case of an interchange between the two armies—it was becoming clear that the fronts were now so close together that the mobile striking force could be switched from one to the other over interior lines almost at will, and that a counterstroke to preempt the intended Allied attack, to be delivered before the tanks were required back at Mareth to fight off the Eighth Army, could be expected at almost any time. The intelligence problem was a familiar one—when and where would the blow fall? Unfortunately, a number of unconnected circumstances combined in the first fortnight in February to befog Ultra's vision, and to make this one of the rare occasions when neither Ultra nor any other intelligence source provided the correct answer; still worse, some of the information which seemed to point toward one proved in the end to be misleading.

The idea of an Axis counterstroke in central Tunisia originated with OKW. The War Diary entry for 19 January recorded an appreciation, based on much the same evidence as that quoted above, to the effect that the Allies would soon attack in the region of Gafsa to prevent the junction of the two Axis armies, and proposed to forestall this by striking toward Bône, or even Constantine, from Sbeitla and Gafsa through Tebessa, where a westward and a northward stroke would meet to cut Eisenhower's frontline troops off from their base in Algiers. It was to be a predominantly German operation; Comando Supremo, which still formally controlled all African operations, was to be given no more than an outline of the plan.

This was the germ of what is generally known as "Kasserine." There is a curiously close resemblance between "Kasserine" and the Battle of the Bulge, in 1944. Each was the last despairing effort of a losing side to delay or even escape its doom by a bold stroke to disrupt the enemy's strategy and to cut his armies off from their base. Each secured initial surprise but failed in the end, partly because the original plan was so watered down before being put into operation that the new objective assigned could not have achieved the original purpose even had it been reached, but mainly because the maximum force that could be mustered was inadequate. Each gained an initial success it scarcely deserved because of an intelligence failure. In each case, the chief victims of the surprise were American. Since "Kasserine" failed either to disrupt Allied strategy or even to delay its execution for long, it might not deserve the attention it has always received but for the shock it administered and the lessons it taught.

OKW appears to have passed on its ideas to Tunisia by some means other than radio (presumably courier, for greatest secrecy), for there was no hint of it in Ultra, yet it seems to underlie Kesselring's review of 24 January, which must count as Ultra's first long-range prediction of a thrust from the south against the Allies in central Tunisia—i.e., the essential element in "Kasserine." Kesselring began by considering Allied intentions, and by insisting that Mareth was the key to the defense of Tunisia. He went on to propose that under cover of preparing to defend Mareth, a mobile group "operating from the south end of the western front" should seize the initiative by thrusting

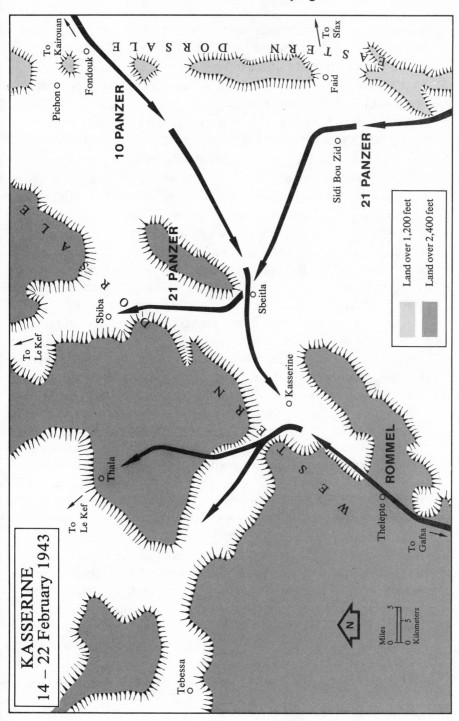

KASSERINE
14 – 22 February 1943

10 PANZER

21 PANZER

21 PANZER

ROMMEL

Pichon O
Fondouk O
To Kairouan
EASTERN DORSALE
To Sfax
Faid O
Sidi Bou Zid O

Sbiba O
Sbeitla O
To Le Kef

Kasserine O

Thala O
To Le Kef

Thelepte O
To Gafsa

Tebessa O

WESTERN DORSALE

Land over 1,200 feet
Land over 2,400 feet

N
Miles
0   5
0   5
Kilometers

toward Tebessa. By renouncing major operations elsewhere, the Fifth Panzer Army should begin at once to assemble such a group round the 21st Panzer behind the southern flank and prepare for a drive westward, or even (if need arose, supposing that Rommel could not hold Mareth) eastward to counterattack the Eighth Army. A few days later, an unspecified authority (it must surely have been von Arnim) poured cold water on this, asserting that there was not enough armor for such an undertaking. Still later, on 31 January, the Fifth Panzer Army announced its intention to make an attack "in the Kairouan area" shortly; the troops engaged in it were to move up on 2 February. Some details followed: the 21st Panzer would attack on Day A; part of the armor would thrust toward Pichon, while part screened this move against an Allied counterattack through Fondouk.[7]

From all this, it appeared that the proposed thrust through Gafsa northward (clearly a Rommel enterprise, if it came off) had at least been shelved, if not abandoned altogether, in favor of a quite different operation, directed by von Arnim and aiming westward at the Pichon-Fondouk route through the Eastern Dorsale, many miles farther north. Herein lay the seed of future error. Allied intelligence officers did not hereafter seriously envisage an operation against Tebessa from the south, nor reflect that the Faid pass was as inviting a way through the mountains as the Fondouk pass—more inviting, indeed, if the northward drive by Rommel had not after all been abandoned and a junction between the two was contemplated. This mistaken reading of the future seemed to gain confirmation from an order for aircraft to transfer to Kairouan to support an operation by the Fifth Panzer Army west and southwest of Kairouan on 10 February—although the description fits Faid and Fondouk equally well. Further, the disagreements between the Axis commanders (which in fact explain von Arnim's independent Pichon-Fondouk plan) and their shortage of men and matériel—both of which were, of course, genuine—took on such an exaggerated importance in intelligence circles that there seemed no reason to

---

[7]In view of the way this operation later misled Allied intelligence, there is a peculiar appropriateness about its German cover name: KUCKUCKSEI ("cuckoo's egg").

expect serious danger. General Mark Clark, Eisenhower's deputy and later commander of the Fifth Army, wrote that Brigadier Mockler-Ferryman, Eisenhower's Chief Intelligence Officer (an Englishman), insisted that Rommel had too little petrol and transport to move his armor into Tunisia.[8] Yet Ultra had shown that Rommel had managed to move the 21st Panzer thither nonetheless.[9] A similar fit of overconfidence in ill-founded opinion was to leave American troops once more unwisely deployed and vulnerable on the eve of the Ardennes offensive in December 1944.

As OKW and Kesselring supposed, a plan for the U.S. II Corps to take Gafsa and keep the two Axis armies apart while Montgomery attacked Mareth had in fact been scheduled, but it had been dropped when Montgomery indicated that he could not be ready to tackle Mareth for at least another month. An Axis counterstroke would therefore occur during a period of relative Allied quiescence.

Because of successive changes in the structure of the Axis command, because Rommel and von Arnim could not cooperate with each other, and in the absence of a supreme theater commander after the later Allied pattern, "Kasserine" was not one but three ill-coordinated operations, of which Rommel's memorable action at the Kasserine pass, on 20 February, was only the culmination. In marked contrast with the lavish intelligence Ultra provided in January, at just this time interception of the unprecedented variety of keys (the consequence of the multiplication of operational commands) was incomplete, and decryption exceptionally difficult because of new German security procedures. The result was scrappy and confusing intelligence which made interpretation unusually hazardous, particularly for the relatively inexperienced staffs in Algiers, so that in the end not only was no proper warning given of Rommel's and von Arnim's intentions, but disconnected items were fitted together in such a way as to prolong the plausible but erroneous belief that the main attack would be made at Fondouk rather than Faid or

[8] See Appendix V, "Axis Supplies Before Kasserine."
[9] See p. 198, above.

from the direction of Gafsa. It was Ultra's most notorious and regrettable failure, an object lesson in the drawing of overconfident conclusions from evidence too weak to support them, and a warning against relying too exclusively on a single source of intelligence. As with the British in 1941, human errors of judgment, rather than inadequate intelligence material, were the reason for discomfiture on the field of battle.

A good deal of information was conveyed in a Comando Supremo directive of 11 February: part of it was still in force, but part of it had in fact been superseded by new orders by the time it was decrypted three days later, in the early evening of the 14th. It ordered the Fifth Panzer Army to begin an offensive in the Sidi bou Zid area on the 12th, if possible (in fact, the 10th Panzer's attack on the Faid pass and the 21st Panzer's on Sidi bou Zid had already begun on the morning of the day on which the directive was decrypted), and instructed Rommel to follow this, by the 15th if possible, by attacking Gafsa and exploiting toward Tozeur; Rommel doubted whether he could manage Tozeur as well as Gafsa.

Here two comments must be allowed to interrupt the narrative. In the first place, exploitation toward Tozeur would lead Rommel into the deep western flank of both his enemies, unrealistically far both from their main areas of concentration and from his own chief concern—his often-repeated anxiety about the Gabès defile along the coast a hundred miles away. Secondly, if, as he hinted, he declined the Tozeur operation, his occupation of Gafsa would invite him to exploit in the opposite and more promising direction, into the area in which he suspected the Americans were assembling for their own drive on Gafsa[10]—i.e., toward Feriana and Thelepte—after which either Tebessa or Kasserine would beckon him on. As the map shows, troops moving forward after forcing the Faid pass and occupying Sidi bou Zid would converge with this second line of advance at Kasserine. After reading the Comando Supremo directive, therefore, it would have been wise and farsighted of Eisen-

---

[10] See p. 162, above, for anxiety about this area all through the second half of January.

hower's and Anderson's intelligence staffs not to leave Kasserine out of their calculations, as they seem to have done, particularly since by the time they read the directive they had already known for some twelve hours that there was to be a heavy air raid on Sbeitla in support of an operation by the 10th Panzer on the 14th—which, since Kasserine is a mere twenty miles from Sbeitla, might have suggested that the Kasserine pass was the immediate strategic objective.

Unhappily, there had only been a frustrating and even misleading Ultra preface to the Comando Supremo directive. On 7 February, the Fifth Panzer Army intended an offensive "in the southern sector"—a phrase so vague as to be meaningless in this context—using the 21st Panzer (known recently to be at Maknassy, equidistant from Faid and Gafsa) and another unspecified formation; its air support was to be based at Kairouan and to operate principally south and southwest of that place. This was, of course, the Faid–Sidi bou Zid operation by the 10th and 21st Panzer, but the vague geographical direction from Kairouan suggested the Fondouk rather than the Faid route through the Eastern Dorsale[11] and seemed to confirm the profound misreading of Axis intentions which originated with von Arnim's order of 31 January and had taken firm and lasting root at AFHQ. It made still more probable the surprise the attackers gained not only at Faid but also later at Kasserine. Worse was to come. A particularly tantalizing message was decrypted on 12 February: the Fifth Panzer Army informed air support group that "Day A will probably be 14 February." To what did this refer? The only clue was again the von Arnim order—which pointed at Pichon and Fondouk. An attack was now felt to be imminent, but there was great uncertainty about its location.

The Ultra preliminary to "the Gafsa operation" was only a

[11] The unspecified formation must of course have been the 10th Panzer. In a message decrypted during the afternoon of 12 February, this division had been reported as reaching its assembly area by midday on the 10th; but the area was given as "7949," a coded reference to which there was no clue. Had it been given intelligibly, or had a map showing the meaning been captured, the attack on Faid would no doubt have been deduced in time. On what trifling chances may the outcome of battles depend! The involvement of the 10th Panzer (P.M. 13 VM 3953 0250/14) was probably notified too late to give warning of the attack on the Faid pass.

little more enlightening. There was a steady stream of references to it during the preceding week, but all were confusing rather than helpful: one showed that Rommel and von Arnim both found Comando Supremo's orders so obscure that they were taking no action on them; another implied that the operation might start soon after 11 February; a third disclosed that the approach march was under way late on the 13th; a fourth made it clear that the operation would be controlled by the Afrika Korps, with the 15th Panzer (whose latest known tank strength, dated 3 February, was 56, including 25 of the powerful long-barreled IVs) as its striking force. None, unfortunately, gave the slightest hint of the remoter objectives of the operation, although it must have been obvious that unless it was to stop short with the capture of Gafsa as the close-range protection for Gabès, some kind of stroke at the Allied flank was intended (the main routes from Gafsa all lead either to the coast or to Feriana and beyond). In face of the threat, French and American troops evacuated Gafsa during the night of 14–15 February, shortly before German tanks moved in, and next day Anderson ordered a general withdrawal to the line Feriana-Kasserine-Sbeitla. This led Kesselring to deduce, in the course of the 16th, that an Axis thrust toward Feriana and Tebessa was feasible; Feriana was by that time already in German hands, but this decrypt, signaled at dawn on the 17th, was Ultra's first recent indication of likely future developments. The Afrika Korps was already on the move, but an order for it to dig in at the position it had reached north of Thelepte and to detach a panzer regiment to strengthen the defense of Mareth indicated some hesitation on Rommel's part about the wisdom of further advance. He asked von Arnim's intentions, and later in the evening of the 17th he did not think that, with only 52 German and 14 Italian tanks, he could hold his ground for any length of time, let alone risk continuing toward Tebessa—a move which, though exposing his flanks dangerously, nevertheless held out the distant promise of compelling the Allies to abandon Tunisia altogether.

Time had really run out for the Allied command by now, for their withdrawal had become disordered, and defensive arrangements were sketchy all along the front. These reflections of

Rommel's were the last hint of Axis intentions before the blow fell at Kasserine early on the 19th. Once more, however, Ultra unhappily proved misleading. Ten hours before the signal disclosing Rommel's hesitation was received at AFHQ and First Army, Rommel changed his mind and came to the conclusion that the opportunity outweighed the risk, got Kesselring to agree, and proposed to Comando Supremo that he should thrust at once toward Tebessa. Unhappily, none of this was intercepted. Comando Supremo's answer came with unusual rapidity, but it was too timid ("an appalling and unbelievable piece of shortsightedness," Rommel later called it). Instead of a bold stroke aimed at the Allies' rear, the Italians ordered an advance due north toward Thala and Le Kef, far closer behind the Allies' front and therefore through country where they could more speedily collect reserves to oppose it. The road to Thala lay through the Kasserine pass, where the Afrika Korps (now reinforced by the 10th and 21st Panzer from Faid and Sbeitla, with almost 200 tanks) attacked at dawn on 19 February. All the Ultra information in this paragraph was revealed only between the later afternoon on 19 February and the late evening of the 20th—too late to be of any tactical use, but still valuable insofar as it showed the intended strategic scope of the operation.

The inquest began as soon as the crisis had passed (Kasserine was recaptured on the 24th). How had the disaster come about? Disorganization in the high command was one explanation. Alexander had already been appointed Eisenhower's deputy to coordinate the operations of the First and Eighth armies, but he could not set up even a makeshift HQ for the 18th Army Group in Tunisia until 19 February; one of the first signs of his new and more vigorous direction of affairs was the establishment of the North African Tactical Air Force under Coningham, who worked as closely with Alexander as he had in the desert with Montgomery. The inexperience of Allied troops and their commanders was one explanation of what had happened. As soon as they recovered from their initial shock, British and Americans alike fought back determinedly, but intensive training and the replacement of the discredited Fredendall by Patton at II Corps were the remedies here. (During the battle, Montgomery had been conducting a "Study Week" in Tripoli to drive home the lessons of his experience, while sardonically noting the discomfiture of lesser men in Tunisia who had declined his invitation to attend it.) The wholesale importation of officers from Cairo, who "could hardly escape giving the impression of professionals arriving to teach amateurs their job," was another means to the same end. [12]

But the chief fault had lain with intelligence. Had the direction of the enemy's thrusts been more accurately foreseen, the defenders might have been better prepared to meet them. Eisenhower at once demanded the dismissal of Mockler-Ferryman ("a pure theorist without practical experience," Montgomery called him) for predicting the attack too far north, and blamed him severely in his postwar *Crusade in Europe*. The semi-official diary kept by Eisenhower's aide Harry Butcher adds that Mockler-Ferryman had relied too heavily on a single source of information, Ultra. As has been made clear already, his mistake was not so much excessive reliance on Ultra as forgetting (or not possessing enough operational experience to realize) that although everything Ultra said was true, in the sense that there was no need to assess the reliability of each bit of information before using it, yet it had always to be borne in mind that higher authority might hold a different opinion from that of the author of a given decrypted message, that even the author himself might change his plans after issuing it (as Rommel had done), and—most important—that there were usually vital links in the chain of information that did not appear in Ultra at all. Air reconnaissance (which appears to have been lacking on the critical days) or prisoners secured by active patrolling, Mockler-Ferryman or his operational superiors should have remembered, could insure against this form of inadvertent

---

[12] Only a few days later, the Axis rectified its own parallel defects—had Rommel's and von Arnim's operations been better coordinated, "Kasserine" could have been a spectacular victory for it. Army Group Africa was now set up under Rommel to coordinate the two converging armies (VMs 4967, 4974); its staff was composed mainly of Rommel's men. This was neither the first nor the last time that both sides were simultaneously afflicted by similar ills and adopted similar remedies, but it is a reminder that neither had been well placed to control events during the recent fighting.

error. An even better insurance could often be given by the Y Service, but the efficient exploitation of lower-grade intercepts in Tunisia only began with the formation of the 18th Army Group.

Like Shearer when he miscounted Rommel's tanks in January 1942, Mockler-Ferryman suffered for his mistake.[13] Insofar, however, as each paid the penalty for being wrong when inexperienced in what always remained a difficult and delicate art—that of using Ultra in battle—some sympathy can be felt for both of them.

Medenine, Mareth, Wadi Akarit

As if in repentance for letting the new boys down, Ultra now lavished its bounty on the old hands of the Eighth Army, providing daily bulletins about Rommel's next move. It had, of course, long been appreciated that if his Tunisian attack stalled, Rommel might switch his armor back east for a preemptive strike at the Eighth Army before it could breach the Mareth Line, but his change of direction came with astonishing speed. Comando Supremo's orders to break off the attack and Rommel's to move across to the other front were issued in quick succession late on 22 February, and both were in Eisenhower's and Montgomery's hands by the following evening.[14] (Fliegerkorps Tunis's version of the plan included the forecast that after smashing the Eighth Army's spearheads, the German armor would return whence it came to mount another attack on the Fifth Panzer Army's front.) Fashionable Eighth Army jargon arrogantly had it that in rushing back and forth so hastily

---

[13] See Appendix VI, "The Intelligence Aftermath of Kasserine." Churchill was unfair when he told Alexander that enigma had given "ample warning" of the attack (Gilbert vii.349).

[14] On reading these signals. Churchill sent Montgomery a copy of a note he had written in August 1941: "Renown awaits the commander who first, in this war, restores the artillery to prime importance on the battlefield, from which it has been ousted by heavily armoured tanks," adding, "if Rommel tries to chop up your spearheads in the next few days he may easily bring about an encounter battle on terms unexpected by him." (Gilbert vii.358–59).

Rommel was behaving like a "wet hen" skittering brainlessly across the farmyard. It was in the same spirit of pride that Montgomery told Alexander that he would positively welcome an attack, but in later years he confessed to having felt some anxiety until he had completed regrouping, his force having become unbalanced. He could not know that Axis opinion was still deeply divided about prospects. Keitel now shared Warlimont's pessimism (see Appendix V) and admitted to "serious misgivings about our whole position in Tunisia," but Kesselring and Ambrosio (Chief of Staff of the Italian Armed Forces since the dismissal of Cavallero earlier in the month) were convinced that the Allies had suffered such heavy losses in the recent fighting that they would be compelled to postpone their next offensive for a month or six weeks, thus giving Rommel his opportunity. Rommel himself, dispirited again after his burst of activity, saw no chance of a more than illusory success, and repeated his recommendation of a retreat to the hills of Enfidaville in northern Tunisia.

It was quickly evident that the whole of the German armor was to be thrown against the Eighth Army, the 10th Panzer again joining the desert veterans 15th and 21st Panzer. The strength—31,000 men and 135 tanks—the rate of progress eastward, and the plan and date (4 March) of the intended attack at Medenine (which the Eighth Army had occupied on 17 February) were all fully documented by 1 March.

Rommel's chief quartermaster set out his fuel requirements on 1 March in such a way as to imply that the "intended operation" had been deferred until the 6th or later. The "known units" were on their way to their jumping-off positions on the 3rd, under orders to follow two thrust lines, both of which pointed at the southern edge of Medenine. By dawn on 6 March it was confirmed that the attack would take place that day, but the warning was not needed.

Not even before Alam Halfa had Ultra so completely foreshadowed the pattern of future events. Thus forearmed, Montgomery prepared an impregnable all-round defense, with 600 antitank guns dug into the ground to kill off the tanks before they could get at the infantry, and with 400 of his own tanks

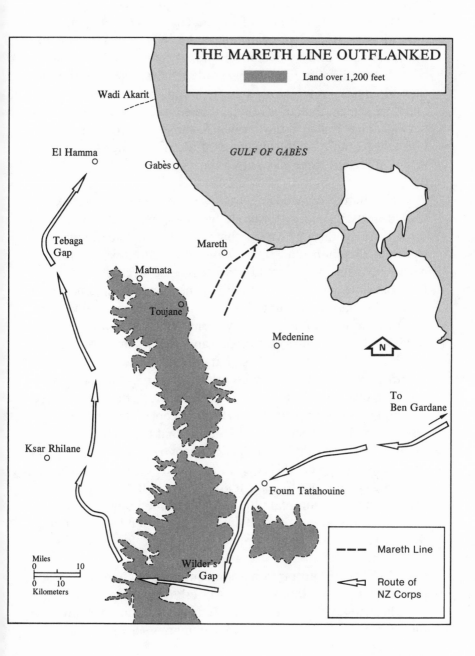

THE MARETH LINE OUTFLANKED

Land over 1,200 feet

Wadi Akarit

GULF OF GABÈS

El Hamma

Gabès

Tebaga
Gap

Mareth

Matmata

Toujane

Medenine

N

To
Ben Gardane

Ksar Rhilane

Foum Tatahouine

Miles
0   10

0   10
Kilometers

Wilder's
Gap

– – – Mareth Line

Route of
NZ Corps

ready for a counterattack should one be required. Everywhere the assault recoiled in face of the defenders' fire, and soon the ground was littered with burning tanks.[15] Not an inch did the attackers gain, and by evening Rommel called the battle off.

So total a failure—perhaps made all the sourer by the fact that his desert veterans had been humiliated under the command of a mere Italian (General Messe had taken over the renamed "First Italian Army" when Rommel was given the Army Group)—completed the collapse of Rommel's health. He left Africa for good three days after the battle.

The battle of Medenine underlined the security risk involved in using Ultra operationally. A captured document convinced Army Group Africa that the British had known the strength, direction, and time of the attack in advance. Reconnaissance from the air could have suggested strength and direction, but hardly time. Kesselring felt that someone had betrayed Rommel's plan, and pointed an accusing finger at Messe. Fortunately, no inquiry into security seems to have been made. The sinking (through Ultra) of three supply ships on 7 March did nothing to relieve Axis fears, but it caused Kesselring to ask Goering to improve convoy escort and to order special protection of a convoy due to reach Tunisia on the 12th. Three of the ships were sunk nevertheless. Hitler accepted Kesselring's advice on the 14th, when he told Doenitz that the Sicilian narrows "must teem with ships to protect the convoys." As Rommel had just found, however, this was simply a part of his obstinate but erroneous belief that if Tunis fell Italy would fall too, and hence of his policy of reinforcing the bridgehead, although it had long been evident that even a "teeming" defense could not guarantee the arrival of sufficient supplies to hold out for more than a short time.

The flow of Ultra information continued at its recent steady pace during the preliminaries to Mareth over the next fortnight and throughout the battle itself. Indeed, as a comparison with the 18th Army Group's Y Service summaries shows, on occasion

---

[15] See Appendix VIII, "Tank Returns," A.

it was even a speedier source of tactical intelligence. (Astonishingly, for a time Ultra also provided more frequent and more accurate tank strength returns from all three panzer divisions. Kesselring expected an attack on the Mareth position "in the immediate future" on 10 March and assigned the task of reducing its impetus by breaking up troop concentrations to the German and Italian air forces. Yet, although Fliegerkorps Tunis usually had 15 or 20 reconnaissance aircraft ready to operate, out of a total of about 130 machines of all types, reconnaissance seemed to be only intermittent and halfhearted, partly because of bad weather but also partly because on several days "restrained operations" were all that was ordered. Early on the morning of the 19th, however, a report of the results of a sortie undertaken about midday two days earlier showed that scattered groups of vehicles had been seen on tracks leading south from Foum Tatahouine through "Wilder's Gap," and then north again toward Ksar Rhilane; later the same day, another report (this time only a few hours old) indicated a concentration of 4,000 vehicles near Ksar Rhilane as a suitable bombing target. These messages represented the discovery of Freyberg's New Zealand Division (raised temporarily to corps status for the purpose) on its outflanking march through the Matmata hills, by a route pioneered by the Long Range Desert Group soon after Christmas, to take the Mareth defenses in the rear by striking via El Hamma to the coast at Gabès. Alexander wrote that Montgomery did not try to keep this move secret, in the hope that it would distract attention from the frontal assault he also intended to make; Montgomery himself claimed that the New Zealanders were sighted "sooner than I had hoped." In any case, it seems to have been Ultra which first revealed that the column had been sighted.

An appreciation drawn up by Messe on 19 March and evidently intended for von Arnim's eyes (von Arnim had succeeded to the Army Group command on Rommel's departure) predicted the two-fisted British attack which began just after midnight on the 20th, but timed it for three days later. This appreciation showed that both Freyberg's "left hook" (then nearing the crucial gap between the Djebel Tebaga and the

Djebel Melab, which was still undefended but into which the 164th and 21st Panzer divisions were hastily drafted) and Patton's II Corps at El Guettar were believed to be stronger than the defense. What reserves had the Army Group? inquired Messe, adding that he would rather save his army by withdrawing under pressure to the shorter line of the Wadi Akarit than allow it to be annihilated by defending Mareth to the bitter end.

The frontal assault having come to a standstill,[16] on 23 March Montgomery made a swift change of plan, reinforcing the "left hook" and inserting an additional "short hook" directed on Toujane and Beni Zelten in the center. This shift of the Eighth Army's weight over to its left wing was soon observed, and the fate of the Mareth defenses declared to depend on the outcome of the fighting there.

Twelve hours before Broadhurst's tactical innovation[17]— clean contrary to standard Air Staff doctrine—of concentrating heavy bombers to give close support on a narrow front to ground troops (who in this instance followed up with the afternoon sun at their backs and shining right into their enemy's eyes), the number of battle-worthy tanks the 21st Panzer had ready to face the advancing infantry was reported as only 44, with another 55 under repair. On the British side, the 1st Armoured Division, with just 100 more tanks than the 21st Panzer, pushed on through the night of 26–27 March to the outskirts of El Hamma.[18] The Mareth Line, outflanked and untenable, was evacuated in haste, but most of the defenders got away: "The Tebaga gap attack won the battle, but could not make a victory of it," the official history declares.

---

[16] A detailed description of the defenses built and building (they included sixty kilometers of minefields and eighteen of antitank ditches) on 19 February had long been available (VMs 4789, 4839).

[17] Air Vice-Marshal Harry Broadhurst was now commanding the Desert Air Force.

[18] "If we punch the hole, will the tanks really go through?" Freyberg had asked. "Yes, they will, and I am going with them myself," replied Horrocks, and was as good as his word. The exchange reflects both the heat which still remained in the old infantry-armor feud and the irritation Freyberg felt at being apparently superseded at the moment of crisis by a regular corps commander when Horrocks and the 1st Armoured Division were sent to reinforce him, an irritation Montgomery tried to assuage by tactfully sending identical orders to them both, heading his letters "My dear Generals" (Horrocks, *Full Life*, 152; de Guingand, *Operation Victory*, 258).

*   *   *

The main preoccupation of the Axis command on the morrow of Mareth was not so much withdrawal to the better defensive position along the Wadi Akarit as the provision of the wherewithal to defend it. Von Arnim told Kesselring that all air transport space should be reserved for ammunition and petrol, which were more urgently needed than anything else; the situation was "desperate . . . even a few hours may make all the difference." Kesselring replied that everything possible was being done in the air,[19] but that bad weather had delayed the sailing of a convoy (one ship from which was known to have blown up in Naples harbor). The fact remained, ran von Arnim's immediate rejoinder, that ammunition and fuel stocks were low and that no ships were on the way. Confusion and muddle by the various supply authorities with a finger in the pie now made matters worse. On one and the same day, 30 March, von Arnim repeated his demand that only matériel, not men, should be flown over until further notice, and OB South's supply office announced its intention of sending up to 1,500 men a day by air! Against all reason, Hitler's policy of reinforcement was evidently still prevailing over the more rational views of those on the spot.

The order to occupy the "final line" along the Wadi Akarit on 30 March became known early on the same day, only a few hours after it was issued, but already an Italian labor force was being sent 150 miles farther back to prepare defenses along the steep scarp above Enfidaville; this would represent the surrender of the whole coastal plain south of Kairouan. Useful intelligence during the short interval before the Akarit position came under attack were several tank returns (they were sometimes difficult to interpret, owing to the frequent changes in the subordination of panzer divisions to different commands) and evidence to corroborate the pressure II Corps' aggressiveness

---

[19] Fifty-two Ju-52s were at that moment flying the first of two operations planned for that day, and it was later claimed that a total of 165 Ju-52 and 9 six-engined Me-323 sorties had been made, with more 323s expected to arrive on Goering's orders (VMs 7632, 7638, 7644). As a result of this and much similar information, within a week the RAF had laid on the highly successful Operation FLAX to shoot down Axis air transport (MME iv. 358, 415).

round El Guettar was taking off the Eighth Army by holding the
10th and 21st Panzer divisions many miles away from the Mar-
eth-Akarit area. The fighting along the Wadi Akarit was over in
a single day; the 164th Division was in retreat by 1600 hours on
the sixth, with the rest to follow after midnight, and as usual the
Italians were not to be told until the last minute. As Messe dis-
consolately said, "It was not a good battle."

Renewed quarrels between the Axis partners ensued. Von
Arnim complained bitterly to Kesselring that Messe had moved
several Italian divisions back to Enfidaville without his consent,
but during the seventh he himself was thinking of moving the
whole Army Group thither—he had ordered the 10th Panzer
back there the night before—provided he received enough petrol, for most of the German troops (including even the 21st
Panzer) were retreating on foot for lack of it.

The Eighth Army followed up fast, but once more the enemy avoided encirclement; this time the fault lay not so much
with the Eighth Army itself as with the 6th Armoured Division
of the First Army, which took so long to capture the Fondouk
pass that the Afrika Korps had escaped northward before it
could debouch from the hills to block the way. By 13 April the
bridgehead had been reduced to an area bounded by an approximate line Enfidaville—Beja—the coast at Cap Serrat.

Tunis

By the time the Anglo-American advance slowed to a halt in
mid-December, six or seven weeks after the landings, there had
been time for the Axis to supplement the telephone system of
the settled area enclosed by the bridgehead with military land
lines, and the doubly lessened need for radio meant that from
Christmas 1942 onward the Fifth Panzer Army sector generated
very little Ultra save that derived from naval keys covering supply and shipping movements. Serious military activity was confined to the south, the empty desert sector where radio was the
indispensable means of communication. Thus, as has already
been evident, the Cairo and Algiers commands were well served

by Ultra throughout the Kasserine and Mareth operations. But the desert phase, which had lasted since the winter of 1940–41, ended at the Wadi Akarit. As the front moved swiftly northward, the flow of army Ultra diminished because land lines reduced radio traffic and thus made the cryptanalysts' task more difficult; in April and May, army keys were broken only intermittently and, as a rule, two or three days late. By the time it came to a sudden stop at Enfidaville, in mid-April, the Eighth Army was sensing the changed conditions in another quite different way as well, by discovering that its desert experience did not equip it for mountain warfare.

Both sides realized by now that there could only be one outcome to the campaign, and that the Axis could not hold out much longer. The Allies were anxious for victory at the earliest possible moment, so that they could proceed to invade Nazi-dominated Europe. During the Casablanca conference in January, Eisenhower had bet Alexander that Tunis would fall by 15 May, but the Chiefs of Staff still hoped for an April date, and there were anxious debates about the minimum time required to assemble equipment and train men for a seaborne assault on Sicily; after much questioning by Churchill of what seemed to him the excessively long interval demanded by the soldiers, HUSKY was set for July.

The horizon of strategy, then, was already passing beyond the shores of Africa, and there was little more that Ultra could have contributed to victory in Tunisia, even if there had been more of it in April and May.

After Enfidaville, the focus of intelligence was primarily on two interlocking questions: tactical opportunities for the *coup de grace,* and Axis plans for evacuation. Hitler had in fact already rejected Kesselring's plea to be allowed to comb out specialist personnel and send them home, on the ground that this would have a bad effect on morale. Ultra did not discover this, but pointed in the right direction by revealing that it was at Hitler's personal order that three more battalions of the Hermann Goering Division were to be sent in April, and by continuing to report the Tunis and Bizerta unloading figures almost every day, along with the flight times of the Ju-52 and Me-323 convoys, which were steadily bringing in unwanted reinforcements. It was often possible to give notice of these flights in time to offer tempting targets to the RAF; the numbers shot down were seldom reported, unfortunately, and the size of the "bag" on some of the most profitable days is much disputed. There was no evidence of evacuation plans until the very last days, when it was already too late to put them into operation. Beach landing points on Cape Bon were being investigated on 3 May, presumably for this purpose; it was hoped to fly out two or three hundred Italians and Germans on the 9th. Generalmajor Schmid, GOC of the Hermann Goering Division, was to follow on the 10th by Hitler's special order, since he was "the repository of secret knowledge"; but by the time von Arnim asked whether he might send back surplus tank crews (there had for some time been more crews than tanks in Tunisia) and a few other selected specialists, the local naval authorities had come to the conclusion that the Allied blockade made all surface movement impossible.

The straits to which the defenders of the diminishing bridgehead were being reduced was revealed by Army Group's prediction on 27 April of "a complete supply breakdown" unless it received new shipments immediately (it did not; three supply vessels were sunk almost at once), followed by its admission on 3 May that it could no longer guarantee to provide units with ammunition, rations, or even the water they needed.

The tremendous power Alexander unleashed in STRIKE, the final assault for which the 7th Armoured and the 4th Indian Divisions were brought across to assist the First Army, was too much for opposition suffering under such handicaps, and all resistance ceased on 13 May. "We are masters of the North African shores," Alexander signaled in triumph to Churchill. The strategic gains were the recovery of freedom to navigate the Mediterranean, and the consignment to prisoner-of-war camps of nearly a quarter of a million fighting men who might otherwise have opposed the coming Allied assault on "Fortress Europe." The folly of reinforcing failure not success, weakness not strength, was once more exposed, but Hitler still did not learn the lesson.

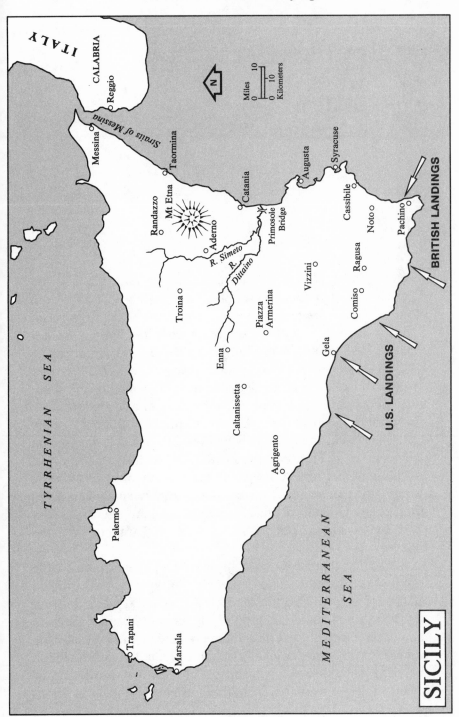

ITALY

CALABRIA

Reggio

Straits of Messina

Messina

Taormina

Randazzo

Mt Etna

Aderno

R. Simeto

R. Dittaino

Troina

Enna

Piazza Armerina

Caltanissetta

Agrigento

Catania

Primosole Bridge

Augusta

Syracuse

Cassibile

Noto

Pachino

Vizzini

Comiso

Ragusa

Gela

BRITISH LANDINGS

U.S. LANDINGS

TYRRHENIAN SEA

Palermo

Trapani

Marsala

MEDITERRANEAN SEA

SICILY

N

Miles

0   10

0   10

Kilometers

9
SICILY
July–August 1943

The campaign in North Africa was still hanging fire
(Montgomery had only just reached Tripoli, and
Eisenhower had not yet renewed the offensive in
Tunisia) when the Casablanca conference at the end of January
1943 decided to aim at finishing it by the end of April and to
follow it as soon as possible by an invasion of Sicily. This proved
an even more momentous decision than it seemed at the time,
for it amounted in the event to the opening of a second front on
the Mediterranean coasts of Europe from which there was to be
no turning back. It was already plain in January that there could
be no landing in France or the Low Countries that year, and yet,
as Churchill said, the Allies would be "a laughing stock if in the
spring and early summer no British or American soldiers were
firing at any German or Italian soldiers." Where else could they
shoot at the enemy but in Sicily, Italy, or (just possibly) the
Balkans?

A major change of heart by the Americans smoothed the
way, but the decision was a genuinely joint one, not a hard-won
victory for the British point of view. Above all, it was a decision
of grand strategy taken on grounds of geopolitics and logistics in
the widest sense of the term—the men, equipment, and shipping
needed for any other course of action could not be assembled in
the right place in time, but enough of each for an invasion of
Sicily would be available in Malta and North African ports as

soon as Tunisia was in Allied hands. Neither Ultra nor any other form of intelligence played any part in the decision, save that all through the spring and early summer Ultra showed that the defenses of Sicily remained slender, and thereby satisfied Eisenhower and other doubters who, in a moment of hesitation (pusillanimity, Churchill called it) at the end of March, had wanted the landing called off if substantial German reinforcements reached Sicily before the assault.

Two question marks hung over the operation, which was code-named HUSKY. First, it would be an operation on a larger scale than anything hitherto attempted; the tactics and the technology required were quite untried, and the Dieppe raid of August 1942 offered an awful warning. Secondly, Sicily was so obviously the likely target—at the end of February, OKW had listed Sicily, Crete, and Sardinia-Corsica (in that order) as probable sites for landings in the near future—that some effective means of diverting attention from it would have to be devised lest strong Axis reinforcements be drafted in and the assault troops be annihilated on the beaches before they could gain a secure foothold. Ultra helped greatly under the second head by revealing the extent of the confusion sown by the deception planners and the persistence of serious error on the part of the Axis all through the period of preparation and even for some weeks after the landing.

When Montgomery, who was soon appointed to command the operations on land, could spare the time from fighting his way to Enfidaville, he objected to the outline plan on the ground that it made the same mistake of excessive dispersion of effort which had marred TORCH, but he put his objections so tactlessly that Admiral Cunningham, the naval commander, accused him of "seeming to think that everyone will dance to the tune of his piping." Here was the unhappy consequence of his victories and the first signs of the attitude which was to cause friction between him and Patton in Sicily and between him and Tedder for the remainder of the war. The conquest of Tunisia was triumphantly completed soon enough to meet the demands of the HUSKY timetable, and before long there were two more boosts to Allied morale. Doenitz withdrew his U-boats from the

Atlantic at the end of May (a happy combination of new methods of destruction by aircraft and surface vessels with new Ultra inroads into the U-boat key compelled him to admit defeat): the United Kingdom need no longer fear starvation, and American troops would not be prevented from crossing the Atlantic for OVERLORD. And six weeks later, Hitler called off his long-planned offensive (ZITADELLE) round Kursk only a few days after it started, compelled thereto by the tremendous strength of Russian resistance and perhaps also by the belated realization that for the moment the Mediterranean front might after all present the greater danger.[1] The tide of war was quite evidently turning.

MINCEMEAT was one of the most successful pieces of deception in military history, and it has become one of the best-known (the Hon. Ewen Montagu, who devised it, published the story in *The Man Who Never Was* in 1953). On 30 April, a British submarine put into the sea off the coast of Spain the body of "Major Martin"—ostensibly the victim of an air crash—and the "dispatches" he carried, with the intent that the Spaniards should find them and bring them to the notice of the Germans. The dispatches had been carefully designed to suggest that Greece and Sardinia were the Allies' real objectives and that Sicily figured only in the cover plan. By 12 May, OKW had accepted the dispatches as genuine, and Hitler—conditioned to acceptance because he had believed since Alamein that the Allies would next attack Corsica or Sardinia and that the Balkans were of more value to them than Italy—had immediately issued a directive listing Sardinia, Corsica, southern Greece, and the Dodecanese islands as danger spots and ordered their defenses to be improved. The next day

---

[1] Hitler had ordered ZITADELLE in June when OKW advised him that it was impossible to defend Italy and the Balkans. Now, inescapably faced with the dilemma of deciding where to make his main effort, he gave the Mediterranean preference over Russia. But for many months yet he failed to decide the corollary: whether to withdraw from the Italian peninsula and defend the line of the northern Apennines or the Alps (as Rommel advised), or whether to defend Italy as far south as possible and fight every inch of the way back if compelled, which Kesselring advocated. ZITADELLE was the last big German offensive on the eastern front. When the Russians struck back, their advance never halted for long until it reached Berlin.

Keitel added further details. These included permission for the temporary transfer of Flak from nothern Italy to protect ports in the same threatened areas, the defenses of which, he emphasized, "are no longer adequate in present circumstances."

Though MINCEMEAT was their prime constituent, the words "in present circumstances" also embraced the effects of another deception which had long been distorting German intelligence. Shortly before Alamein, "A" Force had launched Plan CASCADE to persuade the enemy to overestimate Allied strength in the Mediterranean. It succeeded handsomely; soon German estimates were 50 percent too high and included several entirely "notional" divisions. MINCEMEAT's impact was all the greater because there seemed to be enough troops left in Egypt to mount an invasion of the Peloponnese at the same time as a landing in Sardinia or elsewhere. In fact, there were insufficient landing craft for more than one operation.

The deception was ingenious, and its success seemed complete. Immediately on reading the dispatches, OKW reversed its February opinion that Sicily was the most likely target—and this was ironical, because the February appreciation had been qualified by the remark that "the Allies are practising deception on a large scale"(!). Ultra demonstrated MINCEMEAT's success by showing, more clearly than any other source could have done, that German troop and aircraft movements over the following weeks conformed to the deception; this enabled planning for the assault on Sicily to go ahead in an atmosphere of confidence.

"According to a source which can be regarded as absolutely reliable," OKW told OB South and OB Southeast on 12 May, "large scale landings in the eastern and western Mediterranean are projected for the near future. . . . The cover-name is HUSKY." This was the promulgation, in the form of orders to the theater commanders concerned, of Hitler's new directive, which was thus made known to the Allies within three days of its issue. Only the version addressed to OB Southeast was intercepted, however (that for OB South doubtless went by teleprinter); it made no mention of action expected against Sardinia or elsewhere in the western basin of the Mediterranean, but went on to specify vulnerable points on the Greek coast and islands, predicting that landings would take place there in two or three weeks' time if full strength was intended but that they could be made at any time if lesser force was deemed sufficient. At once OB Southeast and the recently established Balkan Air Command demanded a close watch on Allied troop movements in all the lands bordering the eastern Mediterranean and as far afield as Iran, and called for reinforcements to enable them to deal with the threat: Two fighter Gruppen, a bomber Geschwader, the rest and refit of what was described as the sole army reserve capable of swift movement (a single regiment), 175 locomotives, and 5,000 tons of extra shipping space. Soon the 1st Panzer Division (at that time one of the strongest German armored divisions; it was then being completely reequipped in France after long months of bitter fighting in Russia), with 83 tanks and 18,000 men, was on the move from Brittany to the Balkans, passing through Romania and Bulgaria on its way to the Peloponnese, where it arrived on 14 June.

Reaction to MINCEMEAT was just as quick in Kesselring's command. The capacity of Sardinian ports was to be increased on 13 May, and glider attacks on the island's airfields were feared. The RAF's continual raids on ports and air bases now seemed part of the softening-up process before a landing; Fliegerkorps II felt that the Italians could not cope on their own, and on 24 May called for a Gruppe of Jagdgeschwader 77's fighters to be sent to assist them; by 24 June, this Gruppe accounted for 31 of the 113 fighters and ground-attack aircraft in Sardinia. A steady stream of reinforcements flowed into Sardinia by sea and air, and continued without intermission all through the summer; so frequent and regular were reports of the shuttle service between Leghorn and Corsican and Sardinian ports by the ships *Champagne* and *Roussillon* that they must surely have been left alone on purpose in order to allow the drain of men and supplies away from the mainland and Sicily to continue unhindered. The German garrison of Sardinia was already 5,000 strong by 2 June; this "Division Sardinia," partly composed of drafts for Africa

which had never reached their destination because of the surrender on Cape Bon, was rechristened the 90th Panzergrenadier
Division, and had doubled in strength by the end of the month.
(In a similar way, "Division Sicily" became the 15th Panzergrenadier Division.) On 9 June, Hitler decided to send one of
the newly established assault gun units to Sardinia at once, and
he was considering further armored reinforcements there and
for Sicily; a week later, the transport to Corsica of a unit named
in honor of Himmler, Assault Brigade Reichsfuehrer SS, was
being arranged. On 1 July, 22 tanks, all of which would have
been useful in the coming battle for Sicily, were landed in Corsica.

Information of this type about Sicily was rarer than that
about Sardinia and Corsica during the weeks immediately preceding HUSKY, but whether this was due to the success of
MINCEMEAT or simply to the existence of better cable communications is hard to determine. The Italians were urged on 21
June to emulate the Germans' performance in ferrying 1,000
men, 500 vehicles, and 600 tons of supplies across the Straits of
Messina in a single day, but the War Office was of the opinion
that more reinforcements were by now going to Sardinia. A
whole month earlier, the view that MINCEMEAT was keeping
the defenses of Sicily weak was lent powerful support by an instruction issued by Kesselring's Chief Quartermaster on 25 May,
which gave an early indication of the size envisaged for the German force: a supply base large enough to hold rations for two
overstrength divisions for three months, together with eight or
nine thousand tons of petrol and diesel fuel, was to be established in Sicily. Compared with the forces employed in Tunisia,
this was a tiny garrison, particularly as the Germans had a poor
opinion of the half-dozen Italian divisions in Sicily (within a few
days of the HUSKY landings, Kesselring complained that "half-
clothed Italian soldiers were careering about the countryside" in
stolen lorries). This approximate order of magnitude nevertheless received confirmation from a proposal of 10 June on which
OKW wanted the opinion of Kesselring's Chief of Staff, Westphal. It set out the principle that two "two-part striking groups"
would suffice for the defense of Sicily, and suggested that if the

Hermann Goering Division was ordered to the island (in fact it began crossing the straits on 21 June), the defense could be reorganized as "a kind of two-part Panzergrenadier division." No further large formations were sent to Sicily, but little became known about the number of Germans there after the report of 18 May that Division Sicily (i.e., the 15th Panzergrenadier Division) was six battalions strong, that holdups at the Messina ferry were delaying its expansion, and that it possessed 42 tanks. There were in fact some 200,000 Italian and 30,000 German soldiers (half 15 PG, half Goering) and an equal number of Luftwaffe personnel in Sicily at the moment of invasion. Ultra discovered this, and the proportionate strengths of the two divisions, but the decrypt was not available until 21 July.

How much of all this German activity can really be attributed to MINCEMEAT alone and how much to German strategic ideas independent of, and previous to, MINCEMEAT which would have rendered it necessary even if there had been no deception? OKW had foreseen—how could it not?—that the whole of the southern shore of the Mediterranean would be wide open as soon as Tunis fell. It concluded (as the British Chiefs of Staff did until it became clear that the distance from takeoff airfields precluded fighter cover; the Germans seem never to have made this simple deduction) that Sardinia was the most promising target because it could serve as a jumping-off ground for a landing in northern Italy to take advantage of an Italian collapse and drive the Germans back to the Alps. Hitler was preparing steps to neutralize the consequences of an Italian collapse in the same weeks as MINCEMEAT was launched; there is one Ultra reference to them before the crucial 12 May.[2] In view of the imminence of Italy's desertion of the Axis, it might be wiser to keep the strategic center of gravity in the north and center rather than risk losing valuable troops in what Kesselring was to call "the Sicilian mousetrap." To act thus was in conformity with the advice of Rommel, whose influence was currently dominant in the Fuehrerhauptquartier. The Balkans

---

[2] See p. 230, below.

were another sensitive spot. They were the link between the Russian front and the Mediterranean; they produced half of Germany's oil, all of its chrome, three-fifths of its bauxite, and a quarter of its antimony and copper, and this was transported over the railway linking Athens and Salonika with Belgrade and the north, which required constant protection. The Partisans were a growing threat to the German-held Balkans—three major drives were launched against them during 1943, but in spite of this the Asopos viaduct on the Salonika line was blown up in June[3]—and Hitler feared that the Allies, having got a foothold in Italy, would strike across the Adriatic and join up with Tito as soon as the Italians (who occupied the coastline) surrendered.

All this was sufficient reason for drafting reinforcements to all parts of the Mediterranean—Sicily possibly the least of all— even at the expense of weakening the defenses of east and west. MINCEMEAT was designed (as all successful deception measures must be) to play on existing anxieties and to confuse still further the Germans' strategic planning (already difficult enough by reason of the great length of coastline to be protected), and to force them to spread their defensive screen as widely and thinly as possible. It cannot be claimed to have caused, on its own, all the moves of German troops in the early summer of 1943; but the coincidence of ML 1955 with Hitler's new directive and Keitel's follow-up order is surely proof positive that it succeeded in its purpose of distracting attention from Sicily.[4]

---

[3] See p. 340, below.

[4] There has lately been some discussion of the extent to which changes in German defensive plans in May 1943 can be attributed to MINCEMEAT alone. Clearly, the geography of the Mediterranean basin and long-standing German strategic anxieties preclude an exact measurement of MINCEMEAT's influence, but it may be of interest to record the opinions of two men who held responsible posts at the time:

In mid-May, Oberstleutnant von Plehwe, assistant military attaché in Rome, overheard a telephone conversation between Jodl and his chief, General von Rintelen, in the course of which Jodl shouted, "You can forget Sicily, we know it's Greece" (*Intelligence and National Security* ii, 79).

As keeper of the OKW War Diary with the rank of Major in the Reserve, the distinguished German professor Percy-Ernst Schramm was a prominent figure at the Fuehrer HQ; he saw a good deal of intelligence material, although he was not formally responsible for any of it. On the subject of MINCEMEAT he wrote after the war: "We earnestly debated the question 'Genuine or not? Perhaps genuine? Corsica, Sardinia, Sicily, the Peloponnese?' It is well known that under the influence of the [MINCEMEAT] letters Hitler moved troops to Sardinia and southern Greece, thereby preventing them from taking part in the defense against [HUSKY]" (OKW/KTB iv. 1797).

If Ultra was able in this way to reassure Eisenhower that German forces in Sicily were unlikely at the outset much to exceed the two divisions he had set as the desirable maximum, it also warned him of the arrival of several new formations on the mainland of Italy during the weeks before HUSKY, their precautionary moves toward the south in late June, and Berlin's reaction to the Anglo-American landings—an instant order for two of them to cross the Straits of Messina. Some of these new arrivals were in the early stages of reestablishment after the battering they had received in Russia and were therefore not yet fully fit for battle. Thus XIV Panzer Korps, which had last been heard of at Stalingrad, was evidently somewhere in Italy in late May, had reached Rome before the end of the month, and had its HQ at Cassino by 21 June. On 1 June, the 16th Panzer Division, which had been destroyed at Stalingrad, was leaving Laval, on the Normandy-Brittany border, where it was being reconstituted, for Siena. In late June, the 29th Panzergrenadier Division, destined henceforth to be one of the stalwarts of the Italian campaign, began the journey from southern France to Foggia. Still more transfers from OB West to OB South were announced on 26 June: LXXVI Panzer Korps was to leave France for Italy and to control the 26th Panzer Division at Orvieto and the 3rd Panzergrenadier, which first replaced the 16th Panzer west of Siena—16th Panzer having meanwhile gone farther south—and then moved on to Chiusi, halfway between Florence and Rome.

It was not until 11 July, the day after the landings, that Hitler ordered XIV Panzer Korps (under the command of General Hube, who had led it in Russia and during its subsequent rest and refit in France) to Sicily with the 1st Parachute Division and the 29th PG. Ultra discovered the imminent move of the latter only two days later, and added further details on the 14th and subsequent days. Three separate parachute drops of detachments of the 1st Para Division behind the Catania front were noted on 17 July. Nothing was known of the firepower of the new arrivals, but on 18 June, Berlin had coldly informed Kesselring that his allocation of tanks could not be increased "because of the total tank situation"—i.e., because supply was lagging behind demand.

There was at least equally informative news about the Luftwaffe in the central Mediterranean: it is now known to have increased in strength by about one-fifth between mid-May and mid-July. On 17 June, Oberst Peltz, who had previously been Angriffsfuehrer England (that is, leader of the assault on England), arrived at Piacenza to take up duty as Angriffsfuehrer Sued under Luftflotte 2. A list of units apparently under his command, and of their base airfields, included eleven bomber Gruppen (nominally 330 aircraft), eight of which had until recently been in France or Germany; a return for an almost identical list of units, dated 7 July, showed 148 serviceable aircraft out of a total which, allowing for a few gaps in the figures, must have been about 240. On 23 June, Luftflotte 2 (now commanded by General Richthofen, also from Russia; his appointment left Kesselring free to concentrate on his duties as head of all three services in the Mediterranean) had 153 fighters serviceable out of 260. The total of about 500 aircraft, some 300 of them ready for action on any given day, compares reasonably well with the 750 or so now known to have been within range of Sicily in early July, and the 370 which operated against the landing. This advance warning of the redeployment of the Luftwaffe was of considerable value, particularly when it is remembered that the figures could be reviewed almost every day as strength and serviceability returns came in from each of the units concerned. But Ultra also recorded the still more significant rapidity with which the Luftwaffe was driven out of Sicily and forced to use bases in central Italy too far away for it to render much assistance to the ground troops. Its decline as a fighting force was thereby made apparent; the balance of air power had finally and decisively shifted. By way of contrast, the Allies had almost 3,500 aircraft in the whole Mediterranean—nearly three times the German total for the same area—and they flew 1,300 sorties a day in the week before HUSKY.

From an early stage in the Libyan campaign, it had been an open secret that Germans and Italians did not get on well together: the one did most of the fighting, but the other retained at any rate nominal authority over the defense of their own territory, and this did not make for a harmonious military relationship. The disparity in power still prevailed in Sicily, although there were six or seven times as many Italian as German troops there, but the disparity in determination and will to win had even increased. It was therefore not to be expected that command arrangements for the defense would be smooth. General Guzzoni, GOC of the Italian Sixth Army, had nominal authority over all Axis troops on the island, but he was already playing second fiddle well before the invasion. Ultra gave a hint—it was no more—of the awkwardness of so unnaturally divided a command with the news toward the end of June of the appointment of a special German liaison officer with the Sixth Army, Generalleutnant von Senger und Etterlin, an experienced panzer general; his tactfulness enabled von Senger to use his highly equivocal position to exercise a certain amount of direct command over German troops and to bring some pressure to bear on Guzzoni, as well as liaising between him and Kesselring. Hitler's motive in sending Hube and XIV Panzer Korps to Sicily a fortnight later was a further step toward excluding the Italians from operational control altogether.

Long before this, however, Hitler and OKW had felt profound misgivings about the Italians' ultimate intentions. On the morrow of von Arnim's surrender on Cape Bon, which weakened the Italians' resolution by confronting them with the probability of soon having to fight on their own soil, Hitler began planning what to do should they desert the Axis and change sides. On 22 May he appointed Rommel—who was now regularly attending his daily conferences at the Berghof and behaving (in his own words) as "a sort of acting commander-in-chief of the army"—to assemble a skeleton staff and prepare to occupy northern Italy should the Italians defect. The operation was given the cover name ALARICH. Again, Ultra provided only a tantalizing hint of what was in the wind, and no immediate help toward interpreting its significance. A "Planning Staff Rommel" had been identified at Wiener Neustadt near Vienna as early as 4 May, and on the 20th the message which first showed that XIV Panzer Korps was in Italy included the sentence "I have been transferred to Rommel," in which the former Chief of Staff of the corps explained why he was giving up his post.

In the light of all this, it is not surprising that Kesselring—
for the time being out of favor with Hitler,[5] while Rommel was
at the height of his ascendancy—should have some doubts
whether Sicily could be defended. According to von Senger, he
hoped to achieve his first resounding success as OB South, and
boasted that he would "throw the Allies into the sea," but in a
gloomy appreciation for OKW on 7 July he wrote that German
troops there had only half the supplies they needed, so that if
the Italians' defense failed they could hold neither Sicily nor
Sardinia. Ambrosio, the Italian Chief of Staff, was in fact about
to urge Mussolini to make peace as the only way to avoid the
horrors of a second front in Italy, and some leading Italians
were on the point of approaching the Allies with proposals for
peace. Kesselring, of course, did not know this, but he was almost certainly aware that the Duce was losing popularity even
with his closest advisers—the Fascist Grand Council deposed
and arrested him on 25 July.

In the nature of the case, little of this could be expected to
surface in Ultra. That Kesselring's apprehensions about the
strength of the coming assault were more accurate than those of
the Italians, on the other hand, was apparent in two Ultra reports of 7 July. The Italians were convinced that the Allies had
sufficient landing craft to embark nine or ten divisions, Kesselring that they would suffice for only five British or seven
American divisions, with one other British division to come by
sea and a large glider-borne contingent of both nations by air.
(The true figure was seven divisions in all, four British and three
American, plus four independent British brigades and the airborne troops.) Two circulars from Kesselring struck an almost
despairing note. One warned German Wehrmacht personnel not
to provoke the Sicilians, never to go out alone, and always to
carry side arms; the other instructed airfield defense units all
over Italy and the islands to fight to the last in emergency, but to
make sure that they first of all destroyed the airfields in their
charge. The baseless alarm scares—particularly that paratroops

---

[5] "We were regarded as Italophiles," wrote Westphal, Kesselring's Chief of Staff, stressing Kesselring's loss of Hitler's favor. "We felt that we had been written off" (Westphal,
222). In mid-August, Kesselring even offered his resignation, but Hitler refused to accept it (Mavrogordato, in K. R. Greenfield, *Command Decisions* (1960), 307–11).

had landed or were about to do so—that abounded during the last weeks before HUSKY showed how nervous and jumpy Germans of all ranks were becoming. For what its scanty evidence was worth, Ultra suggested that the morale of the defense was low.

The approach of the HUSKY convoys during the night of 9–10 July was, of course, observed from the air, but their destination was not at first recognized: over four hours after the first Allied troops set foot on shore, 21 ground-attack aircraft took off for Sardinia from their base in Sicily, and late in the evening of the 10th, Berlin was concerned about the effectiveness of cooperation between Luftflotte 2 and GAFSE (GAF Command Southeast, charged with defending the Balkans) if the Allies landed on the Adriatic coast or in Greece. A paucity of decrypts from army keys, particularly during the first few days, restricted the amount of strategic information which could be distilled from the intercepts for much of the Sicilian campaign. Thus two tank returns (they had been rarities of late) were several days old when they became available, although Hitler's prudent decision to reverse his initial impulse and retain the 26th Panzer and the bulk of the 29th PG in Calabria, instead of sending both to Sicily at once, was known in good time; rather more equivocally (had he changed his mind again?), the 26th Panzer and XIV Panzer Korps were expected in Reggio—the Calabrian terminus of the Messina ferry—a few days later.

To spearhead a drive on Catania, the British 1st Parachute Battalion was dropped during the night of 13–14 July to capture the Primosole bridge, which carried the main road across the river Simeto to Catania, ten miles farther north. The first Ultra news of the German reaction, signaled less than twelve hours later, showed how seriously Kesselring viewed the consequent situation: "Can our left flank be strengthened quickly?" he asked von Senger. "If we cannot hold at Catania much longer, I think we ought to withdraw at once to a line between Etna and the sea." He put von Senger in charge of manning this position and scraped up every available able-bodied man, except pilots and aircraft maintenance staff, to plug the gap well enough to prevent the Primosole operation from bearing its intended fruit.[6] Kesselring was, in fact, even more worried than this suggested. In his *Memoirs,* he says that he told Hube (who had just arrived to take over XIV Panzer Korps) that he expected to have to evacuate Sicily, and an entry in the OKW War Diary has Jodl stating bluntly that "Sicily cannot be held." Another pointer to Kesselring's mood was his appointment, also on 14 July, of Oberst Baade (a former regimental commander in the 15th Panzer Division in Africa) to take charge of the area round Messina—soon designated "Fortress Messina"—with authority to bring order into the chaos caused by traffic streaming north on all roads, to stop deserters, and to organize the defense of the straits area against Allied interference with a future evacuation. At Goering's express order, thirty heavy Flak batteries were to be sent to assist him in his task, the forerunners of many more which protected the evacuation with remarkable success a month later.

The attempt to rush Catania failed, and further delay was caused by friction between Montgomery and Patton over the use of a main supply and transport route. But in spite of this, until 17 or 18 July there was still a chance that the Allies might gain the quick victory on which Montgomery had set his heart. Ultra continued to reveal German fears of this, but the most important items were delayed by decrypting difficulties: For instance, neither the news that on the evening of the 16th von Senger thought that the 15th PG's front might collapse and that the Goering Division was down to 30 tanks, nor Kesselring's hesitation whether to bring the main body of the 29th PG over or to keep it in Calabria to fight another day could be signaled until 18 July, and XIV Panzer Korps' belief that evening that it could discern signs of flagging in the British drive for Catania not until the 21st. An order of 17 July, this time signaled almost at once, for means of demolishing Brindisi harbor to be investigated, even hinted that the defenders might soon be pulled back out of the heel and toe of Italy, until Kesselring's decision to defend

---

[6]There is a firsthand account of the Primosole operation in John Frost, *A Drop Too Many* (Buchan & Enright, 1982), 169–85.

Calabria began to become evident on 23 July and was confirmed during the next few days in signals which located all the principal formations in Calabria and Apulia. Meanwhile, Comando Supremo had signified its intention to defend the northeastern tip of Sicily to the last.

Approximately 60,000 Germans and 70,000 Italians escaped to the mainland before the Allies completed the occupation of Sicily on 17 August, and they took a great deal of their heavy equipment with them. Ultra accounted for 15,000 Germans, over 1,000 motor vehicles, 21 tanks, and 50 guns by the evening of the 14th, and was able to show how insistent both Germans and Italians were that nothing which could be removed should be left behind—29th PG, in fact, claimed to have carried away all its arms, equipment, and transport. The narrowness of the straits (only four or five miles across at some points) and the massive array of artillery assembled by Baade and his Italian counterparts—250 or more Flak guns, half of them 88s, put up an antiaircraft barrage heavier than those over London or the Ruhr, according to some accounts, and almost as many in emplacements along both shores protected the sea passage—made all attempts by aircraft or surface vessels to interfere with the ferry traffic almost impossibly hazardous. This was the main reason why there was no "bag" of prisoners comparable to that on Cape Bon in May. ("The conquest of Sicily was complete, but the only surrenders were Italian," Alexander wrote afterward.) Another prominent explanation was the difficulty of collecting all the senior commanders together in one place to concert measures: "Cunningham is in Malta, Tedder in Tunis, Alexander in Syracuse . . . and the truth of the matter is that there is NO plan," complained Montgomery. He might have added that in any case they were all fully occupied in planning the descent on the Italian mainland which had just been agreed as the next stage in Allied strategy and which was to follow in less than a month's time.

However, a widespread failure to make proper use of available intelligence was a major contributory cause of the Axis armies' escape. Immediately on Mussolini's fall, with the defenders already penned into a diminishing triangle of ground in the northeastern tip of Sicily and fearful that they might not be able to construct a defensive front across the Italian peninsula in time if the men, guns, and tanks in the island were lost, on 26 July OKW ordered Kesselring to prepare to evacuate Sicily, Sardinia, and Corsica. On the 27th, Kesselring began planning accordingly, and believed that the job could be done in three days. Ultra did not discover this, but on the 31st, the Eighth Army captured a German map showing that Adrano (which fell a week later) was the key to the final defense line and sketching the evacuation which would become necessary if it fell. Unaware of the captured map, but on the same 31 July, the Joint Intelligence Committee concluded that "there is no sign that the enemy intends the evacuation of Sicily." This astonishing opinion (Patrick Howarth's *Intelligence Chief Extraordinary,* a biography of the ninth Duke of Portland, who was chairman of the JIC at the time, omits all mention of this, at it does of much else which would bear on an assessment of the JIC's role in intelligence matters)—perhaps inadvertently nourished by Ultra evidence that the transport of some men and matériel to Sicily was continuing (it was not restricted to ammunition in short supply until 6 August)—seems to have survived for several days the impact of an Ultra signal of 1 August which, in combination with the captured map, might have been expected to kill it stone dead. In furtherance of Kesselring's plans, a practice ferrying exercise was laid on at four main ferry points for the night of 31 July–1 August. Ultra got wind of it almost at once, only six days after OKW had authorized evacuation, only a couple of days after detailed preparations began, and ten full days before troops started to cross the straits in great numbers on 11 August. Yet on 3 August Alexander and on 5 August Eisenhower still saw no convincing signs of withdrawal, and not until the 14th did Alexander feel certain that evacuation had started. Long before this, however, Ultra had shown XIV Panzer Korps asking on 8 August for extra petrol, diesel, and oil to meet "coming heavy demands on the ferry system." In later signals, XIV Panzer Korps wanted the 15th Panzer and the Goering Division to hold out until late on 16 August in order to guarantee complete

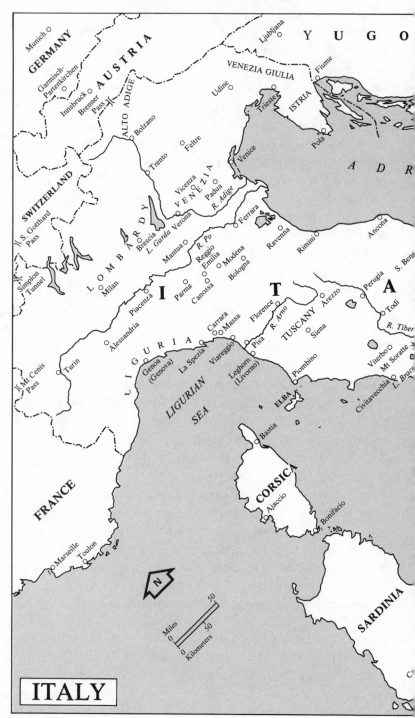

ITALY

evacuation. It was no shortage of intelligence which ensured that its wish was fulfilled.

The last boatloads had scarcely reached the Calabrian shore when self-congratulation began with disdainful criticism of the Allied air and naval forces for not pushing their attacks home more vigorously, criticism which was repeated in later years by Kesselring and which, by its curious failure to admit the effectiveness of the obstacles he himself had put in the way of such action, sits strangely with its author's usual reputation as a commander of insight and ability.

10
THE ITALIAN CAMPAIGN
November 1943–May 1945
Salerno to the Winter Line
(September–December 1943)

Although it is now difficult to believe that the Mediterranean theater of war could have been closed down once Sicily was in Allied hands, the Casablanca decision of January 1943 had left the question open by not attempting to look further ahead than the invasion of the island. The next step was settled at the "Trident" conference in Washington at the end of May, when HUSKY was still six or seven weeks ahead. In their final report to Churchill and Roosevelt, the Combined Chiefs of Staff proposed to instruct Eisenhower "to plan such operations in exploitation of HUSKY as are best calculated to eliminate Italy from the war and to contain the maximum number of German forces," and they directed him to submit operational plans by 1 July. Of the two new objectives thus stated, the first was the more pressing and, it was rightly thought, the more quickly attainable; in the event, an Italian initiative for surrender delivered it just before the Allied landings. This left the second as the sole objective of the new campaign. It called for an open-ended commitment, the eventual realization of which lay in the impenetrably distant future; because of this, it unfortunately soon became a matter of contention between allies—one arguing that heavy pressure on the Italian front would attract enough Germans away from other fronts to bring them substantial relief, the other that the Germans would escape this trap by retreating to the northern Apennines or even the Alps at an early opportunity.

For the moment, the latter view—the American, though it was at first shared by some of the British—approximated more closely that of OKW. In the course of a strategic review, undertaken to discover whether the current distribution of German forces corresponded with the needs of the various fronts, Jodl concluded on 6 September that resources could be spared only from southern Italy—and even there, in view of the likelihood of an Italian defection, only if accompanied by a withdrawal to a shorter and more easily defensible line in the Apennines. Barely a month later, the weight of argument was beginning to swing over to the British side as Kesselring's optimistic counsel to hold the Allies south of Rome prevailed with Hitler over Rommel's cautious advice to withdraw, and as more troops were sucked into the fighting; before long, one German division in five was engaged in the Mediterranean theater.

Plans for landings at Salerno by the U.S. Fifth Army (British X and U.S. VI Corps) under General Mark Clark (AVALANCHE) and by the Eighth Army in Calabria (BAYTOWN) were well advanced when on 15 August, after preliminary feelers since late July, the Italian government of Marshal Badoglio opened negotiations for surrender. Almost three more weeks were consumed in agreeing to conditions, and meanwhile, preparations for the landings continued. In the event, BAYTOWN began a few hours before the "Short Terms" were signed on 3 September; the public announcement of them by both sides was timed to coincide with AVALANCHE on the 9th.

During the weeks immediately preceding the landings, it became clear from Ultra that Allied preparations were not being systematically watched from the air: few reconnaissance flights were made, because few suitable aircraft were available. On the other hand, since it was obvious that landing points would have to be chosen from among the few suitable beaches on a predominantly rocky coast, and that they must be within range of fighter aircraft based in Sicily, there was very little hope of either strategic or tactical surprise. Anticipatory German moves

near the west coast demonstrated this in good time. As early as
16 August, the 16th Panzer Division (which had 100 tanks and a
great many guns and armored troop carriers a week later)
moved to Eboli, just behind the AVALANCHE beaches, the
base from which it played a major role in the first hours of the
landing, and XIV Panzer Korps' HQ opened at Formia, north of
Gaeta; the 15th Panzergrenadier and the Goering Division were
close at hand. If confirmation was still needed, it was provided
in the shape of an explicit forecast that the Allies would land
somewhere in the general area of Gaeta, Naples, and Salerno.
In southern Calabria, LXXVI Corps, with the 26th Panzer, the
29th PG, and the 1st Parachute Division, were all firmly identified from the middle of August onward. All kept well out of the
toe of Italy, and several signs—the first had been as early as the
10th—of air and ground formations retiring northward could be
signaled between 30 August and the early hours of 3 September.
This meant that BAYTOWN would not meet serious opposition
and that Montgomery's ponderous arrangements were unnecessary, particularly the heavy expenditure of ammunition on undefended targets; de Guingand called this using a sledgehammer to
crush a nut, and even Montgomery himself admitted that the
only casualties occurred when shellfire broke open cages in the
Reggio zoo and a puma and a monkey escaped and attacked
some Canadian soldiers. Perhaps the most striking intelligence
about German forecasts did not concern real Allied intentions at
all. Several items showed that the influence of MINCEMEAT
still persisted long after it had served its original purpose and
that later deceptions designed to prolong it were succeeding.
Landings in Corsica and Sardinia were still expected, though not
to the exclusion of others; men and weapons were still being
poured into both islands, and an occupation lasting into the
winter months was envisaged.

Even stronger evidence of German nervousness came from
the Balkans, where, if the Italian army of occupation ceased to
function (and its morale was known to be low), the way would
be open for Allied intervention, and where distance, Yugoslav
and Greek guerrillas, and growing disaffection in Croatia would
make a preemptive German takeover far more difficult to ex-

ecute than in Italy—but also far more necessary, because of Germany's dependence on the mineral wealth of Yugoslavia. Signs that a thorough reorganization and reinforcement of the German Balkan Command was under way first surfaced on 12 August, and its pattern became clear during the next few days. A new army group, F, was being set up under Generalfeldmarschall Maximilian von Weichs, with HQ at Belgrade; von Weichs took over the responsibilities of OB Southeast from General Alexander Loehr, whose Army Group E was now confined to Greece and subordinated to von Weichs. At the same time, a new army (the Second Panzer Army) and several new corps and divisions were identified in Yugoslavia, eight new airfields were being occupied in Albania, and reinforcements were being sent to the Aegean islands.

The weeks before AVALANCHE and BAYTOWN, then, saw the diversion to other parts of the Mediterranean of German forces which, if sent instead to Rommel's Army Group in northern Italy and then brought south under his command, could probably have prevented the Allies from gaining a foothold on the Italian mainland. Through Ultra, the extent and purpose of these diversions were known well before the landings and the Italians' change of sides which they were designed to counterbalance, and it was evident that they conformed to Jodl's reading of the strategic situation quoted above. In view of the subsequent and sometimes acrimonious inter-Allied disputes, it is important to point out that at this early stage Ultra was correctly suggesting that the German reaction was more likely to be retreat than reinforcement. As will shortly appear, when German strategy soon changed, Ultra quickly produced evidence that it had done so. Thus it accurately reflected both sides of the coming argument as they emerged, marking the watershed between them. Here was an intelligence feat of the highest order.

The origins of plans for German action should Italy desert the Axis has already been noted.[1] From the German point of

---

[1] See p. 230, above.

view, an Italian collapse would be even more damaging in the Balkans—where Italian troops constituted a large part of the joint occupying force and whence Germany derived essential imports of bauxite and chrome—than in Italy itself. ALARICH, the contingency plan for Rommel to occupy northern Italy, therefore had a counterpart, KONSTANTIN, under which Germans would replace Italians in Yugoslavia and Greece.[2] Hitler recognized the supreme importance of the Balkans to Germany (and the enduring influence of MINCEMEAT) on 20 July, when, believing that he had stiffened Mussolini's resolve to fight on when he met him at Feltre, in the Alps near Trent, the previous day,[3] he appointed Rommel to command in Greece while keeping open the option of recalling him to Italy later on should the situation demand it. Rommel reached Salonika at midday on 25 July, was summoned to the Fuehrerhauptquartier in East Prussia before midnight on news of Mussolini's fall that evening, and from there was sent straight off to Munich to prepare for the occupation of north Italy in earnest. In Munich he collected round him the staff of Army Group B, but under the cover name of "Rest and Refitting Staff Munich," lest the Italians take fright at the presence of an Army Group headquarters so near their borders and block the mountain passes on the routes into Italy before the Germans could seize them; for the same reason, he was forbidden for the time being to cross the frontier himself. ALARICH and KONSTANTIN were recast as ACHSE, a comprehensive plan for occupying Italy and all Italian-held territory and for subjecting the Italians to German control. (The fall of Mussolini had cleared a major obstacle out of the way. On 14 July, Rintelen, the chief German military representative in Rome, had told OKW that the Duce was the source of the resistance to an increase in the number of German troops in Italy, his main grounds being expense and a loss of prestige.) German troops took over the Alpine passes and began moving south on 31 July.

---

[2] See Chapter 11 for Balkan events at this time.

[3] During the meeting, Mussolini received news that the immediate vicinity of Rome had been bombed for the first time, rather as Churchill had heard of the loss of Tobruk while staying with Roosevelt at the White House. But whereas Roosevelt promptly offered Churchill 300 Sherman tanks, Hitler had only empty words for his decrepit ally.

Although matters of this kind were seldom entrusted to Wehrmacht radio links,[4] Ultra managed to pick up one hint of what was afoot at once, and several more soon afterward. At midday on 26 July—the day after the fall of Mussolini—the German admiral in the Aegean warned his subordinates that the Italians might be negotiating surrender and that, if this happened, they were immediately to take over all Italian communication centers, peacefully if possible but by force if necessary. The condition was not met, so the action was not taken. If signals of 16 and 26 July about army dumps north of the river Po and the arrival of what were said to be the first trains at "supply base north Italy" were discounted as probably referring to Kesselring's command rather than Rommel's (this would have been a wrong deduction, however; the dumps were being got ready for Army Group B), then the first indications of ACHSE came on 5 August, when a message of 30 July was decrypted. It referred to the dispatch of 77 tanks to Garmisch in southern Bavaria and Innsbruck in Austria for the 9th SS Division[5] and SS Division Adolf Hitler, which had been in France and on the Russian front respectively. On 9 August there was an oblique reference to II SS Korps, which had controlled the Adolf Hitler Division in Russia. The Hitler Division was in fact one of six which OKW had alerted for Italy on 26 July in the framework of ACHSE, and soon another of the six made its appearance—the 305th Division, one of those reconstituted after Stalingrad, was addressed at Verona on 14 August.

Far more evidence came on the 19th in two messages trans-

---

[4] Jodl sent a personal representative posthaste to explain ACHSE to Kesselring, rather than risk a "Most secret" teleprint or a radio message in Enigma (SSI 307), and four of the eight copies of the preparatory order for ACHSE issued on 2 August were sent by courier (OKW/KTB iii.1449). None of the cover names mentioned in the text ever appeared in Ultra messages, nor did any of those for the several thrusts launched in the last days of the Tunisian bridgehead (MORGENLUFT, OCHSENKOPF, KUCKUCKSEI), nor WACHT AM RHEIN, the Ardennes offensive of December 1944. High-level complaints of "gross breaches of security" over HERBSTNEBEL, the plan to withdraw across the Po in the spring of 1945, seem to illustrate the same point (see p. 314, below).
[5] The tanks were not consigned to the divisions by name, but to field-post numbers which MI 14 identified with the 9th SS and Adolf Hitler divisions. Since no mention of the 9th SS in an Italian context can be found anywhere, it must be presumed that this identification was incorrect. However, it was quite clear that two panzer divisions were involved; the second may have been the 24th Panzer.

mitted two days earlier. The first put pretense aside by announcing that Rest and Refitting Staff Munich would be known in
future as Army Group B. In the second, Army Group B itself
proclaimed that it had taken over command of all German
troops in northern Italy and that three corps were subordinate to
it: LXXXVII (with the 76th, 94th, and 305th divisions, the last
of which had not yet arrived), LI Mountain (the 44th Division
and Brigade Dohrla), and an unspecified SS Panzer Korps[6] (SS
Adolf Hitler, the 24th Panzer, as soon as it arrived, and the 65st
and 71st infantry divisions). The Army Group enjoined friend-
liness toward the Italians "so long as no hindrance to the execution of military duties is encountered," but authorized the
ruthless use of force to overcome any obstruction. Further, it
commissioned LI Korps to advise special means to protect the
Brenner route to Verona, the main line of communication from
Germany and Austria into Italy. These orders were signed
"Rommel," thus establishing his connection with Army Group
B beyond doubt; but under the rule about "gossipy items," this
fact was suppressed for a week and then signaled only to a severely restricted circle of recipients.

Except that the subordination of divisions to corps differed
in one or two particulars, this signal was identical with what was
later found to be the order of battle of Army Group B in early
September. That it differs in some other respects from that settled on by OKW on the morrow of Mussolini's arrest—notably,
that it falls short of the latter by three divisions—bears witness
to the haste with which Hitler was compelled to act in spite of
his previous apprehensions, and to the extent to which German
manpower was already stretched. Together with the divisions
long known to be with OB South, and with the addition of the
3rd PG and shadowy elements of the 2nd Para Division located
by Ultra in central Italy, these new identifications account for
the entire German force in Italy at the time of the Italian surrender. Every major formation had been reported by Ultra before the end of August. When the northern boundary of the
Tenth Army (a new command just established in southern Italy

[6]Evidently II SS, as was shortly confirmed.

under the experienced panzer general Heinrich von Viet-inghoff)—which might be the same as the northern boundary of OB South—was fixed some seventy miles south of Rome on 22 August, it seemed that Kesselring was being confined to the southern third of the peninsula and the larger part left, at least notionally, to Rommel (this was in fact not so: The Rommel-Kesselring boundary was shortly fixed thirty miles or more south of Florence), even though the function of Army Group B was defined as that of forming "a self-contained strategic reserve in Upper Italy," and none of its divisions had yet penetrated beyond Lombardy. Three tank returns at the end of August gave some idea of Army Group B's striking power: II SS Korps alone had 20 VIs, 65 Vs, nearly 100 IVs, and almost 50 antitank guns, a stronger armored force than had ever been at Kes-selring's disposal.

The strategic value of this intelligence is beyond question. It demonstrated the full extent of the actions which the Germans intended to take in a situation which they feared would come about and which the Allies knew to be imminent, and the force with which they could back those actions. The knowledge could hardly affect tactical plans—AVALANCHE was by now only a day or two away—and it did not necessarily reveal Germany's long-term intentions in Italy. But it did show very plainly that Hitler's immediate reaction to the weakening (and possible fu-ture loss) of his Italian ally was to rob the Russian front and the future OVERLORD area to shore up his suddenly endangered southern front. What it did not show conclusively, however, was how fiercely he would resist an Allied landing, for all the ACHSE divisions remained for the moment under Rommel's hand and none were sent south to Kesselring. Nevertheless, the new moves gave some grounds for hoping that the enemy might assist the Allies in fulfilling the directive to Eisenhower to con-tain as many German divisions in Italy as possible. Unknown to Ultra, Jodl had recently told Hitler, "We are not pinning the enemy down in Sicily; he is pinning us down." To contain as many German divisions in the south by deploying as few of their own as possible was to be the Allies' prime object henceforth, and Ultra was now enabling the first of many arithmetical calculations to be made of the two sides' relative expenditure of effort—the point so long in contention between the British, who did, and the Americans, who did not, believe that a satisfactory balance could be achieved.

The major question still remained unanswered when ACHSE was put into operation immediately the Italian surrender was made known. As soon as they had mastered any Italian resistance—there was not much, for Badoglio ordered none, and most Italian servicemen were only too glad to get out of uniform—would the whole of the new occupying force move south to oppose AVALANCHE and BAYTOWN, would only delaying actions be fought while the main body esconced itself behind prepared defenses in the northern mountains, or would some of the newly arrived divisions be sent back to Russia or the west as soon as the immediate crisis was past? Ultra found the answer in the end, but it could not do so until Hitler had made up his mind which course to follow, and he was not to do this for several weeks yet.

First reactions to AVALANCHE accorded with expectations. Orders (few of which could be carried out) to take over the Italian fleet were in most cases decrypted in time to affect operations, and so were warnings that reinforcements would reach Salerno during 9 September and that the beachhead would be bombed at first light on the 11th.[7] On the 11th too it was learned that Apulia was being almost denuded of troops, Kesselring having ordered all forces, except those required to protect the Foggia air base, across to Salerno "to throw the Allies into the sea. Only by this means can a decisive change in the Italian situation be achieved." By the 14th, when the crisis in the beachhead was already passing, his language was perceptibly less sanguine as he told the Tenth Army that if necessary it might send its "last reserves" to Salerno, but Luftflotte 2 was still talking of an Allied reembarkation and making comparisons with Dunkirk even on the 15th.

---

[7] This speed of service could not be maintained, but tactical information abounded and was usually signaled within twenty-four hours.

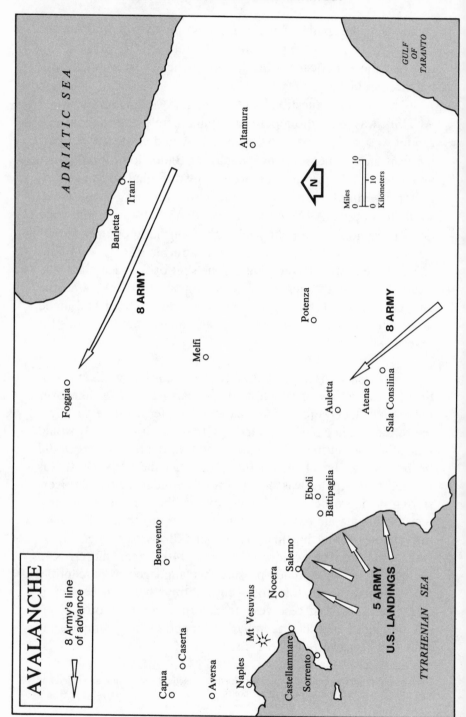

AVALANCHE

⬚ 8 Army's line
   of advance

On the strategic plane, plentiful information made it instructive to observe the rapidity with which the Germans reacted to the rupture of the Axis: troops marching on Rome had taken Civitavecchia and reached Lake Bracciano by midday on the 9th, and Army Group B had moved headquarters into Italy (to the shores of Lake Garda) and believed—too optimistically, it proved—that it had already pacified Lombardy by 12 September, after crushing Communist risings in Milan and Turin. Rommel was soon sending the 24th Panzer Division to Leghorn and pushing battle groups east to Venice, Udine, Trieste, Ljubljana, and Pola, where before long they met stiffer resistance.

No clear answer to the pressing question of whether or not Army Group B's resources would be added to those of OB South were intercepted during these early days; an order that none of its forces should cross the Army Group boundary was rescinded on 14 September, but only small units were released to help Kesselring as his difficulties mounted. Here, it may be, the irresolution which held Hitler in its grip that autumn caused him to miss a golden opportunity. The divided command which he had allowed to persist in Italy, the rivalry of the two field marshals, and the uncertainty which of them would eventually inherit sole authority were all additional obstacles in the way of clear strategic decisions. Rommel, convinced that coastal defense deserved higher priority than concentrating a central reserve inland (witness the stationing of the 24th Panzer at Leghorn), dispersed his forces just as he did later in Normandy, and made no move to strengthen Kesselring's hand; and in any case, he was out of action with appendicitis for a fortnight from 14 September.

The first sign that efforts to wipe out the beachhead were being abandoned in favor of retreat were timed midday 17 September and signaled twenty-four hours later, to be followed by contradictory hints about how far the retreat might go: on the one hand, central and northern Italy were described as forward bases for the air defense of the Reich; on the other, the Air Staff in Berlin was making long-range plans to reallocate surplus ground staffs as soon as central and south Italy were evacuated and the "final defence line" manned. Luftflotte 2 moved its headquarters to Vicenza, in the foothills of the Alps, but OB South only as far as the environs of Rome. During the last week in September, references to XIV Panzer Korps reconnoitering a position behind the river Volturno and to "Blocking Line B" gave the first indications that a stand might be made south of Rome.[8] Confirmation came in a report on 1 October that Hitler considered it of the first importance that as little ground as possible should be given up, particularly on the Tenth Army's left flank along the Adriatic (no doubt because he feared its use as a springboard for a Balkan invasion), and certainty on the 8th, when LXXVI Panzer Korps announced three successive defense lines (though not the dates on which they were to be occupied). It referred to the last of them as "the final winter line" and gave sufficient topographical detail for it to be identifiable as what was later well known as the Bernhardt Line.

The next intended stage was revealed a few days later. Army Group B reported that at Hitler's personal orders, it had reconnoitered an "Apennine position," and suggested certain modifications to a draft (which had not been intercepted) it had recently received. Again, enough detail was supplied to show that the line would run right across the peninsula on the crest of the mountains north of Florence,[9] but there was no indication how soon construction work would start nor when the position was expected to be ready. Its evidence was incomplete, but Ultra had once again done what no other intelligence source could do as quickly or as accurately: it had revealed to his enemies the general direction of Hitler's thoughts about the defense of Italy. Existing accounts of the war in Italy do not draw sufficient attention to the tremendous strategic contribution Ultra made at this juncture.

---

[8] Comparison with OKW/KTB iii.1147 suggests that the B line was an earlier proposal, later discarded, which zigzagged between the Bernhardt and Gustav lines.
[9] This was the later Gothic Line (see Appendix IX). Rommel had proposed a defense line in the Apennines in mid-August (Rommel, 440–41). Hitler's order making it the final stage in the defense of Italy was issued on 12 September, almost immediately after the Salerno landing, as part of a directive for the conduct of the Italian campaign (OKW/KTB iii.1096; see iii.1461–63 for a revision dated 4 October), which the various Ultra references in the previous paragraph evidently reflected. Ultra was thus a fortnight late with definite news (which was, nevertheless, the first received by the Allies) of a major strategic decision but, as so often, had picked up hints of it a good deal sooner.

At last, just four weeks after AVALANCHE, the outline of German strategy for the next few months stood revealed: to hold a line south of Rome through the winter while making preparations to retreat under pressure to a still stronger position in the north later on. These decisions, and the troop movements consequent upon them, were taken, it later became known, at a meeting at the Wolfschanze, Hitler's East Prussian headquarters, at the end of September, when a depressed Hitler admitted that he could see no prospect of victory by conquest but only by prolonging the war until the Allies wore themselves out in vain efforts to win it; time, he insisted, was the overriding need. At the meeting, Rommel and Kesselring bitterly criticized each other's proposed Mediterranean strategies; and although Hitler still postponed a final choice between them, for the moment he accepted Kesselring's view, because by pausing south of Rome now he might gain several months' precious time. He therefore turned a deaf ear to Rommel's cogent objection that any line so far south could be turned by another landing from the sea, and dismissed his advocacy of immediate retreat to a position in the northern Apennines.

Important as this decision was to the western Allies, from the German point of view a still more important consideration underlay it. During the fortnight preceding the Wolfschanze meeting, the alarming progress of the Russian autumn offensive had compelled OKW to undertake a painful reappraisal of the way German forces were distributed among the competing demands of east, west, south, and southeast. In the course of September alone the Russians had recaptured Smolensk, Briansk, and the Donets basin, and were approaching Kiev and Dniepropetrovsk. OKW explained its conclusions on the ground that "because of the tense situation there . . . the eastern front must be given help at the cost of accepting risks in other theaters of war." The consequence was the dispersal of the strategic reserve in Lombardy: the 65th and 305th divisions were on the move south (to Pescara and Rome respectively) on 6 October, the latter being replaced by the 90th Panzergrenadier (it had been garrisoning Corsica, which had just been evacuated); at the same time, the 24th Panzer was off to Russia, while the brutal 162nd (Turcoman) Division came from Germany to Venezia

Giulia and a new SS division (the later-notorious Hitler Jugend) was forming along the Dalmatian coast.[10] These moves, like the decisions about the Bernhardt and Apennine positions, became known within a week or ten days of the Wolfschanze meeting— all the signals concerned were transmitted by 12 October, and most of them several days earlier. Ultra had discovered all this by its now classical method—picking up the essence of high-level decisions which were beyond its reach by intercepting them as they were converted into operation orders at points lower in the military hierarchy.

Until now, the euphoria which had followed the resolution of the initial crisis at Salerno had allowed Washington, London, and Allied HQ in Italy all to convince themselves that the Germans would soon retire northward to the plain of Lombardy. The Joint Intelligence Committee held this view throughout September, Alexander issued a four-stage program on the 21st which provided for Florence and Rimini to be reached by December, and the 15th Army Group Intelligence Summary for 25 September claimed that a quick advance into central and northern Italy was possible. On the very day that he learned that Hitler had ordered the slowest possible withdrawal (but presumably before he received his copy of JP 6048 the same evening), Churchill congratulated Alexander on the rapid progress his armies had made and looked forward to meeting him in Rome at the end of the month, because "everything in our Intelligence goes to show that the enemy's object is to gain time and retire northwards without serious losses. He has not in any case the

---

[10] Similar intelligence about movements between one theater of war and another was frequently decrypted in the course of the autumn and winter. Cumulatively, it was of great strategic significance. Order-of-battle details make tedious reading, however, and a great deal of it will therefore be omitted here. Among the most striking items were the move of the Adolf Hitler Division from Army Group B to the eastern front at the end of October (JPs 8188, 8622, 8658), the slow (in spite of Hitler's demand for haste) departure of the 16th Panzer for the same destination a month later (JP 9971, VLs 37, 976, 1334), and the transfer of II SS Panzer Korps to the west from Army Group B in December (VLs 1026, 2307, 6626). Because in Kesselring's opinion American troops were well trained in mountain warfare (he was presumably thinking of the French mountain troops serving in the U.S. Fifth Army), the 5th Mountain Division arrived in Italy during December to counterbalance them (VLs 107, 1658, 2156). Concern about the approaching exhaustion of Germany's reserves of manpower underlay all: Hitler issued a Fuehrerbefehl for a comb-out of a million men from desk jobs on 21 November (OKW/KTB iii.1295, 1315, 1336–37, 1574–76).

The Italian Campaign 253

strength to make a front against the forces you are now deploying." It is not clear on precisely what evidence these opinions were founded.

Now, in the light of Hitler's decision to make a stand south of Rome, all estimates of rapid progress had to undergo immediate and drastic revision. Alexander, who only a few days earlier had still expected to be in Rome before long, realized by 6 October that a costly assault on the mountain defenses round Cassino would have to be made first: "Here was the true moment of birth of the Italian campaign," he noted in his memoirs. Next day, Churchill spoke of "a drastic change within the last 48 hours," and Eisenhower told the Combined Chiefs of Staff on 8 October, "There will be bitter fighting before we reach Rome." Within only a week of the Wolfschanze meeting, therefore, Ultra was enabling—indeed, compelling—the Allies to alter their whole approach to the Italian campaign to match the change in that of their enemy. The speed with which that alteration could begin was an advantage which must not be allowed to obscure either the fact that the Germans had taken the initiative in the Mediterranean for the first time since the previous summer, or the far more significant conclusion that by committing himself to a protracted defense of Italian soil Hitler was wasting on a secondary campaign men and equipment which OKW had just demonstrated were more urgently needed in Russia, and that this enabled the Allies to fulfill still better their declared purpose of holding troops away from east and west. Alexander lost no time in drawing attention to both aspects of his prompt recalculation of the balance of forces in Italy: whereas in September thirteen Allied divisions had been holding eighteen German divisions in Italy, he pointed out, by mid-October eleven were containing twenty-five, and this startling change gave ground for anxiety as well as for self-congratulation.

By the time Eisenhower set out the reasons for this anxiety in an appreciation he drew up on 24 October after consultation with Alexander, Allied political and strategic decisions were beginning to affect the Italian situation as much as the German. Several of the best and most experienced British and American divisions were withdrawn from Italy during the autumn to prepare for OVERLORD in the United Kingdom—the first of successive amputations the armies in Italy were to suffer for the benefit of the Allied cause as a whole.

The consequences of the change in the Italian balance were foreseeable: a marked slowing of the rate of Allied advance through the "Rain, rain, rain" which General Lucas blamed for the postponement of his attack on the defenses along the river Volturno at the beginning of October, and the mud which soon choked the roads.

During this period, Ultra complemented the strategic service it had just rendered with a steady flow of information which revealed the stages and timing of Kesselring's stubborn retreat through a series of temporary defense positions to the Bernhardt Line, and eventually, when the forcing of the Volturno and Garigliano breached it on a twenty-mile front, beyond the Bernhardt to the Gustav Line and Cassino in December. These months were in fact an exceedingly fruitful period for Ultra. Two and sometimes three batches of Flivo reports were signaled almost every day; frequent situation reports from the Tenth and Fourteenth armies (the Fourteenth Army had been created to take over the residual divisions of Army Group B when the latter was dissolved in November,[11] and remained in Lombardy until it was brought south to deal with the Anzio landing in January) showed how the front line looked from the German side; and occasional appreciations by Kesselring gave an insight into the theater commander's mind. The switch of armor from one sector to another, divisional reliefs or withdrawals into reserve for rest, and the like seldom escaped one or other of these sources, and perspective was lent to the whole by a number of supply returns which listed the current state of German petrol, ammunition, and rations stocks and drew attention to prevailing shortages. Three sets of figures showed the strength of the German armies in Italy. On the eve of Anzio, 300,000 soldiers manned the Gustav Line, there were 125,000 more under the Fourteenth Army in northern Italy, and a grand total of just over 750,000 in Italy all told. Tank returns proliferated in No-

---

[11] See p. 257, below.

vember before unaccountably drying up in December and January. Some were incomplete (the result of slack German reporting, not faulty interception), but the fullest of them, dated 13 November and decrypted within three days, showed 154 tanks ready for action (just over half of them long-barreled Mark IVs), with another 64 under repair in the workshops, supported by markedly more antitank guns—almost 300—than had been available only a few days previously. Analysis made it plain that two divisions, the 26th Panzer and Goering, monopolized two-thirds of the armor; as usual, its whereabouts at any moment could be checked from the daily army situation reports and Flivo bulletins.

On three occasions in December, long decrypts described in detail the defense works (gun emplacements, numbers of mines laid, estimates of the area of artificial inundations, and so on) completed or under construction in the Gustav Line about Cassino, in a switch position behind it, and along the coasts at each end of the line. With this and other Ultra material as a basis to work on, the Allied staffs were enabled to divine the motives behind the new German strategy in almost the words which Warlimont, the head of the OKW Planning Staff, used to Kesselring on 27 December: *"In Italien muss im Hinblick auf dem Westen und Osten sparsam gekaempft werden . . . das heisst, 'Bauen, bauen und wieder bauen'"* ("In view of the situation in east and west, manpower must be economized in Italy . . . this means that your watchword must be 'Build, build, and keep on building'"). At Anzio, and still more in the Liri valley offensive of May 1944, they set out to negate this strategy by breaching the Gustav defenses and attracting scarce German reserves back into Italy.

Although many of Hitler's recent decisions, as reflected in Ultra decrypts, had suggested that he had already come down in favor of Kesselring rather than Rommel as Commander-in-Chief in Italy, the appointment was, in fact, still open while Hitler most uncharacteristically hesitated between them. He seems to have promised the command to Rommel on 17 October, and he defined Army Group B's task as the ancillary one of protecting OB South's lines of communication a few days later. He re-

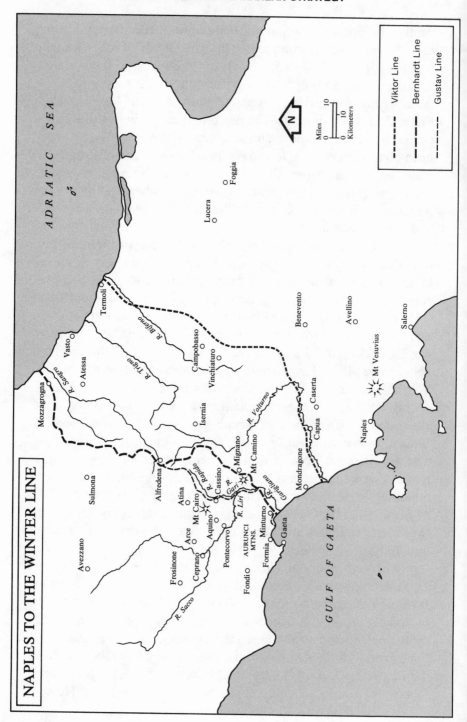

NAPLES TO THE WINTER LINE

ceived Kesselring on the 24th, but the OKW War Diary entry for that day records that "the question of supreme command in Italy is still in the balance." The final decision in Kesselring's favor came on 6 November, the appointment to take effect from the 21st (according to Westphal, it nearly went the other way at the last minute: Hitler changed his mind directly after dictating a cable appointing Rommel). No hint of any of this appeared in Ultra until 20 November, when a message from Kesselring to OKW on the 11th which explained how he would regroup his forces "when he took over command in all Italy" was decrypted. Precisely what this meant was revealed a week later, in a delayed decrypt of the 21st which announced that Kesselring had assumed command of the whole of Italy as OB Southwest and GOC Army Group C. Army Group B's disappearance was confirmed when the new Fourteenth Army succeeded to the control of its divisions and to authority over Italy north of a line from coast to coast through Perugia. But both its whereabouts and Rommel's (he had in fact been sent straight off on 6 November to reorganize the Channel defenses) remained a mystery until both were identified in France in the spring.

All in all, then, throughout the autumn and early winter, Ultra offered a richly woven tapestry of intelligence which provided Allied commanders and their political masters with a panoramic view, constantly kept up to date, of the enemy's situation. Over the same period, however, the Allies gradually lost momentum, and their operations slowed to a disturbing halt. The four days Brooke spent at the Italian front in early December left him with a feeling of acute depression: "Monty is tired and Alex fails to grip the show," he wrote. He returned to London by way of Tunis, where Churchill had taken to his bed with influenza after the Cairo and Tehran conferences. Their conversation led to the Prime Minister's outburst "The stagnation of the whole campaign on the Italian front is becoming scandalous" and to the revival of the plan—which had only just been discarded—to break the deadlock by a landing from the sea at Anzio.

Anzio (January–March 1944)

The plan to put a force ashore behind the German lines in the neighborhood of Rome was conceived by Alexander in October 1943 as a way of using Allied sea power to dislocate the defenses of the Winter Line enough to compel the garrison to withdraw from its fortifications and thus to speed up the Allied advance. It was discarded in November because the necessary shipping was under orders to leave the Mediterranean for OVERLORD before it could be put into effect, and also because it was considered unrealistic to suppose that the Fifth Army could break through at Cassino in time to relieve the small landing force then envisaged. The revived plan provided for a larger force to be landed, so that relief would not be so urgent, but since the departure of the shipping could not be postponed for more than a short time, the landing would now have to be planned and carried out within three or four weeks.

Haste was thus an inseparable ingredient of SHINGLE (the cover name adopted), but a large measure of ambiguity was needlessly added almost at once. Was the principal object to cut the enemy's communications, so forcing him to evacuate the Winter Line, and to make a quick dash for Rome in the resultant confusion? Or was the first priority to build up an invasion force strong enough to withstand every counterattack on its bridgehead and not to advance until this was achieved? Alexander's directive of 12 January took the former line and spoke (as Hitler soon did too) of a "battle for Rome," but it did not lay as much explicit emphasis on the immediate capture of the hills surrounding the beaches as was necessary to the fulfillment of this aim or as he had done earlier himself. Mark Clark, on the other hand, stressed the need to secure a firm hold on the beachhead more than the advance for which it was to be the springboard, entrusted the command of the landing force to a man (Major General Lucas) as much scarred by his experience at Salerno as he was himself, and acquiesced in arrangements for loading the supply ships which prevented the main body of tanks—a prerequisite for any advance inland—to be put ashore until D + 6. The fate of the expedition hinged on these divergences.

The choice of landing place owed nothing to Ultra: Anzio was chosen because its beaches were the most suitable within the range of Allied fighters based behind the main front. From the numerous Ultra reports of possible Allied landings, however, it could be deduced with some confidence that no more fears were entertained about that part of the coast than about any other, and that surprise was therefore likely. Both coasts of Italy, it soon became clear, were believed threatened throughout their whole length (oddly, there were very few references to Civitavecchia, about which the cover planners were busily spreading rumors), together with the eastern shore of the Adriatic and Greece. The Adriatic, even as far north as Venice, seems to have been the most favored. In addition, there were signs that the Germans were interpreting much of their evidence naively. Thus the arrival of aircraft carriers in the Mediterranean was taken to be a way of reinforcing land-based fighters but was not linked with the provision of extra support for a landing, the ships assembled in Gaeta Bay were not thought to portend an assault even as late as 20 January (two days before SHINGLE), repeated human-torpedo attacks on Naples harbor do not appear to have been conceived as efforts to destroy an invasion fleet before it sailed, and the disappearance of landing craft from Bizerta harbor was regarded simply as a mystery to which no solution could be propounded. All this pointed Allied intelligence officers in the right direction, for we now know that early in January, Kesselring told Jodl that in spite of the obvious vulnerability of his flank (Ultra had shown that he was concerned about the coastline near Rome in early November), he did not fear an Allied landing, and that even later Canaris, the Abwehr chief, confidently predicted that there would be no new invasion for at least a month or six weeks.

This careless optimism had its counterpart in Allied circles. At the Tehran conference in November, even the slenderer early version of SHINGLE had been expected to carry the invaders to Rome in a few days, and the Christmas revision at Carthage had been carried out in a spirit of festive confidence which soon spread through the whole command until it became an article of faith that a sure way of breaking the Italian deadlock had been found. The Alban Hills are not as high as Etna or the Enfidaville position, both of which had in turn held up an Allied advance, but they dominate the chosen landing beaches more than seems to have been realized before the expedition sailed, and since they and the Monti Lepini protected the Tenth Army's vital supply routes, the enemy was bound to defend them bitterly unless the invaders captured them in the first rush; Kesselring's sighs of relief when no attempt was made to do so are sufficient evidence. If a foothold on the high ground about Campoleone and Cisterna was not secured during the first few hours, whatever the risk involved, all chance of quick success would disappear, for surprise would only hold the road to Rome open for a few hours. Lucas, with his feeling that the whole affair had "a strong odour of Gallipoli," was emphatically not the man for the job, and the ambiguity of the orders given him is only a partial excuse for his lack of enterprise. However, there were probably only two Allied generals qualified by temperament and experience to take the risk and drive ahead: Horrocks (who had done just this at El Hamma), but he was in hospital with wounds so severe that they kept him out of the fighting for twelve months; and Patton (who had led the drive to Palermo), but he was still under the cloud which had descended on him after the slapping incident in Sicily. In Lucas's shoes, each of them would probably have taken Rome, but it is doubtful whether either of them, or indeed anyone else, could have held it against the weight of counterattack which would have fallen on their tiny mobile force even more quickly than it fell on the Anzio beachhead. It cannot be sufficiently emphasized that there was a profound (and perhaps unrealized) contradiction between the object of SHINGLE—to loosen the defenses south of Rome by threatening them in the rear—and the means chosen to achieve it; the magnetic attraction of Rome and the topography of the Anzio area, irreconcilable in themselves, combined to impose an ambiguity on the expedition which its leaders never resolved and which the courage and endurance of the troops engaged could do nothing to alleviate.

*   *   *

To compensate for the hazards imposed by the nature of the ground, hasty planning, and a less than ideal command structure, Ultra offered regular information about the enemy's order of battle and weapon strength. During January, the Tenth Army's morning and evening reports were intercepted on most days (sometimes both on the same day) and were usually signaled within twenty-four hours. They could be supplemented from the Flivos' graphic accounts (transmitted in an "easy" GAF key) of the current fighting, for the Flivos' duties obliged them to register with their parent Luftflotte or Fliegerkorps the relief of one division by another, changes in corps and divisional boundaries, moves across the front, and so on, as soon as they occurred or even before they took place. No tank strength-returns were intercepted in December and January, and the most up-to-date of them at the time of the landing was that for 1 December 1943. It showed that there were 181 serviceable tanks of all types at the front that day (including 90 IVs and 7 Tigers), plus 54 more under repair, together with 431 heavy antitank guns (37 of them belonged to Antitank Abteilung 525, whose arrival in Italy we had recently reported). When the next similar return (it was dated 25 January but not decrypted until 2 February) showed substantially lower figures after only a week of the Garigliano offensive and three days of SHINGLE, it was clear that the 1 December return had been a sound enough guide in spite of its age.

Only in one instance was any danger to SHINGLE to be apprehended from these reports. Kesselring's order of 14 January for one of the three battalions of the Hermann Goering Division's tank regiment to watch the coast behind the 94th Division meant that he was strengthening the defenses of the southern part of the Anzio area with 30 or 40 tanks (the 1 December return had shown that the division possessed no more than 35 battle-worthy tanks and 27 more under repair).[12] Since

---

[12] The Goering Division had by then been for a couple of weeks under orders to move to France on or after 20 January, but we did not know until 5 February that Kesselring had promptly begged OKW to let him keep it for the time being. His plea was successful, and the division remained in Italy (VLs 3361, 3398, 5576; see footnote on p. 326) until the late summer, when it was transferred to the Russian front (p. 281, below).

Ultra's close monitoring of every division in Italy threw up no other evidence of troops moving into the coastal sector between Rome and the main front, it may fairly be claimed that Ultra enabled Alexander and Clark to arrive at the same conclusion as that recorded in the OKW War Diary (which was, of course, written up after the event), that this sector was "to all intents and purposes unguarded" when the landings took place. Positive confirmation was provided by a Kesselring appreciation of 18 January, which added that on that date there were only two battalions and two engineer companies in Rome, and that they were too weak to repulse even a strong commando operation; but unfortunately this could not be decrypted for another fortnight. Whether this unequivocal statement, had it been decrypted currently, would have been enough to stimulate Alexander and Clark to give Lucas a direct order to seize the fleeting opportunity to advance is pure speculation, but it is solid, contemporary evidence that the road to Rome was indeed wide open for a few hours, as Westphal later asserted.

The nature and extent of the reserves round Rome was naturally a major preoccupation during the weeks of preparation for SHINGLE, because they would make up the first counterattack force; here again, Ultra served the Allied commanders well. In mid-November it disclosed that two new parachute divisions were being set up in Rome, and later that a new headquarters, I Parachute Corps, had replaced Fliegerkorps XI in the capital. Two battle-hardened divisions, the 29th PG and 90th PG, were known to be out of the line in mid-January, and Ultra gave partial confirmation of other evidence that they too were somewhere near Rome. Between them, they could deploy 47 tanks (mostly IVs) and more than 50 assault and antitank guns on 1 December, and so would present formidable opposition if they were near enough to strike within the first few hours of the landing. It was with the object of drawing them away from Rome and Anzio that Mark Clark began his offensive across the lower Garigliano on 17 January, and Ultra was soon in a position to show that his ruse had succeeded. The Allied attack was so heavy that by the next morning General von Senger und Etterlin, commanding XIV Panzer Korps, began to scent serious danger and telephoned Kesselring for reinforcements. Still confident that there was no likelihood of a seaborne landing on his flank, Kesselring agreed to send the 29th PG and 90th PG to prevent the breakthrough which von Senger feared. Only twenty-four hours later, Ultra reported that the first elements of the 29th PG had arrived at the front, and that more help for the hard-pressed 94th Division was on the way; before long it could add that the 29th PG was taking over part of the front from the 94th Division. In the very early hours of the 22nd, just as the fleet was approaching the Anzio beaches, Ultra reported that the 90th PG had followed suit, and that it was under the command of I Para Corps, which had also come from Rome, and that the 3rd PG Division, the only army reserve, was also being drafted into the same area. Before the end of the first day's fighting at Anzio, I Para Corps was known to be fully committed to the Garigliano battle, because it now controlled the 94th Division—which had always been there—as well as the two divisions which had come down with it from Rome. As a corps commander, Lucas did not see these signals, for Ultra was not distributed below army level, but by the time he landed at Anzio his superiors had ensured that he knew that the 29th and 90th PG were both on the Garigliano and therefore could not counterattack during his first hours ashore. The knowledge did not make him any bolder or more inclined to risk-taking.

Was a great opportunity to turn Kesselring's defenses and scatter his army in disorder missed when the assault became bogged down? A close look at the Ultra signals does not settle the Anzio controversy, which will last as long as interest in the military history of the Italian campaign. But it does make clear that the upper echelons of the Allied command knew at all relevant times that they would take the enemy far more completely by surprise than at Salerno, and that nothing stood in the way of an immediate advance of twenty miles to the Alban Hills, or forty to Rome. However, this is not the heart of the matter. Had they advanced, could the invaders have protected the flanks of their deep salient long enough for the striking force at its head to deal Kesselring's Army Group the deathblow? Where were the tanks to make up this striking force? And—just as at the time of the breakout in the following May—should the striking force aim for Velletri and Valmontone to cut the routes that supplied the garrison of the Gustav Line, or for Rome and a dramatic coup? Intelligence about the enemy cannot answer these questions. All that a study of Ultra does show is that if a great opportunity was missed, then the Allied commanders knew at the time that they were missing it.

Alexander at any rate soon reconciled himself to the outcome—whether from retrospective conviction that no more could have been achieved or from a prudent wish not to ruffle American feathers is not clear—but he never resolved the logical ambiguity. Explaining his strategy to the War Cabinet in July, he said that the object of the Anzio landing had been "to cut communications between Rome and Cassino," but the minutes of the meeting record: "It had been suggested that if greater risks had been taken and operations carried out more vigorously, our forces might have advanced further than they did. This might be the case, but [Alexander] doubted if it would have been possible to advance much further than we did." As he spoke, his armies were winning the victories he had looked for six months earlier, and he himself was envisaging an advance into the heart of central Europe in the near future. Present success may well have influenced his thoughts about the past, but he allowed the ambiguity to remain in his official *Despatch* (1950)—the objective was to reach the Alban Hills and cut the enemy's communications, but "the actual course of events was probably the most advantageous in the end"—and in his *Memoirs* (1962), where he wrote that an advance to the Alban Hills might have involved holding too long a line and being wiped out in consequence, yet in the very next sentence criticized Lucas for slowness and for not realizing the great advantage surprise had given him.[13] Even Churchill's often-

---

[13] It is, of course, clear that the six-month delay in capturing Rome extended Kesselring's defensive front from 85 to 120 miles, and drew four more German divisions (which might otherwise have gone to Normandy or Russia) into Italy, thereby continuing to fulfill the directive to contain as many German troops in Italy as possible. I am grateful to Sir David Hunt for pointing this out to me.

quoted gibe—"I had hoped that we were hurling a wild cat on the shore, but all we got was a stranded whale"—is really no more than halfhearted, for he knew that Kesselring could only be dislodged from the Italy he had persuaded Hitler to defend by a blow powerful enough to deserve a far grander metaphor.

The planners had allowed for a rapid build-up of opposition at Anzio, but Kesselring improvised defense measures with astonishing speed and skill, throwing every unit he could lay hands on into the fray one by one with the single object of roping off the assault forces while their commanders remained so strangely passive. Several of these measures were discovered in good time, but this was not the kind of work at which Ultra usually excelled, and its first reports were not of outstanding quality. Before midday on 22 January, XIV Korps had resumed command on the Garigliano, thus releasing I Para—for the moment, responsible directly to OB Southwest—to coordinate the various units as they came up to the Anzio battle; this was signaled early next morning. The move of the first large body of tanks against the bridgehead, ordered the night before, became known late on the 25th through the interception of orders for the 26th Panzer (which had had 40 Mark IIIs, including 13 flamethrowers, on 1 December) to shift across from the Adriatic sector to Avezzano in the mountains east of Rome, and there were indications that two more divisions, the 71st and the 715th, were destined for the bridgehead too.

Next came a major success: the decryption of Kesselring's orders for the 24th, which outlined his plan of campaign so clearly that the signal was given high priority even though it could not be sent until 2 February. The Fourteenth Army was to come south from Lombardy to "throw the Allies back into the sea" (the phrase was repeated in Hitler's flamboyant Order of the Day for 28 January, the decrypt of which Mark Clark still recalled having seen twenty-five years later—yet another premature revelation of Ultra), a new authority (Army Group von Zangen) was to develop the "Apennine position" in the north with maximum energy and also look out for new landings as far south as a line approximately from Leghorn to Ancona,

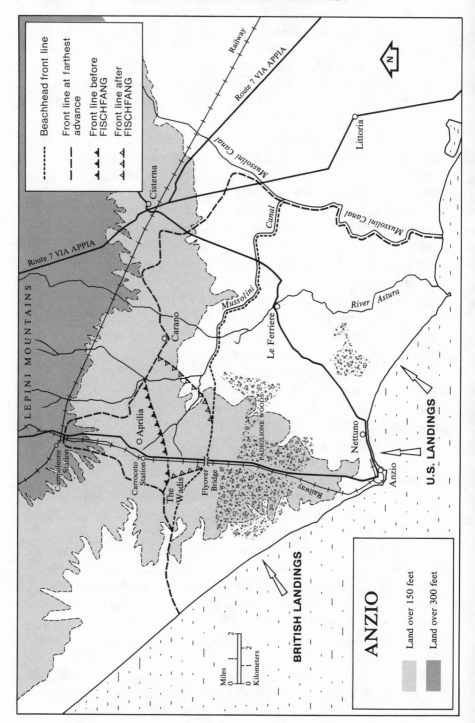

ANZIO

Land over 150 feet

Land over 300 feet

and the navy was to give better protection to coastal traffic in order to relieve the bomb-damaged railways,[14] while Kesselring himself continued to direct the defense of central Italy from his headquarters at San Oreste, twenty-five miles north of Rome.

A still greater intelligence triumph was in store. Hard on the heels of these orders came those for 28 January, signaled soon after midday on 3 February; sandwiched between the two was a tank-strength return for the whole of Kesselring's command dated 25 January, which neatly complemented both. Kesselring's new orders (he stressed the great need for secrecy in handling them) detailed his plan for a large-scale counterattack on the bridgehead, timed to start on 1 February if certain reinforcements had arrived by then but likely to be postponed if they had not. It would strike toward the sea straight down the main road, the Via Anziate, and would be directed by I Para Corps, whose subordinate formations were listed in detail; first objectives and possible directions in which success might be exploited were set out together with a statement of the supporting artillery (with a warning that ammunition was short) and a description of how railway guns would be used to neutralize the fire of Allied warships—which the GAF could not keep down because the Allies had command of the air—and a complete order of battle of the Fourteenth Army for good measure. By correlating the list of formations under I Para Corps with the 25 January tank return—in which the holdings of each formation were listed separately—it was possible to gain a good idea of the scale of the coming attack. At least 25 Mark III tanks, 20 VIs (Tigers), 25 assault guns, and 90 heavy antitank guns were to be employed, and probably many more.[15]

As Kesselring had foreseen, the attack was postponed because some of the reinforcements arrived late, and even a preliminary push to wipe out the Campoleone salient did not start until 3 February. Thus these three interlocking pieces of intelli-

---

[14] Rail traffic, according to OB Southwest on 26 January, was so frequently interrupted that stocks at the front were dwindling, and it was proving impossible to accumulate reserves for the Fourteenth Army's planned offensive (VLs 5336, 5676).
[15] See Appendix VIII, "Tank Returns," B.

gence—together they formed the highpoint of Ultra's contribution to the defense of Anzio—reached Clark and Alexander in plenty of time to warn them of what was afoot. There was no Ultra of importance about the second preliminary stage, which between 7 and 12 February recaptured Aprilia as a jumping-off point for the main effort (code-named FISCHFANG, "Fishing"). A smart piece of detective work by one of the military advisers in Hut 3, made possible by the exact knowledge of the front line which the Flivo reports afforded, enabled him to discern a likely connection between three outwardly unrelated bits of information and predict this third and fiercest stage of the attack just two hours before FISCHFANG finally began on 16 February.

The next three or four days were critical, as the Allied line was gradually pushed back to its position on the first evening, only seven miles from the sea; when he arrived on 17 February as deputy commander of U.S. VI Corps, General Truscott found "a sense of dejection and hopelessness" prevailing in Lucas' underground headquarters. But the defense held, the attackers could get no farther, and by the 18th Kesselring and von Mackensen of the Fourteenth Army (who only twenty-four hours earlier had felt that he was winning) were driven to conclude that they had no choice but to call FISCHFANG off. They made several attempts to renew the attack, but in vain; the tide had turned against them, and their troops never recovered the élan they had showed on the Anzio road during the last few days. The stubbornness of the defenders (made possible, it has been argued, by the resources accumulated only because Lucas had refused to overextend himself at the start by dashing for the Alban Hills), had finally broken them. And at this climax of the battle, Ultra had been a prime instrument of victory. It had risen to the occasion and enabled the Allied generals to read their enemy's intentions before he began to execute them and to know the timing, direction, and weight of his assault; thus it guided them to concentrate their men in the right places and to apply their superiority in guns and planes to maximum effect. The successful defense of the Anzio perimeter in February 1944 was a turning point in the Italian campaign,[16] and there is substantial ground for the claim that Ultra played a conspicuous part in bringing this about; Sir David Hunt, who was one of Alexander's senior intelligence officers at the time, considers it "one of Ultra's most important triumphs."

A hint of preparations to renew the attack could be discerned in several sector changes from 22 February onward, and, more definitely, in requests for photo-mosaics to be ready by the morning of 26 February, and for radio silence to be kept "until D-Day." "Tomorrow's operation" was canceled at midday on the 27th (in fact because of bad weather), but next day OB Southwest ordered an advance on the 29th to establish a bridgehead over the river Astura, only six miles from the shore. The striking power of the divisions involved consisted mainly of some 25 Mark III and 58 Mark IV tanks (with as many more under repair), a very great increase over the last comparable figures in early February. Soon, heavy losses were followed by several reports of withdrawals, and before long both fronts relapsed into a state of comparative quiescence which, apart from the third battle of Cassino in mid-March, was not disturbed until Alexander's DIADEM offensive in May.

Kesselring had shot his bolt; he reconciled himself to the collapse of his own and Hitler's hopes at once and made no further attempt to wipe out the Anzio beachhead. Directly he recognized that the 29 February attacks had failed, he composed a lengthy appreciation in which he set out his intention to stabilize the main front and simply to nibble away at the Anzio perimeter enough to ensure that the Allies' unloading points were always

---

[16] And even in the war as a whole. Siegfried Westphal, Kesselring's Chief of Staff, went off to Berchtesgaden at the beginning of March to explain the Fourteenth Army's failure to Hitler, whose 28 January Order of the Day had made the obliteration of the invaders a prestige and propaganda issue as the defeat of the first of the several invasions of Europe expected in 1944. Westphal told Hitler that the new German infantry divisions were not up to the standard of the old because their training was defective, and that the Allies were getting the measure of German tanks and possessed superior artillery. Shocked by this, Hitler summoned twenty-two frontline officers from Italy; under interrogation, they confirmed what Westphal had said. In his *Erinnerungen*, published in 1975, Westphal added that Anzio convinced him that the war had passed its turning point and could not now be won, but that he had not told Hitler this (MME v.762; OKW/KTB iv.167; Westphal, *Erinnerungen*, 351–53; Kesselring, 198).

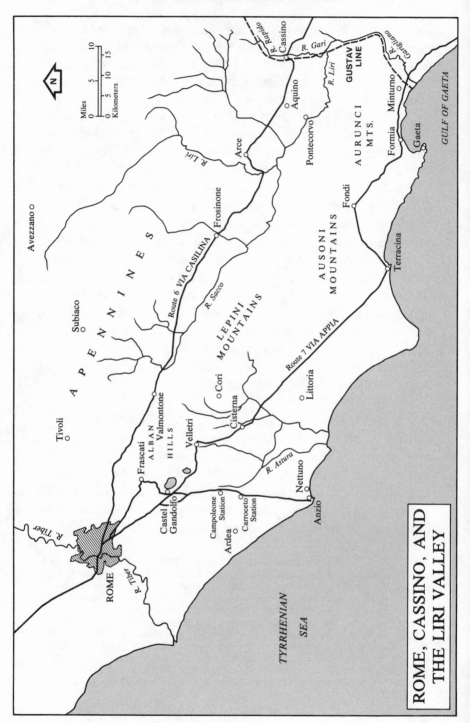

ROME, CASSINO, AND
THE LIRI VALLEY

kept under fire. "A continuation of the attack with the object of completely cleaning up the beachhead will only have prospects of success," he concluded, "if fresh battle-tried divisions can be brought up"—and this, he knew, was out of the question, for he went on to say that he expected to have to surrender more to the west than just the Hermann Goering Division and the Infantry Lehr Regiment (brought up specially for FISCHFANG, this demonstration and training unit had proved a failure in action), which were already under orders to leave Italy. Instead of renewing the attack, he proposed to push ahead urgently with the construction of a new defense line, the C-position,[17] to cover Rome and, "in the most extreme emergency," to withdraw both flanks to it, thus effecting at any rate a small economy of force. But it would take at least two months to prepare the C-position, the purpose of which was to frustrate "any possible attempt by the enemy to break through towards Valmontone or Rome"—a phrase which anticipated and exactly expressed the divergence between Alexander's and Clark's strategies the following May and June.

This is one of the few occasions on which the strategic value of Ultra does not have to be inferred from circumstantial evidence but can be conclusively proved. Kesselring's appreciation was composed on 1 March, and decrypted and sent to London and Allied HQ Caserta on 9 March. On the tenth, Brooke—whose obligatory preoccupation with the broad lines of Allied strategy in all theaters normally precluded the consideration of individual items of intelligence—described it as "a most useful document giving his outlook on the whole of the fighting in Italy." Kesselring's determination, despite the failure of FISCHFANG and the impossibility of mounting another and more successful counterattack, to build new fortifications in order to continue his obstinate defense of an Italian front as far south as practicable (the policy to which he had converted Hitler

---

[17] As early as 20 November, Ultra had reported (VL 982) that "the C-position" was to be reconnoitered; the only clue to its location was that the men who were to mark it out were to go to L'Aquila in the central Apennines, on the southern slopes of the Gran Sasso, the highest mountain in Italy. The line was planned to cross the peninsula from sea to sea at this latitude, but its main purpose was to cover Rome.

six months earlier) combined with Hitler's now well-established penchant for ordering "no retreat" to confirm Brooke in his belief that the best way to assist OVERLORD was to continue the offensive in Italy, and so force the Germans to divert some of their by now limited resources to their southern front. Kesselring recognized that he could not expect fresh divisions for a new attack on the Anzio lodgment area; but if he were himself attacked he might persuade Hitler to send him enough troops to protect Rome—and these reinforcements could only come to Italy at the expense of Normandy or the Russian front. Brooke had repeatedly argued for an Italian strategy with Marshall and the American Chiefs of Staff. Kesselring now enabled him to press his point with renewed vigor. If he was eventually to lose—as he was almost bound to do—over ANVIL (the landing on the Riviera in August, which Brooke thought a mistake because the troops to make it would come from Italy and so reduce the pressure there), he nevertheless secured their present agreement to a new assault on the Gustav Line which, though it could not be mounted within the two months during which Kesselring believed he could complete the new defenses, was to be directed with such skill and prosecuted with such energy in May that a real breakthrough was achieved at last, and Rome fell two days before the OVERLORD landing. A single item of intelligence cannot, and should not, be the sole determinant of strategy, and Brooke had of course always urged "forward" policy in Italy, but the strategic repercussions of this particular decrypt cannot be mistaken.

Preparing the Breakthrough (March–May 1944)

Ten weeks now passed before the May offensive (DIADEM) which breached the Gustav Line, captured Rome, and drove the Germans another hundred miles farther up the peninsula before it lost momentum. Given the geographical constraints and the ill fortune of successive efforts to blast a way through the defensive wall, there were only two options open to the Allied command: either to attempt another amphibious outflanking move farther north, or to recognize that the Liri valley was really the only practicable way forward and devise new and better means of gaining access to it.[18] Prompted by the new Chief of Staff Brooke had sent to revitalize his headquarters, Lieutenant General (later Field Marshal Lord) Harding, Alexander chose the latter. In order to gain the three-to-one superiority in infantry needed to force the Liri valley, Harding proposed that the Eighth Army should come across from the Adriatic and shoulder the main burden of breaking through at Cassino, while the French mountain troops of the Fifth Army tackled the high ground between the Liri and the sea; a little later, U.S. VI Corps would burst out of the Anzio bridgehead at the right moment to cut off the enemy's retreat when the double pressure compelled him to evacuate the Gustav Line. The expected enemy reaction would ensure that "between the main front and the bridgehead we were certain to trap and maul so many German divisions that reinforcements would have to be sent at the expense of the resistance to OVERLORD."

In order to encourage Kesselring and his staff to think that Alexander would choose the alternative of another Anzio-type operation, rather than risk beating his head against the brick wall of the Gustav defenses once more, the deception planners again put about rumors that he had a landing at Civitavecchia, Leghorn, or Genoa in mind, and reinforced them with a bogus wireless network and simulated landing exercises in the bay of Naples. By this means Kesselring was to be induced to disperse his forces to guard his coastal flanks, so weakening the Gustav line and making it easier to assault: that is to say, the reverse of the deception which had been practiced on him in January.

The DIADEM plan was already at an advanced stage while the fate of the Anzio beachhead still hung in the balance in the middle of February, and all its interlocking pieces were moving into position by the time Alexander flew home to explain it early in April. To support it, a scheme (code-named STRANGLE) to

---

[18] Ultra had not been very informative about previous attempts to get through at Cassino and had nothing to say, for instance, about the bombing of the monastery on 15 February. Even Flivo reports seldom dealt in the fine detail of ground positions which would have been required if Ultra was to assist in tactical matters of this kind.

hamper or prevent the movement of German divisions to the battle area and disrupt their supply services by bombing road and rail communications had gone into action on 19 March. The U.S. Strategic Air Force, based on the Foggia airfields, assisted in practicing "interdiction" on the largest scale yet attempted; a novel feature of STRANGLE was the destruction of road and rail bridges, which was now possible with highly trained crews and new precision instruments.

The success or failure of DIADEM depended in large measure on surprise, for if the enemy correctly forecast the Allied plan it would not be difficult for him to frustrate it, so favorable to the defense is the terrain of central Italy. Conversely, the attacker would be greatly heartened, and his prospects enhanced, by the knowledge that the bait of his deception was being swallowed and by evidence that German communications were being cut often and seriously enough to prevent men, petrol, and ammunition from reaching the front when they were needed. In all these and other fields, Ultra provided information which under prevailing conditions could scarcely have been obtained from any other source, certainly not with anything like the same degree of reliability or with the authority which Kesselring's own reports home conveyed. Not for the first time, it was in a period of preparation for the offensive that Ultra's supreme value as a source of intelligence was demonstrated. The success of DIADEM was founded on skillful planning and surprise, and Ultra's part in each was very great indeed.

Toward the end of March, the department of OKH responsible for collecting information about the Allies drew up a survey of their presumed intentions for the summer of 1944. After a long passage about an invasion of France, it turned to the western basin of the Mediterranean, where "new Allied undertakings must be reckoned with," but could not decide whether the French Riviera or the Gulf of Genoa was the more likely target. It correctly stated that the Allies' main object was that of tying down German troops in Italy so that they could not be used to greater advantage elsewhere (although an effort might be made to capture Rome), but added that "it is possible that the continuing attempts to break through at Cassino are meant to create favourable conditions for this by drawing off German forces from the front encircling the beachhead. The object of this operation will be to bring about the collapse of the German defences in southern Italy by cutting 10 Army's rearward communications while simultaneously breaking through its front." Berlin, then, mistakenly believed that Alexander would try to fool Kesselring a second time with the same trick that had been played on him once already; but the rest of this part of the survey came uncomfortably close to Alexander's concept of a two-fisted punch with right and left in turn, first at Cassino and than at Anzio. Kesselring, on the other hand, seems to have expected (as he was intended to do) either a new landing in his rear—he later wrote that had he been Alexander, he would have tried to shorten the campaign by this means—or a breakout at Anzio, but the Ultra indications in March and April suggested a far greater division of opinion among his subordinates than this. Three early reports predicted landings on the west coast, but by the end of March this had been dismissed as unlikely, and from then on various ports up and down the whole length of the Adriatic were favored, latterly because a suspected concentration of landing craft in Bari harbor (in reality they were ships carrying supplies to the Eighth Army, and the "agent" who reported them was a creature of the deception planners) was taken as a pointer, even by Kesselring himself and even after DIADEM was well under way. It was clear from all this not only that the Germans were starting so many hares that they were missing the true scent, but also that they were finding it very difficult to come by information on the subject at all: patrols were bringing in little useful intelligence, and a twice-daily reconnaissance of the Adriatic coastline, ordered on 12 April, was evidently not being carried out regularly three weeks later, in spite of the anxiety about Bari.

Inadequate air reconnaissance was nothing new; heavy Allied raids on the Reich were drawing aircraft from other areas to counter them. It had been impossible in February to cover the western Mediterranean and the African ports in the course of a search for signs of new landings or reinforcements on the way to Anzio, because Luftflotte 2 had too few aircraft to cope with this as well as with its essential tasks over the land battle. Luftflotte 2 had been deliberately depleted in order to strengthen the defenses of France and Germany, but in addition, the GAF was already in the decline from which it never recovered. At least sixteen activity reports were received from Luftflotte 2 between mid-February and the beginning of DIADEM; only three showed as many as 200 sorties a day, and by May the daily total seldom went beyond double figures. Over the same period, the Allies were averaging some 400 sorties every twenty-four hours. In fact, Allied air superiority (4,000 aircraft against 700) was blinding the enemy and making it easier to deceive him;[19] and since most activity reports included statements of the place and time of visual or photographic reconnaissance, the effects of the blinding could be estimated with a fair degree of accuracy. Nothing shows more clearly the Allies' advantage in the field of intelligence: they could observe the enemy's movements while denying him a sight of their own, and by reading his signals could check their own findings by reference to what he was seeing, doing, or intending. The value of this double advantage was most clearly apparent when the Germans failed to spot the transfer of the Eighth Army from the Adriatic coast to Cassino. The transfer was designed to give Alexander the numerical and matériel superiority necessary to strike a heavy blow on a narrow front and break through into the Liri valley at last; Ultra showed that the plan was likely to succeed when it demonstrated that Kesselring was doing nothing to counter a blow which he clearly did not expect, and was even making his defensive task more difficult for himself by taking divisions away from the threatened sector to meet amphibious landings which existed only in an imagination assiduously fed with rumor by the Allied deception staff. A happier combination of operations and intelligence could hardly be conceived.

A large percentage of Ultra during the weeks before DIADEM dealt in one way or another with the consequences of

---

[19] "We had no idea what was going on behind the enemy's lines and could not reconnoitre Naples because of the anti-aircraft fire," wrote Westphal (*Erinnerungen*, 248–49), explaining why the Anzio landing was such a surprise. Von Senger, 218, complains that the Luftwaffe scarcely dared venture into the air during the Cassino battles.

the Allied command of the skies. Looked at as a whole and in retrospect, the signals now seem to show that the policy of trying to cripple the rail network—STRANGLE aimed primarily at destroying the marshaling yards and cutting the railways along a line from Pisa to Rimini, but in addition at interrupting the transalpine routes from time to time by long-range bombing attacks—was far from gaining the success its sponsors hoped for, but at the time the chief impression they gave was of the immense difficulties under which the German supply services were being forced to labor, and therefore of the likelihood of their breaking down altogether. A dozen or more reports of serious damage seemed to testify to the success of the bombing program. Quartermaster returns of ammunition, food, and fuel stocks held by the Tenth and Fourteenth armies were received for thirty out of seventy days between 1 March and 10 May, sometimes for both armies on the same day. Most gave the bare figures, but a few remarked that stocks were adequate. In mid-April, the Tenth Army gave figures for average daily consumption (120 tons of ammunition, 200 cubic meters of petrol, and 50 cubic meters of diesel), making it possible for Alexander's intelligence staff to calculate whether the amounts in stock close to the front were rising or falling as the date of his offensive drew nearer.[20]

Statistics like these formed a solid background for the assessment of the repeated complaints Kesselring addressed to Berlin. One of them, dated 19 March, was a good curtain-raiser to STRANGLE, which began on the same day: many lorries, it said, had been compulsorily surrendered to other theaters, and more were expected to go; the resultant shortage, together with the increased wear and tear on the remainder and the scarcity of spares, meant that men and equipment could not be moved from place to place to meet sudden attacks and that supply columns, already fully stretched, would not be able to cope if the Allied air forces further dislocated the railways. A request to

---

[20] OKW estimated in mid-April (after a month of STRANGLE) that ammunition stocks were higher in Italy then anywhere else, and that there were a fortnight's rations for the Wehrmacht, though less for civilians (OKW/KTB iv.484). See Appendix VII, "STRANGLE."

Berlin for additional construction battalions to repair damaged
roads having elicited only the cold reply that none were available without taking them from Russia, which was out of the
question, Kesselring turned to the headquarters of the organization Todt, without result as far as Ultra knew.

By early April, STRANGLE seemed to be having the desired effect. "Systematic air attacks" on the lines between Florence and Rome were straining the supply situation, complained
Kesselring, and by the end of the month "the continually increasing destruction of railway supply routes" led him to demand the recruitment of much-needed electrical technicians
among Italian prisoners of war in the Reich, since OKH had
turned down a request for Germans. He had already struck a
more sinister note in a message which also accurately identified
the Pisa-Rimini interdiction line: "If operations are to be carried
out, the Italian railways must remain in working order," and in
a final despairing effort he demanded (not for the first time) that
sea transport be increased to make up for what the railways
could not carry (in response to an earlier appeal, German Naval
Command Italy had promised to transport 9,000 tons to Ancona
in April, and another 3,000 south to San Benedetto), forgetting,
perhaps, that Admiral Adriatic had lost a great many ships
lately and had attributed his losses to the weakness of the Luftwaffe and the absence of proper Flak protection round many
harbors. There was, in fact, a good deal more seaborne traffic
up and down both coasts than this implied, but it was so well
monitored by Ultra that it is surprising that sinkings were not
more frequent than they were.[21]

The effect on the Italian front of the manpower shortage
resulting from Hitler's inability to bring any of his vast schemes
of conquest to a conclusion or to pacify the conquered territories
enough to dispense with armies of occupation was apparent
early in May, when Kesselring repeated a Fuehrer order which
referred to "an increasingly strained manpower situation." This
was in fact already to be discerned between the lines of a state-

---

[21] But see, for instance, the successful operations of a "battle squadron" of MTBs in the
Tyrrhenian Sea in March and April, described in Pope, 195–203.

ment of OKW reserves (i.e., troops which could not be moved without Hitler's permission) issued over Jodl's signature toward the end of April: five divisions in the west, one (the Hermann Goering Division) in Italy, some lower-grade or still incompletely organized divisions in Hungary and the Balkans, and a single parachute regiment in the whole Reich.[22] To judge from a survey which his headquarters staff sent to Berlin in mid-April, neither Kesselring nor his divisional generals (a list of their names had just been signaled) had at all a high opinion of the troops under their command. The survey rated each division according to a four-point scale, ranging it from "fit to take the offensive" to "suitable only for static defence." Only two divisions (the 29th PG and 1st Para) reached their own commanders' standards for the top category, but OB Southwest downgraded them both by one point in the scale. (The tenacious resistance of 1st Para at Cassino suggests that Kesselring was too severe, and casts some doubt on the criteria used throughout the document.) Eight divisions altogether were put in the second category, eight in the third ("fit for mobile defence"), and four in the last.

Because they were necessarily more objective, the nine returns of the tanks and guns held by the German armies in Italy during the same ten weeks were of much greater practical intelligence value.[23] Through them, Ultra told as much about the armor and artillery at Kesselring's disposal against the coming offensive as it had ever done about Rommel's striking power in its palmiest African days.[24] During the preparatory stages of DIADEM, this vital evidence about the German capacity to hit back was coming in at an average rate of twice a week. Before March, and again after the middle of May, the average was

---

[22] The Russian front was OKH's affair, which explains its omission from Jodl's statement. The competition for reserves between theaters had recently been the subject of a special study by the Wehrmachtfuehrungsstab, of which Jodl was the head (OKW/KTB iv.56–57; MME vi/1.48).

[23] In addition to these nine complete returns, five fragments (some quite large) also came to light during the same weeks (VLs 9124, 9168; KVs 1086, 1118, 1394, 1849, 3489).

[24] Possibly more. In the desert and Tunisia, the Y Service had regularly intercepted the returns made (in a lower-grade code) by the panzer regiments and the tank-repair workshops. In Italy, these returns were far less frequently transmitted by radio, and Ultra became correspondingly more important.

barely twice a month. What explains the sudden abundance at the time when it was most needed? There are three possible answers (if pure chance be ruled out): more frequent success in breaking the relevant key at one time than another (but why at this particular time?); deliberate intercept policy; and the destruction of teleprinter lines, the natural route for the transmission of long and complicated reports of all kinds. Ultra itself threw up nothing about broken teleprinter lines after STRANGLE, as it was shortly to do in France before OVERLORD, but this proves nothing one way or the other. So little has yet been published about how cryptographic effort was directed and intercept sets allocated that any remark about either must be very hesitant. However, it is difficult to escape the conclusion that a deliberate decision was taken at a high level to devote as many sets and as much bombe time as possible to Italy in March and April, before shifting the main attention of both to western keys and western frequencies. Since land lines were bound to be used in the west (as they had been ever since the end of the 1940 campaign), until the heavy raids of late May and the onset of mobile warfare in June compelled the use of radio, there was nothing to be lost by giving Alexander the best possible service for as long as this would not hinder the greater task on which Eisenhower and Montgomery were about to embark.[25] A decline in the volume of Mediterranean Ultra as a whole soon after the invasion of France seems to confirm this.

Analysis of the seven tank returns intercepted between 21 March and 12 May shows that after the Anzio fighting the number of tanks and assault guns (but not of antitank guns) in Italy rose slightly until late April and then leveled off. The last return before DIADEM, that for 5 May (signaled on 8 May), showed that Kesselring's armies then possessed 18 Mark III tanks with 5cm guns (10 of them flamethrowers), 47 IIIs with 7.5cm guns, 160 IVs, 58 Vs (Panthers), and 43 VIs (Tigers); divisional artillery comprised 180 assault guns and 616 heavy

---

[25]The reason for the small volume of western Ultra during the spring of 1944 is discussed in Bennett, 65–66.

antitank guns.[26] Since each division appeared under a separate heading, it was possible, by correlating the divisional figures with the enemy order of battle which intelligence staffs kept constantly up to date, to see the distribution of heavy weapons over the two fronts and in reserve at a glance. There were no tanks on the main front (where, of course, the ground was unfavorable over most of its length), and nearly 100 were being held back, away from where the action would be; over 50 of these were with the Goering Division, which ever since early March had been guarding the coast about Leghorn against a landing the Allies had no intention of attempting.[27] On the opposite side of the peninsula, a new headquarters, the Venetian Coast Command, was created to protect the head of the Adriatic, also erroneously believed to be under threat. Further, the 90th PG, with its large complement of antitank guns, had also been set to needless coast-watching at Ostia, and the 29th PG (one of the only two divisions which had been considered for a top-category rating) and its 40-odd tanks had disappeared from the Flivo reports and had therefore to be regarded as out of the line. Three of Kesselring's best divisions were thus known not to be immediately available to meet an emergency. The war of nerves which Allied cover-planners had been waging for the last two months was having the desired effect of preventing Kesselring from concentrating his forces where they would soon be most needed, and of compelling him instead to insure against imaginary risks by distributing them piecemeal about Italy. In addition, it had managed to conceal the date of the assault: nothing in the Flivo reports—which were intercepted with unusual frequency and completeness about this time—during the first days of May gave the slightest ground for thinking that the enemy guessed what was about to happen.

To cap all this, Ultra had recently shown how OB South-

---

[26] An additional 7 IIIs, 24 IVs, 26 Vs, 5 VIs, 80 assault guns, and 48 antitank guns were stated to be under repair; some of them would no doubt have been returned to service by 11 May.

[27] OKW took the threat to this part of the coast so seriously that in March it suddenly canceled its earlier plan to convert the Goering Division to Panther tanks and send it to France, and retained it in Italy instead (VLs 8045, 8633, 9801; KVs 149, 3563; OKW/KTB iv.100).

west proposed to conduct the defense if compelled to retreat. A long message from his Chief Engineer on 15 April listed the fortified positions, several of them in front of Rome, which were under construction between the Gustav Line and the mountains fringing the plain of Lombardy—the future Gothic Line—as well as at various points along the coast; their approximate strength and imperfect state of readiness could be judged from the number of mines and tons of concrete used in each.[28] The stages of a fighting withdrawal, and the last line of defense which Kesselring had yet envisaged, were here clearly displayed; as so often, the least superficially exciting of Ultra signals could provide the best strategic guidance.

During the ten weeks between the crisis at Anzio and the opening of the May offensive, the Allied intelligence and planning staffs had been well served by their most reliable source, which had poured out information of the kind they needed at just the right time. No other source could have shown anything like so convincingly how well the cover plan was succeeding in its purpose of deception, nor have monitored the enemy's supply situation so comprehensively. It had counted Kesselring's tanks twice a week, and demonstrated not only how little the GAF was seeing (that could be guessed already, because there were so few hostile aircraft in the sky) but just what Luftflotte 2's reconnaissance pilots were managing to miss or misunderstand—and therefore how well the secret of the Allied preparations was being kept; it showed with the absolute certainty denied any other source how unbalanced the opposing armies had become, with some of their best divisions away on fool's errands far from the real danger points. Cumulatively, rather than by sudden or dramatic revelation, Ultra had laid bare the enemy's weaknesses, and if it is true that DIADEM was "one of the great masterpieces of generalship" during World War II, then Ultra deserves a share of the credit.

DIADEM: The Great Advance, May–July 1944

Fortified by so much knowledge of their enemy, the Allied commanders could press forward with confidence, but it would have

---

[28] See pp. 288–289, below.

been unreasonable to expect that Ultra would help them as much during the battle as it had done during the period of preparation for it. The bombing which paralyzed Army Group, the Tenth Army, and XIV Panzer Korps headquarters for the first thirty-six hours of DIADEM no doubt owed something to Ultra, which had located all three not long beforehand, but Ultra did not discover the most convincing of all proofs that the attack would take the Germans by surprise—the absence on leave of several senior generals.[29] It was unfortunate, too, that a recent slight tendency to delay in decrypting become more pronounced just as the battle began, delaying, for instance, news of an alarming shortage of ammunition in the Cassino sector and the first sign that reserves were being moved up to the Gustav Line.

Flivo reports often gave a comprehensive review of events on the whole front or large sectors of it, but even when decrypted and signaled within a few hours, they will in all likelihood have done no more than confirm what the Allied commanders already knew from their own forward units; that this was realized at the time is evident from the merely moderate priority accorded to most of them. More indicative of OB Southwest's waning powers of resistance was the news that there were not enough reserves to plug the hole which the Canadians punched in the 90th PG's front on 23 May (Allied gunfire was already making it impossible for the division to man its defense properly four days before this), so that the evacuation of Pontecorvo and Terracina was unavoidable. Some idea of the expedients to which Kesselring was being reduced in order to keep his line intact could be gleaned from a series of messages which began with a report from Army Group von Zangen in Lombardy on 13 May to the effect that the newly set up 278th Division, stationed in Istria, was now fit for limited offensive purposes; very soon Kesselring replaced it in Istria (where, however, he

---

[29] Quoting Winterbotham, 114–15, CTA, 42, asserts that Ultra revealed the absence of the Tenth Army commander, von Vietinghoff, soon after the fighting began through a message from Kesselring demanding his return. There was in fact no Ultra signal to this effect, nor is there any sign of several others ascribed to this period by Winterbotham which, had they existed, would have been of great importance (for instance, Kesselring's order to withdraw from the Gustav Line). It is a matter of regret that an official publication should thus have inadvertently given currency to error. For further details, see *Journal of Contemporary History* 16 (1981), 139–40.

still feared diversionary landings) with an untrained reserve division, and before long the 278th Division was identified under the Tenth Army in the Liri valley.

By this time, Alexander had already given orders for the Anzio breakout to start on 23 May. His choice of date was partly governed by the knowledge that Kesselring was progressively committing his only mobile reserves to the Liri valley battle. Ultra located the 26th Panzer, an important part of these reserves, there early on 20 May, and reported it wilting under heavy pressure forty-eight hours later, but was not so successful as when Kesselring fell into the same trap before Anzio; patrols, aerial reconnaissance, and lower-grade signals intelligence provided most of the information available to Alexander, as was usual under battle conditions. The Hermann Goering Division, for instance, must have been picked up by other sources well before it reappeared in Ultra, for it was already under incessant air attack as it moved south by road to plug the gap which threatened to open between the Tenth and Fourteenth armies at Valmontone. There was no hint of von Mackensen's bitter complaints at the removal from the Fourteenth Army of the 26th Panzer and 29th PG, without which he felt unable to withstand the powerful drive from the Anzio beachhead which he expected at any moment, but—contrary to some accounts, and to von Mackensen's own erroneous assessment—at least one of his subordinates rightly judged that the blow would be delivered in the Cisterna sector and not down the Via Anziate, which had hitherto been the axis of operations favored by both sides.

The general pattern of intelligence remained the same throughout the battle for Rome. The link-up between the two fronts on 25 May passed unnoticed by Ultra, and there was nothing to explain Clark's strange behavior in halting the advance, which threatened to cut the Germans' main escape route at Valmontone, and directing his Fifth Army straight for Rome instead, thus denying Alexander the Churchillian "cop" which his battle orders envisaged, and perhaps throwing away the chance of greatly shortening the Italian campaign for the privilege of ensuring that Rome was an exclusively American prize.[30] Churchill had already informed Roosevelt that Alexander's "prime purpose" was the destruction of the German forces, and Alexander explicitly told Churchill on 18 May that when the right moment came, "the Americans will break out [from Anzio] to get astride the enemy's communications to Rome." Ultra's prosaic and piecemeal account of the Tenth and Fourteenth armies' escape from a trap which, had it closed on them, might have been even more disastrous than that other and greater trap at Falaise in Normandy at the end of the coming August does not do justice to the drama of the occasion.

On the other hand, a series of messages, some of them very long and detailed, bore witness to the disarray of the German divisions now fleeing northward as fast as they could go. Von Mackensen (who was on the point of being dismissed for failing to halt the thrust from Anzio) made a very gloomy report on the state of the Fourteenth Army on 27 May. The morale and fighting power of the infantry were declining, he said, and three divisions had been badly mauled; there were too few trained NCOs; many guns had been smashed in the fury of the enemy onslaught ("the whole June production" of assault guns had just been allocated to Italy to make up for recent losses);[31] there was a serious shortage of tractors; tanks were constantly breaking down on long journeys; and Allied armor had driven straight through the 362nd Division because, like other new divisions, it had too few antitank guns. Next day Kesselring added some supporting figures: 420 of the 540 antitank guns in Italy were out of action (some divisions had lost three-quarters of their holdings), and losses like this could not be made good from stocks south of the Alps. "On 30 May," writes General Jackson, describing how the

---

[30] It is unfortunate that Gilbert's account of these events (vii.785) is marred by the assertion that the division which Mark Clark had directed on Valmontone "was forced to a halt before reaching its objective." In fact, Clark ordered it to change direction, and its commander protested. According to Brian Harpur (*The Impossible Victory* [Kimber, 1980], 103–16), in 1964 Clark convicted himself of national and private ambition and excused his contravention of Alexander's orders on the ground that he was following Roosevelt's instructions. On his way home from the Cairo and Tehran conferences in December 1943, Roosevelt had in fact met Clark in Sicily and urged him to take Rome before OVERLORD.

[31] However, only 165 tank and assault guns together were delivered to OB SW between 21 May and 10 June (OKW/KTB iv.582).

U.S. 36th Division exploited the gap it found in the defenses of the Alban Hills, "the first indication of the coming collapse of von Mackensen's army was spotted almost simultaneously by Kesselring and Truscott."[32] The two signals just quoted, transmitted on 30 and 31 May respectively, will have given Ultra's firm and immediate support to this deduction from the way the battle was going. The situation could only be eased, thought Kesselring a week later, by powerful fighter and ground-attack reinforcements to the Luftwaffe, but he did not say how the additional aircraft were to be found in the week of OVERLORD. On the same day, his staff informed Berlin that his armies had suffered 38,024 casualties by 2 June (17,000 of them in the last two days), and that between 200 and 250 tanks—about half the original total—had been lost. There followed an assessment of infantry strength, artillery stocks, and serviceable antitank guns for each division, expressed as percentages of the 11 May figure; only two divisions (apart from two others which had not been engaged) were given a 50 percent rating, most scored only 30 percent or 40 percent, and in several cases the antitank gun figure was as low as 10 or 15 percent of what it had been six weeks earlier. (The 362nd Division, about which von Mackensen had complained, and the 90th PG, which had borne the brunt of the early fighting, were assessed at only 5 percent.)

Elated by his success and the "irresistibly high" morale of his armies, only three days after the fall of Rome Alexander ordered an immediate advance to the approximate latitude of Pisa and Rimini. Ultra evidently contributed to his bold decision in three respects. The high German casualty rate was clearly one, and the continued decline in the effectiveness of the Luftwaffe was another: during the first month of the DIADEM offensive, Ultra missed only four of Luftflotte 2's daily reports of the number of sorties flown by its aircraft; the average works out to about 70 sorties a day, and 100 was exceeded on only eight occasions. Thus the emergency had brought a reduction, rather than an increase, compared with previous figures,[33] whereas the

---

[32] Truscott now commanded U.S. VI Corps in the beachhead.
[33] See pp. 275, above.

Allied scale of effort was constantly rising; the decline became still more marked as aircraft were shortly withdrawn from Italy to meet the even more pressing needs of the eastern and western fronts.

But the third way in which Ultra prompted Alexander's decision to "go for the kill," although his own forces had already been weakened in favor of OVERLORD, and soon would be again for ANVIL, was probably the most powerful of all. His decision clearly rested on the belief that Kesselring would not be able to steady his beaten armies, now that they were on the run, into an orderly retreat from one prepared position to another. Alexander did not know, when he issued the order for advance on 7 June, that Kesselring was about to warn Hitler that he might have to abandon Italy altogether in order to prevent the destruction of his Army Group, or that Hitler had already ordered the rebuilding of the front as short a distance north of Rome as possible (the message from Jodl conveying the Fuehrer's instructions to Kesselring was not decrypted and signaled until 9 June). But he was aware that Ultra evidence which had been accumulating since the autumn of 1943 showed that there were no prepared defenses in central Italy, and that quite recently even the fortifications of what was later famous as the Gothic Line, in the Apennines north of Florence[34]—an ideal defensive position—were far from complete.

Alexander therefore had good reason to think that if he allowed Kesselring no time to pause and consolidate, by the end of the year he could "bounce" him out of every locality in which he might try to stand south of the river Po. He even went so far as to tell the Chiefs of Staff and General Wilson (who had succeeded Eisenhower as Supreme Allied Commander in the Middle East at the end of 1943) that "neither the Apennines nor even the Alps should prove a serious obstacle." But between Alexander and the achievement of his ambition lay the obstacle of defenses in the mountains north of Florence, which might by now have been improved enough to slow down or even halt his progress. The Ultra evidence about them touched the highest

---

[34] See Appendix IX, "The Gothic Line." The preparation of a line of defense works in the northern Apennines seems first to have been advised by General Roatta, then Chief of the Italian General Staff, shortly after the invasion of Sicily (OKW/KTB iii.799–800).

levels of strategic decision-making during the next few crucial weeks, as Alexander's plans for a quick advance clashed with the policymakers' itch to take divisions away from Italy to furnish a landing in the south of France in support of OVER-LORD.

The first Ultra mention of an "Apennine position" had been on 12 October 1943. It had followed hard upon surveys undertaken by Rommel and Army Group B in response to Hitler's order, issued on the day of the Salerno landing, that defenses should be constructed there. Sufficient descriptive detail of the proposed line (which seems to have corresponded fairly closely to that finally chosen, although there were substantial differences at each end) was provided in Army Group B's report to enable aerial photography to keep an eye on what, if any, construction work was being done during the winter. Toward the end of January 1944, in the same signal which gave away his plans for dealing with the Anzio landing,[35] Kesselring ordered Army Group von Zangen, a new command recently set up in northern Italy, to "develop the Apennine position with the greatest energy," and he repeated his orders a week later, particularly emphasizing the need for special attention to the eastern end of the line at Pesaro on the Adriatic.

The prospect, thus held out, of an eventual necessity for the Allies to assault a formidable line of fortifications in difficult mountain country was suddenly made to look far less grim and daunting by two long reviews of work in progress drawn up by Kesselring's Chief Engineer in April and May. Statistics of labor employed, concrete emplacements constructed, mines laid, and barbed-wire fencing erected revealed the exact course of the defense line for the first time and demonstrated the widely varying states of readiness in different sectors; analysis showed that protection against coastal landings (the Allies had no intention of making any, but the deception planners were continually suggesting them in order to confuse the enemy) was being given priority over the preparation of a fortified line across the peninsula, and that quicker progress was being made near the western

---

[35] See p. 265, above.

end than near the eastern, while the mountainous section in the center was receiving the least attention.[36] It was noticeable, also, that neither of the two reviews suggested that any part of the project was being tackled with special urgency, so that an extraordinary outburst of frankness by Hitler in mid-June came as less of a surprise than would otherwise have been the case. After declaring that the Apennine position was the "final blocking position" and that "an Allied entry into the plain of Lombardy would have incalculable military and political consequences," Hitler went on to complain that (as a recent inspection by General Warlimont of OKW had found) nothing at all had yet been done to prepare defenses over long stretches of the line and to order that "the misconception, existing in the minds of commanders and men alike, that there is a fortified Apennine position, must be scotched once and for all"; OB Southwest was to withdraw to it as slowly as possible so as to gain time for "the mighty labours for months to come" which were required if the defenses were to be developed properly.

The impact of this astonishing new piece of intelligence was immediate. Alexander had decided on a rapid advance northward and had issued his optimistic forecast on 7 June, three weeks before Hitler's directive—which had been signed on 13 June—could be decrypted on the 27th. Between these two dates, the Combined Chiefs of Staff had debated Alexander's proposal to cross the Po and drive on into Austria (to which the Americans objected as sinister central European adventuring by the British to the detriment of OVERLORD) and had ruled on 13 June—curiously, the same day as Hitler's directive—that he should stop at the Pisa-Rimini line and lose seven more divisions to ANVIL, the landing in the south of France to which Eisenhower and Marshall were so attached and Churchill and Brooke so hostile. Alexander at once protested against the ruling. Marshall's counterargument centered on his conviction that the Germans would not defend the northern Apennines but would retire to the Alps of their own volition—so that Alex-

---

[36]Figures to support this conclusion will be found in my paper "L'Ultra e la linea Gotica," in G. Rochat, E. Santarelli, and P. Sorcinelli, eds., *Linea Gotica 1944* (Franco Angeli, 1986).

ander would be beating the air, rather than attracting divisions from OVERLORD, if he advanced beyond Pisa and Rimini. Unconvinced, because sure in his own mind that Kesselring would defend the northern Apennines, Alexander next appealed to Brooke and Churchill, and the debate was still raging when on 27 June all parties concerned received the signal in which Hitler described the Gothic Line as "the final defense position" to keep the Allies out of Lombardy.

Brooke hailed the signal as "all-important . . . the most marvellous information," which proved the correctness of his long-held opinion that the Germans would retreat only under pressure: "there could now be no argument that the Germans were about to retire in front of us" (as Marshall and most other Americans maintained, crediting Hitler with a rational rather than his normally emotional strategy), he wrote in his diary. Since Kesselring was now known to be under orders to contest every foot of ground, it followed that ANVIL was unnecessary, because it could only be mounted at the expense of the Allied armies in Italy and would attract no more troops away from von Rundstedt's front in France than Hitler was already guaranteeing without it. (This was to be proved a sound deduction when, directly after the Riviera landing, Hitler ordered the immediate evacuation of the south of France.)

By the time Hitler's revelation about the weakness of the Gothic Line was decrypted, however, Alexander had been ordered to halt at Pisa and Rimini, and the moment when ANVIL must be finally approved or abandoned was fast approaching. Political considerations outweighed military—notably, the need for French troops to fight on their own soil again at the earliest possible moment, and the Americans' refusal to countenance any extension of an Italian commitment they had never liked. The British Chiefs of Staff quoted the Hitler directive to their opposite numbers on 28 June, and Churchill did the same in a last agonized effort to change Roosevelt's mind on 1 July, but all in vain. The Americans remained adamant; ANVIL got the go-ahead on 2 July, and Alexander lost more divisions ("The ghost of ANVIL hangs heavily over the battlefield," he wrote to Churchill). Churchill was unrepentant; he told Roosevelt that this was "the first major strategic and political error for which we two have to be responsible," and before long was cruelly pointing out that "Eisenhower's operations have been a diversion from this landing, instead of the other way round, as the American Chiefs of Staff imagined"—indeed, that five divisions had been moved to his front, "which would not have happened if we had continued our advance here."

It is only infrequently that the impact of a single piece of intelligence upon strategy at the highest level can be detected with such clarity. Did it come just too late to affect the final decision, or was ANVIL predetermined already because the sheer weight of the Americans' contribution to the war effort guaranteed them the last word in any dispute? Probably the latter, but it is nevertheless of some interest to speculate for a moment whether the consequences of this particular decrypt would have been different had it been possible for all parties to the dispute to read Hitler's instructions on the day they were issued instead of a fortnight later. Had Alexander been able to refute Marshall's arguments with hard evidence instead of opinion, however well founded in experience that opinion might be, it is just possible that ANVIL might have been canceled and Alexander's forces allowed to remain undiminished. If so, the Allies would almost certainly have been able to break the Gothic Line and reach the Po before April 1945 (when they eventually did reach it), and might therefore have been able to accelerate the collapse of Germany by bringing pressure to bear upon the Reich from the south in the autumn of 1944, before Eisenhower had crossed the Rhine or the Russians the Vistula. The incidence of a cryptographic problem may here have influenced the outcome of the war—and thus, perhaps, the partition of Europe and the chronicle of the postwar years; we may be in the presence of one of the great might-have-beens of history.

As, undeterred by the rejection of his plans and the depletion of his forces, Alexander nevertheless pressed northward in July hard on Kesselring's heels, he could draw strategic inferences of major significance from several communications the latter sent to Hitler and OKW. "I have been forced to conclude," Kesselring wrote on 11 June, "that successive crises in the fighting have been exacerbated by ammunition shortage," and went on to order corps and divisional commanders "to ensure prompt and adequate deliveries by ruthless means," even by closing roads to all other traffic—forgetting, perhaps, that less than a month back the Chief Quartermaster of the Tenth Army had pointed out that this was just what the formations for which he was responsible could not do, because they had too few lorries of their own to fetch supplies for themselves. The railways too were strained almost to breaking point, according to Kesselring; the Allied successes had prompted a wave of sabotage at a time when reinforcement battalions, hitherto used to guard the tracks against saboteurs, could no longer be spared for this purpose because they were urgently needed to replenish the frontline divisions. The only solution was to punish guerrillas with the utmost severity and to turn a blind eye to officers who overstepped the customary restraints.

Soon Kesselring called on the Fourteenth Army to report the state of its divisions for Hitler's information. Two of the answers and part of the digest Kesselring made for the Fuehrer were intercepted. They made sorry reading: the best division included one exhausted and three weak battalions out of eight; the worst consisted of only three weak battalions in all and had no heavy antitank guns and only 16 pieces of light artillery; the remainder fell somewhere between the two, with fighting strengths rated III or IV on the usual four-point scale. As early as 12 June, Kesselring knew that he could keep the 715th Division instead of handing it over to OB West as originally envisaged, but its poor condition was revealed when OKH issued particulars of the reorganization planned for it and the 65th Division: they were to have only 22 percent of the standard equipment of a 1944-pattern infantry division. A long indent for new weapons for the 94th and 305th divisions at the end of June ended with the note "The Army Group cannot provide this without depriving other divisions," and the wretched state of these other divisions was shown up by the announcement that in the future those in I Para Corps (perhaps the strongest in the peninsula hitherto) would be known simply as battle groups under the names of their commanders, so reduced were they in numbers. I Para Corps' casualty list for April, May, and June bore independent witness to its failing strength. The consequence of this decline in his battle strength was that Kesselring received substantial reinforcements before the end of June.[37] The direct and speedy result of DIADEM could thus be seen as the fulfillment of the instruction to Alexander to attract troops to the Mediterranean theater and keep them away from Normandy, where Montgomery had not yet broken out of the ring which von Rundstedt had managed to throw round the bridgehead.

A few Panther tanks had been detected on the way from Germany in early June, and Panzer Abteilung 504's strength in Tigers was recorded twice, but no comprehensive tank return of the kind so familiar in March and April had been seen for several weeks when that for 23 June was intercepted. Under three headings in particular it bore startling witness to the destruction wrought by the Allied offensive and fully supported Kesselring's complaints. In comparison with the returns of early May, the numbers of serviceable Mark IV tanks and heavy antitank guns were down by three-quarters, and those of assault guns by nearly two-thirds;[38] only Tigers, the newest and heaviest type of tank, remained fairly steady, though many had been damaged.

These figures depressed and exasperated Kesselring as much as they presumably encouraged the Allied command, and he complained bitterly to Jodl and OKW. The matériel superiority of the Allies (ten to one in assault guns and tanks, he claimed) could only be counteracted by great mobility on the part of the Germans, but "as has been proved almost daily," the means to achieve this were lacking. Heavy antitank guns had often been blown up because they could not be hauled away, and it had been impossible to prevent even small parcels of Allied armor from breaking through, because antitank guns could not be shifted into new defense positions. Since 1 June, the

---

[37]See p. 295, below.
[38]See Appendix VIII "Tank Returns," C.

Army Group had received a total of 523 tractors,[39] but even a single mortar detachment had lost 42 since 11 May; to make his artillery, Flak, and heavy antitank guns sufficiently mobile, he needed 700 tractors. Similarly, the number of serviceable tanks had "sunk to a threatening degree" because damaged machines could not be towed away and because there was a shortage of spare parts: 21 tanks of Panzer Abteilung 216 had been blown up, for instance, because there were no spares to put them back into service, and this sort of thing was having a bad effect on the morale of tank crews and on their sense of responsibility for their weapons.

There was a rare consistency in the complaints about losses of weapons during the first six weeks of DIADEM, particularly losses of antitank guns (the only effective defense against the onrush of armor in open country), and the statistical backing given them by the 23 June tank return was impressive. The Allied staffs were doubtless not slow to draw the obvious deduction, and this, like the evidence that the eastern end of the Gothic Line was the weaker, may have played a part in the decision to make the next thrust along the Adriatic coast in order to gain entry into the broad Romagna plain, which, it was widely but erroneously believed, would offer "good tank going."

The Assault on the Gothic Line (July–December 1944)

The DIADEM offensive was in some respects the climax of the Italian campaign. The fall of Cassino at long last and the expulsion of the enemy from Rome monopolized the headlines, but during the same weeks Ultra gave repeated proof that Allied pressure in Italy was fulfilling the obligation which had been laid upon it at Cairo and Tehran—to attract German strategic reserves south of the Alps and thereby assist the western and eastern offensives. Five divisions were reported arriving in Italy

---

[39] OKW/KTB iv.582 has 52 in an otherwise identical sentence. The sense of Kesselring's argument seems to require the lower figure; a German signaling error may explain the higher.

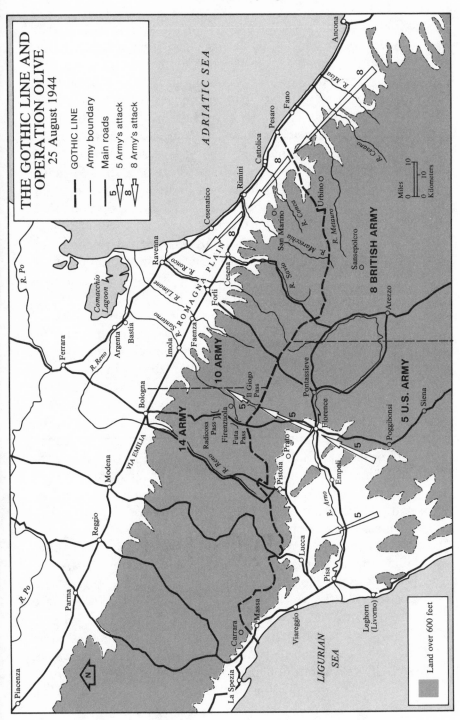

THE GOTHIC LINE AND
OPERATION OLIVE
25 August 1944

GOTHIC LINE
Army boundary
Main roads
5 Army's attack
8 Army's attack

from other theaters—two from the west (19th and 20th GAF), one from the Balkans (42nd Jaeger), one from central Europe (16th SS), and one from the Ukraine (34th Infantry)—and the 715th Division was shown to be staying in Italy instead of moving to the west as planned. All these moves (except that of the 34th Division) were known by early June, soon after Hitler ordered them. The erosion of Kesselring's armies, which was making continual reinforcement necessary, was also demonstrated only a little later in signals which showed that 20th GAF mustered only 430 men on 30 June, and by its amalgamation with 19th GAF division before the end of July. On the opposite side of the ledger, the Hermann Goering Division, which had long been held back in Italy against OKW's original intention of sending it to France, was now at last called away in mid-July—but to the eastern front by the Russian offensive in the Pripet Marshes area leaving its tanks behind.

During June and July, the U.S. Fifth Army lost 40 percent of its strength and 70 percent of its air component to Eisenhower's command—the departing French contingent included the only highly trained mountain troops in Italy, who would soon be sadly missed in the assault on the Gothic Line—while two inexperienced divisions from the Middle East took over the sectors of veteran formations on the British Eighth Army front. Thus diluted and progressively reduced to a secondary role, the Allied force was nevertheless still expected to attract German troops into Italy and to hold them there by an aggressive conduct of operations. In these circumstances, order-of-battle information—held by many since desert days to be Ultra's chief contribution to intelligence—became of primary importance from the strategic point of view, since it could show whether the task was being accomplished well or ill. In the course of the two months immediately preceding the next Allied offensive (OLIVE, which began on 25 August), two new arrivals (the 98th and 237th divisions) and two departures (the 3rd and 15th PG, both to the west) were recorded, but the most striking items were those which proved that ANVIL (now renamed DRAGOON) was not fulfilling its ostensible purpose. An order for the only panzer division in the south of France (the 11th

Panzer) to move north to Chartres was canceled on 11 August because of the threat of imminent invasion, but within only forty-eight hours of the landing on the Riviera coast it became clear that no new German formations would be attracted down from northern France, where the battle of the Falaise pocket was raging. On the morning of 17 August, Hitler ordered the main body of Army Group G to retire up the Rhône valley with all speed,[40] while its two easternmost divisions (the 148th and 157th) withdrew across the Franco-Italian frontier into the welcoming arms of the 90th PG at Cuneo (whither it had been sent to strengthen the new German-Italian Army of Liguria, which had been set up in mid-July to protect the Gulf of Genoa against a landing); the two divisions passed thereby from von Rundstedt's to Kesselring's command. The news of Hitler's order was signaled in the early afternoon of the same day and usefully reassured the Americans chasing Army Group G up the Rhône valley that their right flank was not in danger, but they also gave conclusive, though retrospective, proof that from the military point of view DRAGOON had been wasted effort; Hitler's response to it was evacuation, not reinforcement, so that the landing brought Eisenhower no relief. Ultra had more than once pointed unmistakably toward this conclusion, and Brooke had foreseen the outcome when he urged that invading the south of France would accomplish no more than threatening to do so[41]—a deduction which was no doubt at least partly based on repeated Ultra indications that the threat had been causing mounting anxiety at all levels of the German command since the end of 1943.

The desired order-of-battle information could come from a variety of sources: from orders, like those already quoted, by Hitler or OKW for single divisions to move from one theater to another; from Flivo reports locating the battle headquarters of

---

[40] The Ultra narrative of Army Group G's hasty retreat is sketched in Bennett, 151–54.
[41] Foreign Armies West had perceived this with great clarity six weeks before DRAGOON. The Allies were trying to tie German troops down in the south of France, ran an appreciation on 30 June, by a war of nerves and the threat posed by their own forces (which were known to be limited) in North Africa. But there was no sign that ships were being got ready to lift these forces, and the Allies would attempt a landing only if and when the war of nerves failed (XL 689).

the divisions composing the corps to which the particular Flivo was attached, because from them transfers could be deduced, an accurate and up-to-the-minute map of dispositions in the front line maintained, and the extent of reserves in the rear estimated; from tank- and gun-strength returns, which might by their arrangement reveal the move of a formation from the Tenth to the Fourteenth Army or the reverse; from railway-movement reports, which often showed how many trains carrying a division into or out of Italy had completed their journey by a given date; and from reports on the fighting strengths of divisions in each corps and each army. Reports of the last type classified divisions on the usual four-point scale and often included an estimate of their motorized or horse-drawn mobility. Several examples were received during the slow autumn advance to the Gothic Line, and they showed that few divisions except the 26th Panzer and 29th and 90th PG ever escaped, even momentarily, from the third category ("fully fit for the defensive") into the second ("fit for limited offensive operations").

Shortly before Christmas, the first OB Southwest rations-strength return for six months showed that there were approximately 100,000 more men (nearly 1,100,000 against just under a million) and 50,000 more horses in Italy on 20 December than on 25 May. Casualties were less often and less usefully reported in Ultra, but two signals showed up the difficulty the Germans were having in maintaining the fighting strength of the troops at the front. In ten days in about the middle of September, the 4th Parachute Division lost just 5,000 more men than it received by way of replacements, and by mid-November OB Southwest was reporting that casualties were no longer being made good by new drafts coming up from the Reich. As long ago as July, a comb-out of the GAF in all theaters had been instituted under the grandiose cover name WALKUERE, with the object of finding men to fill the gaps in the army's ranks.

Indications like these of the failing strength of German divisions and of their low battle-worthiness proved the value of the Italian campaign to the Allied cause, and demonstrated the superiority of Ultra over other sources of intelligence on matters of strategy. Ever since February, when Harding had planned

DIADEM so as to attract the maximum number of German divisions into the cauldron of Cassino and aimed to use the Liri valley as a killing ground, a deliberate policy of attrition had been applied as continuously and as ruthlessly as the repeated reductions in Allied strength permitted. Now the dividends were coming in. Not even the valiant parachute divisions, the cream of the remaining German infantry, were rated capable of a sustained offensive, but merely as fit for the stubborn but perpetual rearguard actions to which Hitler and Kesselring had condemned them by insisting on holding a succession of lines across the peninsula rather than retiring in one bound to fortifications in the Alps which could have been made impregnable with far fewer men. Casualties in frontline combat could be discovered, at least approximately and in the short term, through the Y Service and from the interrogation of prisoners. Only Ultra could find out whether and to what extent reinforcements were being regularly drafted in to compensate, and only Ultra could tell Alexander and his staff how Kesselring assessed the capacities of the formations under his command. Ultra made it clear that, as the Combined Chiefs of Staff had demanded, some of the best German divisions were being kept busy far away from the two fronts whose topography was more favorable to advances which could strike more directly at the heart of Hitler's Reich, and that they were being ground down in the process. This was a great service to the Allied cause, but once more it could not be intelligence alone which proved the strategy right. The richest reward was in the figures which Alexander quoted in his final dispatch: although progressively starved of resources and of experienced troops, although always the attacker in conditions where the odds in favor of the defense were longer than usual, nevertheless he had not thrown away lives recklessly in order to win the war of attrition. By May 1945, Italy had cost the Germans 536,000 casualties, but the Allies only 312,000.

To maintain a million men in arms in Italy and to keep them properly supplied was becoming more and more difficult for the Germans, particularly after Luftflotte 2 moved to Vienna in September, thus still further diminishing the protection against air attack which could be given to road and rail transport.[42] Bomb damage to the railway system was regularly reported in September, October, and November, together with lists of the stretches of line open or closed to traffic and estimates of the time required for repairs. Things were so bad on the Brenner route in early September that Hitler proposed to construct a second section of track between Bolzano and Trent, and on 18 November, General von Vietinghoff (temporarily promoted from the Fourteenth Army to deputize as OB Southwest after Kesselring was injured in a road accident) was not only compelled to forbid artillery support "to the previous lifesaving extent" in order to stockpile ammunition for use against the "large-scale attack on Bologna" which he expected in the near future (a shortage the previous month had provoked OB Southwest's Chief Quartermaster to say that "every delivery delay caused by rail cuts causes a crisis"), but also to tell OKW that the planned move of the 71st Division from Istria to Bologna was very risky on two counts: first, because the almost complete lack of aerial reconnaissance meant that he had no idea whether it would be safe to denude Istria or whether an Allied landing there was likely, and second, because in consequence of the "difficult railway situation" the move would take at least three weeks.[43]

Fuel stocks were even harder hit than ammunition by delayed deliveries and by the waning output of the remaining oil plants in Germany and occupied territory. Goering imposed restrictions on the use of petrol by the whole Luftwaffe at the beginning of September and tightened them severely two months later (all operations were to be "ruthlessly cut down" and some discontinued altogether—for instance, night ground-attack sorties). An Air Ministry comment appended to a signal announcing the aircraft-fuel allocation for October suggested that it was about one-twelfth of normal; the GOC of LXXVI

---

[42] Luftflotte 2 had, however, never managed more than a couple of dozen sorties a day in the fortnight before DRAGOON, in spite of the pressing need to discover the preparations for it and to establish the sailing and movements of the convoys (XLs 4436, 4577, 4700, 4826, 6209, 6352, 6766).

[43] The distance from Istria to Bologna is no more than 150 miles.

Korps, in Lombardy, complained in the same week that he had been told that he would get no more petrol for motor vehicles until the middle of the month and that he had therefore had to fix the permitted maximum daily consumption at an absurdly low level; and in mid-November, the Tenth Army reported fuel so short that some divisions could not even carry out tactical movements for lack of it.

Despite their seemingly factual nature, there is a subjective element in these outbursts which is impossible to measure yet essential to discount. Freer from it, but less frequently intercepted than in the spring and early summer, were OB Southwest's returns of serviceable tanks and guns.[44] Comparison of the figures in them with those from earlier returns shows conclusively that in the second half of the year new deliveries hardly made good natural wastage: Army Group C began the OLIVE battles with some 30 fewer tanks of the older patterns (III and IV) than it had held a short time before, but although it had recouped these and other losses by December, the total was still a little short of what it had been in May. Newer types (Panthers and Tigers) showed comparatively small fluctuations, presumably because their thicker armor made them less vulnerable. The number of assault guns tended to rise slightly, but most striking of all was the continued decline in all types of heavy antitank gun, holdings of which in December were only two-thirds of what they had in May.

Only very occasionally was there anything to lighten this gloomy picture, and when there was it never applied to aircraft fuel. According to the German navy on 16 October, 49 additional ships (representing 300,000 tons of cargo space) had come into service during the previous three weeks, with the result that seaborne supplies were almost back to normal, and a long report from the quartermaster department of OB Southwest at the end of November included the phrase "supply situation at present assured," but these two stood almost alone. In retrospect, this means that the Ultra evidence, if taken *au pied de la lettre*, was misrepresenting the true facts by suggesting that the interdiction

---

[44] See Appendix VIII, "Tank Returns," D.

program was having the desired effect and was well on the way to strangling the German armies in Italy altogether by so restricting their supplies that they could neither fight nor maneuver.[45] That this was not the general case—however near disaster particular units or formations might come at one moment or another—became apparent as fighting continued with undiminished ferocity and autumn turned into winter without either an Allied breakthrough or a German collapse. Under strength, exhausted, periodically short of weapons and ammunition, and often immobilized by lack of petrol though Kesselring's troops were, they continued to resist with a determination which used the favorable terrain to the best defensive advantage, and they managed to retreat in good order and unbroken line until Alexander was obliged to call off the last stage of his offensive in late December, still a vital few miles short of Bologna and Route 9, the main Milan-Rimini road which provided the Germans with superb lateral communications behind the Apennines. By the time the Ardennes offensive had run its course in the west, there were no better troops in the Wehrmacht on any front than those in Italy, despite the hammering they had received. If transferred to either of the other two fronts, they might even now have prolonged the war; earlier, their impact could have been incalculable.

Since they had still nurtured high hopes of a decisive victory and an early advance to the Alps or even into Austria long after those who designed grand strategy had deprived them of the means to achieve it, and since Ultra sometimes encouraged them to see the weakness of their opponents in colors more lurid than faithful, it says much for the good judgment of the Allied

---

[45] The reasons for this, apart from the operation of chance, cannot be fully ascertained until thorough histories of the internal organization of Bletchley Park and of the Y Service are published. Intercept stations were, of course, directed to listen to frequencies known to be most productive of intelligence, and priority on the bombes was given to the keys most likely to yield valuable information. But an ineradicable element of randomness was introduced by fading and interference on the one hand and by the intractability of some keys on the other, to say nothing of a natural German preference for telephone and teleprinter when the RAF and USAAF had not destroyed the transmission lines, and the natural predilection of hard-pressed field commanders to make the most of their difficulties in the hope of extracting much-needed supplies from their superiors. All the same, the disproportionate gloom of the intercepts is more than a little puzzling.

commanders in Italy that they never allowed themselves to become infected with the overoptimism which ran riot elsewhere in August and September, and were never lured by it into acts of military imprudence. Even the usually hardheaded Brooke was not immune from the infection, and on 6 September he and the other British Chiefs of Staff, on board the *Queen Mary* en route for the Quebec conference, solemnly debated whether, in view of Germany's evidently approaching collapse, they should begin withdrawing troops from Europe for the war against Japan. It is far easier now, when a long run of Ultra signals can be analyzed at leisure, than it can have been then to discern a common pattern or stereotype in many of the complaints of shortages,[46] and in consequence to suspect that they do not so much display objective truth as conceal it beneath emotive verbiage—a suspicion which, once roused, quickly dispels the temptation to take them literally or to believe that they proved that victory was just round the corner.

OLIVE was planned at even shorter notice than SHINGLE and entailed an even sharper reversal of ideas. At a hasty meeting with Alexander and Harding on Orvieto airfield on 4 August, General Leese (who had taken over the Eighth Army when Montgomery came home for OVERLORD) persuaded them to abandon their previous intention of attacking the central sector of the Gothic Line north of Florence and to substitute a thrust on the Adriatic coast, where there were no mountains to obstruct progress and there was a chance to outflank the whole German position by a quick penetration of the least well-prepared sector of the defenses,[47] followed (it was hoped) by armored exploitation across the plain as far as the river Po after a fashion not seen since the desert. One objection to the change was that an Adriatic attack was being represented as the Allied purpose under the existing cover plan because the real intention was a drive for Bologna by the direct route through the Apennine passes north of Florence: now truth was suddenly to be-

---

[46]For instance, compare the wording of the complaints on pp. 278, 293, 301, above.
[47]See pp. 289, 294, above, and CTA 299–302 for detail. Warlimont confirmed the weakness on the Adriatic in June (OKW/KTB iv.579).

come falsehood, and vice versa, and so swift a change might reduce credibility and increase danger. The operation began on 25 August, just three weeks after the Orvieto meeting, but its results fell far short of what had been hoped for (the operation orders called for exploitation as far as the Po), largely because the Germans contested each successive river line quite as bitterly as they had defended the mountains round Cassino a year earlier.

The essential prerequisite for OLIVE had been that the Eighth Army should transfer unnoticed back eastward to the Adriatic coast from which it had come for DIADEM. The move was carried out between 15 and 22 August, by night to prevent observation from the air, but before it had begun Ultra was already giving good reason to believe that the deception planners were once more successfully fooling the enemy. An agent had convinced Foreign Armies West by 8 August that the Eighth Army had moved its headquarters to Siena(!) and that its left boundary had been shifted *westward* between Florence and the sea; on the 12th, three days before DRAGOON, Kesselring declared a first-degree alarm for the whole area west of a line Pisa-Reggio-Mantua (partly, no doubt, because he was still inclined to construe the rumors of an imminent new landing as another Anzio-type threat to his own western flank rather than to von Rundstedt's southern). Right up to the start of OLIVE, there was not a shred of evidence in Ultra to suggest that the Germans knew that the Eighth Army had crossed the mountains again or realized where the blow was about to fall, and even a fortnight after DRAGOON and four days after the beginning of OLIVE, the continued presence of the 42nd Jaeger, 16th SS, and 26th Panzer divisions west of the Apennines showed that Kesselring had still not grasped the pattern of Allied strategy.

At the beginning of September, the Eighth Army was held up on the Coriano ridge and prevented from reaching open country, and when the Fifth Army delivered the second of Alexander's "two-handed punches" in the center, it gained ground only slowly. By the 21st, both armies had made a little progress, but neither had achieved the desired breakthrough: the Eighth Army had reached Lombardy but was bogged down in what

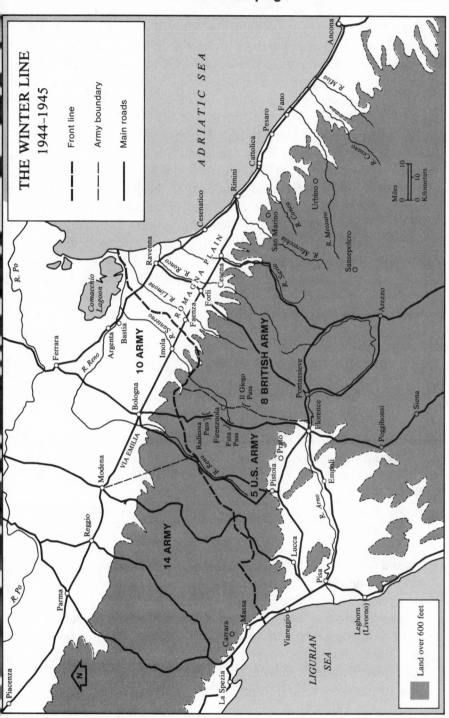

THE WINTER LINE
1944–1945

Front line
Army boundary
Main roads

ADRIATIC SEA

R. Po

Comacchio
Lagoon

Ferrara

R. Reno

Argenta
Bastia
Imola
10 ARMY
Bologna

VIA EMILIA

Modena

Reggio

14 ARMY

R. Po

Parma

Piacenza

Ravenna

R. Ronco
R. Limone
R. Senio
R. Montone

ROMAGNA PLAIN

Forlì
Faenza
Cesena
Cesenatico

Rimini

Cattolica

Pesaro

Fano

Ancona

R. Misa

R. Cesano

R. Metauro

Urbino

R. Conca

R. Marecchia

San Marino

Sansepolcro

Arezzo

R. Savio

8 BRITISH ARMY

Il Giogo
Pass

Radicosa
Pass
Firenzuola
Futa
Pass

R. Reno

5 U.S. ARMY

Pontassieve

Florence

Poggibonsi

Siena

Pistoia
Prato

Empoli

R. Arno

Lucca

Pisa

Leghorn
(Livorno)

Viareggio

Massa
Carrara

La Spezia

LIGURIAN
SEA

N

Miles
0   10
0   10
Kilometers

Land over 600 feet

came to be called "the battle of the Rivers," and the Fifth Army now held the passes but had ground to a halt five tantalizing miles short of Bologna and Route 9. The cost had been high, and a temporary pause was necessary at the end of October. So far, the purpose of containment had been fulfilled, but the mounting demands of the Russian front (on 22 September, Army Group South Ukraine reported that five corps and sixteen divisions "must be considered smashed") soon sucked the 44nd and 71st divisions out of Italy, replacing them only by the lower-quality 710th Division from Scandinavia. Even so, renewed Allied pressure achieved little, and the offensive was eventually called off toward the end of December. Alexander had meanwhile succeeded Maitland Wilson as Supreme Allied Commander, Mediterranean, but the outbreak of civil war in Greece (which the Germans had recently evacuated) had compelled him to reduce his striking power in Italy still further by sending British troops to Athens and then to spend a hazardous few days there himself.

The Last Offensive (January–May 1945)

Like DIADEM, OLIVE petered out because Alexander's depleted armies could not generate quite enough momentum to penetrate the last barrier thrown up by a stubborn defense. The three-month pause which weariness and winter weather now imposed served also to see the cryptanalysts through a difficult patch of their own. New refinements of Enigma were introduced in January 1945—notably the encoding of call signs and repeated changes of frequency—and time was required to find answers to the resultant problems. All were eventually solved, but at a price. The volume of traffic decrypted in January and February was less than had been customary in the autumn, and most keys took longer to break than formerly, so that the interval between German transmission and English translation was in future seldom quite as short as it had usually been in the past. The position was much brighter in both respects by March, however, and something like what we had come to regard as normality was restored by the time the final offensive opened on 9 April.

During the pause in operations, a certain delay in decrypting mattered less than it would otherwise have done. Just as in the west, abundant material the value of which was not much diminished if it was only available several days late was accumulated during the first three months of 1945, and from it precious inferences could be drawn about the state of the enemy's forces, their deployment, and their readiness to meet attack at the points where it was planned to strike first. Alexander had been told not to attempt more than limited operations while the final decision was being sought in other theaters of war. His determination not to be a mere spectator of a victory won by others, but to be an active—indeed, a leading—participant in it nevertheless dictated strict economy of effort. In this situation Ultra provided much-needed help, and in much the same ways as before: throughout the strategic planning stage, and over the first tactical moves of the battle itself.

Eight complete OB Southwest tank- and gun-strength returns were decrypted during the first three months of 1945, three of them within a few days at the end of March and the beginning of April, the most useful time; from them emerged a clear picture of Kesselring's situation on the eve of the offensive. The most striking feature of the whole series was the very slight change in the figures from one return to another. The number of tanks in the armored formations remained almost constant, but was still lower than previously.[48] This showed that little if any of the wastage resulting from the autumn's fighting was being made good and confirmed an earlier impression that scarcely any new deliveries were coming in from the factories in the Reich, while also suggesting that the repair workshops behind the front were still managing to restore to service most of the tanks damaged in combat or halted by mechanical breakdown. The only significant exception to the general rule was the 26th Panzer; for some unexplained reason, its holding of Mark IVs sometimes dropped to

---

[48] Compare the autumn figures on p. 301.

about 65 before returning to a norm of 85, and it acquired 25 Panthers from I Panzer Regiment 4 (which had long had that number) when the latter disappeared from the Tenth Army's order of battle in February. With the assimilation of I Panzer Regiment 4, the restriction of tanks in Italy to a small handful of readily identifiable formations became more marked than ever. Apart from the 26th Panzer (with 85 IVs and 25 Vs) and the 29th PG (between 40 and 50 Vs), only Panzer Abteilungen 212 (40 IVs) and 504 (35 Tigers) possessed more than a very few (the 90th PG never had more than 3 now, nor did the 16th SS before it left for Russia in early February). It followed that so long as the whereabouts of these four was known (the first two, at any rate, were regularly reported in Ultra, and doubtless daily by the Y Service), the enemy's striking power could be precisely located and either confronted or sidestepped at will. The advantage this gave was to prove of inestimable value in the first critical moves of the offensive.

Weekly reports on the state of divisions were more numerous in the spring of 1945 than they had been previously, and frequently contained more information.[49] Most conveniently, there were more from the Tenth Army, guarding the plain eastward from Bologna to the Adriatic—the sector where the attack was to be made—than from the Fourteenth Army. The series opened in the middle of January with a gloomy report from General Lemelsen, commanding the Tenth Army. The recent lull in the fighting round Bologna, he said, had enabled him to improve the training of the troops in that sector, but not on the rest of his front. The Ardennes offensive and a spell of home leave over Christmas had raised morale, but although replacements were coming through faster than before, the position was still not good enough. Small arms and petrol were short, and mobility was only some 60 percent even in the motorized divisions (in the 16th SS, it was down to 35 percent).[50] Retrospec-

---

[49]Notably about the tanks and guns held by each division. Thus these returns corroborated and (where they filled gaps in the series of tank and gun-returns) complemented the figures discussed in the last paragraph.

[50]The surrender by OB Southwest of 380 lorries and 100 trailers for the Ardennes offensive was doubtless partly to blame. Because this was far fewer than he had been ordered to give up, Kesselring was peremptorily ordered early in January to explain the shortfall and to say why most of these handed over were badly in need of repair (BT 3388). The universal shortage of motor transport was again illustrated in an order of 8 February for 350 tons of lorry space to be sent off to Army Group Vistula (BT 4930).

tively, Lemelsen's remarks showed how near the German line had been to snapping when Alexander called a halt in December, but careful study of the dozen or so weekly reports intercepted during the next three months showed that steady progress was being made to strengthen it. Mobility rose to about 80 percent in most cases, though of course it remained completely dependent on a regular supply of petrol (and horse fodder too, in the case of the infantry divisions); estimates of fighting value rose in parallel, and the 1st Para, 90th PG, and 98th Divisions joined the 26th Panzer and 29th PG in being rated as capable of taking offensive action. By far the most valuable feature of these returns to Allied intelligence, however, was the light they shed on changes in the order of battle. The lists were drawn up by corps, so that the affiliation of each division, antitank detachment, and so on could be read off at a glance— and an absolutely reliable check made on information derived from battle contact and other sources. Furthermore, by displaying the lineup across the whole front, these returns revealed the strongest and weakest sectors and the disposition of the armor with the utmost clarity. As will be seen, the three or four such returns which came in during the period immediately before the 9 April offensive proved invaluable in this respect.

The Allies' enormous superiority in mobility and firepower was now more apparent than ever, and Ultra helped to exploit it to the full. Berlin was evidently at its wits' end to find enough ammunition to meet the insatiable demands of three hardpressed fronts. An OKW order of 10 January proceeded from the axiom that these demands could only be satisfied (because raw material was in short supply, manufacture hampered by air raids, and transport delayed by blocked railway lines) if the use of ammunition was restricted to essential targets and the strictest economy observed elsewhere. In spite of this, however, so many shells were being fired off on quiet fronts that reserves were not being accumulated. Yet reserves were essential. Pursuant to this order, Army Group C was instructed next day on the economies to be made and the reserve stocks to be built up. A month later, OKH warned all army groups that the February allocation would be 30 percent down on the previous month, and that future allocations would be made for ten days at a time, instead of monthly.

Petrol was similarly rationed. Berlin forecast that OB Southwest would receive 1,500 cubic meters for the last ten days of January, but that even this might be subject to cuts if the situation on the eastern front made it necessary. By mid-February, the outlook was still worse, and Jodl peremptorily ordered OB West, OB Southwest, and OB Southeast to impose a "ruthless limitation of operations" because of the critical fuel situation.

It may have been this circular which stung Kesselring into an angry correspondence with Jodl on which Ultra was able to eavesdrop briefly at the end of February. Answering on the 23rd a communication of Kesselring's which Ultra had not reported, Jodl said that "the overall ammunition and fuel situation" would not permit an increase in Kesselring's quotas in the foreseeable future, in spite of his "admittedly difficult situation," because of low output from the factories, the loss of coal-mining districts, and continuous attacks from east and west. Kesselring would therefore have to accumulate his own reserves for "the large-scale battles which must be expected," and even the prevailing daily ration of four rounds of light and two rounds of medium field howitzer ammunition(!) could no longer be justified.[51] As for fuel, Jodl continued, current allocations exceeded current average consumption by 94 cubic meters a day, and reserves would have to be built up out of the surplus. Kesselring accepted this, but told Jodl that he could only stockpile reserves if supplies came through regularly—which they had not been doing of late—and complained that he had not had fair compensation for fuel used up in moving a division out of Italy in accordance with orders. All this, he concluded, meant that he would have the greatest difficulty in conducting operations "in a situation which is approaching a climax."[52] His Chief of Staff

---

[51] Howitzer shells had been in short supply, and the subject of repeated complaint, for several months past. The Allies were also suffering from a shortage of shells, but it was far less severe and was overcome by April.

[52] A similar crisis was reached on the Hungarian front a month later. Army Group South telegraphed baldly on 4 April, "Ammunition and fuel so short that conduct of operations can no longer be guaranteed" (BT 9870).

added a telltale postscript: only two or three supply trains a day had crossed the frontier between 10 and 24 February, whereas a minimum of five was needed even in quiet periods; the result had been a dangerous decline in buffer stocks.

The precise impact of petrol and ammunition shortages could be observed at close quarters in a series of stock returns which—whether by good fortune or good management it is now impossible to determine—were intercepted in unprecedented numbers at this time. More than half of them concerned the Tenth Army, and the remainder were divided equally between the Fourteenth Army and the Army Group quartermaster. When the key to the pro forma used in ammunition returns was worked out at the beginning of January, the way was opened to running checks on Kesselring's angry generalizations and to a reliable estimate of how long the Tenth Army's guns could keep up a barrage against the coming attack before they were silenced for want of shells.[53]

Kesselring's claim that he had not had proper compensation for petrol consumed in transporting a division out of Italy (according to his Chief of Staff, Berlin had ordered priority to be given to this over incoming supply trains) implied that the railways—for which Kesselring had repeatedly demanded more coal—could not do the job, and that the task of carrying the division at any rate part of the way had fallen on road transport, which was still less able to perform it. Petrol, indispensable for the motorized divisions, which could win or lose the battle for the Lombardy plain, was instead being burned up in strategic transfers from front to front, and the lifeblood of Army Group C was draining away with it. The move to which Kesselring referred was presumably that of the 16th SS to Germany (en route for its eventual destination in Hungary); ordered out of Italy on 3 February, it left the front line on the 6th and started to move on the 10th, but its last elements were not out of the country until the end of the month. By that time, the 715th Division had been on its way north for several days, and it was to take even

---

[53] The calculation could be the more exact because eight of the Tenth Army returns were rendered during the last weeks before the Allied offensive.

longer to complete its journey than the 16th SS had done. Only four trainloads had managed to cross the Brenner pass by 1 March, and the last was not clear until the 21st; that is to say, it took the 715th Division more than a month to travel from the southern edge of Lombardy to the Austrian side of the Brenner, a distance of less than 150 miles! Churchill presumably had these two examples in mind when he wrote that the Allies' thirty-to-one superiority in the air kept the Brenner closed for nearly the whole of March and delayed two divisions on their way to the Russian front. Isolated from the Reich and almost imprisoned in Italy by the rupture of their communications, OB Southwest's still relatively coherent armies could not even serve as a pool from which to draw reinforcements to stem the onslaught from east and west. Driven up against the Alps, they soon had no choice but surrender.

For as the number of sorties flown by the Allied air forces rose during the spring of 1945, the interdiction program began to bite in real earnest, and the mounting tide of purely factual evidence made it less necessary to be skeptical about emotional complaints of shortages. Before the end of January, Kesselring (just back from sick leave) told OKW that an emergency transport plan could be extended until 1 March if he used up all the coal in Italy, but that he would have to impose severe restrictions—tactical troop movements would only be permitted "as far as absolutely necessary," for instance, and the transport of materials for building defensive positions would have to be curtailed. Allied bombing of the Brenner had just reached a new peak, ran his report for 28 February. All the passes into Germany were still closed; not only was the move of the 715th Division being hampered, but all attempts to build up stocks to meet the impending Allied offensive were being crippled. Protesting a month later against an order to surrender Flak batteries for home defense, his successor, von Vietinghoff,[54] pointed out that the protection of his supply routes depended almost entirely

---

[54] Kesselring was appointed OB West on 8 March. On the 12th, von Vietinghoff was recalled from the Baltic front (where he had taken over Army Group Kurland when Kesselring returned from leave after his car accident) and assumed command of Army Group C as OB Southwest on 19 March (BTs 4713, 6970, 8415).

upon Flak, and that whereas in January the Allied air forces had made 1,800 sorties against the Brenner out of a total of 18,000 all told, the figures had now risen to 3,700 out of 20,000.

No train crossed the Brenner on 22 March (the last tanker in the Adriatic was sunk the same day), and from then on the route over the pass was almost always blocked. Efforts to disentangle the resultant traffic congestion were disturbed by harassing raids on the marshaling yards at Udine, where there were 24 raids and 12 guerrilla attacks within a short period up to 8 April. Before the 9 April offensive had been in progress a week, von Vietinghoff felt bound to inform OKW and OKH that his petrol stocks would last at most a fortnight at present rates of consumption, but a proportionately shorter time if it became necessary to make large tactical moves in such a hurry that "improvised means (ox-drawn vehicles)" were ruled out. His forecast proved remarkably accurate.

Roughly as he had been treated by his political masters and their military advisers, Alexander could reflect, if he was shown some of the Ultra signals in January, that his opposite number was in far worse case. On 21 January, Hitler ordered commanders down to divisional level to report every decision they took to him personally and at once, so that there would be time for him to countermand their orders if he thought fit! He had already once more repeated his parrot cry "Yield no foot of ground," and the two together effectively undermined Kesselring's authority and tied the hands of all his generals. Once they had submitted to the loss of some of their best divisions, on the other hand, Alexander and Clark were free to make their plans without further interference.[55] The repetition of Hitler's parrot cry could only reinforce their conviction that these plans were not likely to be disrupted by a strategic German withdrawal to the Alps. A withdrawal was now militarily more advisable than ever, because it would economize forces and give the defenders

---

[55] Alexander had succeeded Wilson as Supreme Allied Commander, Mediterranean at Christmas 1944. Mark Clark took over the 15th Army Group, and Truscott the Fifth Army. The Eighth Army had been under the command of Lieutenant General Sir Richard McCreery since October, Leese having gone to Southeast Asia.

the advantage of the higher ground, presenting the Allies with the awkward task of winkling out the garrisons from one prepared position in the mountains after another. Such a plan was known to exist: would it be put into effect? Ultra had long ago noted the cover name under which (it later appeared) the plan went, but had lost track of it after two references on 21 September. In the first of them, Kesselring's new Chief of Staff, Generalleutnant Roettiger, rebuked those concerned for their "repeated gross breaches of security during preparatory work for HERBSTNEBEL." Rather naturally, he gave no clue to the meaning of the cover name then, and was presumably responsible for its disappearance from radio communications thereafter, but he did himself inadvertently lift the corner of the veil in another message to the effect that in the event of HERBSTNEBEL, no river crossing was to be allowed to fall into the hands of the enemy.

In his *Memoirs* (published in 1962), Alexander wrote that he learned about HERBSTNEBEL "through our Intelligence," and soon realized what it signified. The German word means "autumn mist," for which the Po valley is notorious. In the present context, therefore, it must be the cover name for a withdrawal thither or beyond—following, of course, an evacuation of the Gothic Line.[56]

Shaken by his losses in the retreat through central Italy, and fearing that in consequence he might not be able to defend Lombardy (which would have allowed Alexander almost to fulfill his ambition of reaching the Alps by August 1944) Kesselring had in fact just been trying to persuade Hitler to sanction HERBSTNEBEL and allow him to withdraw to the so-called Lower Alps position. Hitler rejected his request at once, on 23 September. Kesselring tried again with new arguments on the

---

[56] Alexander proceeds to remark upon the "danger of having a secret cover-name with a built-in clue to its meaning," a mistake the Germans often made, the Allies seldom (but SHINGLE for Anzio suggests a beach, and it was Churchill himself who chose ARMPIT to denote a landing at the head of the Adriatic). If Alexander learned of HERBSTNEBEL from Ultra, this was a justification of the policy (introduced in November 1943; JP 8944 is the first example of it) of transmitting the German cover name once, though an English substitute thereafter. Curiously, in view of the authorship and purpose of the DIADEM plan, the substitute for HERBSTNEBEL suggested by the random list then in use turned out to be HARDING.

27th, but was again refused permission, partly on the ground of the psychological shock to German opinion of an unforced retreat. Finally, on 5 October, the Fuehrer repeated his order to hold the existing line "not only into the late autumn, but to the bitter end" *("nicht nur bis Spaetherbst, sondern ueberhaupt")*. He again rejected a less drastic plan for a phased withdrawal to the line of the rivers Ticino and Po on 22 February when Kesselring renewed his plea once more as the prospect of another Allied offensive loomed closer—"a death sentence for the Army Group in Italy," the Chief of Staff of the Fourteenth Army called it. None of these decisions found its way into Ultra, but the 21 January directive envisaging that Hitler might cancel even divisional commanders' orders, which did, left little room for doubt that OB Southwest would be made to stand his ground, and that therefore his Army Group could be enveloped and annihilated if its defenses could be pierced on a wide enough front for the Allied armor to be loosed into its rear areas. Alexander's plan for the final offensive was to achieve this and to destroy Army Group C south of the Po before it could escape into the mountains beyond.

The promulgation of a cover plan to facilitate this was hampered by an initial uncertainty whether the U.S. Fifth Army or the British Eighth Army should attack first, west of Bologna or south of Lake Comacchio respectively, but the enemy's nervous response to every imagined threat, soon reflected in Ultra, was a good augury for success. When, early in March, the newly arrived U.S. 10th Mountain Division (later to be one of the spearheads of the advance) was "blooded" in a small but vital operation to improve the Fifth Army's starting line, it made such rapid progress that the 29th PG was brought across from its fruitless coast-watching in Liguria to halt it. Shortly after this, Ultra showed OB Southwest disputing Foreign Armies West's opinion that no large-scale offensive was impending; he argued—in terms which showed "A" Force's success in planting "notional" divisions on his intelligence section—that the Allies still had ten or twelve formations (four of them experienced and three armored) as yet uncommitted behind the front. Only twenty-four hours earlier, Lemelsen (deputizing as OB Southwest during the interval between Kesselring's departure and von Vietinghoff's return from Russia) signed an agitated appreciation of likely developments at the head of the Adriatic. Recent talks between Alexander and Tito (they had met in Belgrade toward the end of February), the announcement of the general line Graz-Trieste as the boundary between the eastern and the western powers, and Tito's claim to Slovenia, he began, all suggested that a Partisan drive northward from Croatia would be timed to coincide with "the expected Anglo-American offensive" in Italy. In consequence, he was anxious about the defense of the area on both sides of his boundary with OB Southeast, where there was no unified command. To improve it on his own side, he would have to take troops away from the Istrian peninsula to strengthen the weakly held district on the mainland behind.

A cover plan issued by Jodl the same day, 12 March, showed that Berlin was more concerned about the situation farther north in Hungary (six weeks earlier, IX SS Corps had been at its last gasp in Budapest, which the Russians occupied on 13 February), whither the 16th SS and 715th divisions had just been sent. To disguise their movements, the creation of new parachute divisions was to be announced and a bogus wireless network was to suggest that the 715th Division was going to Istria. How the pretense of setting up new parachute divisions could operate as a disguise for something else was not made clear, and in any case there was soon a reversal of roles which turned cover plan into reality in the same way that OLIVE had replaced an originally "notional" attack on the Adriatic coast. Barely a week after Jodl issued his plan, Keitel, his immediate superior in OKW, countermanded it with the statement (clearly in line with Foreign Armies West's opinion just recorded) that, in view of the withdrawal of Allied troops from Italy and of the critical position in Germany (Hodges with the U.S. First Army had been across the Rhine at Remagen for a fortnight, Patton and Montgomery were about to follow suit), Hitler had decided to set up two new parachute divisions, and that I Para Corps in Italy should dispatch 6,000 men as cadres to Holland immediately. Seven trainloads, evidently of these men, had left by the end of the month. Since 1st Para and 4th Para divisions, which provided these cadres, had been returning strengths of 13,000 or 14,000 each, this meant that Hitler had taken nearly a quarter of von Vietinghoff's best infantry away from the defense of Bologna (where I Para Corps was stationed) just as two Allied armies were about to converge on the city. The news could not fail to encourage the Allied command, nor would it be easy to find a better example of the interdependence of the three crumbling German fronts.

To return from Hitler's anxieties to von Vietinghoff's, however, Alexander himself testified to the value of news of the 29th PG's next convulsive move in demonstrating the success of the Allied deception planners in playing on German fears of an amphibious landing at the head of the Adriatic, fears which had, of course, been a familiar feature of Ultra for many months before von Vietinghoff's recent forecast of joint operations with Tito. The reference is to two signals of 21 and 23 March, which were transmitted on the 24th and 31st respectively. In the first, OB Southwest reported that the 334th Division had relieved the 29th PG behind Bologna, and that the 29th PG was assembling as Army Group reserve south of the Po between Mantua and Ferrara, near the river crossing at Ostiglia. The second showed that a reinforced regiment group of the division had by now crossed the Po northward and was heading for Padua, clearly in order to keep a watch on the coast northeast of Venice.[57] This latter signal must have reached Allied GHQ and Eighth Army just as the commandos were beginning their capture of the "spit" between Lake Comacchio and the sea, an action which kept alive the threat of a landing but really served as the extreme arc of the "right hook" by which the Eighth Army was about to drive for the Argenta gap in the inundations south of the lake in order to penetrate the German lines in force and begin the work of destroying Army Group C.

Plainly, von Vietinghoff had inherited Kesselring's well-

---

[57]This was another success for the Allied deception planners, who had labored to suggest that a landing was intended somewhere north of the Po. In fact, Alexander's naval advisers had assured him that the water there would be too shallow for a landing (Alexander, "Allied Armies in Italy," 2959n).

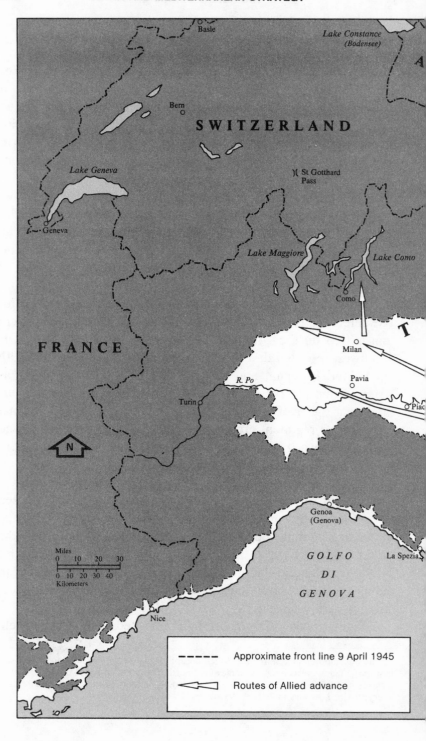

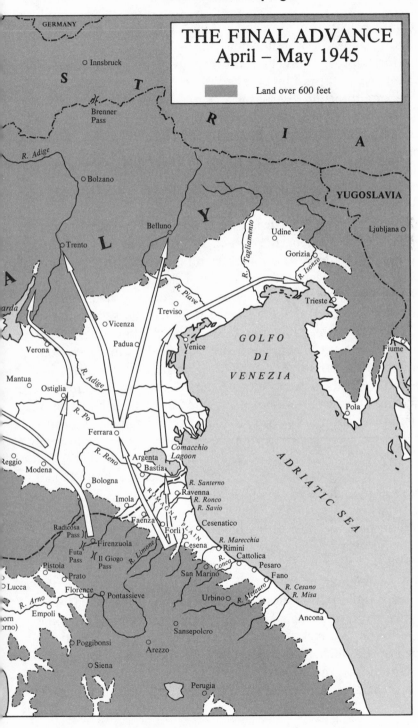

THE FINAL ADVANCE
April – May 1945

Land over 600 feet

GERMANY

S   T

Innsbruck

Brenner
Pass

R. Adige

Bolzano

R
I
A

YUGOSLAVIA

Belluno

Y

R. Piave

Udine

Ljubljana

Trento

L

Gorizia

R. Isonzo

R. Tagliamento

Vicenza

Treviso

Trieste

Padua

Venice

*GOLFO
DI
VENEZIA*

A

Verona

Fiume

Mantua

R. Adige

Ostiglia

R. Po

Pola

Ferrara

A
D
R
I
A
T
I
C

Comacchio
Lagoon

Reggio

R. Reno

Argenta

Bastia

Modena

Bologna

R. Santerno

Ravenna

S
E
A

Imola

R. Ronco
R. Savio

R
O
M
A
G
N
A

Faenza

Cesenatico

Radicosa
Pass

P
L
A
I
N

Forli

R. Limone

Cesena

R. Marecchia

Rimini

Firenzuola

Futa
Pass

Il Giogo
Pass

San Marino

R. Conca

Cattolica

Pistoia

Pesaro

Prato

San Giovanni

Fano

Lucca

Florence

Pontassieve

Urbino

R. Metauro

R. Cesano
R. Misa

R. Arno

orn)

Empoli

Ancona

rno)

Sansepolcro

Poggibonsi

Arezzo

Siena

Perugia

known proclivity for misreading Allied intentions, but not (as
the next few weeks were to show conclusively) his predecessor's
flair for improvisation and recovery from his own mistakes.
Soon he sent more of his scanty mobile reserves hurrying off in
the wrong direction. Early on 5 April, Ultra showed that the
90th PG was under orders to move, and twelve hours later that
it was to join LI Korps under the Fourteenth Army, which
would place it at least as far west as Modena. The message on
which these two signals were based originated on 2 and 3 April
respectively. The intention to move the 90th PG therefore ante-
dated the U.S. 92nd Division's push down the west coast at Carrara, which began on 5 April. Part of the 90th PG was, however,
switched from Modena to meet it. On the same day, the 29th
PG was told to draw its supplies from the Tenth Army "when it
arrived"—an indication that the rest of the division was at that
moment following the regimental group already mentioned—
and after a period of radio silence it joined the signals net of
XCVII Korps (which had long been charged with the defense of
Istria) on 6 April. There were still slight delays in decryption,
but before the offensive opened on 9 April, all this information
was in the hands of Alexander, Clark, McCreery, and Truscott,
who could thus begin what was intended to be their final operation in the comfortable certainty that two of the enemy's strongest divisions were far away from the places where he would need
them most.

During the next few days, it emerged that the 29th PG had
been destined for service still farther afield, for XCVII Korps
was transferred from OB Southwest to OB Southeast on 10
April at the same time as the boundary between the two major
commands was shifted eastward to the line of the Isonzo, which
implied that the 29th PG would end up somewhere in Slovenia.
(Von Vietinghoff had opposed both changes and wanted the
boundary sited thirty miles to the west, along the Tagliamento.)
This last absurdity seems to have been averted soon after the
Eighth Army's attack, for a tank return of 10 April showed the
29th PG still under the Tenth Army; by the time it returned to
the battle zone, the division had lost 3 of its 47 tanks and burned
up a great deal of precious petrol in its fruitless wanderings.

Once more Ultra had done valuable service in showing that the enemy commander was unbalanced, with two of his strongest divisions wrongly placed to meet the coming attack. We were less fortunate with the third, the 26th Panzer. No news of its activities was reported during the first fortnight of April, but its unchanged complement of armor was known.

Tactical surprise—doubly ensured by an artillery program in the last hour before the infantry attack which so confused the enemy that the assault troops were across the monstrous barrier of the flood-banks along the river Senio before he realized that they were coming—was almost a guarantee of quick and total victory, for Hitler's policy of no withdrawal denied his generals a second chance once the crust of their defenses was pierced. The vital bridge at Bastia was in the Eighth Army's hands by 14 April, the day the Fifth Army moved up to the attack; the Eighth Army was through the Argenta gap and on the way to Ferrara by the 17th, and the Fifth Army across the Via Emilia on the 20th. With the Po and its broken bridges behind them, the German armies could not escape destruction.

In conditions like these there is very little left for military intelligence to do; a fluid battle moves too fast for it to keep up. To a remarkable extent, however, Ultra managed to overcome this handicap during these last weeks of the Italian campaign, because some of its most illuminating items were decrypted with unaccustomed rapidity. Von Vietinghoff's review, already quoted,[58] of the way the deteriorating situation might develop and his forecast that ammunition stocks might be exhausted and his entire Army Group immobilized by lack of petrol within a fortnight was dated 14 April and signaled at midday on the 16th, for instance. Still more striking, both for speed and content, was a nine-page appreciation which had immediately preceded this review. Von Vietinghoff dispatched it to Berlin early on the 14th, only an hour or two before the Fifth Army attacked and the Eighth Army crossed the river Reno; the first half was signaled just over twenty-four hours later, the remainder at dawn on the 16th. It offered a complete justification of Alexander's

---

[58] See p. 313, above.

strategy, conclusive evidence of the disarray of Army Group C, and unmistakable pointers to future German moves. Few Enigma intercepts gave a clearer picture of the state of affairs behind the German lines, and it is so perfect an example of what Ultra at its best could do that it is worth quoting at length. "Large scale offensive . . . exceeds all previous fighting . . . weight of Allied material never before experienced . . . intention to destroy German armies confirmed by unspecified English source: 'considerable relief for us when the Germans did not retire but gave battle' . . . Allied air force attacking every recognisable target by day and night . . . signals communications repeatedly destroyed, so control of operations impossible during greater part of day . . . movement of even smallest reserves, tanks and guns well-nigh impossible . . . 98, 362, 42 Jaeger and 26 Panzer divisions exhausted or broken . . . even rearward positions cannot be held . . . voluntary surrender of salient sectors necessary to obtain reserves, especially as II U.S. Corps must be expected to attack near and west of Bologna any day and breakthrough there would endanger entire western part of front[59] . . . if Allies cannot be halted at northwest corner of Lake Comacchio,[60] forces needed to prevent breakthrough into Po plain can only be obtained from I Para Corps[61] . . . if intention of OKW is to continue to keep British and Americans away as long as possible from Reich fortress[62] . . . Army Group must withdraw to Po-Ticino position . . . this would take at least 14 days . . . only in that way can valuable region be preserved for German war potential until decisive final battle." Even after this, it took von Vietinghoff nearly another week to ask for freedom of action; needless to say, he received the usual stony answer, "There will be no withdrawal," and was left to derive what comfort he could from the reminder that in spite of everything he was better placed to carry out his task than any other theater commander. Alexander knew what Hitler had told him during the afternoon of the 22nd, barely twenty-four hours later than von Vietinghoff himself.

---

[59] II Corps attacked at 0900 hours on the morning this appreciation was sent out.
[60] Where the Eighth Army had been pushing forward fast since 8 April.
[61] Holding the sector just east of Bologna.
[62] See Appendix X, "Italian Defenses, or an Alpine Fortress?"

One or two items, on the other hand, lost the edge of their value through lapse of time. Von Vietinghoff's intention of trying to carry out Hitler's instructions by creating a new line along the Po—perhaps always a vain hope, in view of the chaos in Army Group C—was of merely academic interest because by the time it became known his front had irreparably collapsed and the Tenth Army was in precipitate flight. Jodl's exhortation to all to fight hard against "the Bolshevik arch-enemy," but not to mind losing territory to the British and Americans, was a sign of the end—but also a sign that there was still a flicker of life in the command system which had done so much harm to the German cause, for nevertheless all transfers of troops from west to east (the two fronts were now only a few miles apart) still required the sanction of OKW!

With the surrender of Army Group C,[63] signed at Caserta on 29 April and set to come into force on 2 May, a million men laid down their arms. It was "a remarkable end to a campaign whose primary object had always been limited to strategic containment," but whose architect was determined to triumph over the adversity imposed upon him. It has been said that the progressive withdrawal of troops from Italy made Alexander resemble a man "promoted chairman of a company about to go into liquidation," or "the director of a magic-lantern show." His achievement was all the greater for the partial truth these exaggerated similes contain: the final victory was "his most impressive exploit, because it was thought to be impossible."

---

[63] See Appendix XI, "Operation SUNRISE."

11
YUGOSLAVIA
1941–1945

German armies invaded and occupied Yugoslavia and Greece in the spring of 1941; Bulgaria and Romania submitted without a fight. The Nazi domination of the Balkans remained unbroken, though increasingly challenged, until the autumn of 1944. Contact with the west was denied to the whole area from the Adriatic to the Black Sea and the Aegean for the first two of the intervening years and only partially reestablished from the middle of 1943. Little news came out and only a few brave men could get in after the collapse of the British attempt to shore up the Greeks' self-defense against aggression in 1941. A social structure which, though riven by national rivalries, had long concentrated wealth and power in the hands of a few behind a façade of monarchical government ensured that part of the resistance to the invader would aim at restoring the prewar conditions; part, on the other hand, wanted to take advantage of the situation to inaugurate social and political revolution as well. Each type of resistance welcomed help from outside, its political color dictating its preference between east and west as the source of aid. From the Anglo-American and the Russian points of view alike, both forms of resistance were at first welcome because both might weaken the common enemy. Which, however, would be more effective in fighting him? And which would be more likely to disturb the political future of the Balkans? Time alone would reveal the answer to the first question, and the second would not arise until then.

To aid anyone willing to resist the Germans by guerrilla warfare and sabotage of communications was a natural aim for all the Allies when they could spare resources from their own immediate needs. Particularly as time went on and their own prospects improved, however, reliable information about the occupied territories became an even more urgent requirement. Above all, it was desirable to know which of the two main resistance movements was inflicting the greater damage on the enemy, in order that resistance might be directed where it would bring greatest benefit to the Allied cause.

Ultra provided a great deal of information about Yugoslavia,[1] but (at any rate as far as evidence yet open to inspection goes) only from the middle of 1943 onward. This chapter sets out to examine it, and to show how far it assisted in this task. Ultra intelligence about Yugoslavia could never be used, however, in the way Ultra was used in North Africa and Italy. Since no Allied army ever operated in Yugoslavia, no Ultra was sent thither, and its operational use was restricted to supply-dropping and naval activity in the Adriatic, both of which could be organized from bases in Egypt or Italy; the Yugoslavs were dependent on their own intelligence-gathering resources in their long struggle against the invader.

The German invasion of Yugoslavia in 1941 was an immediate success in the sense that it drove the royal government into exile and that the invaders occupied Serbia, worked with the Italians in Dalmatia, and set up with them the "independent" puppet state of Croatia, but not in the sense that the administration they imposed was universally accepted by the population. Resistance never entirely ceased in a country so mountainous that the invader could not keep it all under surveillance, and within a few months it found a leader in Colonel Draža Mihajlović, a Serbian army officer who established his headquarters at Ravna Gora, in central Serbia, in mid-May. Mihajlović adopted and adapted the Chetnik (the word means "guerrilla fighter") organization for guerrilla warfare which had framed Serbian resistance to the Turks in the nineteenth century, but his followers could claim no monopoly of this ancient and hon-

---

[1]But far less about Greece, too little to warrant a section about Greece here.

orable title. Other more or less similar groups, owing little or no allegiance to Mihajlović, also used it, and it will be important later on to keep the distinction prominently in mind: many who called themselves Chetniks were not under Mihajlović's orders, and the actions of Chetniks cannot always be taken to indicate Mihajlović's attitude or policy unless the allegiance of those who performed them is known for certain.

Mihajlović led a movement of resistance to the German occupation, but he was not a resistance leader according to any recognized pattern. As a serving officer, he was not cut out to be the head of a popular movement; as a Serbian, his appeal was mainly to the national feeling of Serbs. His object was to save Serbia from a repetition of the bloodletting of World War I, but not necessarily to preserve the Karadjordje dynasty. Conservative rather than radical, though aware of the need for change in a monarchy whose social and political character was still that of the previous century, he was essentially nonpolitical. But he was temperamentally opposed to communism, though not anti-Russian. His strong desire to protect the Serbian race meant that he was anxious not to provoke reprisals which he could neither prevent nor avenge. A brutal massacre in Kragujevac at the end of October, following upon Keitel's order for the shooting of up to a hundred Yugoslavs for every German killed by the resistance, convinced him that premature heroism would do more harm than good; and he informed the British government, with which he first made contact in August, that he would not resist actively until the Allies were in a position to invade the Balkans and bring him assistance.

Josip Broz was completely different in antecedents and motivation. Born into a Croatian peasant family, he was captured by the Russians in 1915 while serving in the Austrian army, and after the 1917 revolution he became a dedicated Communist. He worked for the Bolsheviks in Moscow for several years, but returned to Yugoslavia and served a prison sentence for his Communist activities. In 1940 he was secretary of the underground Yugoslav Communist party and was already using the cover name Tito. There is some dispute whether he began to stir up resistance to the German occupation before

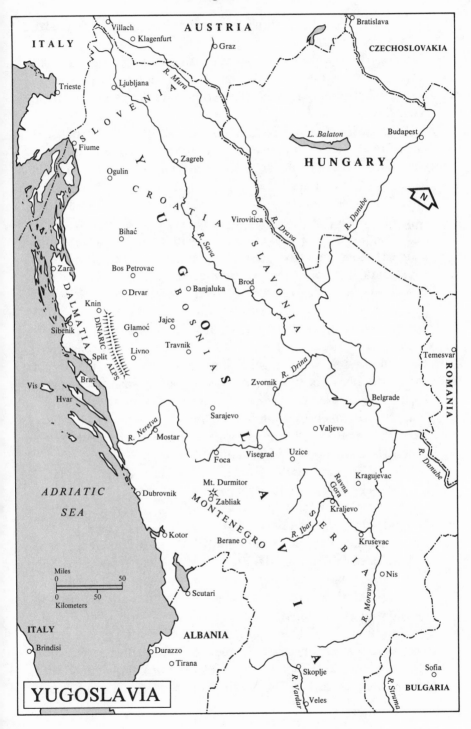

YUGOSLAVIA

BARBAROSSA, but he was certainly doing so soon afterward. If he came a little later into the field than Mihajlović, he had one significant advantage over him: the Yugoslav Communists were not numerous in 1941, but their recruitment and loyalty transcended race and creed, the two bitterly divisive elements in Yugoslav society.

Centuries of Turkish domination had added a Muslim minority to the existing division between Orthodox and Catholic Christians, and had deepened rather than eroded the mutual hostility of the several racial groups (Slovenes, Croats, Bosnians, Serbs, Montenegrins, and Albanians) which had been thrown together into a single heterogeneous state by the Treaty of Versailles: the national unity upon which successful resistance to the invader might be grounded was far to seek.

Communist and Moscow-oriented though Tito was, his embryo movement was neither directed nor materially supported by Stalin, perhaps mainly because until late in 1943 Russia could not spare resources for anything but her own struggle for survival. If Tito expected Russian aid, he was soon disillusioned. He could look for none from Britain, partly for the same reason and partly because prewar Britain had had no love for communism and was slow to moderate its hostility even after the Russian alliance which Churchill proclaimed in June 1941. To share a common enemy is no recipe for instantaneous friendship, between states as between individuals.

Thus Tito was on his own from the start. Equally isolated by distance and German victories, so was Mihajlović, but he could confidently look for at least tokens of friendship from Britain, which was already giving shelter to the royal government in exile. During the autumn of 1941, Britain recognized him as leader of the resistance, and King Peter appointed him War Minister in the exiled government. Pursuant to the policy of "setting Europe ablaze" with which Churchill had inaugurated the Special Operations Executive (SOE) in June 1940, a little money and a British liaison officer (Captain, later Colonel, Hudson) were sent to him in September 1941, but Hudson was soon reporting by radio that Mihajlović was not campaigning with much energy and that Tito—who had briefly freed a district of

Serbia which became known as the Republic of Užice and declared himself supreme commander of the people's liberation army—was much more active.

This news attracted less attention in London than might have been expected. Because it was obviously going to be impossible to provide material help on a useful scale in the foreseeable future, the British government's policy and the Chiefs of Staff's military judgment were in fundamental accord with Mihajlović's belief that he should bide his time until conditions were more favorable and that armed revolt would be premature until then. Tito spurned Britain's first advances, made through Hudson ("The sun will not rise in the west," he said), and scored several quite spectacular successes on his own before the German First Offensive drove him out of Užice and established on a permanent footing the hideous regime of reprisals which Mihajlović was determined to avoid, and with indifference to which he charged the Partisans (as Tito's followers were beginning to be called).

The autumn months of 1941 saw two unhappy developments. Mihajlović and Tito met several times but could not agree to work together. Their followers were more intransigent. Civil war broke out between them in November and the breach was never healed; five years later, Tito, by that time head of state, saw to it that Mihajlović was tried and executed for treason. More sinister, and even now not easy to comprehend, were the first of several occasions on which Mihajlović appeared to be collaborating with the occupying forces. This was to carry his policy of nonprovocation to extremes, because it meant that he was not only doing nothing to hasten the coming of the better times to which he professed to look forward but was actively delaying their arrival. Except in Serbia, where it was simplified into a means of preserving Serbian authority, his reasoning was too subtle for most Yugoslavs, and by the end of 1941 Chetnik numbers were static or declining, but Partisan numbers were growing.

Mihajlović continued to lie doggo for most of 1942, but a decisive change came over Tito's fortunes as the months passed. Forced out of Užice, he wandered by a circuitous route south through Montenegro to Foča; driven thence by the Third Offensive, he turned northward and embarked on the 115-day "Long March" deeper into Croatia via Jajce to Bihać, where by November he had cleared a broad enough "free territory" to hold an assembly of representatives of the liberated areas and to proclaim himself the leader of a national army which aimed at the foundation of an all-Yugoslav national state. Broadcast and then published in the western press, the declaration established Tito by the end of 1942 as an independent figure on a European scale instead of merely a puppet of Moscow.

Hudson's radio was off the air in the early part of 1942, but by the summer the British were not without news—incomplete, confusing, and contradictory at the time, and still obscure today—about events in Yugoslavia.[2] However, what little positive action could be taken was not based on conclusions drawn from the evidence but was instead governed by preconceived notions. Everyone seems to have known by that time that most of the fighting was being done by Partisans, not Chetniks, but Foreign Office policy—with which military opinion concurred for its own reasons—was to continue supporting King Peter's government and its War Minister, Mihajlović. SOE London was bound by this superior authority.

Thus the British attitude toward Yugoslavia remained substantially unchanged until late in 1942. The preconception that Mihajlović deserved support because he represented the "establishment" which the Axis had overthrown still colored the reading, by those in authority, of any information which came into British hands, even when (as was increasingly the case) it pointed to the conclusion that Tito was putting up far more effective resistance than Mihajlović, and even when it came from a reliable source.

Taking their lead from Churchill, who in December 1941 had ordered that preparations for the liberation of the oppressed peoples of Europe should be based on the principle "By themselves they will never be able to revolt," civil and military authorities alike were convinced that resistance could not succeed

---

[2]See Appendix XII, "Missing Links in the Chain of Yugoslav Intelligence," A.

by its own unaided efforts but depended on British or Allied intervention. Thus although the Chiefs of Staff had begun to realize in March that Balkan resistance might be helping the Allied cause by compelling the Axis to divert substantial forces thither, and although they were persuaded to allot two of their scarce long-range aircraft to SOE for supply-dropping, in May and June they directed SOE (which had already told Mihajlović to "await the decisive hour") to prevent a premature rising in Yugoslavia. This attitude of mind was closely related to what has been called the "T. E. Lawrence complex" which was then so prevalent in government circles—the belief that Britain could direct and control the time and manner in which each oppressed country was to be liberated, just as she had tried to do twenty-five years previously, and that Tito and Mihajlović could be induced to work docilely toward this end under British guidance and Mihajlović's local leadership. These beliefs rested on an out-of-date, almost Palmerstonian, conception of Britain's place in the world and on a grossly optimistic overestimate of her resources in men and matériel. They derived in part also from an inability to grasp the inflexible nature of the Communist creed. The DDMI Minute quoted in Appendix XII, A, is full of this outlook, which is even more strongly marked in a Minute of Eden's in April 1943; it can still be traced as late as August 1944—only a month before Tito "levanted" to Moscow—in a memorandum of Churchill's calling for Tito to make a public declaration that he would not impose communism on Yugoslavia after the end of the war.

In combination, these ideas long exercised a stultifying influence on British policy. Their grip was not significantly loosened until early in 1943, but circumstances were already suggesting that they should be discarded as outworn during the months when Alamein and TORCH were making closer contact with Mediterranean resistance movements both possible and militarily desirable.

The first sign of coming change, and of a realization that there could and should be a relationship between the Allied campaign in North Africa and the Yugoslavs' struggle in their homeland, came in late September 1942. Through SOE Cairo,

Alexander asked Mihajlović to cut the Balkan routes along which supplies were delivered to Rommel. With the same object in mind, an SOE party under Colonel Myers and Major Woodhouse was parachuted into Greece; before the end of November, they had blown up the Gorgopotamos bridge on the Salonika-Athens railway and effectively put this important arterial route out of action for six or seven weeks. The link between two theaters of war, which had hitherto always been considered in isolation, became still more manifest when planning for HUSKY (planning began in January 1943) required that as many Axis divisions as possible should be kept away from Sicily. Deception was one way of achieving this—the role of MINCEMEAT in luring German troops into the Balkans has already been discussed—and increased support to the resistance was another. But to which resistance movement?

Mihajlović did not respond to Alexander's request, but remained so inactive that British patience began to wear thin. Conversely, on the testimony of his self-appointed chronicler, Vladimir Dedijer, Tito was at once convinced by TORCH that although operating independently, the Partisans were already working in partnership with the British and Americans because they were causing the diversion to the Balkans of divisions which would otherwise have gone to Tunisia. (His perception of this novel state of affairs was shared by his enemies: The OKW War Diary dates the impact of the Partisans on the conduct of the war as a whole from the autumn of 1942.) With Hudson, now able to report more fully and more frequently than hitherto, giving a confident opinion that the Partisans' organization was far superior to Mihajlović's, by Christmas 1942 SOE both in London and in Cairo was beginning to realize that it might be worthwhile to contact the Partisans and enlist their cooperation. The Foreign Office, too, had doubts but stuck firmly to its pro-Mihajlović stance, and in mid-December Eden went so far as to consider the possibility of an approach to Tito, only to reject it.

By the end of 1942, then, circumstances invited a reassessment of British policy toward the Balkans in general and Yugoslavia in particular, and the process began early in the New Year. Before considering it, however, it is necessary to emphasize how little is certain about the nature and amount of intelligence concerning the Balkans which was available at the end of 1942 and the beginning of 1943. The subject is still veiled in an obscurity which the publication of *British Intelligence in the Second World War* has done little to dissipate.

Very few Balkan signals were transmitted over the Bletchley–Middle East link until the late spring of 1943: the move of the 5th Mountain Division into Greece in September 1941 and out again in November, the order of battle of the Italian occupation forces in Croatia in October, and evidence that the Italian Siena Division was being transported to Africa from Greek ports make up the whole tally, together with two solitary pieces of information in the whole of 1942. One of these noted the appointment of Generaloberst Loehr, hitherto commanding Luftflotte 4 in Russia, as Oberbefehlshaber Suedost and GOC Twelfth Army in July; another, in mid-September, showed Berlin warning Loehr, a month before Alamein, that the Allies might soon seek to regain their former ascendancy in the Mediterranean and might begin by assaulting Crete,[3] the depletion of whose garrison by the hasty transfer of 164th Division to Africa they had appreciated.

There are three possible explanations for this paucity of information. In the first place, no key specifically for use in the Balkans was decrypted until the spring of 1942. Secondly, so long as Rommel was beating at the gates of Egypt, Middle East commands had their hands too full to bother much with the Balkans; security regulations forbade the dissemination of intelligence to those who might be interested in it but who could not make use of it, and so most of the information which may have been available will have been restricted to teleprints or typed reports, which are still withheld from public view. Lastly, some police, Abwehr, and Sicherheitsdienst hand ciphers were being decrypted in both London and Cairo; some fragments of evidence from these sources can be found quoted in official corre-

---

[3] This marked another success for the deception planners, who had circulated rumors of a coming assault on Crete.

spondence and reports in the Public Record Office, but no systematic collection of it appears to exist.

The process which eventually led to the abandonment of Mihajlović and to the transfer of British support to Tito began in Cairo in January 1943. Early in that month, Brigadier Keble, the new Chief of Staff to the recently appointed head of SOE in Cairo, Lord Glenconner, handed certain decrypts of German signals to two of his subordinates, Captains Deakin and Davidson, pointing out that they showed the Partisans in a far better light than other information, notably that the Partisans were frequently enough in action against the Germans to cause them to mount such severe countermeasures that troops were being held in the Balkans instead of going elsewhere—that is to say, that the Partisans were in effect helping Britain and her allies. A fortnight after Keble's initiative, Ultra's first—and still isolated—important contribution to Balkan intelligence lent confirmation to his words: three signals of 17 January gave advance notice of an anti-Partisan drive (Operation WEISS, which began on 20 January) by four German, four Italian, and two Croat divisions.

On his way back from Adana, where he had been trying to persuade the Turks to enter the war (an unwise scheme which fortunately came to nothing), Churchill passed through Cairo at the end of January. Churchill interviewed Keble, who brought with him a memorandum which he, Deakin, and Davidson had drawn up for GHQ Cairo.[4] Churchill took a copy of the memorandum back to London. Based on the continuing inflow of decrypts, it made a strong case for British support to the Partisans, not to the exclusion of Mihajlović's Chetniks but in addition to it. The report stirred Churchill's interest and ensured an unprecedented measure of attention to the Partisans' doings at the highest level.[5] A dispatch from Colonel Bailey (who had re-

---

[4] Most accounts state that Keble arranged for Deakin, not himself, to show Churchill the memorandum, because Deakin had worked for Churchill before the war and therefore might get a better reception than a total stranger. Sir William Deakin assures me that this is incorrect.

[5] See Appendix XII, "Missing Links in the Chain of Yugoslav Intelligence," B.

cently become senior British liaison officer with Mihajlović), recommending separate spheres of influence for the two leaders, also contributed to the same end.

On his return to London, Churchill sent Keble's paper to Lord Selborne, head of SOE, and ordered "close contacts with the Jugoslav leaders." For a moment, Whitehall was even tempted to outdo Cairo by considering—what no one had yet envisaged—a complete break with Mihajlović, but the Foreign Office would go no further than to agree that assistance should be given to both. The Chiefs of Staff were somewhat cooler, but were prepared to allow four more Halifax aircraft to drop supplies to the Partisans.

During these same weeks, Mihajlović unwittingly drove a nail into his own coffin by a violently anti-British tirade (said, however, to have been delivered under the influence of plum brandy) to Bailey, whose report of the incident "hit the British government like a bombshell" and led Churchill to warn King Peter's government that if Mihajlović did not mend his ways, British support might be removed elsewhere. Tito escaped from the perils of WEISS, but had to force the crossing of the river Neretva against so much Chetnik opposition that he embarked upon negotiations with the Germans in mid-March (they were serious enough to involve Loehr in person at one stage, but ended without result), in the course of which his staff declared that the Chetniks were the Partisans' main enemy. London and Cairo were both aware of these negotiations by the middle of April.

The occupying powers were in fact negotiating with both sides at the same time, for Bailey reported more evidence of Mihajlović's collaboration in March and, as we now know, General Roatta, commanding the Italian Second Army, had recently maintained that he could not do without the Chetniks' support and had stood out against a German demand that they should be disarmed—a situation which disturbed Warlimont enough for him to make representations in Rome.

Against this background, the profound uncertainty in British circles about what was really happening in Yugoslavia stands out sharply. A Minute about what was to be done to exploit a successful HUSKY which Churchill sent to the Chiefs of Staff on 2 April contains this sentence: "I believe that in spite of his present naturally foxy attitude Mihajlović will throw his whole weight against the Italians the moment we are able to give him any effective help." Yet only a few days later the Yugoslav government in London, at British instigation, rebuked Mihajlović for stating publicly, "The Italians are my only support," and it was gradually becoming clear in April that in spite of WEISS the Partisans were gaining the upper hand in the civil war and were fatally weakening the Chetniks.

While all this was going on, Ultra was becoming a little more informative. There were five signals in February. Two dealt with reinforcements to Crete, and two more showed that the pattern of command in the Balkans was being reorganized—the Twelfth Army was upgraded to become Army Group E, with authority over the Italian Aegean Command—and three more German divisions were being drafted into Attica. These signals doubtless confirmed Berlin's September warning to Loehr and suggested the very real fear of a British attempt to open the Aegean which tormented Hitler and OKW even before MINCEMEAT and several weeks before Ultra first lent substance to the suggestion at the beginning of April. (There were in reality no British plans to open the Aegean, though MINCEMEAT hinted at them, but in April the Chiefs of Staff debated whether to seize a bridgehead at Durazzo to facilitate future operations in Yugoslavia.) A handful of signals in March and April pointed in the same direction and showed that the reinforcement of southern Greece was being severely hampered by the inadequate carrying capacity of the Belgrade-Salonika line and derailments caused by sabotage of the track in Greece.

Only in May 1943 did Ultra begin to be a regular source of intelligence about the Balkans: signals were transmitted on twenty of the thirty-one days in the month, and this rate was maintained throughout the summer. For the first time, too, Ultra began to bear directly on the operations of Partisans and Chetniks. On 15 May, a decrypt of the 5th described a conference between Warlimont and Comando Supremo and plans for action against Mihajlović by the Italians. No indication of where this would take place was given, and the connection between it and a German thrust "mainly from the north-west" was not clear; this was, however, evidently Operation SCHWARZ, which began in Montenegro on 15 May and lasted a month. On the same day, another decrypt (this time only twenty-four hours old) showed the Prinz Eugen SS Division under constant attack around Mostar (a little to the west of the chief SCHWARZ area) and alleged that the Partisans were striking at Serbia from Montenegro. This signal also showed that German-Italian disagreements over the right way to handle the Chetniks were continuing, and soon another revealed Warlimont trying to pour oil on troubled waters by offering to exempt the Montenegro area of operations from the disarming order. By the middle of May there had, in addition, been a large handful of signals giving the locations of German and Italian formations in Yugoslavia as well as all the evidence for the success of MINCEMEAT which has already been described.[6]

It was in an atmosphere composed of all these disparate elements that two Canadian Yugoslavs were briefed from the latest SD intercepts before they were parachuted into Yugoslavia on 20 April with orders to find out whether the Partisans were willing to accept a British mission. When an affirmative answer and full information about the progress of SCHWARZ were received, Deakin and a few companions jumped on the night of 25–26 May with such pinpoint accuracy that he and Tito met at once and escaped together from the German ring just before it closed round them. Shared dangers helped Deakin to ensure the success of the mission in establishing friendly contact with Tito as he extricated himself from the German trap, turned the Long March back on itself, and headed once more northwest toward Jajce and Bihać. Deakin's radio reports for the first time provided the British, through the instrumentality of SOE Cairo, with regular and reliable news of Partisan doings and showed on better evidence than before that they were a far larger thorn in German flesh than the Chetniks;

---

[6] Above, pp. 222–227.

but they also made it clear that the Partisans were an independent force, led by a guerrilla fighter of remarkable ability, which had to be reckoned with on its own valuation and could not be treated as a mere appendage or offshoot of British policy.

These were important developments which before long began to transform Mediterranean strategy as Yugoslavia came to be regarded as parallel to Italy in significance because both fronts were serving the same purpose—to divert German attention from east and west. A further phenomenon also strikes the historian of intelligence. It can hardly be a coincidence that Ultra signals about the Balkans greatly increase in number from the moment that London and Cairo began to take a greater interest in the area in the spring of 1943. It cannot yet be actually proved that material of the type which was now regularly signaled had been available in equal measure earlier but had been hidden from the eyes of those in the Middle East who might have used it to inform themselves better about the way the Axis was being forced to concentrate men and equipment in the Balkans, but it is almost impossible to escape this conclusion. At all events, the story of intelligence about wartime Yugoslavia takes on a new dimension in the summer of 1943 as Ultra begins to play a part in it comparable to that which it had been playing in North Africa for the past eighteen months. By the time the Chiefs of Staff Committee discussed the subject toward the end of June, Ultra had shown that over thirty German, Italian, Croat, and Bulgarian divisions were in Yugoslavia, most of them engaged in operations against the partisans, and before long Churchill called for a summary of recent Balkan Ultra, "as I want to have an absolutely factual presentation of the whole scene and balances."

One vital contrast with North Africa (and soon Sicily and Italy) must be stressed, however. There, signaled intelligence could be used, with due caution, by British generals to guide their strategy and tactics. In Yugoslavia there were neither generals nor armies, but only British liaison officers assigned to Partisan and Chetnik commanders; only tiny British forces ever operated even briefly on Yugoslav soil, and none of the usual security arrangements for the delivery of Ultra signals were ever made. Even had the British ever landed in force, the risks would probably still have been too great. Tito was immeasurably stronger and more secure on the anniversary of Deakin's parachute drop than he had been the year before, but nevertheless his headquarters at Drvar were overwhelmed by a well-planned German raid and he himself was nearly captured on 25 May 1944. There is a particular illustration of the way in which the risk of Ultra's becoming compromised in Yugoslavia was regarded: by breaking Tito's radio code, the Germans sometimes managed to discover the pattern of the recognition lights to be displayed on a Partisan airfield when a supply drop was expected, and distributed their knowledge in Enigma to those whose might use it to shoot down the aircraft. Any resultant Ultra signal always bore the note: "Comment by 'C': Not to be passed to units in the field."

The escape of the main body of Partisans ("very well led and militarily superior, about 15,000 strong") from the pincer movement of SCHWARZ could be watched in successive Ultra signals which were often only twenty-four hours behind the events they described, until the operation was declared at an end on 15 June with the claim that 7,500 Communists had been killed and 16 of their guns captured for loss of just over 3,000 German lives. (Self-delusion reached still greater proportions at Hitler's headquarters, where the compilers of the War Diary recorded the performance of the 7th SS (Prinz Eugen) and 1st Mountain divisions as having "touched the limits of the possible" and asserted that there was no coherent body of Partisans left.)

While this, the first thoroughly well-documented Partisan action with British blessing, was in progress, a new line of policy toward the Yugoslav resistance was being hammered out. The Foreign Office remained favorable to Mihajlović, but the Chiefs of Staff in London and the Middle East Defence Committee in Cairo (which asserted that "the Partisans are the most formidable anti-Axis element in Jugoslavia"), both with the benefit of Ultra, became increasingly hostile. Churchill seems to have espoused both points of view at the same time. Out of the clash of opinion there emerged by the end of June an agreed policy—to support both Mihajlović and Tito, Tito being warned that if he used British supplies to fight the Chetniks, he would be denied help in future.

On the night of 20–21 June, the Asopos viaduct on the Salonika-Athens line was blown by an ELAS party under SOE direction. This was part of the cover plan called ANIMALS, which had been devised to carry on the good work begun by MINCEMEAT of distracting the Germans' attention from HUSKY by persuading them that a large-scale landing in southern Greece was intended. Ultra reported the destruction of the viaduct by the following afternoon, adding that a temporary bridge was on order from Hungary, giving a preliminary estimate that through traffic would not be possible "for a considerable time" (it was not resumed until 1 September) and erroneously attributing the act to sabotage by Greek workmen employed to strengthen the structure. Many other cases of sabotage in Greece were reported, and the force guarding the alleged six hundred bridges along this vital supply line was enlarged. When in May and June several divisions (including the 1st Mountain, one of the four which had spearheaded SCHWARZ), all of them hastily reequipped so as to be ready for action again on 5 July, were ordered out of Yugoslavia to southern Greece to join those like the 1st Panzer which had already been drafted there, it was plain that the HUSKY cover plans were, for the time being at least, doing more to focus Axis attention on the Balkans than the activities of either Tito or Mihajlović. Fears that the Allies might be contemplating a seaborne descent upon Greece, the Aegean, or the Dodecanese persisted long after the landing in Sicily (which was held to have called for only 30 or 40 percent of the Allied shipping in the Mediterranean) and led to a demand for more tanks at the end of July. In addition, OB Southeast was reminded of the need to ensure proper protection of the vital bauxite traffic over the Croatian railways (the target for which was set at the astonishing figure of 35,000 tons a day from the Mostar mines to the main Belgrade-Zagreb line).

Very little striking intelligence is to be found in the Ultra signals between HUSKY in early July and AVALANCHE and ACHSE two months later. In some respects this merely reflects a period which was comparatively quiet, but in others it is more surprising. There is nothing, for instance, to show the extraordinary reversal in Tito's fortunes which these months witnessed: whereas in May he had only escaped by the skin of his teeth from SCHWARZ, by the late summer he had liberated a large part of the puppet state of Croatia between Zagreb (where "Communists" burnt the railway station down on 3 September) and Sarajevo, 150 miles farther south, and from there westward almost to the sea. The apparent absence of news of these developments may, however, be in part an illusion. As Balkan decrypts and signals multiplied, although there was still no possibility that any save those that provided shipping targets in the Adriatic or the Aegean could be used operationally, the danger loomed that processing them might take away from more pressing Italian business a disproportionate share of the time of intelligence officers and signals personnel in Hut 3. It therefore became customary from July 1943 until the end of the war to pare nonurgent Balkan items down to the bald facts, to allow them to accumulate for several days at a time, and then to send an omnibus signal incorporating a bunch of them under some such heading as "Jugoslav summary, x date to y date." The average length of these signals was perhaps six hundred words, but a significant number of them were two or three times as long, and there were often ten or a dozen a month. Patient investigation of them with the aid of a large-scale map might provide a remarkably detailed narrative of German countermeasures and hence of the doings of Partisans and Chetniks in the last two years of the war. Such an investigation would be out of place in a study of strategy, though, and has not been attempted here.

Memory suggests a further point. As already indicated, several new breaks into Balkan keys were made during the spring and summer; this can scarcely have been accidental, but is more likely to have been the consequence of an instruction to the cryptanalysts to produce more information about a new area of military and political interest. The result was a flood of decrypts, many of minimal intelligence value (in a rebellious occupied land, every trival communication had to go by radio), which would have overwhelmed the Hut 3 translation parties and intelligence officers and grossly overloaded the three daily teleprint and report series, which had already grown to gigantic proportions. Many of them, memory recalls, were carefully scrutinized for anything of value (which was, of course, processed in the ordinary way), while the German texts of the remainder were preserved untranslated. If these still exist—which seems doubtful—a still more detailed story could be told.

In sum, then, in a complete reversal of the situation a few months earlier, by the late summer of 1943 there was a surfeit of information about Yugoslavia, a good deal of which remains to be exploited by historians.

Ultra preserves, like flies in amber, two vestiges of the successive changes in the German command structure in the Balkans and Italy which were proposed in July and August, but their full meaning escaped understanding at the time. Three days after Rommel's twelve-hour tenure of authority in Greece as GOC Army Group B on 25 July[7]—of which, of course, the Allies knew nothing—a message (signaled as ML 9625 on 2 August) referred cryptically to a coming separation between Army Group B in Salonika and Army Group E in Belgrade. The next relevant news was on 18 August, in a two-day-old inquiry by the Chief of Staff of Army Group F (a formation which had never previously been recorded) for permission to establish a communications squadron for Army Group F in Belgrade; a comment to the signal conveying this information confessed to an inability to explain the contradictions, and although von Weichs was identified as GOC Army Group F in Belgrade by 23 August, it was not clear until the end of the month that on 26 August he had succeeded to the title of OB Southeast, and that Loehr's Army Group E in Greece and the Second Panzer Army in Yugoslavia were subordinate to him.

The chief concern of both Germans and Yugoslavs in the second week in September was by quick action to wring the

[7]See p. 243, above.

greatest possible advantage from the Italian surrender. The Germans professed themselves satisfied with the results of ACHSE, but it was the Partisans who won the race in Yugoslavia. Although, as he complained, Tito was given no warning of what was about to happen, he moved swiftly into Italian-occupied Dalmatia and by persuasion or force took possession of enough arms and equipment to double the size of his field army and to make it so much more formidable than hitherto that he was able to enlarge the area of territory he controlled very considerably. By the end of October, von Weichs was constrained to tell Hitler that "Tito is our most dangerous enemy" and that beating the Partisans was more important than repelling an Allied landing. Little news of the Partisans' successes came to light through Ultra until an intelligence report of 24 September to the effect that in pursuance of Tito's order for their main effort to be concentrated in northwestern Croatia, a large body of Partisans was moving in that direction from Split via Knin; this was shortly confirmed by a Foreign Armies West appreciation which added that Chetnik activity in southwest Serbia had also increased of late—welcome ammunition for those, now largely confined to the Foreign Office, who still thought Mihajlović a force to be reckoned with.[8]

Army Group B became, through its radio network, a rich source of information as soon as it moved into Lombardy under ACHSE, and the situation reports of the Army Group itself and of its subordinate formations opened up an area hitherto almost closed to Ultra and revealed that the Partisans' northward shift was bringing them into very close contact with the resistance in Slovenia, thus making clear the severity of the resultant threat to Hitler's strategy of obstinately holding on to Italy and the Balkans. From the start, these daily bulletins showed the Germans endeavoring to push eastward into Venezia Giulia and Slovenia, claiming (prematurely, as their own signals soon revealed) that they had quickly pacified Istria and its neighborhood. By 10 October they were meeting stiff Slovenian

---

[8]Some of the sabotage in southwest Serbia at this time was organized by British liaison officers acting contrary to Mihajlović's instructions, and so was presumably known to the Foreign Office.

resistance on a north-south line through Ljubljana and Ogulin and were engaging "guerrillas" who had crossed the old Austrian frontier. A list of the battle headquarters of formations under the First SS Panzer Army showed them still occupying the same line at the end of November.

In comparison, there was far less broad strategic information about the Sixth Offensive, the first phase of which ran from mid-September to mid-October and aimed at the recapture of the former Italian territories which the Partisans had seized, although many tactical details were recorded.

The most practically useful single Balkan item, in all probability, was one dated 3 October which estimated Partisan numbers in the Split-Dubrovnik area at between 160,000 and 200,000, for this was the section of coastline most accessible from the naval and air supply base on the island of Vis, which was reconnoitered and developed in September and October, as well as being not too far distant from the inland town of Visegrad, where a Chetnik party put the narrow-gauge Belgrade-Sarajevo line out of action for several months by blowing a bridge on 5 October.

The revelation of an extremely serious shortage of shipping in the eastern basin of the Mediterranean was another useful service which bore on the growing supply traffic to Tito across the Adriatic from Termoli in Italy. As soon as the evacuation of Elba and Corsica was complete, OKM ordered on 22 September, a large number of R-boats (small motor minesweepers/minelayers) were to be transported overland from Genoa to Venice and possibly onward to the Aegean—a kind of reverse mimicry of the Venetians' feat five hundred years earlier in sailing warships up the Adige and hauling them on rollers over the hills to Lake Garda to fight the Milanese. Motor gunboats operating from the coastal-force base at Bari sank seven out of the nine large German vessels which did try to break out to the Aegean in mid-October. One of the best-documented Adriatic naval engagements was the affair of the *Niobe* (a small cruiser of 1899 vintage, sold by Germany to Yugoslavia in 1926), which was bombed (evidently after an Ultra warning on 19 December) as it lay in wait to ambush Partisan groups crossing between islands from Hvar to Brac, ran aground, and was then torpedoed; Admiral Adriatic complained that three weeks' planning at Mostar had thus been rendered "unsatisfactory" (!), and the incident counts as one of the most important successes gained by the British coastal forces. Other intercepts at the turn of the year gave elaborate planning details, often with ample advance warning, of a host of small operations by which the Germans managed to regain almost all the Dalmatian islands they had lost in September. The sequence in which it was proposed to tackle the islands was laid down by the Second Panzer Army on 2 December, and over the next six weeks it was possible to keep track of the progress made and to interfere with it when practicable.

It will have been information of the above types which, although little of it could be turned to advantage, was Ultra's main contribution to military intelligence in the Balkans in the second half of 1943. In common with other sources, Ultra cast only an uncertain and flickering light on the matter of chief political concern—whether or not to abandon Mihajlović and channel all aid to Tito. An intercepted German appreciation of 29 August described Jevdjević, a Chetnik commander only loosely connected with Mihajlović but on good terms with the Italians, as prepared to recognize many features of the prevailing situation, ready to work with the Germans if they would help against the Partisans, and believing that Mihajlović concurred in general with this attitude but would prefer to deal with the Partisans on his own rather than with German support; he had not, however, been in recent contact with Mihajlović. Even though there might be reason to doubt the last disclaimer, this was very far short of an indictment of Mihajlović as a collaborator. Another equally inconclusive piece of evidence was not strictly Ultra, though passed over the Hut 3 teleprinter to our usual London recipients; quoting an intercepted communication between Abwehr Belgrade and Abwehr Zagreb, it recorded the signing of a treaty on 19 November between OB Southeast and one of the independent Chetnik commanders, Lukacević, under which there was to be a cease-fire in the Ibar valley district of southern Serbia, so that both parties could undertake joint action against the Communists. Mihajlović's name was not mentioned, but his headquarters was known to have been in the same area recently. By the end of the year, there was still no proof from what was by now the Allies' largest and most reliable source of intelligence that Mihajlović was personally involved in any act of collaboration, and only a couple of Abwehr decrypts at the beginning of December to implicate him.

There was therefore nothing to stand in the way of Maclean's "blockbuster" report of 6 November,[9] which recommended the discontinuance of support to Mihajlović and more aid to Tito, who now controlled twenty-six divisions and more than 200,000 men. Tito would undoubtedly set up a Communist regime in Yugoslavia after the war, but the Allies could not in any case control the Partisans and had better leave them to work out their future system of government for themselves. (This process in fact began three weeks later at the National Congress which met at Jajce on 29 November, proclaimed Tito Marshal and Prime Minister, and left open the questions of restoring the monarchy.) Founded on the evidence against Mihajlović which Deakin and others had collected, this chimed in well with Churchill's own strategic preferences. ("Great prizes lie in the Balkan direction," he had told Alexander on 29 July, qualifying this after AVALANCHE only by reserving priority to operations in Italy and insisting "Although we cannot fight a Balkan campaign ourselves, we ought to use enough force to stimulate others to do it."[10] The Supreme Commander in the Mediterranean, General Wilson, was firmly of the same opinion. In November he

---

[9]Brigadier Fitzroy Maclean, M.P., had been sent in September by Churchill to take over from Deakin (who, however, remained to assist the new mission until November) as his senior officer and to be responsible for British political advice to Tito. The story of his interview with Keble on his arrival in Cairo [Auty and Clogg, 223–24.] is irresistibly comic. In a parallel upgrading, Brigadier Armstrong superseded Bailey as head of mission to Mihajlović.

[10]Churchill remained an enthusiast for the ill-fated Cos-Leros expedition of autumn 1943, the only strategic benefit of which was the temporary diversion of a hundred or two German aircraft from the Russian front at a cost of nearly 5,000 men and 26 cruisers, destroyers, and other naval vessels. The combination of what appeared to be unwise direction and inept execution with forces inadequate to their tasks was so uncomfortably reminiscent of Crete and the early desert campaigns that—particularly as it occurred at the same time as the slowdown in Italy after Salerno—the effect was extremely depressing just when the fortunes of war seemed at last to have taken a turn for the better. See Appendix XIII, "Cos and Leros."

gave Mihajlović an ultimatum: prove your will to fight Germans by blowing two bridges on the Belgrade-Salonika railway by the end of the year, or forfeit British support. Mihajlović remained inactive, and the threat was carried out.

Amid the welter of "special operations," each with its own cover name, which fill the Ultra records—themselves now more voluminous than ever before—in late 1943 and early 1944, a few stand out. Viewed as a whole, they reveal the Partisans' astonishing progress since the autumn and von Weichs' terror at losing control of his (and still more Loehr's) 750-mile-long line of retreat back to the Reich. KUGELBLITZ ("Thunderbolt"), V SS Korps' effort to flush out and destroy three Communist divisions northeast of Sarajevo, which failed when the Partisan main body escaped on the night of 15–16 December, was one of the chief features of the second phase of what the Partisans called the Sixth Offensive. Many of these operations foretold attacks on the coastal islands to protect German seaborne traffic and prevent supplies from reaching the Partisans. Both objects would be advanced by the capture of the Allied base on the island of Vis, and under the name FREISCHUETZ ("Marksman") plans toward this end were repeatedly made throughout the spring, only to be as often postponed as the difficulty of mounting a powerful enough expedition became evident. Doenitz strongly advocated the operation, and OKM put forward a new plan on 6 April, but by that time Army Group F feared the logistical consequences of the shipping losses that might be incurred and the local naval authorities protested that they could not guarantee to resupply the expedition once it had landed, because of the "catastrophic air and strained sea situation"—thus confirming the two chief services the Allies were rendering to the Partisans.[11] Hitler eventually accepted these arguments of prudence and postponed FREISCHUETZ indefinitely on 23 April.

SCHLUESSELBLUME ("Cowslip") was to be seven interlocked operations in the second half of March by the 1st Moun-

[11]The RAF flew over 1,000 sorties during ROESSELSPRUNG (see p. 348, for instance), and by July were "paralysing seaborne supplies south of Split" (XL 1095).

tain and 42nd Jaeger divisions, and hoped to destroy guerrilla bands in western Slovenia by driving them into a valley in the mountains which lie between the rivers Sava and Drava, south of Virovitica—this at the same time as guerrilla activity had "flared up again" on the opposite bank of the Sava near Ogulin.

Signs that the urgent demands of other fronts were beginning to attract troops away from the Balkans in spite of the evident need to retain them there were not lacking, though rather patchily covered by Ultra. Thus at the end of December the 114th Jaeger Division was ordered from northern Dalmatia to Cassino (to release the Goering Division for France, though this latter move in fact never took place), and its anti-guerrilla actions en route could be traced in great detail. But the sudden switching of four divisions into Hungary in March—to reinforce those already falling back before the Russian advance, and to hold the line of the Carpathians—only became fully clear after the event.

On 25 May 1944 (the day the Cassino front joined up with the Anzio beachhead and preparations for D-day entered their last phase), a combined air and ground undertaking code-named ROESSELSPRUNG ("Knight's Move") attempted at OB's Southeast's orders to capture or kill Tito at his headquarters at Drvar in the Dinaric Alps between Sibenik and Bihać, where he had been settled since midwinter and where he felt so secure that he had even considered giving up mobile warfare and establishing a permanent stronghold. Tito had evaded capture for nearly three years, and his followers had continuously increased in number, while OB Southeast's hold on the Balkans was visibly weakening: all else having failed, ROESSELSPRUNG was a bold but despairing attempt to paralyze the Partisan leadership by novel means. There were three Ultra references to ROESSELSPRUNG before the raid, and nearly a hundred aircraft were moved to Croatia at short notice and for a limited period, but good German security saw to it that none of these messages gave the slightest clue to the meaning of ROESSELSPRUNG or hinted at any connection with Tito. A moderately complete account of ROESSELSPRUNG can be reconstructed from Ultra signals, but only with the benefit of hindsight and with the help of other evidence.[12]

Tito managed to escape by crawling out of a window and scrambling down a mountainside; rescued, he was flown to Bari for a few days and then to Vis, where he set up his headquarters and was for the first time isolated from his armies—which nevertheless quickly recovered from what might have been a disaster and soon regained all they had temporarily lost: the Drvar raid was no more than a momentary setback to the Partisan advance. From Vis, Tito visited Alexander at his advanced headquarters on the shores of Lake Bolsena in August, and then Churchill in Naples. Their conversations were friendly, but Tito soon began restricting the movements of Allied missions; the new Yugoslavia would be beholden to none, for, as he was to tell Fitzroy Maclean when explaining his flight to Moscow, "We are an independent state." Back on Vis at the end of August, to find Romania deserting the Axis to join the Allies, thereby "opening the door of the Balkans to Stalin's armies," and the Germans beginning to evacuate Greece, he suddenly flew off secretly to Moscow, not to reappear until he and the Russians entered Belgrade together in mid-October. These were not matters on which decrypted enemy signals could be expected to reveal much of value; it was a shot in the dark when an unspecified source claimed, in the immediate aftermath of the Drvar raid, that Tito had flown to London and would go on to Moscow.

It was a sign of increased Allied concern with Yugoslavia that an interservice Anglo-U.S. headquarters to coordinate trans-Adriatic operations was established at Bari on 1 June under the title "Balkan Air Force," and that it was provided with an Ultra link almost at once. The answers to two procedural signals about minutiae of army and GAF order of battle, preserved by chance in the files for late December, hint at the attention with which Ultra signals were followed at Bari, although

---

[12]This paragraph is based on a paper entitled "Ultra and Drvar" which I read to the Third Anglo-Jugoslav Colloquium on the Second World War at the Imperial War Museum in December 1982; it has since been published in *Journal of Contemporary History* 22 (1987), 195–208. It is unfortunate that Gilbert (vii. 779) gives further currency to the erroneous belief, stated in BI iii/1.165, that Ultra had given advance warning of German intentions. My paper shows this belief to be completely unfounded.

they could of course still not be used in the way that others were used by the Fifth or Eighth armies in Italy. Attention of this kind will have been particularly close after the inauguration on 1 September of a program, code-named RATWEEK, in which the Balkan Air Force and the Partisans worked together to harass the German retreat through Yugoslavia: for instance, a long complaint from von Weichs to Himmler, on 2 October, that he was at his wits' end to cope with the Russian advance northeast of Belgrade at the same time as heavy partisan pressure from the southeast; and a series of signals pointing out that the Germans could not afford to keep divisions idle along the coast waiting for an Anglo-U.S. invasion which was now considered unlikely, because there was urgent need for them to oppose the Russians farther inland, explaining Hitler's consequent order for coastal defense to be withdrawn into the mountains (the chosen line was approximately sketched out) in order to economize forces, and producing some details of the way in which these orders were to be implemented. Many other signals passing on orders for the successive evacuation of Dalmatian ports and harbors provided useful information to the British coastal forces, and an indication of the six routes by which Army Group E, having evacuated Greece, was now retreating northward, 250,000 strong, doubtless helped the RAF and USAAF to select bombing targets.

Evidence of the Germans' predicament continued to accumulate during the last months of the war: further movements of Army Group E and its deployment in December to assist Army Group F, whose functions it took over in March; an appreciation of the movements and intentions of Partisan brigades in January; instructions from Jodl to OB Southeast for the conduct of operations in the second half of February; OB Southeast situation reports galore, right up to the bitter end; and surprising proof that OKW was still trying to find ways of extricating what remained of OB Southeast's forces from the Russians' grasp and helping them toward Klagenfurt and the British as late as 5 May, the date of the general surrender.

Very little that was either new or of much interest emerged about the attitudes of Mihajlović and Tito during these months.

Some Chetniks were said to be fighting Russians southwest of Krusevac between Nis and Belgrade in August 1944, at the same time as others, bearing allegiance to Mihajlović, were fighting Germans. But within a few days the Abwehr officer of the Second Panzer Army reported that a German envoy was having conversations with Mihajlović in an endeavor to arrange common action against communism, and V SS Mountain Corps explained the sudden hostility of Chetniks in Bosnia and their sabotage of the Brod-Sarajevo railway by supposing that they had been promised an Allied landing on the coast in the near future. By 3 November, a delegate from Mihajlović was offering to assist Army Group E's retreat through the neighborhood of Sarajevo and to cooperate fully if the Allies were to announce the independence of Yugoslavia and to hand it over to Bolshevism; Army Group E was uncertain how trustworthy the offer was, however, because it was sure that Mihajlović was intent on striking the best bargain for himself and might well change sides unless handled adroitly.

This was all, apart from continuing evidence of Chetnik-Partisan conflict.

Finally, something should be said about an operation which is variously termed "the Istrian option" or "the Vienna Alternative." It never took place, but it engaged the attention of almost every major figure on both sides at one time or another, and Ultra was the source of a great deal of intelligence which would have been highly relevant had the operation ever materialized. Curiously enough, it was first mooted in an Allied cover plan and in anxious German imaginings. In the autumn of 1943, JAEL, the first draft of the OVERLORD cover plan, sought to implant the idea that the Allies would land in Istria; those who conceived it probably did not know that the ground had been partly prepared for them by an OKW appreciation of the previous February to the effect that the Allies had enough troops to open the Aegean but not enough to press on to the Danube, and were likely to attempt the former before long. Roosevelt combined Istria and the Danube at Tehran by suggesting an advance from the head of the Adriatic to Vienna; Churchill took it up enthusiastically and became one of its most persistent advocates.

Kesselring's fears had a much closer bearing on the operation which was contemplated in the summer of 1944 than any of this. As soon as he realized how disastrously wrong had been the overconfidence with which he assured Jodl, shortly before Anzio, that he did not fear for his open coastal flanks, he fell prey to constant apprehension that the same trick might be played on him again. From January 1944 onward, Ultra was full of alarmist reports—many of which he obviously took seriously, for his reactions were betrayed by the troop movements he ordered—and no part of the coastline was more frequently mentioned than Istria.

Such, in brief outline, was the background to Alexander's proposal, made directly after the capture of Rome in June 1944, to advance rapidly to the Po valley (he expected to reach it by August) and then exploit either westward to Genoa and France or to Venice and northeastward on into Austria; he made it plain that he much preferred the latter. The Chiefs of Staff received the proposal coldly, the Americans with outright hostility, for it would be impossible to mount both it and ANVIL at the same time, and they greatly preferred ANVIL. The scheme presupposed that Kesselring, his armies weakened by DIADEM, could be kept on the run until he reached the Alps, and in June this was a reasonable if slightly optimistic expectation. But the removal of the French and American divisions for ANVIL in August, in succession to the British divisions which had already left for OVERLORD, and the construction of the Gothic Line, behind which Kesselring rallied his troops, put paid to this hope. The "Vienna Alternative" never got beyond the status of an ideal third stage which might, if all went well, follow the two already envisaged: current operations, and those designed to follow directly upon them.

Two strategic and tactical considerations which had seemed to favor a thrust on Vienna in June turned steadily against it as time passed. Any such thrust would inevitably have to expose both its flanks. If Tito would undertake to protect the right, there would be no danger from that quarter; but as his attitude became more and more independent from the late summer onward (his friendly attitude toward Alexander at Lake Bolsena could not disguise an at best ambivalent attitude toward a British landing in either Istria or Dalmatia), this became increasingly doubtful. On the left flank, an Army Group C in the demoralized state in which it appeared to be in June might have presented no serious threat, but Kesselring managed to pull it together, and as the eastern, southern, and western fronts came closer together, troop movements from one to another became easier for the German command (Ultra supplied many examples of divisions being switched from one to another), and the force would be very vulnerable to a counterattack launched from the mountains of Austria, Bavaria, or Bohemia as it advanced through the "Ljubljana gap" in Slovenia to the Buergenland and Vienna.

Nevertheless, the proposition died hard. Alexander came to London in July and pressed it very strongly at a Cabinet meeting on 7 July, and he continued to hanker after it, although few seem to have agreed with him except Churchill (and Stalin, who, no doubt tongue in cheek, suggested during the Moscow conference in October that Britain should invade Istria as the first step toward a joint assault on Vienna). Proposing what was surely a riskily watered-down version of Alexander's original scheme, the British Chiefs of Staff recommended that Wilson should send four divisions to Vienna if Germany collapsed, and in the heady atmosphere of exhilaration between victory at Falaise in August and defeat at Arnhem in September, the Quebec conference authorized this. The second Quebec conference has been described as the nearest the "Vienna Alternative" came to being realized, and it was not until late in November, with something approaching a winter stalemate on all fronts, that the four-division scheme was canceled.[13]

By taking Budapest on 13 February 1945, the Russians made it impossible for an Anglo-American force to win the race for Vienna, and their capture of that city on 13 April presented Alexander with a *fait accompli*. The Allied move into Venezia Giulia in May was not a diluted version of the "alternative" but a different and much smaller operation; the firm yet delicate negotiations which were needed to avoid conflict with the Partisans over Trieste serve to underline the perils which would have attended the larger operation.

---

[13]For a full account, see my article "The Vienna Alternative: Reality or Illusion?," *Intelligence and National Security* iii (1988), 251–71.

12
Toward an Assessment

Is an objective assessment of the value of Ultra in the direction and conduct of the war now possible? The published opinions of generals and statesmen are few, banal, and uninformative: Eisenhower's letter to the head of the British SIS in July 1945, for example, to the effect that Ultra had been "of priceless value" to him and had "simplified my task enormously" is completely unenlightening. At second hand, it has been said of various generals that they welcomed or avoided Ultra briefings—that Patton did,[1] but Montgomery and Mark Clark did not, mold their actions in the light of intelligence—but airy charges like these are not to be taken seriously unless they are well attested and come from a reliable source. According to the testimony of Sir Edgar Williams, for instance—and what better witness could there be?—Montgomery listened to Ultra as willingly after Alam Halfa as before.[2] Medenine and Falaise support this view; Arnhem and the slow pursuit after Alamein seem to contradict it, but much else besides intelligence of necessity governed both these actions.

This is a reminder that an attempt to assess the significance of any type of intelligence must never forget that no statesman

---

[1] But only from August 1944 onward, after XL 5027 had given the first indications of Hitler's Mortain offensive, which led to the annihilation of two German armies in the Falaise pocket (Parrish, 223–26).
[2] Correspondence with the author, July and August 1986.

and no general is ever likely to take an important decision solely in the light of intelligence about the enemy. The constant factor in military decisions is the inconstancy of circumstances which, as they change, are bound to vary the weight which can be attached to intelligence. Thus Montgomery could reap the full benefit of his foreknowledge of Rommel's battle plan at Medenine because he had enough antitank guns to bring the attackers to a dead stop, whereas two years earlier, Wavell's and Freyberg's foreknowledge of Student's plans for the attack on Crete could not make up for a weapon state inadequate for the defense of the island. Just as shortage of men and weapons may rob intelligence of almost all its value, so the attitude of allies (or even neutrals) may restrain or redirect military action: we need look no farther than ANVIL for an illustration. Consequently, a veil of doubt and uncertainty always obscures the intelligence historian's vision.

Examples have been given in the foregoing pages of the beneficial use (within the limits imposed by security) of single items of tactical intelligence at the level of an army command or the equivalent, but the number of such cases is not unlimited, nor is their value outstanding. The main evidence for a true assessment of Ultra must be sought elsewhere.

Ultra's part in shaping strategy is much harder to determine. At the level of theater commander, Combined Chiefs of Staff, or War Cabinet, a single item of intelligence, however "juicy," can hardly ever be the sole determinant of action; accumulated information and deductions from it, the enemy attitudes and capabilities it reveals, will usually be far more decisive. The regular monitoring of Axis supplies and perhaps even more the regular order-of-battle information which Ultra provided continuously from the summer of 1942 onward are examples of this; the latter, for instance, told Alexander that he had achieved the three-to-one superiority in infantry between Cassino and the sea which he required for the DIADEM offensive, and Flivo reports of divisional movements and locations helped him to decide the timing of the breakout from the Anzio bridgehead.[3]

---

[3] Interview with Field Marshal Lord Harding of Petherton, who was Alexander's Chief of Staff at the time, 2 September 1982.

All in all, then, the question "What influence did Ultra have?" is not as easy to answer responsibly as it seemed in the first flush of excitement, when Ultra's existence had been admitted but no signals were yet opened to inspection; books written ten or more years ago are frequently inaccurate and misleading. The signals tell, on close examination, a much more complex tale than was then supposed. But even a perfect understanding of them cannot yield a completely satisfactory assessment of their part in shaping operations, for the direct (as distinct from the probable) link between knowledge and action is often missing. However, maturer reflection during the last few years has increased and deepened an estimate of Ultra's value rather than diminished it.

The most fascinating, but also the most elusive, element in all historical inquiry is not to establish the mere sequence of events but to discover the reason why they fell into a particular pattern. It is consequently most unfortunate that the senior Allied commanders were not invited to set down in confidence their thoughts about the use Ultra had been to them while their memories were still fresh in the years immediately after the war. Their judgments would have been no less fallible than those of any other human, but they themselves were better informed on this specific point than anyone can now hope to be. The failure to record their opinions has deprived later generations of probably the single most valuable ingredient required in any attempt to assess the practical value of an intelligence source more profuse in quantity and more reliable in quality than any to which the combatants in previous wars—or the Germans in World War II—had access, and has forced us to rely uncomfortably often on probability, the dangerous argument of "must have been." The masses of documents, Ultra and other, which are now available cannot be an entirely satisfactory substitute for the recollections of the participants—though they may provide a salutary check on the accuracy of survivors' memories—for as a rule they record facts or decisions, not the reasons for them; like the minutes of meetings, they habitually gloss over the debates and disagreements which precede an awkward choice between alternative courses of action. The records of one set of meetings—those of the Joint Intelligence Committee, whose task it was to analyze and digest intelligence and report on it to the Chiefs of Staff and the Prime Minister—might make up for the lack of firsthand accounts of Ultra's value, but they have not yet been released into the public domain.

Like their British counterparts, U.S. admirals and generals left no record of their use of Ultra. On the other hand, the intelligence officers attached to U.S. commands in northwest Europe in 1944–45 to receive Ultra and bring deductions from it to the notice of their superiors were required to write an account of their experiences. As junior officers (most were captains or majors), they knew little of the wider context and nothing of the responsibilities of command. Their accounts throw up several straightforward examples of tactical Ultra, but only one of strategic significance in the Mediterranean: the Hitler order to evacuate southern France directly after the ANVIL/DRAGOON landing prompted the U.S. 6th Army Group into quicker and more carefree pursuit because it showed that a flank attack on it from across the Alps was improbable.

Because so little firsthand evidence survives, all that can be done today is to use the documents to examine actions strictly in the light of what the combatants knew at the time. But this is to rely on circumstantial evidence, a notoriously untrustworthy guide. *Post hoc* is not necessarily *propter hoc;* the murder may not have been committed by the obvious suspect. Circumstantial evidence cannot reveal motive; although a decision may appear to depend on intelligence, it may really have been taken for quite different reasons. Since no other course is now open, however, the risk must be run. On this basis, what conclusions can safely be drawn about the part played by Ultra during four years of war in the Mediterranean?

Despite the many examples of Ultra leading the Royal Navy and the Royal Air Force to their targets—the convoys that supplied Rommel's armies—major influence cannot be claimed for it with quite as much confidence in 1941 as in 1942 and later; the technique of interpreting the signals was as yet imperfectly understood, and it is notoriously difficult to assess economic evidence in absolute terms. However, a striking foretaste of the source's future possibilities had been given as early as the battle for Crete in May—barely three months after Mediterranean Ultra began to flow freely—and arguably something more as well. If Rommel had received all the reinforcements destined for him, he would presumably have been able to achieve more than he actually did. May it not be, then, that with the petrol and weapons Ultra sent to the bottom he might have broken through to the Nile Delta at Christmas 1941 or at some time during the next six months? Did Ultra's part in halving German aircraft fuel stocks in the forward area during the summer and early autumn and in reducing reserves in Tripolitania by 90 percent make it in effect the savior of Egypt? If this is granted, then Ultra must be accorded a large part of the credit for preventing the disasters of that period from being a great deal worse than they actually were. A British recovery would have been far more difficult in January or June 1942 from a base far up the Nile valley than it actually was in August and September from the Delta.

One reason for the disasters of early 1942 was the absence, until midsummer, of regular Ultra news of the ground situation. This contributed toward the serious errors made by the military intelligence staffs in the Middle East, whose unaided estimates of Panzer Army's tank strength were very inaccurate until the summer, and although Ultra correctly forecast the date of Rommel's May offensive, it gave no advance warning that he would strike for Tobruk by a circuitous route round Bir Hacheim, foreknowledge of which might perhaps have prevented some of the worst British command errors.

Cryptographic advances gradually corrected this imbalance. Order-of-battle information (considered by some to have been Ultra's most valuable contribution, especially later on in Italy) became more plentiful, up-to-the minute tactical news helped Auchinleck halt Panzer Army's progress on the line of defenses being hastily thrown up at Alamein, and careful analysis of the great bulk of logistical information which was now coming in made it possible for the first time to appreciate fully the handicaps under which the enemy was operating, and to bend every effort toward making his predicament still worse.[4] Before long it was plain that he was barely managing to live from hand to mouth, and that the resumed heavy air and sea attacks on his communications were reducing his tactical options to the single and increasingly difficult task of survival. The weeks before Alamein marked an indubitable strategic success for Ultra.

It is not surprising that the rising tide of partnership between intelligence and operations should have ebbed with the TORCH landing, nor that many of the Eighth Army's mistakes should be repeated in Tunisia, for all the Americans and most of the British—fighting soldiers and intelligence staffs alike—were without battle experience. At Kasserine in February 1943 an intelligence failure coincided with a command failure to bring about a sharp, though temporary, reverse. More interesting for the present purpose, however, is the apparent cooling of the partnership in its original home, the Eighth Army. The seeming disregard of Ultra in November and December 1942 is instructive, for it shows up the difficulty of rediscovering motive forty years on. The Ultra evidence suggests that Montgomery missed several chances of utterly destroying Panzer Army between Alamein and Tripoli. Was he rightly deterred from taking risks, on the other hand, by the difficulty of supplying his spearheads so far from base, by the knowledge that his army was still incompletely trained and that part of it more than half expected another "Benghazi handicap," or by a temperamental preference for "balance" and meticulous preparation over disorderly haste? His own published accounts make no attempt to resolve the conflict or to explain how he reached his decisions. The riddle must now remain without an answer, cloaked by the dark saying of Sir Edgar Williams that "The brilliant improvisation

---

[4]The late Lieutenant General Sir Terence Airey, who was Alexander's Chief Intelligence Officer from August 1942 onward, pointed out to me in a conversation in August 1982 how items of these and other kinds could be combined to yield valuable intelligence. Ultra evidence that base petrol stocks were rising might suggest a coming offensive; then, later on, Y Service reports that a particular division or divisions had been ordered to send lorries to top up its or their petrol tanks from army dumps, and Flivo announcements of divisional movements in Enigma might complement this by giving tactical warning that the attack was about to take place.

which cut off the Italians at Beda Fomm in February 1941 was not in Montgomery's repertoire."

The hiatus in the intimate relationship between intelligence and operations ended with the invasion of the Italian mainland, and from then until the end of the war there followed a succession of instances in which positive evidence or clear inference reveals the unmistakable impact of the one upon the other. The political and military directive to Eisenhower—to attract as many German troops to Italy as possible and hold them there—required for its fulfillment as complete a knowledge as could be attained of the enemy's proposed defensive strategy, the line or lines on which resistance would be ordered, the number and weapon strength of the divisions to be employed, and, above all, whether he was reinforcing or reducing his forces in Italy. Because the Allies had at first mistakenly anticipated an unopposed march of liberation northward through Italy, and because Hitler was for some time in doubt whether to fight or to evacuate the peninsula, the timeliness with which these things could be discovered was of special importance. It must be counted among Ultra's greatest services that it found the answers to all these questions almost as soon as Hitler had made up his mind what to do. The disclosure, at the beginning of October 1943, of Hitler's intention to stand firm south of Rome was of immediate and decisive importance, for it showed him prepared to fall willing victim to Allied strategy and bound to respond in future to every sign of pressure by releasing troops from other theaters to man successive defense lines in Italy. Only the necessity of removing battle-hardened British and American divisions to England in readiness for OVERLORD, and later for ANVIL, stood in the way of extracting maximum advantage from this knowledge.

Alexander had been transferred from Cairo to Algiers in February 1943 as Army Group commander, a post he continued to hold until he succeeded Wilson as Supreme Allied Commander Mediterranean in December 1944. Like so many others, he left no record of his debt to Ultra, but two[5] of those who worked most closely with him in Italy are well qualified to speak

---

[5] Three, until General Airey's untimely death in 1983.

for him and to describe his reliance on Ultra: Lord Harding, his
Chief of Staff for twelve months, and Sir David Hunt, who, as
Lieutenant Colonel GSO 1, was Airey's deputy as Chief Intelligence Officer and later assisted Alexander in writing his official
Despatches (in which it is consequently possible to discern some
of the influence of Ultra on operational decisions by judicious
reading between the lines). Their unanimous testimony is that
Alexander paid close attention to intelligence,[6] particularly to
Ultra, that it sharpened his instinctive "feel" for the battle, and,
by frequently letting him know the orders under which his opposite number, Kesselring, was operating, enabled him to turn
to still greater advantage the insight into the German military
mind which his experience of commanding German troops in
Latvia in 1919–20 had first given him. In Lord Harding's opinion, it was only Ultra's proof that the Allied campaign in Italy
was continuing to draw German divisions away from east and
west that lent cogency to Alexander's demand to be allowed to
retain enough troops, despite the losses inflicted on him for the
benefit of OVERLORD and ANVIL, to keep up the pressure
which the Combined Chiefs of Staff directives had laid upon
him: that is to say, that in this respect Ultra had a decisive influence upon long-term strategy in the Mediterranean theater. The
case of Army Group B, which was drafted into Lombardy at the
time of the Italian surrender to overawe the population and to
form a strategic reserve, is but one illustration among many of
the value of order-of-battle information; before long, some of
Army Group B's divisions were found to be dispersing to other
theaters and others to be moving southward to the Italian
front—i.e., Ultra showed that part of the strategic reserve was
still being kept away from other fronts to fight an unnecessary
campaign in Italy.

Foreknowledge that the enemy was not expecting the Anzio
landing reassured the Allied command in January 1944, but the
potentially critical intelligence that the road to Rome was open
for a few hours was not, in the peculiar circumstances, of any

---

[6]In correspondence and discussions with the author, 1982–86. I should like to express
my particular gratitude to both of them for the kindly patience with which they have
received my inquiries.

practical use at all. A month later, Ultra's warning of Kesselring's plan for a lethal counterattack played a crucial part in saving the bridgehead from being obliterated—"one of the most valuable decrypts of the whole war," which is credited with converting Mark Clark from skepticism to respect for Ultra. Of equal value was the revelation, after the counterattack had failed, of Kesselring's intention to construct further defense lines south of Rome, for it confirmed that the best way to relieve pressure in east and west was still to maintain a lively initiative in Italy. Like the preparations for Alamein, the preparation for the DIADEM offensive in May—a prime example of this initiative—gained a great deal from the regular analysis of German resources; the happy combination of intelligence and operations was particularly well displayed in Ultra's demonstration of the enemy's weaknesses and his ignorance of Allied plans.

Ultra was unquestionably prominent in the conflict of opinion about the strategy to be followed after the fall of Rome. Aware that the fighting round Cassino had fulfilled its purpose of weakening the opposition, Alexander wanted to "go for the kill" at once; had he not had to surrender several French and American divisions for ANVIL, he might have achieved his purpose—to reach Lombardy by autumn. Piquancy is retrospectively added to the furious debates between the British and American Chiefs of Staff in June by the realization that a single most revealing decrypt—it showed that nothing would be gained by a landing in the south of France which was not already ensured by prosecuting the Italian campaign actively—was delayed by cryptographic difficulties until too late to affect the issue. This may have been one of the turning points where history failed to turn: this single piece of intelligence, had it been available sooner, might perhaps have led to a different decision, a quick and overwhelming victory in Italy, an end to the war in 1944, and a different partition of Europe.

The same pattern of intelligence which preceded Alamein and DIADEM was repeated in April 1945 for the *coup de grace*. Ultra showed that German tank losses were not being made good and that once more some of the best divisions had been successfully lured away from real to imaginary danger points by

Allied deception and a misreading of Allied intentions. As they celebrated victory in May, Alexander and Mark Clark could console themselves for the depletion of their forces in 1943 and 1944 by reflecting that they had fulfilled the duty laid upon them by holding some of the best German troops away from other fronts and had gone far beyond it by defeating them roundly into the bargain. It would be difficult to overrate the assistance Ultra had given them at every stage.

Although, unhappily, it is not easy to provide entirely satisfactory proof in every instance, there can be no doubt that this general conclusion is sound. Many things have changed since World War II ended more than forty years ago, weapons and signals intelligence among them. Would a similar generalization hold good today, or has past experience taught the present nothing? For instance:

Do the British and American armed services still accord intelligence the prime position it had won by 1945? The conduct of operations in Vietnam and the Falklands suggests that they do not. If General Sir Frank Kitson's recent *Warfare as a Whole* is any guide to current opinion, then there has been an alarming regression to the state of mind which prevailed in the 1930s, for General Kitson allots only one paragraph to intelligence among his many proposals for reforming the British army.

Could intelligence be distributed to the field commanders who could use it in time to assist them in their operations? Gordon Welchman, the former head of the Enigma decryption team at Bletchley Park, who later worked in the communications field for many years, seriously doubted this when he wrote *The Hut Six Story* in 1982, and the introduction of long-range missiles with nuclear warheads has speeded up operations so much since 1945 that decisions must be taken far more quickly than forty years ago.

Was Ultra unrepeatable, or could signals intelligence provide military intelligence in comparable quantity, quality, and reliability today? The answer is, very properly, secret. We can only hope that it could, but meanwhile we should certainly prepare an intelligence system ready to meet all circumstances.

Intelligence is no more exempt from the consequences of

scientific discovery than gunnery or submarine warfare, but the lineaments of some timeless principles may nevertheless be discerned in the experiences of the past. Among them is the necessity to scrutinize intelligence and its sources closely enough to avoid errors like those of 1941 (when Ultra told less about Rommel's strength and plans than seems to have been realized), 1942 (when Ultra gave more hints of the tank reinforcements Rommel was receiving than Cairo ever supposed), and 1944 (when the ineradicable human tendency to fit new information into existing patterns of thought caused the German intention to attack in the Ardennes to be construed as defensive preparations). Finally, the Pacific war provides a valuable reminder that no source, however good, will ever tell all: after the battle of Midway, which he had helped Nimitz to win by skillfully interpreting Japanese decrypts, Admiral Layton shudderingly reflected that "radio intelligence, which had provided us with the key to victory, could just as easily have been our undoing."

This book has dealt with historical events which, though more recent, belong as irrevocably to the past as the Battle of Hastings. The novel intelligence methods devised between 1940 and 1945 could not be applied again without modification, but there is every reason to suppose that new inventions and discoveries do not completely sever continuity, because they do not completely obliterate the human fallibility upon which all intelligence ultimately depends, and that it is therefore reasonable to believe that the past may have something to teach the present and the future. A historical study of the relation of intelligence and strategy in World War II may therefore appropriately end with an urgent plea that the lessons and experiences of the 1940s should be borne prominently in mind by those whose duty it is to defend the western alliance today.

APPENDIX I:
Signals to Commands Abroad*

Very approximately, the number of signals dispatched daily from Hut 3 to commands abroad at different periods was as follows:

March–November 1941	10 or less	First clashes in the desert
December 1941–May 1942	30–40	CRUSADER
June–October 1942	70–80	Tobruk to Alamein
November 1942–April 1943	90–100	Alamein to the surrender in Tunisia
May–June 1943	70–80	Between campaigns
July–September 1943	100–120	Sicily and Salerno
October 1943–March 1944	70–80**	Anzio
April–May 1944	80–100	DIADEM
June–August 1944	120–140	Advance to Florence; D-day and Falaise
September 1944–April 1945	90-100	The Gothic Line, OLIVE; Arnhem, crossing the Rhine

*See p. 20
**Signals were sent to SHAEF and other western commands from January 1944.

It is of some interest to note that fewer than 2,000 signals were dispatched during the first six months, only about 8,000 by the fall of Tobruk in June 1942, and 15,000 by Alamein. By the end of the war, almost 100,000 had been sent.

In the early days, only two or three headquarters in Egypt were served, but the service was progressively extended, and by 1945 sixty or more navy, army, and air headquarters had at one time or another been recipients.

Signals were prefixed OL, MK, etc. (usually 9999 of each series), as quoted in the reference notes. The complete series, in historical order, was OL, MK, MKA, QT, VM, ML, JP, VL, KV, XL, HP, BT, KO. All are now in the Public Record Office, in class DEFE 3, together with the small C series.

APPENDIX II:
The Mood of Early 1941*

The extent to which ill-founded optimism and even wish fulfillment seem for a moment to have replaced a sound grasp of
reality in the spring of 1941 is well illustrated in a cable Churchill sent to the acting Prime Minister of Australia on 29 March,
on the morrow of the naval victory over the Italians at Cape
Matapan and two days after the Simović coup d'état in
Yugoslavia (but also two days after the first Enigma evidence
that German troops were massing against Yugoslavia as well as
Russia). The change of government in Yugoslavia, wrote Churchill, had suddenly turned LUSTRE from "a military adventure
dictated by noblesse oblige" into "a prime mover in a larger
design" to protect the Balkans from Hitler. Yet it had long been
known that German troops were concentrating in Poland and
the northern Balkans for the attack on Russia which Churchill
had himself predicted as long ago as June 1940, and the Enigma
messages of 27 March had just given a very clear pointer to current German intentions: an order for three panzer divisions to
move from the Balkans to Cracow was canceled within twelve
hours of the Simović coup. The scale of preparations for BAR-
BAROSSA, the attack on Russia, was known to be so great that
it now seems an inescapable inference that the temporary diver-

---

*See p. 34.

sion of only a few more divisions and the necessary supporting aircraft would be enough to overwhelm everything Britain and all her possible Balkan allies could bring against them. After the narrow escapes of the Battle of Britain and from invasion in 1940, followed by the long-drawn-out winter Blitz, the Simović coup and Matapan, coming within forty-eight hours of each other, seem to have provided so welcome a relief that they clouded judgment in a rosy haze and created a feeling that (as Alan Moorehead wrote at the time) "fortune was with us and the Greek adventure could go forward with success."

APPENDIX III:
Auchinleck, Montgomery, and Rommel*

Needless to say, Ultra throws no light on the other aspect of the controversy—whether or not Auchinleck was prepared if necessary to retreat first into the Delta and then up the Nile valley. (General Richardson, who was ordered by Auchinleck to draw it up, outlines the plan in *Flashback,* 104.) Here again, the search for a solution in absolute, black-or-white terms has obscured the military realities. A "worst case" plan (and Auchinleck's was never more than this) carried a psychological risk, because it was bound to invite the defenders to look over their shoulders to the rear from time to time, instead of concentrating their whole gaze to the front and on the enemy. However important it would have been, in the event of defeat at Alamein, to keep the army 'in being' to protect Gulf oil, there is no doubt that by proclaiming, "Here we will stand and fight; there will be no further withdrawal. . . . We will stand and fight *here*. If we can't stay here alive, then let us stay here dead," Montgomery raised the morale of the Eighth Army at a stroke. His words struck the psychological note which suited the circumstances; they had the desired effect at the time, and they formed one of the foundations of victory at Alamein. But this must not prevent the historian from recognizing that no distinction can be drawn *in principle* between Montgomery's proclamation of 13

---

*See pp. 133, 148.

August and Hitler's repeated "No retreat, fight to the last man and the last round" edicts. Only *different circumstances* made the one right and the others always wrong. But for Hitler's misplaced bravado on 3 November, Rommel could have saved more men, tanks, and guns to fight another day, although he had lost the battle of Alamein; at the beginning of the previous August, on the other hand, the Eighth Army did not lack resources sufficient to hold off any attack Panzer Army could mount, but for a moment it had lost purpose and direction. In absolute terms, "No retreat, no surrender" can hardly be justified except when there is no alternative—retreat or rescue being impossible, and surrender dishonorable.

Rommel faced the same situation in the weeks after Alamein as Auchinleck after Tobruk, and his description of it sets out the rationale of the 'army in being' viewpoint. Commenting on Mussolini's order to resist to the end at Buerat, he wrote, "How did Mussolini imagine such actions were fought? I had really done all I could to arouse some understanding of the art of desert warfare in our higher commands and had particularly emphasized that to concern oneself with territory was mere prejudice. The all-important principle was to keep on the move until a tactically favourable position for battle was found, and then to fight."

APPENDIX IV:
A Shortened War?*

It is by no means certain that an earlier capture of Tunis would have shortened the war. Presumably the invasion of Sicily would have come before July 1943, for the British Chiefs of Staff had been considering it even before Alamein, and an earlier invasion of Italy might well have followed. More rapid progress would have been made than in HUSKY or AVALANCHE, since far fewer German troops were deployed in the peninsula in the spring than in the autumn of 1943.

It is very much less likely that OVERLORD would have been brought forward, or that it could have succeeded if it had taken place earlier than the summer of 1944. Neither British nor American war production was even approaching full spate by the end of 1942, nor had either country yet unfolded its maximum air power. Victory in the battle of the Atlantic was still six months away, and the supply line across the ocean was therefore still insecure. It was only the experience that the Eighth Army gained in fighting its way from Alamein to Mareth which made it the highly efficient fighting machine it was by the spring of 1943; it had not reached that stage by Christmas. United States troops were entirely without combat experience in 1942; Kasserine taught lessons which were learned with amazing rapidity, but

---

*See p. 162.

Kasserine was not until mid-February 1943. By contrast, the German army's strength was only just beginning to wane after Alamein and Stalingrad (January 1943), and its level of training was still higher than that of the Allied armies or than its own was when it faced the Normandy landing eighteen months later. Moreover, had an early capture of Tunis denied Hitler the chance—which in the event he foolishly took—of reinforcing North Africa, most of the 230,000 Germans who surrendered on Cape Bon would have been in arms on D-day, whether that had been in 1943 or 1944.

Any invasion force that could have been put ashore in northwest Europe in 1943 (and it is very doubtful whether the necessary landingcraft and other matériel could have been assembled) would have been far too weak and far too short of equipment, preparation, and properly trained commanders to survive for more than a short time; either withdrawal or annihilation would have tended rather to lengthen than to shorten the war.

Brooke's reasons for deferring OVERLORD until 1944 are even stronger in retrospect than they were when he urged them against Americans itching for action and Russians scornful of delay. Later arguments to the contrary appear feeble and ill-conceived beside his solid wisdom.

Little of this can have been in Montgomery's mind, however, as he shaped the tactics of pursuit. On the other hand, he knew that an intention to open the Mediterranean by invading Italy (GYMNAST) had been in the air since mid-1941 or earlier, and that in the autumn of 1942 the Chiefs of Staff were anxious to complete the clearing of North Africa as quickly as possible so that they might plan future strategy with a free hand. It is against this background that his dilatoriness in pursuit must be judged. (See chapter 7.)

APPENDIX V:
Axis Supplies Before Kasserine*

The bearing of the Axis supply position on its offensive capability in February 1943, and above all the Allied estimate of it, is a crucial question to which it is not easy to give a clear answer. That the position was very bad is uncontested. Warlimont visited Tunisia between 5 and 14 February (Ultra gave notice of his trip but knew nothing of the report he made after it), discussed supply at length with all three senior commanders, and reported back to Hitler (who listened to only part of what Warlimont had to say before flying off to visit the south Russian front). His main points were these: at the current rate of sinkings, there would be no supply ships left by June or July; ammunition, fuel, and food were desperately short, as they had usually been since the start of the African campaign, and the best monthly rate of inflow that could be expected was less than half what was required; and it was scarcely safe to risk the planned strike against Tebessa. In sum, the Axis position in Tunisia was "a house of cards."

Warlimont's views were, of course, not known in London or Algiers, but much of the material on which he founded them were common knowledge. Since the beginning of January (the situation then is discussed on page 179, above), two reports

---

*See p. 203.

from Rommel showing that his army was living from hand to mouth for ammunition, petrol, and rations, daily unloading returns from Tunis and Bizerta (now usually detailing cargoes, including tanks), and the known sinkings (many caused by Ultra and almost all reported in Ultra)—notably that of the tankers *Thorsheimer* and *Baalbek,* sent to the bottom with over 8,000 tons of fuel at the height of the Kasserine battle (a comprehensive return of army-fuel stocks at Tunis, Bizerta, Gabès, Sfax, and Sousse enabled its exact impact to be assessed)—had combined to show how desperate the situation was. (Formal confirmation of this came at the end of the month with the release of the February unloading figures for all the Tunisian harbors.) To conclude, therefore, as the intelligence staff at Algiers did, that the Axis had not the resources to mount an offensive was not unreasonable.

What this thoroughly rational conclusion overlooked was the known "bullish" attitude of both Kesselring and Rommel and the latter's record of attempting the impossible and bringing it off. The intellectual problem involved in balancing these two opposite considerations against each other is reminiscent of that in the desert in 1941, and the wrong conclusion was again reached for the same reasons. It is probable that the Cairo staff, with their hard-won greater experience, would have come to a less cut-and-dried conclusion on the same evidence.

Had Mockler-Ferryman known of an intercept about Rommel's health decrypted as long ago as 25 January, he would no doubt have felt still more confident in his reading of the rest of the Ultra intelligence, and Eisenhower would have been less justified in his subsequent complaints about it. But under the procedures introduced after the security alarm over the news of Rommel's illness in August 1942, no mention of this decrypt was made to commands abroad. It recorded the opinion of Rommel's doctor, Professor Horster, that Rommel had been unwell since the previous summer: his symptoms included low blood pressure, physical and mental fatigue, and sleeplessness, and the medical recommendation was that he should leave Africa to resume the interrupted treatment and stay in a European climate for some time.

The recommendation was accepted, but no date had been set when, noticing how precipitate was the American withdrawal after the Faid–Sidi bou Zid attack on their flank, Rommel saw a sudden chance to strike through Tebessa at Eisenhower's rear, cast off the depression which had been plaguing him, briefly regained his old energy, and took the defenders of Kasserine by surprise.

APPENDIX VI:
The Intelligence Aftermath of Kasserine*

A short-lived attempt has recently been made to exonerate Mockler-Ferryman. In his biography of Eisenhower, *The Supreme Commander* (Cassell, 1971), 173, Stephen Ambrose accepted Eisenhower's account, as most writers have done. Ten years later (*Journal of Contemporary History* 16, p. 165 n. 17), he claimed to have evidence that Mockler-Ferryman had made no mistake and had only been dismissed because Eisenhower had to balance his sacking of Fredendall, the American II Corps commander responsible for the faulty troop dispositions, by getting rid of an Englishman too. Ambrose relied on what he had been told that the second volume (then being written) of the British intelligence history would say. This volume, published in 1982, does try to exculpate Mockler-Ferryman, but rather unconvincingly. In *Eisenhower* (Allen and Unwin, 1984), 227–29, Ambrose returned to his earlier version; he did not refer to *British Intelligence,* nor did he link the two dismissals. In fact, although Mockler-Ferryman was dismissed immediately (20 February), Fredendall survived until 6 March before being replaced by Patton. Mockler-Ferryman was replaced by Major General Kenneth Strong, who remained with Eisenhower until the end of the war.

---

*See p. 209.

APPENDIX VII:
STRANGLE*

Most modern accounts—for instance, STC 451 and MME v. 816—credit STRANGLE with little more than nuisance value and point out that supplies always did manage to get through. But when STRANGLE began in March 1944, there were high hopes that the unprecedented severity of this offensive against an army's means of living and fighting might suffice on its own to paralyze Kesselring's force into defeat. (Were comparisons ever made, one is now inclined to ask, with the air and sea assault on Rommel's trans-Mediterranean supply routes in 1941 and 1942? These, in fact, twice came a good deal nearer to strangling Panzer Army Africa than STRANGLE did OB Southwest's command, but never managed to achieve that object. There was a lesson to be learned here.)

After only a month of STRANGLE, Air Marshal Slessor, C-in-C RAF Middle East and deputy to the American General Eaker as commander of the Mediterranean Allied Air Forces, had begun to realize that its best prospects were far more modest, and by the middle of June had become convinced that air power alone "cannot enforce a withdrawal by drying up the flow of essential supplies nor entirely prevent the movement of strategic reserves to the battlefront."

---

*See p. 277.

The problems inseparable from the assessment and interpretation of bomb-damage reports and the contradictory nature of the conclusions to be drawn from them are well illustrated in a long (twelve-page) report from the German Director of Transport in Italy nearly a year later. By going into exceptional detail and by ranging right across northern Italy and beyond, from Turin and Milan in the west to the Brenner and Ljubljana in Slovenia, it conveyed an impression of the tremendous damage which a single day's raids could do. But the Director of Transport went on to say that much of the damage had been repaired at once and that the rest would be made good before long. And since this was a late decrypt (26 February 1945, signaled 3 March), the repairs would all have been completed by the date of the signal.

By showing how quickly apparent devastation could be put right, this one report represents the whole strategic bombing controversy in miniature.

APPENDIX VIII:
Tank Returns

A. (see p. 212)

The number of tanks destroyed in the battle of Medenine was reckoned as "at least 50" at the time and as 52 in Alexander's Despatch and elsewhere. On the day after the battle, returns from the three panzer divisions showed only 41 tanks as total losses (this figure is also given in GS iv.347), but nearly twice as many under repair. However, the total of the four heads under which the returns were compiled is over 200, and this does not tally with previous Ultra information. A summary covering the whole of the Italian First Army, dated 8 March, gave 85 runners, which, with the addition of 40 or 50 total losses, agrees well enough with the 145 stated to be fit for action the evening before the battle. [VM 6065.]

B. (see p. 267)

The returns gave exact figures of tanks of each type, serviceable and under short or long repair (seven and fourteen days respectively), for each formation. The workshops could carry out repairs very rapidly, and the approximate figures in the text therefore make some allowance for tanks returned to duty in time for the attack. (A fragmentary return for 28 January shows, for instance, that a few assault guns had been damaged during the intervening three days and a great many Mark III's repaired.) The Hermann Goering Division, which was to take part in the attack, made no return on either day. The latest available information about it dated from 1 December, when it had 20 serviceable IIIs and 15 IVs, with 15 and 12 respectively under repair. A further element of uncertainty about the totals arose from the fact that there had as yet been no return of the weapon strength of the reinforcements coming up to operate under I Para Corps; they included one unit (I Panzer Regiment 4), for example, which was later found to have 50 or 60 Mark Vs (Panthers).

C. (see p. 293)

The returns are set out below in tabular form for easy comparison. Figures in parentheses are tanks or guns under repair.

	III	IV	V	VI	Assault guns	Heavy A/T guns
5 May KV 3190	47 (24)	160 (26)	58 (12)	43 (5)	181 (80)	616 (48)
12 May KV 3791	53 (17)	148 (36)	49 (21)	43 (5)	(194?) (45)	681 (34)
23 June XLs 30, 129	42 (15)	39 (73)	43 (2)	35 (40)	72 (42)	173 (49)

D. (see p. 301)

Only three substantially complete returns were signaled during the second half of 1944. Occasional small gaps in them have been filled from a few fragmentary returns in order to make the calculations in the text. The pro formas changed several times, but each new version quickly yielded up its secrets. The May and June figures are tabulated opposite (Appendix VIII, C).

Among many other useful features of these returns was the fact that the weapons of each division were listed separately. This showed, for instance, what a high proportion of the armor and heavier weapons was concentrated in the hands of only two divisions (the 26th Panzer and 29th PG) and meant that when a Flivo reported that his division had been moved to another part of the front, a fairly accurate estimate of the alteration in the offensive or defensive strength of both sectors could quickly be made, and the enemy's intention to attack or fear of being attacked could be deduced.

APPENDIX IX:
The Gothic Line*

The defensive position in the northern Apennines was known simply as "the Apennine position" in the autumn of 1943, and this was its only title for the next six months. It was renamed "Gothic Line" on 24 April 1944, but the older description also remained current. Ultra did not know of the change until 18 May. As the realization grew that it might not be strong enough to keep the Allies out, "Gothic Line" was replaced by "Green Line" on 15 June, but the Allies never adopted the new name. "Green Line" appeared in Ultra almost at once, but at first confused interpretation.

The second change was made lest the Allies derive propaganda advantage from capturing a defense position named after the Goths. Perhaps someone remembered that it was not far south of the new defense position that the Ostrogoths had suffered in 552 the defeat at the hands of the Byzantine general Narses which had extinguished their sixty-year-old kingdom, and Hitler thought it a bad omen!

Sixth-century reminiscence affected both sides. Mark Clark boasted not only that he had deprived the British of the glory of capturing Rome, but also that he was the first general to take the city from the south since Justinian's general Belisarius.

---

*See p. 287.

The Gothic Line ran fifteen or twenty miles north of Alexander's objective, the Pisa-Rimini line, for the greater part of its course, but somewhat to the south of it from the crest of the Apennines to the Adriatic.

Fuller details on the Gothic Line are given in my article "L'Ultra e la linea Gotica," in *Linea Gotica 1944* (Milan, 1986), pages 125–41.

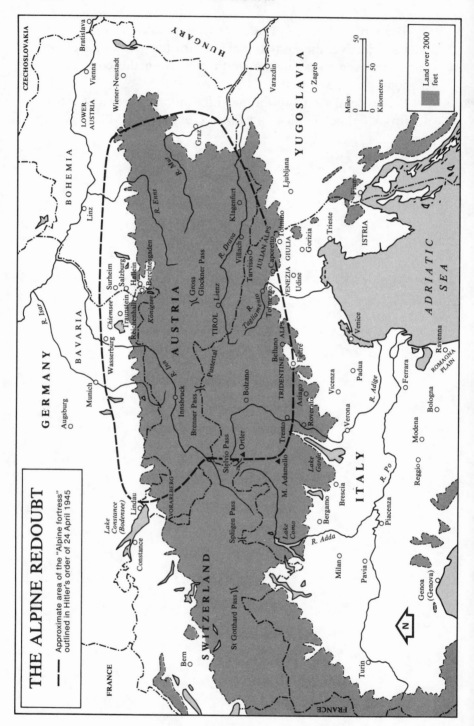

THE ALPINE REDOUBT

— — — Approximate area of the "Alpine fortress" outlined in Hitler's order of 24 April 1945

Land over 2000 feet

Miles
Kilometers

APPENDIX X:
Italian Defenses, or an Alpine Fortress?*

How much was Ultra able to tell the Allied command, during the final months of its advance to victory, about the last defense lines with which Hitler hoped to protect the Reich, and about their possible effect on Allied strategy? The principal object of Allied strategy on the Italian front in this last phase of the war was to destroy Army Group C in Lombardy, but another object—second in time but almost equal in importance— was to link up (either by an advance on land through Venice or by an amphibious operation across the Adriatic) with Tito's Partisans as far east as possible in order to ensure that Venezia Giulia, Trieste, and Fiume should remain in the orbit of the western powers. Beyond this, a third and more grandiose objective had earlier been prominent; known sometimes as "the Vienna Alternative," it called for Anglo-American forces to be pushed through the so-called Ljubljana gap to make contact with the Russians in Lower Austria.[1] Each of these objects deserves individual examination. Fortified defense lines in the mountains, should any have been prepared, could hinder the attainment of them all. Army Group C might take refuge behind them in an effort to escape destruction, and a force occupying them would

---

*See p. 322, above.
[1] See pp. 351–353, above.

be a constant threat to the flank of an advance toward Trieste, Ljubljana, or Vienna. Furthermore, such fortifications might also approximate to the outermost defenses of the "Alpine fortress" to which some believed that the last unrepentant Nazis intended defiantly to retire.

The unopposed occupation in May 1945 of all the territory that still remained unconquered at once exploded the myth of an Alpine fortress, for no convincing trace of such a thing could be found; but it would be mere wisdom after the event to brush aside for this reason the considerable body of Ultra evidence which seemed to suggest that a fortress in the Alps was really being prepared during the spring of 1945, particularly because (as already hinted) it was very difficult at the time to distinguish between the preparation of a final defense line for Army Group C and the construction of the southern wall of a hypothetical fortress. (So far as either was more than imaginary, it appeared afterward that the two were in fact identical.) A look at this evidence may serve to explain the hold the myth gained over some minds that spring and to dispel the charge of scaremongering which is sometimes made. Ultra gave ample ground for believing that a last defensive position was being prepared in the Austrian Alps, and none for doubting that it was as real a part of the enemy's plans as experience had shown the Gustav and Gothic lines to be. Since far more information accumulated about what could be construed as the southern wall of a fortified area in Upper Bavaria and the Tirol than about its northern face, however, and since this information came in over a longer period of time, it is important to note the paradox that the myth took far deeper root at SHAEF in Versailles than at AFHQ in Caserta. A supposed Nazi redoubt round Berchtesgaden was taken to be one of the necessary bases of strategy in Eisenhower's unfortunate attempt to coordinate his own plans with Stalin's at the end of March, for instance, but there is no sign that the possible existence of an impregnable fortress and its garrison on the left flank of an advance into Istria and beyond had any influence at all on Alexander's plans for these enterprises.

At some stage during his three-month tenure of authority over northern Italy in the late summer and early autumn of

1943, Rommel ordered the preparation of a *Voralpenstellung* (Lower Alps defensive position) running from the southeast corner of Switzerland via Lake Garda in a curve round the southern edge of the Tridentine and Julian Alps to Gorizia and Trieste. Rommel thought it a good position, open only to the objection that it could be turned and rolled up by a landing in Istria. In September of the same year, shortly after the Salerno landing, OKW called on OKH to set up several new army staffs in Italy, among them one for a *Befehlshaber der Sicherungsgebiete Alpenvorland* (GOC Lower Alps Security Areas).

More than six months later, in mid-May 1944, Ultra picked up an echo of all this in a message thought to originate with the Tenth Army (responsible for the eastern half of the German line in Italy), detailing part of the course of a *Voralpenstellung* running from Sondrio, on the river Adda, close to the Swiss frontier thirty miles north of Bergamo, in an easterly direction via Lake Garda to the Adige valley at Rovereto and on to Asiago, north of Vicenza. The message broke off at this point, but the line could be conjecturally (though confidently) completed in September from an OKH order for the development of a defense line joining the Lower Alps position at Tolmino (forty miles north of Trieste) to the Jablonica pass in Silesia. If the conjectural extension followed the lower Alpine slopes, as the western section did, then its route would be roughly Asiago-Feltre-Belluno-Tolmezzo and along the Julian Alps south of Tarvisio to Tolmino—almost precisely the line recommended by Rommel but with the important addition of an eastern section which surrenders Istria but cannot be outflanked. In the interval between these two intercepts, a Hitler order of 29 July was decrypted. It supplemented one of the 26th (not reported by Ultra) and ordered the construction by the Lower Alps Command of additional defense lines to prevent an Allied penetration into the Udine basin. In furtherance of his policy of walling in what remained of the Reich[2]—*Festung Europa* had shrunk to *Festung Deutschland*—Hitler had in fact issued a directive on 26 July for the construction of several positions in northern Italy, and had

---

[2]The Swiss frontier, which of course needed no defense, connected the Lower Alps position with the West Wall at Basel either northabout via Constance or southabout via Geneva.

varied and added to it on 29 July (the above intercept) and 3 August. Some paragraphs confirm the conjectural extension of the Lower Alps position proposed above, others call for three new lines branching out from it—one from the Piave valley above Belluno to Trieste, the others from unspecified junction points to the Gulf of Venice—and all are to be built because "the enemy is certain to attempt to thrust northwards in the direction of the Udine basin." Before long, Ultra took up the story again, showing the expansion of a small existing staff into Headquarters, GOC Lower Alps (*Alpenvorland*); a similar defense headquarters for the Adriatic had already been in existence for at least a month.

It would be reasonable, then, to sum up the twelve months from September 1943 to September 1944 by saying that Ultra had managed to give a fair impression of German plans for the defense of the Alpine front and Venezia Giulia, but that nothing so far had even hinted at either the move of any senior headquarters behind the Lower Alps defenses in readiness for a "last-ditch" stand or any fortified enclosure other than that of the whole Reich.

That just such a move was contemplated first began to emerge at the turn of the year. In December and January, cables were being laid, telephone exchanges set up, and staff accommodation constructed for an OB Southwest headquarters in several mountain villages along the Pustertal, which joins the Adige valley immediately below the Brenner pass and connects with the Drava valley and the Salzburg-Klagenfurt route. Only construction and maintenance personnel were yet in occupation, but GOC Lower Alps was among the many departments of OB Southwest's staff allotted offices there. In January 1945, a 12,000-strong Organisation Todt detachment (which OB Southwest soon found indispensable, because defensive positions had to be constructed "on a large scale") started work on a defense line from the Tagliamento valley near Tolmezzo to the Drava near Lienz, and it was reasonable to surmise that its purpose might be to protect both the Pustertal complex and the road and rail routes to Austria and Bavaria from Trieste, Ljubljana, and the southeast. Additional color was soon lent to this surmise by two further developments. In February and March, evidence began to accumulate that a larger and more important headquarters complex was being prepared in the Salzburg-Berchtesgaden district, and it gradually became clear that the Berlin directing staffs of OKW, OKH, and OKL would split into two parties as soon as the Allies drove a wedge into central Germany, the southern party going to the Salzburg area.[3] Right at the end of March, special protection was ordered for a number of particularly vital bridges and stretches of railway track on the Salzburg-Klagenfurt and the Innsbruck-Pustertal-Lienz-Klagenfurt routes, together with two spurs between Klagenfurt and the Alpine passes on the lines to Udine and Ljubljana—that is to say, all the main transport arteries from Germany to Italy and Yugoslavia through the high mountain areas which were alleged by rumor to be the site of the national redoubt to which the most fanatical Nazis would retreat.

An Alpine fortress or redoubt, should one exist, would extend over the greater part of Wehrkreis XVIII (the home defense and recruitment district comprising southern Austria, with headquarters at Salzburg), and it was therefore of some interest that in December 1944 OKW reserved to itself responsibility for the defenses south of the river Drava (responsibility for those north of the river—facing the Russians—was transferred to OKH, which had always directed operations on the eastern front) and delegated day-to-day authority for construction and survey work as far west as Lake Constance to Wehrkreis XVIII, on the understanding that it would cooperate with OB Southwest through General Jordan, who had already been identified as GOC Lower Alps. It was also noticeable that OKW loosely defined the defenses it was interested in as lying along a line Varazdin-Ljubljana-Lake Constance, because the western half would evidently more or less coincide with that of the *Voralpenstellung*. A cryptic statement by the Chief of Staff of Wehrkreis XVIII toward the end of March 1945 that no place in Wehrkreis XVIII was intended to be a fortress was difficult to interpret, because it depended on a message which had not been

---

[3]The separation did not in fact take place until 20 April.

intercepted, but it was permissible to understand it as meaning that no single place would be fortified because the whole Wehrkreis was to be a fortress. If it did in fact bear this meaning, it is evidence for an awareness at a comparatively low command level of preparations for defending the Tirol a good month before Hitler proclaimed "an inner fortress" on 24 April. Only one other Ultra signal came anywhere near suggesting the existence of a defended mountain zone until well after this date. Von Vietinghoff's reference on 14 April to keeping the British and Americans away as long as possible from "the Reich fortress" and to a planned withdrawal in order to preserve its "war potential" was evidence that the concept (but, of course, not necessarily the reality as well) was familiar in more exalted circles, and this too was before Hitler's proclamation.[4] There were half a dozen explicit references between 27 April and 2 May, but decryption delays meant that none could be signaled until 1 May, two days after the capitulation was signed. Three of them mentioned defenses on the northern face of the "fortress," and two of them were concerned with provisioning it from Bohemia—by then the only part of the Great German Reich still free from invasion.

By the time Hitler called for the creation of an "inner fortress," it was, of course, far too late to organize its defense, because the German government had collapsed. But there was perhaps another reason too. Hitler's sketch of the boundaries of the fortress area confirms what could already be inferred— though by a perhaps risky application of the argument from the negative—from the Ultra signals, namely, that the *Voralpenstellung* was also the southern wall of the fortress and that there were no further defenses behind it along the higher slopes. (There had been no mention of such defenses in Ultra, but radio communications are unreliable or useless in mountain country, and land lines might have carried a great deal of intelligence which could not be intercepted.) Army Group C made no attempt to occupy the *Voralpenstellung* because the speed of the Allied advance denied it the chance to do so; OB Southwest's

---

[4]See p. 322, above.

headquarters had got no farther than Bolzano when U.S. troops cut the Brenner road behind them and penetrated within what was to have been the defensive ring, and this, quite as much as the swift advance of the U.S. Seventh Army to Berchtesgaden and Salzburg which Eisenhower had ordered, put paid to any thought of mounting a defense of the "fortress" at this late stage. Perhaps the supreme tribute to Alexander's victory lies in the fact that the southern face of the "fortress" was never manned, because he had already compelled its only possible garrison to lay down its arms on the plain of Lombardy.

APPENDIX XI:
Operation SUNRISE*

It should occasion no surprise that Ultra contributed nothing to Operation SUNRISE, the tortuous and protracted negotiations for a German surrender which had dragged on inconclusively since they were initiated in February as a result of peace feelers by Obergruppenfuehrer Karl Wolff, the SS and Police Commander in Italy. Wolff and the few others in the secret on the German side would naturally avoid committing anything which might be construed as treason to an Enigma cipher to which others besides themselves had the key, and they presumably communicated by different means. A message of 18 April to the effect that his staff wanted Wolff back in Italy to deal with a general strike in Turin was innocuous enough, since Wolff was widely known to be visiting Hitler. Of somewhat greater interest were messages from Kaltenbrunner, the infamous Chief of Security Police, and others about the necessity to negotiate with the Allies, but they were all so late in April that they were of historical interest rather than practical value.

---

*See p. 323.

APPENDIX XII:
Missing Links in the Chain of Yugoslav Evidence

A. (see p. 330)

See, for instance, Auty and Clogg, 28, 239–40, and Davidson, 103, for a discussion of what evidence was available to SOE in 1942; PRO.WO 208/2014 (DDMI Minute, forwarded by CIGS to Prime Minister, 3 June 1942) and GS iv.386 (cf.iii.558) for the military and political angle.

An Enigma key which Hut 6 christened Raven was first broken in February 1942 and was read regularly thereafter. It served the Twelfth Army and later Army Group E. It is impossible to believe that the only two worthwhile items it carried for the next twelve or fifteen months were those noticed on p. 333, above,[1] and it is therefore to be presumed that most Raven items were teleprinted or typed for home consumption only. (Since Cairo was more concerned with Rommel than with the Balkans for most of 1942, the absence of signals is understandable.) It is therefore permissible to assume that in 1942 London possessed a perhaps considerable body of Ultra information about southeast Europe, and that this material still exists but is inaccessible, so that nothing yet in print has been able to take

---

[1] The key from which a signal was derived cannot, of course, be identified with certainty from published evidence, but these two were surely Raven decrypts.

account of it. (It is noteworthy that for every other front except the Russian, the release of the signals has given access to at least the most important items, and that the Balkans in 1942–43, where British interests were increasingly involved, is a glaring exception.)

The 1942–43 material may—or, of course, may not—bear on the Tito-Mihajlović issue, but it is in any case extremely regrettable that this controversial matter is deprived of evidence which might well clear up questions which are obscure and much debated today.

British Intelligence in the Second World War leaves a great deal unexplained under many other heads as well. For example, BI iii/1.501–3 reveals that Abwehr Enigma as well as Abwehr, Police, and Sicherheitsdienst hand ciphers were being read in England in 1942, and some of the latter in Cairo as well, and BI iii/1.139 n.9 quotes examples of information from one or other of these sources (which one is not specified) being included in CX/MSS teleprints, along with translations of Wehrmacht Enigma material. But these teleprints (and the many lesser items which would have been included in the supplementary typed reports) have not been released for inspection.

None of the above-mentioned material was signaled to the Middle East—presumably because it was inconceivable at the time of Gazala and the loss of Tobruk that Cairo could make any operational use of it. But intelligence which was not worth signaling in 1942 may be of crucial historical value today, for it may throw light upon some of the obscurer passages of Anglo-Yugoslav relations.

Very few signals of any kind (all are listed on pp. 332–333) about the Balkans were in fact sent to the Middle East over the usual route before the second half of May 1943, and it can be asserted with confidence that these few were all derived from normal Wehrmacht Enigma or from Italian naval intercepts relating to ship movements and occasionally to the Italian-occupied Dalmatian littoral.

The picture only began to change in the summer: by then, several Wehrmacht Enigma keys specifically for use in the Balkans were being read with some regularity; after Alamein, the

Allies' horizons were widening to include the Balkans; and British policy was beginning to look with more favor on Tito. But these changes had scarcely begun when the Keble report was presented in January and the Deakin mission to Tito was parachuted onto Mount Durmitor in May.

B. (see p. 334)

The received explanation of these events runs as follows:

The decrypts which Keble showed Deakin and Davidson were of Abwehr, Police, or Sicherheitsdienst hand-cipher intercepts (exactly which is not clear, but the balance of opinion favours SD; some traffic of all three had been decrypted in Cairo since the summer of 1942). These decrypts told a very different and far more favorable story about Tito and the Partisans than other information available, either in Cairo or in Whitehall (to which, apparently, they were for some reason not forwarded). Keble's action broke security regulations. But how did he come into possession of decrypts which were not normally circulated to SOE? In a previous post, Keble had been privy to Ultra, and it is usually said that either by his own artifice or others' oversight he had remained on the Ultra list when posted to SOE, and now, unauthorized, he passed on his knowledge to others not within the charmed circle. Ultra was so closely guarded a secret, and the "need to know" principle so sternly applied, that this is hard to believe, and in any case it raises two further problems. Keble had certainly seen Ultra in the past; he had served in MI 14, the War Office department dealing with the German army, and his last posting had been as head of the intelligence section in Cairo which (not very successfully, as events showed) analyzed the flow of supplies to Rommel, using Ultra as its main raw material (his successor was Enoch Powell: see p. 101 above). As has been shown, however, none of the Ultra so far signaled from Hut 3 bore on the Tito-Mihajlović issue at all. Were hand ciphers classed as Ultra in Cairo? Or has one truth—that Keble had formerly seen Ultra—been allowed to obscure another—that it was not Ultra which he showed to Deakin and Davidson? The latter seems the more probable, though it is worth noting that no precise and formal definition of Ultra is to be found in *British Intelligence,* and it is not absolutely impossible that the meaning of the word "Ultra" was sometimes stretched to cover the product of ciphers other than Enigma.

An additional argument frequently employed to explain the shift away from Mihajlović and toward the Partisans may be mentioned in passing. Davidson had left-wing sympathies at this time, and one of his assistants, James Klugman, was a Communist and had been a member of what it is now fashionable to call the "Cambridge Comintern." Out of these unquestionable facts, some have constructed the theory that SOE Cairo plotted to promote the Communist cause. The evidence for this supposition appears to be entirely circumstantial and impressionistic. It should be noted, moreover, that the potentially anti-British nature of Communist-directed resistance movements was already becoming known at this same time through Woodhouse and Hammond in Greece, who warned that there was a link between ELAS in Greece and the Partisans in Yugoslavia.

Because these areas of serious doubt still exist, it is greatly to be regretted that fuller information has not been made public. The controversy which has always surrounded the whole question of British policy toward Mihajlović and Tito has recently been reawakened by the prejudiced and often ill-founded arguments of Nora Beloff in *Tito's Flawed Legacy;* it cannot be stilled until exact information about the evidence upon which crucial decisions were taken is available.

APPENDIX XIII:
Cos and Leros*

Originally conceived in August 1943 as a descent on Crete and Rhodes (which the Germans had long anticipated), the plan suffered its first blow at the Quebec conference, where its scale was drastically cut down because there were not enough landing craft for three expeditions and AVALANCHE and Burma were given precedence. The second blow came when, on the Italian surrender, the Germans occupied Rhodes so quickly and in such strength that an assault with the British forces available was clearly hopeless. Cos and Leros were occupied instead as bases from which to harry Aegean shipping, but they could only be spared small garrisons and were much too far from the nearest Allied airfields in Cyprus and Cyrenaica for fighter cover to be provided in case of need. The Germans attacked Cos on 3 September and captured it in two days; Leros on 12 November took twice as long to subdue.

Ultra was less successful in giving warning of the danger to Cos than to Leros. Nothing specific followed a general and long-range warning issued on 14 September as British troops landed there, but bombing raids began almost at once and air reconnaissance at the end of the month, and there was a threefold increase in the number of GAF Command Southeast's daily sor-

*See p. 346.

397

ties. (The rate was usually below 100 a day throughout July and August, but rose to nearly 200 before the end of September, and to between 250 and 300 in October as reinforcements were steadily brought in.) This casts doubt on the validity of the charge in MME v.544 that "British intelligence had not detected the Germans' preparations."

A report from General Mueller, GOC 22nd Division on Crete, about the fighting on Cos was not available for signaling until early on 5 October, but it was followed within a few hours by another which spoke of landing craft being sent to Syros (halfway between Athens and Leros) "in view of future operations." The obvious deduction that this might betoken an assault on Leros was strengthened a couple of days later by news of a convoy sailing from Athens to nearby Cos, now in German hands. The assault was several times postponed, and full details about it provided, and what appeared to be the order for attack on 11 November was signaled just before 0100 hours the same morning; a repetition next day showed that there had been yet another postponement. Two timely reports of tough British resistance preceded another at midnight 14–15 November to the effect that the invaders' situation was "critical," and that victory depended on the landing of heavy arms that afternoon.

APPENDIX XIV:
How It Was Done

Decrypting Enigma

Machine encipherment was still a novelty in 1939. The Enigma machine had been patented in 1919 and marketed without much success during the 1920s by a German firm as a means of safeguarding commercial secrets. It used a system of wheels or drums to complicate the path followed by an electric current when a key on its keyboard was depressed, thus making the relationship between the letters of the plaintext and the enciphered version so erratic as to be undiscoverable by any process of decryption then known. Soon after they seized power, the Nazis bought up the patent and improved the machine, and by the late 1930s it was in use by all branches of the Wehrmacht. It looked like a rather large and clumsy portable typewriter, but it was compact and sturdy enough to stand up to rough treatment. The electrical circuits it contained were immensely complicated, but anyone could learn to use it. Thus it was ideal for its purpose—simple in operation, yet it could make radio signals secure against the eavesdropper. Its only drawback was that it did not print out the encrypted text; instead, each letter was lit up in turn on a display screen, so that two or more operators were needed, one to type out the plaintext, another to copy down the encrypt as each letter appeared. The three wheels or drums could be chosen from a set of five and were interchangeable; each had an outer metal rim which could be locked to it in twenty-six different positions, one for each letter of the alphabet. Each time a key was depressed, the right-hand wheel moved on one place (i.e., made one twenty-sixth of a revolution); once in every twenty-six times the wheel also moved; and all three moved together when the middle wheel had made a complete revolution—just in the way a car's odometer does. The current passed through all three wheels and a fixed drum (the *Umkehrwalze*), which sent it back again by a different route. Later on, another complication was introduced: after leaving the wheels, the current was made to pass along loose wires ending in *Stecker* (plugs), which could be plugged in pairs into the machine in any order. The positions of the wheels and the order of the plugs were frequently changed in accordance with standard instructions; there was usually one major rearrangement every twenty-four hours, with minor adjustments at shorter intervals. In addition, the sender chose different settings of the wheels for every message, telling the receiver what he had done by means of an "indicator"—two groups of three letters with which every message began. (The receiver would set his wheels to the position shown by the first group, and by decrypting the letters of the second group discover the setting at which the body of the text could be decrypted.) In order to decipher a given group of traffic, it was necessary (and sufficient) to know the choice and order of the three wheels, the positions of their outer rims, and the *Stecker* pairings. Wheels and rims together could provide something over a million possible arrangements, and the introduction of the *Stecker* pairings multiplied this to a total of approximately 150 million million million possible but unpredictably different versions of a single original text. It might take months—perhaps years—of unremitting application by a roomful of expert mathematicians to find the right solution to even a single day's key, and the Germans therefore believed that an Enigma message could safely be transmitted by wireless in ordinary Morse code, for although it was sure to be intercepted, it would certainly be unintelligible. They never seriously questioned this belief.

The Polish government, fearful that it was to be Hitler's next victim and anxious for warning of his army's moves, trained a party of mathematicians and set them to work to break the Enigma cipher; they devised a machine to test possible solutions and read many signals until the Germans introduced new complications into their procedure in 1939. France and England were also tackling the problem, and the three countries began to concert measures, most notably when the Poles handed over a reconstructed Enigma machine to the British shortly before the outbreak of the war. Anglo-French cooperation continued until the fall of France in 1940, after which all the work was concentrated at Bletchley Park.

Possession of an Enigma machine gave indispensable familiarity with its circuits, but otherwise did not help toward reading its messages; for this, it was essential to discover the settings used, and the mathematical problem thereby posed was formidable indeed. Only a machine could consistently defeat the machine; certainly nothing else would do if the messages were to be read in time to be useful. A young Cambridge mathematician, Alan Turing, who had worked on the theory of a universal calculating machine, was brought together with cryptanalysts skilled in all the tricks of their trade, and they had the benefit of the Poles' experience with the machine they had constructed. By the early summer of 1940 an electromechanical engine (always referred to as the bombe) had been built at Bletchley and had proved its designers' genius by decrypting several days' traffic.

Human ingenuity had to give the machine a start, however. In theory, the bombe could try out all the millions of possible solutions to a day's key, but it would take an immensely long time to do this. And how was it to tell its attendants that it had come upon the right solution because it had found one that was in German, not gibberish? Before starting the bombe, it was necessary to make a correct guess at the original version of a bit of the text. In the early days it was sometimes possible, because of the slack cipher discipline of some of the Luftwaffe signaling staff, to guess the initial settings of some of the messages, and this provided decrypts of the last three letters of their indicator groups. The first breaks were achieved during the spring of 1940 in this way—that is, by hand and without the help of the bombe.

Before long the Germans tightened up their cipher discipline, but by that time the damage had been done. For as soon as a few days' traffic had been read, a second careless habit was discovered.[1] The tightening up of cipher discipline had made future breaks by hand impossible or hopelessly laborious, but the second bad habit was enough to start the bombe off and to give it a good chance of finding the right solution to the day's key.

Success came just in time for the Battle of France and the Battle of Britain, though as yet it was by no means always possible to break a given day's key while it was still current. If the bombe occasionally faltered, however, it never failed: the flow of decrypted messages was already regular and remunerative enough by February 1941 for shift-working round the clock to be necessary for the intelligence staff which translated and appraised them. From then on, the output showed a constant tendency to rise, except for rare and fortunately brief intervals. Temporary declines in the volume of traffic accounted for one or two of these intervals and progressive improvements in the Enigma machine for others. But although these improvements eventually raised the number of possible versions of a given plaintext to over 10^{33}, none of them proved unsuperable.

All three branches to the Wehrmacht used Enigma, but differently, and within each service different forms of it were used for different purposes. Thus by 1945 there were more than a dozen species, so to speak, of naval Enigma—one for surface ships in the North Sea and the Atlantic and another for U-boats in the same area, a third for Mediterranean surface vessels, a fourth for Mediterranean U-boats, and so on. Naval Enigma proved difficult to break, and the first successes were not gained until early in 1941. GAF Enigma was easier game—partly because there was much more of it, so that the cryptanalysts' foundations were laid sooner, partly because of the slack signals discipline resulting from hasty expansion and low-grade oper-

[1] Military operations call for regular reports from the front line back to headquarters; they are likely to be rendered at much the same time each day and may be of much the same length. Thus there is a reasonable chance of identifying them on external evidence alone. If the same opening formula is used every time, decryption becomes immeasurably easier.

ators—and it was the first to be broken, in late spring 1940. Again, there were several "species"—one for general GAF use in northwestern Europe, another for the Mediterranean, several for aerial reconnaissance and army cooperation in particular theaters of war. A great deal of ground information was thus transmitted over GAF links (the Flivos—*Fliegerverbindungsoffiziere,* air liaison officers—were later one of our most prolific sources of information about the panzer divisions or corps to which they were attached), but in the desert it was a severe handicap that army signals discipline was good enough to delay regular decryption of army Enigma until 1942. All told, there were almost fifty different army and air Enigma keys, several of which might, in the last two years of the war at any rate, be "running" at the same time, at least one of them currently.

Signaling Ultra

As soon as decrypted messages were plentifully available, a new requirement promptly became evident. Cryptanalytic skill and mathematical insight were no longer enough; an exact and fluent knowledge of German and an aptitude for intelligence work were now also needed if the miracle was to be exploited to the full. The two sets of qualities complemented each other; the latter was only called for because of the success gained by the former, of course, but henceforth it was just as essential.

Inescapable differences between the best methods of handling intelligence by the three British services now imposed organizational distinctions. Evidence about the movements of German surface vessels and U-boats could be properly appraised and acted on only by those who knew where British ships and convoys were—that is to say, by the Admiralty, which was an operational command headquarters as well as a government ministry. Naval decrypts were therefore translated at Bletchley Park and teleprinted, almost without annotation, to the Admiralty, which rerouted convoys or took other necessary action. Similar considerations scarcely applied to army and air intelligence. Except for advance news of German bombing raids on English targets (for which the Air Ministry acted in the same way as the Admiralty did for all naval intelligence), very little of it could be immediate and operational in the circumstances prevailing during the winter of 1940–41. The War Office and Air Ministry had much in common with each other, and many things distinguished the attitude of both toward Ultra from that of the Admiralty. A common intelligence organization for these two services was therefore set up at Bletchley Park. It was always known as Hut 3,[2] even after it moved into more convenient brick premises; it was this organization which I joined in February 1941, and it is only Hut 3 and its output with which this book is concerned.

As soon as the Germans invaded Yugoslavia and Greece and began to intervene in Africa in the spring of 1941, a further common characteristic of army and air Ultra became evident, and this too shaped our organization in a fundamental way. Like the Naval Section, Hut 3 teleprinted its hottest information to ministries in London (less urgent material was typed and sent up by bag), but in addition it had already begun to annotate and elucidate each item from background information derived from previous decrypts and accumulated in its card indexes. The swift movement of events in Greece and Cyrenaica, and the direct bearing of Ultra evidence on the fate of British troops there, soon made it plain that much would be gained if the decrypts were fully processed in Hut 3 and if signals based on them were immediately sent to commands in the field. Many perhaps vital hours would thus be saved. The first signals were sent to Cairo in March 1941. Other receiving stations were established as need arose—the air and naval headquarters in Malta and Alexandria were the next—until by the time the Allied armies broke out of the Normandy bridgehead in July 1944, Hut 3 was currently serving forty or fifty subscribers in northwest Europe, Italy, and the Mediterranean. Each of these subscribers was serviced by a Special Liaison Unit, a signals and intelligence link established for this sole purpose and operating under stringent security rules.

---

[2] Decrypts were supplied to Hut 3 by Hut 6. In a similar pairing, Hut 8 supplied Hut 4 (the Naval Section).

The veil of official secrecy which had hidden Ultra was lifted in October 1977 when some 25,000 of these signals, covering the period November 1943 to August 1944, were placed in the Public Record Office.[3] Subsequent releases have completed the series from March 1941 to May 1945.[4] These signals are the evidence upon which this book is based. Each signal drew its authority from one or more decrypts, which were themselves translated and teleprinted *in extenso* to the service ministries along with copies of the Hut 3 signals derived from them. The teleprints have not been released. Because the Hut 3 signals were not only checked meticulously at the time of drafting for accurate statement of fact and appropriately qualified comment but also rechecked later on both in the Hut and in London, it is safe to assume that their wording fairly represents the information received, though usually in summary form. Moreover, nothing which was regarded, either at the moment of receipt or during subsequent rescrutiny, as being important for the conduct of Allied operations was left unsignaled. Even unsupported by the teleprinted translations, therefore, the signals represent all the Ultra that was sent to field commands and all that was thought worth sending. The evidence used here is the same as that which was in the hands of the chief intelligence officers on the staffs of Eisenhower, Alexander, and Montgomery.

What most of the signals lack, however, is more than a hint of the considerable intelligence servicing which almost every decrypt needed and received. The full meaning of the information conveyed by a message was only rarely self-evident from the translation alone, and it was usually necessary to draw out its significance by providing it with a context and setting it against a background as like as possible to that which would have been in the minds of the German sender and receiver. With the aid of Hut 3's extensive indexes, built up from previous messages, this could nearly always be done in considerable detail, and the teleprint annotated accordingly. An order for a panzer division to move from one part of the front to another, for instance, obviously gained added significance if a note pointed out that we

---

[3] A larger number of the (far shorter) naval teleprints were also released. These covered rather different dates.
[4] See Appendix I.

already knew that several others were going in the same direction, or that the new message countermanded previous orders. Little of all this intelligence work appears in the signals, however, partly in order to save scarce signaling time and partly because recipients would draw the same deductions from the same evidence. These annotations—always introduced by the word "Comment," to distinguish them clearly from the text of the German message—were much scantier in the signals than in the teleprints.

By early in 1941, a convenient flow of work and a suitable division of labor had been discovered by experience; it remained substantially unchanged for the rest of the war.

At whatever hour of the day or night a key was broken by Hut 6, decrypts were immediately passed to the translators in Hut 3. Partly for historical reasons dating back to prewar recruitment, partly by chance, the translators were largely civilians, although almost all the rest of the Hut's personnel were in uniform. From mid-1943 onward, an ever-growing number of Americans joined us. So interdependent was every phase of the work and so enthusiastic was everyone to play a part to the best of his or her ability that Hut 3 was from the start, and always remained, a good example of that interservice and inter-Allied cooperation which kept the wheels of the Anglo-American Supreme Command turning smoothly, but which completely eluded the Germans, although they possessed the formal framework for it in the OKW. This spirit of cooperation had to withstand quite severe strains, particularly when an essential expansion of staff brought some overcrowding. On days when several keys were current at once and critical operations were on hand in both theaters, an eight-hour tour of duty could be very tiring, because it required repeated shifts of attention from Normandy to Italy and back again and because it called incessantly for absolute accuracy and continual alertness against errors of judgment while at the same time demanding that everything be done as quickly as possible.

The translators' first duty was to analyze a message possibly corrupted in transmission, suggest emendations where necessary, and expand the many abbreviations used. When they were satisfied that they had produced an English version which fairly represented the sense of the German, the translators handed text and translation to the air and military advisers, service officers who sat opposite each other at the next table in the production line. One or other, as the case required, would use the resources of the huge card indexes maintained by his section to explore the significance of the text before him—for a correct and lucid translation could still present severe intelligence problems. There was also a naval adviser ready to deal with such naval messages as might have wider significance; decrypts from German and Italian naval sources played an extremely important role in guiding British naval and air attacks on the shipping which carried supplies to Rommel across the Mediterranean from Italy and Greece to Libyan ports, and in helping British army headquarters in Cairo to estimate how long the available stocks of food, fuel, and ammunition could sustain the successive German offensives. Having solved his problems as best he could, the adviser annotated the translation accordingly, decided whether the item merited a signal to commands abroad, drafted the signal if he so decided, and then handed it over to the Duty Officer for checking and final approval before it passed to the signals officer and his staff of teleprinter operators and coding clerks. Over two hundred such signals were sent on D-day, 6 June 1944, but a rate of a thousand a week had already been common for almost two years. (See Appendix I.)

Duty Officers knew German and the intelligence background well, but their prime function was to be responsible for everything rather than to be as expert as their colleagues in any single field. Theirs was a twofold responsibility. The first was to see that translation and signal both faithfully represented the sense of the original, looking for misconceptions which incautious wording might accidentally convey to recipients of a signal, and ensuring appropriate changes where necessary. A partially corrupt text, a translation unavoidably loose because of the imprecision of the German original, difficulty in drawing confident conclusions from a perhaps incomplete intercept—all these might lead to uncertainties, the exact nature and degree of which it was essential to make clear to recipients, who in some instances might possess evidence capable of resolving them provided they were told exactly what was certain and what doubtful.

As well as overseeing the observance of standard conventions like these, the Duty Officer was responsible for ensuring that strict security was maintained. Nothing must be signaled which openly revealed the source, nothing sent to a recipient which did not directly concern him—the criterion was his "need to know" its content, which must be of "value, not interest" to him—and various groups of recipients had to be kept informed on an all-or-none basis lest consultation among them be frustrated.

Behind the sometimes hectic activity of these frontline troops lay several research departments whose specialized knowledge was indispensable. One of them combined a rigorously academic understanding of grammatical niceties and precise shades of meaning with a knack of divining the correct expansion of novel German abbreviations and a trained mechanic's repertory of technical terms: it invited the Duty Officer to veto inspired guesses at baffling texts if they did not meet its exacting standards, and it knew the meaning of the long German names for the working parts of radar sets and rockets, tank tracks and self-propelled guns (without which the significance of repair-shop reports and supply returns could not be grasped). Another section took on longer-term research projects where only the careful sifting of accumulated evidence could solve a problem. Supply returns for both services were normally rendered according to a pro forma, for instance, but the pro forma was unintelligible without a key to the numbered paragraphs. Given enough examples and the dexterous juxtaposition of scraps of information and plausible hypotheses, the key could almost always be found in the end—and commands informed how many tanks and guns a panzer division possessed, or how many serviceable aircraft there were in a bomber squadron and how many under repair in the workshops. When the Enigma used by the German State Railways (first broken in the summer of 1940) was found to contain little more than strings of six-figure consignment numbers, it was this department which painstakingly distilled a meaning from the mass of superficially uninteresting and unrewarding detail, managed to associate some of the consignment numbers with army or air force units, noted how destinations and the timing of movements converged on Germany's eastern frontier in the spring of 1941—and forecast the invasion of Russia. A third section concentrated on the inscrutable but tremendously important traffic which carried instructions about navigational beams to the long-range bomber Gruppen and (later on) provided valuable clues to the research going on at Peenemuende and to the construction of V-weapon sites for the bombardment of London.[5] A fourth undertook to assemble and collate German identifications (mainly derived from the German Y Service, which studied the external features of undecrypted wireless traffic and located transmitters by direction-finding techniques) of British and American formations and their ideas about the Allied order of battle. Its studies were of immense value, particularly in the weeks immediately before and after D-day, because they showed the success of the Allied deception plan in creating the impression that the Normandy landings were only secondary and that the main invasion would come in the Calais area.

These research departments had some contact with the world of non-Ultra intelligence outside Bletchley Park and were able to utilize information thus gained to assist and accelerate their work. But they were alone in this. Hut 3 existed to purvey pure Ultra, not to adulterate it with anything else. No teleprint or signal ever bore footnote or comment derived from anything except Hut 3's own card indexes, save that map references were interpolated into frontline reports, etc., as an aid to quick understanding. No hint of forthcoming Allied operations normally reached the Hut, so that we remained "pure." This "purity" was in some respects a hindrance, and no doubt meant that we sometimes sent information needlessly or when it was already out of date, but it ruled out all possibility that we might uncon-

---

[5]Because of the peculiarly complex and technical nature of this material, it was early removed from the normal flow of work and diverted to a special section in Hut 3 which was in direct contact about it with the Air Ministry. The use made of it is fully described in R. V. Jones, *Most Secret War.*

sciously read our evidence in the light of extraneous knowledge, and left it entirely to intelligence staffs in the field to assimilate Ultra to other sources, judge between them if there were discrepancies, and present their commander with a single picture.

This "purity" had one unforeseen consequence. It meant that we followed the fighting from the German point of view exclusively, and knew much more about most German divisions and some German generals than we did about any on our own side. Rommel, Westphal, and Bayerlein were more familiar figures than ever Eisenhower or Montgomery were, the 90th Light Division so daily an acquaintance during the African campaign that there was even a sort of temptation to rejoice when it scored a success. No doubt the mood belonged, as with the general public, to the desert war; it faded soon after Rommel left Africa early in 1943.

Is it possible to discover how much Ultra contributed to the whole intelligence picture? The preceding chapters are an attempt to answer this question, but several points deserve special emphasis.

(i) Because Hut 3 was told nothing about Allied intentions, nothing in the signals themselves indicates their relative value (save, of course, insofar as the priority given to each is a guide to the opinion of those who drafted it). In order to try to estimate this fairly, I have always compared the signals with the actual course of events as it is now known from official histories and from the memoirs of leading participants, setting what we knew in Hut 3—and the time at which we knew it—beside what happened (so far as this can be reconstructed) and pointing out the similarities and—where necessary—the contrasts and discrepancies. Essential though it was, in order to ensure a sound frame of reference, this has meant risking unconscious hindsight, and I have tried to be continuously on my guard against it. For Ultra, in common with all other military intelligence, became available piece by piece in no very logical order as a pattern of largely unforeseeable events gradually unfolded itself, while a historian more than forty years later cannot entirely obliterate from his mind an awareness of their outcome.

(ii) Since every Ultra item carried weight because of its unimpeachable authenticity, however, common sense suggests that a very close estimate of its importance can be obtained through a careful study of the timing of Ultra intelligence. For where an Ultra item can be shown to have arrived in time, it is not likely to have been disregarded. The history of most Enigma messages can still be traced from German time of origin to the moment at which the Ultra signal derived from it was sent off. Reasonable allowance must then be made for transmission time, for decoding upon receipt, and for consideration by the intelligence officer who received it and by the commander who might act upon it. Where this still leaves an interval before the action described in, or consequent upon, the signal, it may be presumed that the Allied commander's measures were taken in the light of the Ultra information. Thus Ultra gave ample warning of Rommel's intentions before Alam Halfa and Medenine, enabling Montgomery to take appropriate measures to frustrate them.[6] Few cases are as simple or as obviously important as these, but I have been at pains to give full evidence about timing so that the probable bearing of information upon decisions may be estimated as exactly as possible.

(iii) A still more serious danger in this line of thought is the assumption that Ultra's chief value lay in the realm of battlefield tactics. This was almost certainly not the case. Even in the most favorable circumstances, tactical information might arrive too late to be useful. The unspectacular accumulation of evidence about the Germans' supply situation, which Ultra made possible, may in the long run have proved more valuable because it enabled long-term trends to be analyzed and pressure to be brought to bear on tender spots. This type of information did not depend for its value on being up to the minute; it could be almost equally useful even when a week old. It first came into prominence in Africa during the summer of 1942, when Ultra enabled a close watch to be kept on Rommel's petrol and am-

---

[6]See pp. 142–46, 209–12.

munition supplies and gave foreknowledge of the restrictions on
tank movements and aircraft sorties which the sinking of even a
single cargo could bring, as well as providing tactical targets in
the shape of convoy movements. Somewhat more intermittent,
but of even greater interest, were the long statements of the
number of their battle-worthy tanks and guns periodically rendered by army corps and divisions, for they permitted the regular monitoring of the enemy's combat readiness in a way no
other source could have made possible. The evident importance
of Ultra's almost daily advance warnings of GAF operations,
even that of rare and outstanding items like the plans for Alam
Halfa and Medenine, must not take too much of the limelight
away from material of a quite different and less glamorous kind
which, recurring at regular intervals, acquired a value all the
greater because it was cumulative.

(iv) Since it was the secret operational communication of one
German headquarters with another, every Enigma message was
authentic and reliable. There was no need, as with agents, to
wonder about the good faith of the source or the soundness of
his judgment. But no message had more authority than that of
the officer who sent it, nor more reliability as a guide to his
superiors' intentions than the extent of the knowledge they allowed him to have or the initiative to which his rank entitled
him. It was perhaps easier for the Hut 3 intelligence officers
then than it is for the reader of today to keep constantly in mind
the caution this imposed. Every Ultra signal had to be suitably
attributed (for instance, "Fliegerkorps II's intentions at 1045
hours ninth were . . .") so that it carried within itself an indication of the credence it deserved as a forewarning of events to
come, and it was not uncommon—to take a very simple case—
for a signal stating the operations proposed by a Fliegerkorps to
be followed within the hour by another announcing that the parent Luftflotte had countermanded them in favor of a different
target.

(v) The scope of the intelligence Ultra could provide was restricted by the natural preference of rearward headquarters and

senior commanders for telephone or teleprinter over radio. A large number of very secret and very important messages, the content of which it would have been extremely useful to know, were for this reason never received at all. But as instructions had to be disseminated nearer and nearer to the front, so the chance that all or part of the original order would become accessible through transmission over the ether began to rise. Again, it could be tantalizing to intercept the answer to a question which had evidently been asked by landline (destruction of the line by sabotage or bombing could prevent the answer going by the same route), for the one was unlikely to be fully comprehensible without the other, and once more laborious analysis and comparison with parallel evidence was necessary before a plausible conclusion could be drawn and useful intelligence extracted.

For although Ultra was absolutely reliable when it appeared, it could not be relied on always to appear when needed or to answer every question explicitly. Deliberate wireless silence could muffle it completely. A crucial intercept might be missed perhaps because weather conditions or fading temporarily blotted out a radio link while it was carrying an important message. A few hours' delay in breaking a particular key might bring vital information too late for it to be used effectively. The failure of Eisenhower's intelligence staff to foresee Rommel's attack on the Kasserine pass in February 1943 vividly illustrates the difficulties which could arise.[7]

(vi) From a totally different angle, there was the necessary restriction imposed by our own security regulations upon the use of Ultra. The number of those allowed to know about it was strictly limited both at home and in the field. Commanders were strictly forbidden to order any action which might imperil the source by seeming to be ascribable only to the reading of Enigma traffic—thus, for example, ship movements and concentrations of tanks had to be confirmed by aerial reconnaissance, and seen to be observed, before they could be bombed. Ultra was too strong a medicine to be taken neat; unless it was diluted

---

[7] See pp. 196–207.

from less secret sources, the consequences might be disastrous—it might be compromised and so lost for the future. For similar reasons, no Ultra signals were sent direct to commands below the level of an army headquarters or the equivalent, and anything passed to corps or division had to be disguised in the form of an operational order. The number of those in the secret was kept to the minimum compatible with effective use. How severe these limitations were in practice, Hut 3 never knew; its duty was done when it had dispatched its signal.

(vii) Lastly, it has to be remembered that Ultra was not the only source of military intelligence. It did not replace the traditional sources but was a superb addition to them because it provided what they could not, and because it came straight from the horse's mouth. The traditional sources remained of great value in their own way. Agents might hear things which had not been signaled; low-grade ciphers used in the front line carried tactical details of immediate (if also ephemeral) value if broken at once; prisoner interrogation and aerial reconnaissance could confirm that the orders conveyed by Ultra were actually being carried out. Thus the old and the new were complementary, each yielding information beyond the reach of the other. To say this is in no way to diminish the importance of Ultra but to see it in its proper light; to recognize that Ultra could not do everything is to appreciate the complexity of the intelligence puzzle as it was painfully put together when there were battles to be fought and a war to be won. The consensus among intelligence officers attached to field commands whose after-action views are known is that blending of all sources was vital, but that Ultra was chief among them. And here again, of course, the question "How much Ultra, how much the rest?" cannot be answered from Hut 3's signals alone—except by observing how little of what is thought worth recording by the operational histories they failed to reveal.

Ultra's successes were in fact in some respects its own worst enemies at the time, and it is essential that the occasional and temporary mistakes of the past should not be repeated now, or false beliefs become engrained. Ultra was not omniscient, and could not be, for the reasons already given. But because it was so nearly omniscient so often, there were a few occasions when something like the opinion "If it's not in Ultra, it can't be true" seems to have prevailed in some quarters. It is not my main purpose to inquire whether this led to errors by Allied commanders, but at the risk of repetition it is worth making two points, both of which are illustrated in the subsequently notorious cases of the surprise the Germans achieved at Kasserine and in the Ardennes. Bletchley's bombes could not decrypt what had never been encrypted in Enigma or sent over the air, and so deliberate wireless silence could make vital information totally inaccessible to Ultra. Because of the consequently unavoidable gaps in the story told by Hut 3's signals, these had to be very carefully interpreted before either being made the basis of command decisions or discarded as unhelpful. The fact that they could occasionally be misinterpreted throws into sharp relief the predicament of generals thrust back upon traditional methods of intelligence gathering alone, and by contrast highlights the service Ultra was able to render on nearly every other occasion.

To return to the original question: How far can Ultra's contribution be measured? Churchill, Eisenhower, Alexander, and others paid such handsome tributes at the end of the war that there is no doubting its incalculable value. It put the Allied general into the position of a chess player whose opponent announces his moves in advance and explains why he makes them. None of the generals, unfortunately, seems to have left a considered account of his opinion of Ultra or to have compiled detailed examples of the use he made of it. But it is a fair presumption that the possession of Ultra did not dispense generals from any of their traditional responsibilities. They still had to plan their attacks and carry them out; Ultra simply helped them to apply force most economically and with maximum effect. Insofar as one of the novelties which distinguished Ultra from older forms of intelligence gathering was that it was not the monopoly of the battlefield general because it was produced far behind the front, Ultra may indeed have somewhat increased a general's burdens; for he must always have been aware that his political chiefs were in the secret too, saw the same decrypts as he, and were therefore in a good position to breathe down his neck should they choose to do so (as Churchill often did during the desert campaigns of 1941–42).

Sweeping suggestions have been made that the revelation of Ultra would make it necessary to rewrite the history of the war. The evidence presented here does not altogether bear them out. On the other hand, while neither the frequency with which Ultra was able to give Allied commanders forewarning of exceptional strokes planned by their enemies nor the tremendously detailed day-to-day information about the German army and air force it collected (only a comparatively small proportion of which could be included here without overloading the pages) is likely to lead to a wholesale revision of prevailing views about those commanders' actions, Ultra must surely modify them by showing that vital decisions were, or ought to have been, taken against an intelligence background which was sometimes markedly different from what has hitherto been supposed.

Notes

CHAPTER 1: Beginnings—and Rommel

16 "...is to betray the country": Rohwer and Jaeckel, 335.

16 after World War I, for instance: Strong, 34

18 been a resounding victory: Beesly, *Room 40,* 160–62

20 scarcely any trained intelligence offers: see, for instance, Bond, Wark.

21 Boniface or Agent OL: Churchill was still using the name Boniface in late 1944; see PRO. CAB 80/88, CoS Octagon 7th Session, Appendix 1, and Colville, 294. For Agent OL see OL 1650.

23 (... forcefully restated by General Sir David Fraser): Fraser, *And We Shall Shock Them,* 136.

24 and a precautionary change of cipher: Churchill was himself very concerned to ensure that the security regulations were properly observed; there are good examples of this in Gilbert vi. 896, 863–66, 1233, 1242.

25 about the middle of August: Sir Edgar Williams, in PRO.WO 208/5575. See p. 105 below.

27 local counterattacks, but no more: OKW/KTB i.253–54.

27 ... opposition from the soldiers: Colville, 284.

27 "...are subordinated to aiding Greece": Churchill iii.17.

28 of Russia and the Balkans: BFP i.523–25; BI i.357–58, 451–55.

29 for a few more days: Kennedy, 75, de Guingand, *Generals,* 23, 47.

29   it was Wavell's grievous error: Compare Carver, *Dilemmas,* 22: "Wavell must carry a large share of the blame."

30   as a practical proposition: Connell, *Wavell,* i.335; Lewin, *Chief,* 81, 95.

30   and recommended immediate aid: Churchill iii.63.

31   Tripoli which he had hitherto urged: Gilbert vi.924, 955, 959, 1010; Carver, *Harding,* 67; Churchill iii.56–57.

31   ardent supporter of the expedition: See Colville, 360–61.

31   which expressed the contrary opinion: de Guingand, *Generals,* 22-23, 28-29. In *Operation Victory,* 79-80, de Guingand listed ten military reasons why "an intervention in Greece never had a chance of success."

31   (. . . overcame Churchill's previous hesitation): Gilbert vi.1013–14.

31   in their possession: BFP i.532-33.

32   share their inevitable disaster: Quoted in Carlton, 178.

32   halting an invader really were: Lewin, *Chief,* 109.

32   being stripped its defenses: Jackson, *Africa,* 94.

32   the German buildup in Libya: BI i.391–93.

32   (. . . already planning evacuation!): de Guingand, *Generals,* 36–37.

33   ". . . largely discounted it": Connell, *Wavell,* i. 384-85.

33   "up to the middle of February": Wavell, 3425.

33   as Eden eventually concluded: Rhodes James, *Anthony Eden,* 235.

33   retired list before long: Bond, 53.

33   ". . . in the last year or two": Liddell Hart, *Memoirs,* ii.238.

34   took exception to them: Ibid., i.252.

34   (". . . is indispensable to successful men"): Gilbert vi.731.

34   ". . . not Archie's strong suit": Fraser, *Alanbrooke,* 340.

35   which Churchill demanded: Churchill iii.93; MME ii.150.

35   ". . . greatest calamity": Rhodes James, 241, 251.

35   to the Middle East in any case: BI i.372, 392, 394–95, 397, 415, etc.

35   of the British positions: OLs 6, 8, 13, 15, 17.

35   1944 was completely misread: Bennett, 154, 189.

36   ". . . dangerous dispersal of forces": Bryant i.248.

36   the government had yet made: Gilbert vi. 1203

37   (". . . to Tripoli without fighting"): Halder ii.272.

37   appeal to Berlin: OKW/KTB i.306-8.

37   controlled some 450 aircraft: MME ii.47.

37	dive-bombers and twenty fighters: MME ii.14.
37	"for a considerable time": PRO.WO 169/19; BI. i.389.
37	". . . considerable risks in Cyrenaica": Connell, *Wavell,* i. 388.
37	". . . grasp of what is possible": Halder ii.305.
38	objective for the following spring: Ibid., 315.
38	Tobruk in the autumn: Ibid., 324.
38	was expressly ruled out: OKW/KTB i.1010.
38	given freedom of action: Rommel, 109, 111.
38	decrypted quickly and signaled: OL 27.
38	made to drive him back: Connell, *Wavell,* i.395; Churchill iii.180.
38	(. . . is no signal on the subject): BI i.395.
39	shortages of petrol and ammunition: OLs 63, 73, 74, 92, 94, 184, 187, 189.
39	flights had to be restricted: OLs 212, 213, 217, 218, 226.
39	possible loss of Egypt: Connell, *Wavell,* i.415.
39	to restrain him: Halder ii, 377–78, 388.
41	(". . . specialist in armoured troops"): OL 201.
41	at dawn on 4 May: OL 211. The text in Halder ii.388 is somewhat different.
42	again at Churchill's insistence: GS ii.526; Connell, *Wavell,* i.488.
42	". . . decisions of his career": Irving, 99–100.
42	took no part in BATTLEAXE: details in Lewin, *Afrika Korps,* 68-69.
43	single report on 18 May: OL 368.
43	later common in the West: Bennett, 89, 122, 135n.
43	now frequently reported: OLs 214, 281, 527, 533, 549, 555, 569—this showed a high servicability rate on the eve of BATTLEAXE—585, 639.
44	Secret Service's Russian decrypts: Beesly, *Room 40,* 8–20, 46–62; Andrew, "British Secret Service . . ." in *Historical Journal* 20 (1977), 679-83; R. S. Churchill, iii.179, 337.
44	". . . his solution into military terms": Quoted in V. Bonham-Carter, *Winston Churchill as I knew Him,* 53, from J. B. Atkins, *Incidents and Reflections,* 126. Atkins was the *Manchester Guardian* correspondent in South Africa, where he and Churchill worked together for a time.
44	". . . out of empty hats": Rhodes James, ed., *"Chips": The Diaries of Sir H. Channon* (Weidenfeld & Nicolson, 1967), 362.

44	". . . the picture is lost": Bryant i. 723.
44	". . . they are born strategists": quoted in Hamilton i.523.
44	"his menacing power was overwhelming": Zuckerman, 255.
44	he became Prime Minster: Soames, *Clementine Churchill,* 291.
44	him friends a year later: Gilbert vi.1170, quoting Colville, 428.
45	position "very serious": OLs 259, 269.
45	the French in Tunis: OLs 584, 618.
45	just before BATTLEAXE: OLs 328, 587.
45	lorries and coastal shipping: OLs 335, 544, 561, 608, 637.
46	the whole Russian front: Creveld, 68; Westphal, *Erinnerungen,* 117–20. Figures for sinkings are in MME ii.58 and Roskill i.439.
46	with a monotonous diet: Mellenthin, 45; Schmidt, 70.

CHAPTER 2: The Limitations of Intelligence

47	toward the Yugoslav frontier: OL 20; BI i.371.
47	military attaché in Belgrade: OL 67.
47	reconnoiter Belgrade and Athens: OLs 28, 29, 30, 31, 32.
49	changed to 0600 hours: OLs 34, 35, 37.
49	in under four hours: OL 44.
49	recording the advance on Belgrade: KOTS 40, 49. The KOT series, carrying Ultra to British army and air headquarters in Greece, ran from 27 March to 23 April, overlapping the OL series a little at each end.
49	traffic on the same day: KOT 51.
49	Aliakhmon River on 15 April: KOT 72.
49	to advance on Athens: KOT 108, OL 152.
49	was signaled: KOT 126.
49	signaled early next morning: OL 146.
50	on the 21st respectively: KOTs 42, 102, 110.
50	". . . security our source": KOT 120.
52	as the starting date: BI i.415.
52	followed on 25 April: Trevor-Roper, 68–69.
52	assigned first priority: Gilbert vi. 1065, 1072.
52	to defend the island: Davin, 458; MME ii.124.
52	defense at short notice: de Guingand, *Operation Victory,* 82; Fergusson in Carver, *War Lords,* 219. Davin, 138, excuses Brigadier Hargest for the loss of the Maleme air-

field partly on the ground that "he was still tired from the campaign in Greece."

52	on 9 April: KOT 28
53	on the same day: KOTs 29, 31.
53	on 17 April: KOT 80.
53	indicating any particular target: KOT 114.
53	signaled with high priority: OLs 156, 158, 164, 167, 169, 173, 174.
53	General Freyberg personally: unnumbered signal 1845/28 April in PRO.DEFE 3/894.
54	". . . maintaining utmost security": OL 2166. It had been announced on 28 April that signals intended for both Cairo and Crete would be numbered from 2000 upward to distinguish them from those for Cairo alone, which were still in three figures. The choice of so low a number for the starting point of a new series suggests that those who made it did not foresee a long life for Ultra! It also explains why the OL series was brought to an end abruptly in November, when it was realized that the Cairo numbers would soon repeat those already used for the Crete series.
54	attack from the air alone: OLs 2154, 2155.
54	and antiaircraft positions: OLs 2167, 2168.
55	90 Ju-87s were available: OL 2170.
56	(. . . date on the 19th): OLs 339, 341, 370.
56	to revise their tactics: OL 424.
57	landing from the sea: Davin, 40.
57	he was reinforced beforehand: MME ii.126.
58	rumor even a year later: Horne, 255–59.
58	leave again on the 19th: OLs 278, 340, 351, 361.
59	receipt of this signal: OLs 389, 390; OLs 411, 423, 428, 431 also mention breakdowns.
59	expedition were sunk at sea: MME ii.136–37; Roskill i.441.
59	destroyers *Kelly* and *Kashmir:* OLs 415, 417, 419, 421.
59	in advance, for example: OL 370.
59	not begin until evening: Davin, 110, 133-34; MME ii.133.
59	that the gap existed: Davin, 180-81
59	afternoon of 21 May: MME ii.154.
60	spirit of some units: OLs 424, 442.
60	hold on the island: OLs 401, 404, 422, 428, 459, 474, 475, 485, 486, 506.
60	merely historical interest: OLs 499, 510.

60	". . . Axis attempt at capture": de Guingand, *Operation Victory*, 86.
60	to suppose, with Roskill: Roskill iii.390.
61	Hunt in *A Don at War*: Hunt, 46.
62	". . . so expensive to garrison": Cf. MME ii.148; GS iii.112; Fraser, *Shock*, 140.
62	only ten days later: Churchill iii.241; cf. MME ii.124.
63	same two airfields: OLs 261, 267, 272, 287.
63	by the same route: OLs 350, 380, 400.
63	(. . . one paragraph of it): OL 457.
64	during the next fortnight: OLs 386, 429, 461, 547, 576.
64	could take part in it: OLs 398, 496.
65	could be prevented: OLs 559, 572, 581, 596.
65	off the Syrian coast: OL 591.
65	still only under consideration: OL 720.

CHAPTER 3: Restless Interlude

69	at the end of July: GS iii.176–82.
69	(. . . force would require): Westphal, *Erinnerungen*, 126–27.
69	directive of 14 July: Trevor-Roper, 83–85.
69	(. . . inquiry in October 1940): Liddell Hart, *The Other Side of the Hill*, 233.
70	hung by a thread: Halder iii.48, 95.
70	the front by road: Creveld, 69.
70	his planned offensive: Rommel, 155; cf. Lewin, *Afrika Korps*, 95, and Jackson, *North Africa*, 144.
70	of the Russian front: Overy, 43-44.
71	about equal proportions: MME ii.281, iii.107.
71	(. . . during September, for instance): Roskill i.524.
71	by Westphal and others: Westphal, *Erinnerungen*, 120; Irving, 116.
71	(. . . identified most of them): e.g., OL 1518.
71	direct air strategy: GS iii.14, 235.
72	(. . . the points identified): OL 853.
72	without compromising the source: see PRO.AIR 40/2 323; Clayton, 159, 164; Gilbert vi.1233n.
72	back to Taranto: OL 674.
72	again a month later: OLs 801, 825, 829.
72	a faster vessel: OLs 861, 873, 888, 895, 897, 899, 901, 962, 969, 988, 1059.
73	Malta-based submarine *Unique:* OLs 936, 938, 954; Roskill i.525.

73	of "special intelligence": OLs 1145, 1149, 1192; MME ii.279; Roskill i.526; BI ii.285.
73	to Alexandria and Malta: OLs 1151, 1183, 1202, 1211, 1221.
73	from Greece in September: OLs 809, 1141.
73	to Greece in June: OLs 527, 532, 541.
73	traffic on 1 November: OL 1759.
73	in twenty-four hours: OLs 1587, 1601.
73	Thus a signal: OL 1835.
74	88mm Flak ammunition: OLs 1847, 1850, 1858, 1868, 1881; MME iii.103–4.
74	(. . . promised through Benghazi): Roskill i.533.
74	stayed for a fortnight: OLs 1963, 1984, MK 58.
74	be hastily improvised: OLs 1793, 1795, 1811, 1814, 1859; MKs 81, 93, 116, 191, 202.
74	"inexplicable," for example: Ciano, *Diary,* 395, quoted in Mellenthin, 57n.
75	Ultra had identified: OLs 497, 642, 692, 751, 969, 1719, 1781, 1852. No breach of security was in fact involved by the Malta signal (Gilbert vi.1233n).
75	or more returns: OLs 819, 976, 982, 1004, 1078, 1105, 1204, 1348, 1568, 1669, 1700, 1805, 1904.
76	battles round Sollum: OLs 768, 787, 835.
76	(. . . to attack Sollum): Halder iii.95, 131.
76	to Berlin as well: OLs 874, 881.
76	to sink the Bellona: OLs 861, 873, 883.
76	(. . . petrol to Benghazi): OL 1774.
76	journey from Tunis: OLs 1020, 890, 872.
76	better fighter control: OL 2021.
76	(. . . Naples the same day): OLs 1227, 1322.
77	Benghazi in late November: OLs 1475, 1478, 1490, 1537, 1613, 1656.
77	end of the month: OLs 1839, 1844.
77	wrangles about sharing it: OLs 637, 1228, 1332, 1343.
77	the Italian air command: OLs 958, 1049, 1528.
77	and transport arrangements: OLs 1635, 1670, 1678, 1790.
77	sent in by U-boat: OLs 1558, 1570, 1627.
77	troops by destroyer and JU-52s: OLs 1525, 1597, 1643, 1683, 1752.
78	". . . his forces against us": Gilbert vi. 1228.
78	at the end of October: Quotations in this paragraph are from Churchill iii.479–81, 486–88.
78	of buoyancy and confidence: Connell, *Auchinleck,* 335.
78	according to Westphal: Westphal, *Erinnerungen,* 124.

79	sinkings known from Ultra: e.g., OLs 954, 1009, 1216, 1221, 1396, 1487, 1604, 1880.
79	(". . . in so much as existing"): Gilbert vi.1130.
79	anything like decisive effect: Calrocoressi, 109; similarly Creveld, 72: "At no time, except perhaps during August and November 1941, did the aero-naval struggle in the central Mediterranean play a decisive part in North Africa."
79	Force K's brief reign: GS iii.235–36.
81	". . . find no better": Fraser, 297; cf. 134, 162, 187. He had made the same lament before; Bryant i.259
82	". . . degree than at present": Auchinleck, 374.
82	in the Mediterranean: OL 880.
83	at dawn on the 11th: OL 1098.
83	was at Derna: OL 1089. OL 1164, dated 15 September, reported the 21st Panzer's withdrawal to its starting position the previous evening, and thus confirmed that the operation was over.
83	to reinforce the warning: OL 1139.
83	air and ground commands: OL 1127.
84	action for a month: OLs 1170, 1230.
84	". . . Panzergruppe's future plans": OL 1208.
84	two or three more weeks: OLs 1175, 1192, 1259, 1318, 1374, 1379.
84	Panzergruppe's main preoccupation: OLs 1475, 1490, 1493, 1509, 1587, 1613, 1656, 1697, 1784, 1812, 1834, 1884.
84	preparations were complete: OLs 1643, 1698.
84	Panzergruppe's "projects": OL 1789.
84	88mm Flak ammunition: OL 1837.
84	by 20 November: OL 1795.
84	plan (made in mid-October): GS iii.231.
84	fuel dumps were established: OLs 1865, 1902, 1962.
84	three or four days: OLs 1994, 1998.
85	up to the attack: OLs 1770, 2008, 2015; MME iii.38.
85	sector of the defenses: OLs 1832, 2027, 1908.
85	assembled at Derna: OLs 1933, 1934, 1982.
85	dangerously close range: MME ii.263, iii.29-30, 434–44; BI ii.705-18.
86	under Fliegerfuehrer Afrika: OL 2029.
86	(. . . dive-bombers for escort duty: OLs 990, 1975.
86	ready for CRUSADER: MME iii.14.

CHAPTER 4: CRUSADER

88	(. . . on the 14th): OL 1952.
88	on 1 November: OL 1770.
89	on its way to Cairo: OLs 2008, 2015.
89	reported in Enigma: OLs 1179, 1953, 1973; MK 133. Cf. Cruikshank, 22–24, Shaw, 91.
90	". . . savage bull in a hencoop": Moorehead, 221. Cf. Liddell Hart, *Tanks*, ii.103.
90	designed Crusader to provoke: Barnett, 99.
90	choice of Army commander: But now see Carver, *Dilemmas*.
91	delivery on 26 November: MKs 217, 309, 241, 247, 249, 251.
91	". . . caught up with Rommel": Irving, 135.
91	his dash for the wire: MK 138.
91	had so abruptly deserted: Westphal, *Erinnerungen*, 137.
91	intercepted almost every day: MKs 56, 122, 191, 207, 249, 283, 333, 361, 403, 453, 482, 506, 514, 654, 666, 702, 710, 784, bearing dates between 20 November and 16 December, and in almost every case decrypted and signaled within twenty-four hours of the German transmission.
92	been on 8 November: MK 52; cf. p. 75 above.
92	"catastrophic" by 26 November,: MK 251.
92	jeopardized by the shortage: MKs 116, 133, 202, 241, 247, 249.
92	Ju-52 was laid on : MKs 177, 320.
92	at the same time: MKs 136, 260.
92	fighters from Germany: MK 45.
92	to Benghazi the next day: OL 1797; MK 81.
92	be destroyed at once: Gilbert vi. 1243–44.
92	"of the utmost urgency": MKs 167, 191, 202.
92	the "maddening muddles": Carver, *Tobruk*, 149.
93	". . . Tripolitania" for granted: MK 1394.
93	on the 23rd: MKs 669, 1241.
93	on 12 December: MKs 485, 493, 593, 605.
93	*Ankara* reached Benghazi safely next day: The *Ankara* story can be pieced together from MKs 664, 698, 777, 801, 811, 879, 895, 906, 910, 917, 931, 932, 974, 976, 998, 1000, 1027, 1111, and 1249. With scarcely an exception, all these signals were dispatched within a few hours of the original messages on which they were founded. Most

of the originals were Italian naval decrypts, which would usually have been incorporated in Admiralty signals to the British fleet commander even sooner.

94 ". . . Luftwaffe to Sicily": GS iii.233–34.

94 chiefly being exercised: GS iii.443, MME iii.21, 98; OKW/KTB ii/1.97; Trevor-Roper, 104–6.

95 Russia dated 2 November: OL 1767.

95 (. . . arrived in mid-December): MK 888.

95 forward of the town: MKs 496, 670, 675, 708, 783, 788.

96 command setup correctly: MK 613.

96 evidence to suggest it: MK 834.

96 (. . . so almost at once): MKs 916, 930.

96 about fuel supplies: MKs 1027, 1080.

96 considerable time to come: MK 1302.

96 (. . . for later that day): MKs 1649, 1656.

97 (. . . and 5 January): MKs 506, 1690.

98 evacuation of Cyrenaica: MKs 702, 710, 744, 894, 1080, 1514.

98 moment to strike: Mellenthin, 87–89.

98 in this convoy: MK 801.

98 panzer company to Tripoli: MKs 993, 1031, 1274, 1585, 1734.

99 ". . . enemy is hard pressed": Connell, *Auchinleck,* 422–23; Churchill iv.20.

99 attack before February: *London Gazette,* 15 January 1948, 317, 348.

99 were decrypted: MKs 1000, 1027, 1111.

100 one of the vessels: MK 801.

100 announced on 3 January: MKs 1551, 1555, 1582, 1605, 1639.

100 (. . . of antitank guns): OKW/KTB ii/1.200.

100 expected to dock shortly: MKs 1847, 1866.

100 available at short notice: OKW/KTB ii.243; Auchinleck, 348

100 basis of calculation: BI ii.336; MME iii.140.

100 ". . . forces began to advance": Auchinleck, 348

101 hitherto been the case: Bryant i.336–39; de Guingand, *Operation Victory,* 105–6; Jackson, *Africa,* 193; Hamilton i.522–23; PRO.WO 208/3575.

102 ". . . end of the line": Young, 121.

102 the autumn of 1941: Gilbert vi.1226.

102 ". . . telegraphese figures—can be": MME iii.199.

102 another three weeks: Connell, *Auchinleck,* 429.

102 offensive in the spring: GS iii.450.

103	offensive (my italics): Churchill iv.276.
103	eve of Crusader: MME iii.14; Gilbert vi.1217–64.
103	not advance the discussion: Churchill iv. 262–64.
103	strain Churchill was under: Bryant i.338. See also Soames, 313–14.
105	". . . rather than valuable": PRO.WO 208/3575; cf. BI ii.333.
105	el Eisa early in July: Kahn 472–77; Irving 142–45, 180.
105	consequences were momentous: Behrendt, 278–88, Eng. tr.
106	forbidden to move at all: OKW/KTB ii/1.98; Westphal, *Erinnerungen,* 146; Irving 144.
106	on the southern flank: MKs 1943, 1960.
106	". . . intended ground operations": MKs 1975, 1983.
106	surprise had been secured: MK 1991; MME iii.142, 147.
106	". . . the illusions remained": Fraser, *Shock,* 178.
107	hours on 25 January: MK 2075.
107	the British command: Irving, 145.
107	(. . . "a source in Egypt"): MKs 2160, 2421, 2754.
107	sent the previous day: MKs 2118, 2136, 2142; Connell, *Auchinleck,* 443. Here, it will be noted, is another occasion on which Connell in effect let out the Ultra secret, apparently with impunity.
108	before Mechili and Derna: MK 2208.
108	correct shade of meaning: MKs 2710, 2718.
108	it at the front: MKs 2434, 2471.

CHAPTER 5: Descent to Disaster

109	Kesselring's bland assurance: Kesselring 122; Macksey 117.
110	in April or May: GS iii.446–47.
110	sense in June 1941: Trevor-Roper, 78–82.
111	(". . . the Caucasus at all"): GS iv.35.
111	". . . the enemy elsewhere": Auchinleck, 383.
111	for June, or resign: Kennedy, 225–26; GS iii.458–59; Bryant i.380; Churchill iv.275–76; MME iii.204.
111	the coming desert battle: Auchinleck, 323, 388–90.
112	Hamilton: Hamilton i.626, 652–53.
113	was only 1,150 tons: MME iii.135.
114	they carried was lost: MKs 4922, 5068; MME iii.183.
114	Tripoli on 23 February: MKs 2898, 3052.
115	". . . regaining air supremacy": MKs 3422, 3429. The same order is noted in MME iii.210.

115	". . . to meet all demands": MK 4074.
115	a sixth as hitherto: MKs 3552, 3659, 3702, 3943, 4035, 4274, 4296, 4398, 4616, 4921, 5205, 5348, 5753, 6112.
116	by the middle of May,: MKs 4750, 4778, 4783.
116	would be supplied in May: MKs 4827, 5101.
116	"coming projected operatons": MK 5066.
116	petrol from 1 June: MKs 4967, 5051.
116	until 4 and 5 May: OKW/KTB ii.102-3; GS iii.445.
116	(. . . to his corps commanders): Irving, 152.
116	"if they arrive in time": MKs 5432, 5603, 5611.
116	on 15 May: MKs 5576, 5602.
117	tractors on OKW: MK 5066.
117	next two or three days: MK 5656.
117	". . . positions is imminent": MK 5834, signaled just as the German attack began.
117	(. . . at the same time): MK 5812.
117	importance of the operation: MKs 5860, 5889.
117	was on the alert: De Guingand, *Operation Victory,* 109; *Generals at War,* 180. The same, for instance, in Jackson, *North Africa,* 204; Fraser, *Shock,* 212.
117	at the critical moment: Carver, *Harding,* 70, 74.
118	of the fortifications: MK 3235.
118	by the end of May: MK 4594.
118	again on 23 May: MKs 4796, 4880, 5755.
118	mentions each in May: MKs 5140, 5270, 5274, 5280, 5311, 5401, 5507, 5561, 5581.
118	Alexandria one or two: MKs 5140, 5401, 5667.
118	Italian tanks on 11 March: MK 3324.
118	six weeks later: MK 4815.
118	(. . . for the latter!): Rommel, 198.
118	of the German offensive: MK 5059.
119	only 159 and 87: Auchinleck, 379; OKW/KTB ii.288; MK 3324.
119	return of 6 May: Auchinleck, 384; MK 5059.
119	the field on 25 May: ME iii.220.
119	by air and sea: MME iii.175.
119	appointed a planning staff: Westphal, *Erinnerungen,* 154–55, 159; Irving, 148; OKW/KTB ii.100.
120	beyond the end of June: GS iii.454.
120	he had captured Tobruk: OKW/KTB ii.102; MME iii.195.
120	that could be mounted: E.g. MKs 3711, 3870.

120	leaving its equipment behind: MKs 2082, 2902, 3343, 3852.
120	in the immediate future: MK 3739.
120	new bases on 28 April: MK 4686.
121	given to the signal: MK 5209.
121	if Rommel was victorious: OKW/KTB ii.104.
123	forecast on the twenty-fifth: Connell, *Auchinleck,* 504, 517; Auchinleck, 390.
123	was a serious mistake: Carver, *Tobruk,* 168–69.
123	had been "considerable": MKs 6054, 6064.
123	with 270 on 6 May: MK 6389; MME iii.231 gives a similar total.
124	the next few days: MKs 6423, 6676, 6840.
124	antitank gun fire: MKs 6146, 6729.
124	as far as Benghazi,: Connell, *Auchinleck,* 539; Auchineleck, 392.
124	playing a waiting game: MKs 6272, 6293, 6460.
124	of some air support: MK 6375.
124	intentions were already apparent: MKs 6402, 6431, 6473, 6492.
124	(. . . fell in empty desert): Mellenthin, 104.
125	soon as he got back: MKs 6388, 6489, 6553.
125	as good as his word: MME iii.237.
125	(. . . sharp rebuke in Enigma): MK 6555.
126	support were also common: E.g., MKs 7322, 7323, 7327.
127	perhaps saved Tobruk: Cf., however, Fraser, *Shock,* 216–27.
127	it to be thwarted: MKs 6657, 6670.
127	British retreat eastward: MK 6747.
127	(. . . 16 June, for instance): MKs 6860, 6924, 6933, 6945.
127	afternoon of 18 June: MK 6999.
127	climax on the 20th: MKs 7034, 7054, 7056, 7082.
128	Alamein four months later: Churchill iv. 343–44; Bryant i.408.
128	movements of British troops: E.g., MKs 7354, 7358, 7382.
128	The Axis infantry was 22/6, MK 7241, 0846/22.
128	been taken in Tobruk: MKs 7274, 7288, 7289, 7330. MK 7306 gave a full account of the capture of Tobruk.
128	By thus penetrating beyond the Egyptian frontier: 1700/22, MK 7288, 0109/23.
128	final assault on Malta: OKW/KTB ii.103.

129	Kesselring vehemently expressed: 0500/23, MKs 7322, 7323, 1031/23.
129	". . . a warrior only once": OKW/KTB ii.440–48, 616.
129	". . . position in Africa": Lewin, *Afrika Korps,* 175; cf. Jackson, *Africa,* 238.
129	was stiffer than expected: MK 7677.
129	761 were believed serivceable: MK 7603.
129	After a postponement: 3016 MKs 7868, 7872, 1439/3.
129	Rommel determined to launch: 1800/29, MK 7818, 2209/29.
129	the British position: MKs 7967, 7985.
129	and resistance stubborn: MKs 8038, 8067, 8096.
129	"the condition of the troops": MK 8135.
129	four sorties a day: MKs 8185, 8191, 8194.
130	new landing grounds: MK 8186.
130	That evening Rommel called a halt: 2100/3, MK 8137, 0015/4.
130	hardening British resistance: MK 8247.
130	over to the defensive: MK 8239.
130	The next evening's situation: P.M. 14, MK 8254, 1511/5.
130	500 of them: MKs 7339, 7846, 7937.
130	employed on 5 July: MK 8341.
130	drained Crete of petrol: MKs 8295, 8298, 8129, 8157, 8158, 8363. The same shortage of petrol on Crete occurred repeatedly, e.g., MK 9247.
130	became available again: MKs 8212, 8253, 8366.
130	have to be reduced: MK 8179.
131	became a total loss: MKs 7400, 7410, 7451, 7466, 7484, 7500, 7505, 7518, 7663. Santoni unaccountably omits *Avionia* from his list of ships sunk "per documentata attività Ultra" on p. 340.
131	(. . . Mersa Matruh on 5 July): MKs 7490, 8251, 8318.
131	additional antitank guns: MK 7581.
131	for shipment to Libya: MK 8667.
132	plan to lure Rommel's main body southward: Barnett, 212; Lewin, *Afrika Korps,* 183.
132	(. . . claimed a breakthrough): MKs 8558, 8644.
132	before Rommel could react: MK 8868.
132	in *The Desert Generals:* Barnett, 2nd ed., 216.
132	"run out of steam": interview quoted in Hamilton i.592; cf. 595.
133	influenced Auchinleck's moves: E.g., MKs 7868, 7893, 8067, 8137, 8239.
133	". . . battle and saved Egypt": Barnett, 217, 244.

134	". . . had forced upon us": Rommel, 253–57.
134	Brigade's "Balaclava charge": Mellenthin, 134; Irving, 183.
134	fighter aircraft serviceability: MKAs 7, 84.
134	air transport moving: MKs 8337, 8197.
134	take time to assemble: MK 8569.
134	(. . . men and 400 tanks): MKA 1083.
134	occupation of Egypt: MK 8612.
134	maintain establishment standards: MK 9066.
134	statement of casualties: MKAs 190, 377.
134	". . . and agreed to them": MKAs 191, 375, 1067, 1380.
134	to the Libyan frontier: OKW/KTB ii.107.
135	Ramcke Brigade over: MKAs 916, 1079, 1104.
135	Loehr, OB Southeast: MK 9551.
135	from Crete on 3 July: MKs 8295, 8298.
135	the next two days: MK 8235.
135	middle of the month: E.g., MKAs 534, 715, 767.
135	needed on 23 July: MKA 161.
135	Africa during July: MKA 946; Irving, 185, quotes the lower figure for 26 July also given in MKA 387.
135	(. . . Brigade) from Germany: E.g., MK 9393; MKA 1097.
135	regiments arrived in Africa: MK 1294.
135	15th and 21st Panzer Divisions: MK 5814, MKA 1810.
135	antitank guns per battalion: MKAs 806, 949, 1319, 1480, 1490, 1494, 1858.
136	in the Tobruk docks: MK 8896.
136	2,000 until early August: E.g., MKAs 1257, 1572.
136	1,000 tons a day: MKAs 1272, 1371, 1354, 1518, 1628, 1852.
136	ammunition on 31 July: MKs 8567, 9195, 9196: MKAs 787, 799, 826.
136	*Rondine* on 20 July: MK 9595.
136	a few days later: MKA 184.
136	of getting a berth: MKA 843.
136	(. . . known well in advance): MKAs 53, 79.
137	stabilization of the front: E.g., MKs 8256, 8632, 8690, 8903, 9048, 9195, 9250, 9259, 9364; MKAs 22, 25, 1022 1079, 1402.
137	mid-July and mid-August: E.g., MKs 6689, 6693; MKAs 1367, 1368, 1376, 1423, 1435, 1441, 1473.
137	1,000 and 2,000 thereafter: E.g., MKs 6828, 8514, 8797; MKAs 1841, 2375; QT 252.
137	2 June and 31 July: MK 6256; MKA 795.

137	12 and 23 July: MK 9088; MKA 577.
137	no large consignments: E.g., MKs 9030, 9440; MKAs 142, 290.
137	many more in August: MKA 937.
137	96 Italian tanks: MKAs 795, 1012, 1083.
137	and 173 Italian tanks: MKA 1741.
137	in the recent fighting: Rommel gave similar figures, Rommel, 245, 263. Compare MKA 1760 on "actual" as distinct from "battle" strength.
137	to meet the new need: MKs 8920, 9149, 9177, 9195, 9340. At the end of September, QT 2473 reported the success of "corsetting" as a defensive measure.

CHAPTER 6: The Eighth Army's First Victories

139	". . . This was exhilarating": Churchill iv. 412.
139	". . . the poor flies out": Churchill iv.414; de Guingand, *Operation Victory*, 139.
140	". . . and in fact dangerous": Hamilton i.618.
140	to make his preparations: Hamilton i.623.
140	to his desert headquarters: 12/8, MKA 1776, 2239/13.
140	Cairo to Wadi Halfa: MKA 1335.
140	of occupation in Egypt: MK 8913.
140	office in Rome: 12/8, MKA 1880, 0545/15.
140	the Qattara Depression: 13/8 MKA 2096, 2122/17.
142	Until early in August: 15/8, MKA 2094, 2095, 2146/17.
142	success very unlikely: see also MKA 2291.
143	as Montgomery himself claimed: Montgomery, *Memoirs*, 103-4; Montgomery, *Alamein to the Sangro*, 4.
143	". . . out for the top": Barnett, 266.
143	in his official *Despatch:* Auchinleck, 395–98. It will also be found in Connell, *Auchinleck*, 937–44, and Barnett, 331–37.
143	himself did name it: Auchinleck, 367.
144	". . . was virtually undefended": de Guingand, *Operation Victory*, 141.
144	training in the Delta: Hamilton i.634.
144	Montgomery verbally himself: de Guingand, *Generals at War*, 187–88.
145	(". . . obviousness," thought Alexander): Alexander, *Memoirs*, 21–22.
145	Others thought the same: For instance, de Guingand, *Operation Victory*, 142; Carver, *Harding*, 92; Horrocks, *Full Life*, 108; cf. Hamilton i.653–54.

145	". . . El Alamein position": Rommel, 277.
145	"greatness and genius": Carl von Clausewitz, *On War,* ed. M. Howard and P. Paret (Princeton, 1984), 71.
146	Another twenty-four hours: 27/8, QT 301, 0811/29.
146	others had preceded it: MKAs 2311, 2316, 2407, 2604, 2635, 2699, 2704; QTs 42, 77, 83, 101, 153, 301.
147	match for the "Specials": MKAs 1741, 2493; QT 396. MME iii.383n gives almost exactly the same figures for 30 August as QT 396 for the 28th. British figures from Hamilton i.662–64.
147	of Blitzkrieg tactics: MKA 2615.
147	had authority over Rommel: QT 40.
147	was in constant attendance: QT 300.
148	(. . . until about 8 September): QT 941.
148	was expected there: MKA 2623; QTs 410, 473.
148	"the hecatomb of the tankers": quoted in Santoni, 176.
148	(. . . quartermaster in Rome): QT 417.
148	appreciation of 18 August: MKA 2282.
149	same twenty-day period: MKAs 2623, 2624.
149	*Pozarica* on 23 August: MKAs 2523, 2568.
149	petrol from their allies: QT 142.
149	most of the fighting: QT 378.
149	sailing program next day: QTs 60, 136.
149	". . . guarantee can be given": QT 136.
150	already been signaled: MKAs 2596, 2614, 2647.
150	petrol in barrels: QTs 100, 229,232,389.
153	soon at the bottom: QT 254, 256, 310, 331.
150	had actually arrived: QT 396.
150	(. . . to affect the fighting): QTs 396, 417, 467, 563, 688, 704.
150	(bombed and set on fire): QTs 604, 607, 658, 733, 758.
151	was sunk on the way: MME iii.327, iv.25, 210.
151	too short of supplies: Kennedy, 264.
151	shortage of petrol: 2/9, OT 585, 658, 0306/2.
151	(. . . plateau in the south): QTs 585, 658, 844.
152	Rommel later stressed: QT 658: Rommel, 284–85.
152	(. . . on 29 August): QTs 417, 941.
152	ready to meet it: QT 1427.
154	". . . came into its own": WO 208/3575.
155	their vigour in action: GS iv.68–69; Bryant i.503–14; Hamilton i.752, 819–37.
155	ran out in October: Bryant, i.506.
155	discovered in the 10th: QT 1144.
155	immediately flew to Europe: QTs 1578, 2228. It was pre-

sumably the new caution about "gossipy" items which held up QT 2228 for three days after the intercept translated as C 29.

155   Austria on the 17th: QT 4152.

157   Four tank returns: QTs 2609, 3533, 4180, 4234.

157   in the Afrika Korps: QT 4234. The figures in MME iv.9 are almost identical but show also another 20 (mostly IIIs) under repair.

157   1,000 tanks all told: MME iv.9, 30.

157   part of Panzer Army: QTs 2038, 3709, 4225, 4595.

157   soldiers for combat duties: QT 2103, C 49.

158   and 50 dive-bombers: E.g., QTs 3025, 3753, 3983, 4064, 4142, 4217.

158   supported Eighth Army: GS iv.62.

158   found to reduce them: QTs 2454, 3111, 3402, 4106, 4139.

158   of sea transport: QTs 3102, 3621.

159   rates of consumption: QT 1394.

159   had consumed vast quantities: QT 2410.

159   cause of several complaints: QTs 1822, 2091, 2256.

159   sign of its delivery: QTs 2242, 2318, 2541.

159   six months, commented Ciano: GS iv.64.

159   rations had been necessary: QTs 2644, 2964.

160   high sickness rate: QT 3024.

160   ". . . decreasing through illness": QTs 3059, 3117, 3193.

160   he could not keep: QT 3102.

160   particularly ammunition and food: QT 3231.

160   the complete tanker program: 15/10, QTs 3712, 3785, 1731/17.

160   had been torpedoed: QTs 3868, 3915, 3973.

160   of the German troops: P.M. 20, QT 4077, 1708/22.

160   leaving aside new deliveries: 20/10, QT 4119, 0044/23.

162   open in about that time: QTs 1590, 1637, 1670.

162   planned to overwhelm: QTs 1863, 2003, 2053, 2234.

162   . . . Siwa, on the ground: QTs 2347, 2362, 2519, 2812, 2981, 3051, 3387, 3506, 4049.

162   known fairly accurately: E.g., QTs 3110, 3195.

162   of the Qattara Depression: QT 3359.

163   coast road as well: QT 3319, 3409; cf. MME iv.26-27.

163   both eye and camera: E.g., QTs 3844, 3944, 3966.

163   "Quiet day. No change": QTs 3944, 4051, 1700/22 QT 4143 0820/23, QT 4221; MME iv.18, Cruickshank, 32. The success of the deception—MELTINGPOT and the LDRG at Jalo—received confirmation just after the battle began. QT 4242, dispatched at 1523/24, reported that

on the previous evening Panzer Army had been expecting the main thrust to come in the south.

163   on the first morning: QT 4259.

163   evening of 25 October: QT 4394.

163   next day or two: QTs 4211, 4357, 4421, 4424, 4431, 4438, 4447, 4588, etc.

163   ". . . up against it": Rommel, 313.

163   come, it was believed: QTs 4709, 4713, 4751.

163   Crete from Greece: QTs 4592, 4599, 4603, 4615, 4756, 4767.

164   to be relied on: QT 4682.

164   being forced to recognize: Rommel 308; QTs 4516, 4545, 4550, 4554, 4628.

164   on the 31st: QTs 4818, 4921; but cf. Hamilton i.828–29.

164   (. . . it on 31 October): QT 4958.

165   ". . . precisely calculated instructions": OKW/KTB ii.697, 754; Halder KTB iii.528, 531; GS iv.32.

165   first reported that: early P.M. 2, QT 5086, 1555/3.

165   for a fighting withdrawal: P.M. 2, QT 5098, 1835/3.

165   turned against him: 1200/3, QT 5207, 1411/4.

165   Rommel wrote later: Rommel, 321.

165   a nominally prepared position: 4/11, QTs 5292, 5340, 1059/5, 2215/5, 1059/5, 2215/5. Two misprints in the account of these events in BI ii.449-50 need correcting. Page 449, note 301, should refer to QT 5207, not QT 5027. Rommel's request for permission to retire to Fuka, said in the asterisked note on page 450 to have been decrypted on 6 November, was in fact decrypted and signaled on the 5th as QT 5292.

CHAPTER 7: The Slow Pursuit Across Libya

167   Panzer Army was already doubtful: 1900/4, QT 5295, 5302, 1236/5.

167   Rommel had decided that: 1300/5, QT 5482, 0842/7.

167   as a halting place: QT 5530.

167   the evening of 7 November: P.M. 7, QT 5567, 0445/8.

167   behind the Agheila position: A.M. 7, QT 5763, 0121/10.

167   during 10 November: P.M. 9, QTs 5794, 5797, 1615/10.

167   brought forward in time: QTs 5877, 5893, 5959.

167   Hitler and Mussolini jointly warned Rommel: 10/11, QT 5946, 0942/12.

170   ". . . and dealt with later": Hamilton i.732; my italics.

171   of Montogomery's generalship: De Guingand, *Operation*

Victory, 212–14; Montgomery, *Alamein to the Sangro,* 25; MME iv.82, 88, 96.

171 so-called *corps de chasse:* Barnett, *Desert Generals,* 287–99, 309-13; Carver, *Alamein,* 184-202; Liddell Hart, *Second World War,* 318–19; Lewin, *Montgomery,* 93-94; Jackson, *Africa,* 329; Irving, *Fox,* 229; Hamilton ii.11–44; BI ii.450–61.

171 had on the ninth: QTs 5265, 5794.

171 as he repeatedly said: Montgomery, *Alamein to the Sangro,* 38; Montgomery, *Memoirs,* 146; de Guingand, *Victory,* 216–71.

172 (. . . restated by General Fraser): Fraser, *Shock,* 252.

172 (. . . 10 and 20 November): QTs 5785, 6597, 6626.

172 would have reached Agheila: QTs 6591, 6680.

172 Rommel's opinion that: A.M. 17, QTs 6433, 6437, 0815/18.

172 with fuel and rations: QTs 6065, 6162, 6166, 6614.

172 not yet being taken: QT 6261.

173 was "almost immobilised": ATs 6231, 6253, 6257, 6266, 6319, 6360, 6371. The same point is made in Rommel, 352.

173 from Benghazi as intended,: QT 6374.

173 again on the 17th: QT 6433.

173 distance on 18 November: QTs 6403, 6436, 6482, 6597.

173 was no longer possible: QT 6495.

173 ". . . increased petrol supplies": Hamilton ii.62.

173 frontier on the 12th: QT 6122.

173 earlier the same day: QT 6015.

173 Rommel's subsequent account: Rommel, 337–58; esp. 354–55.

174 he did this quickly: Montgomery, *Alamein to the Sangro,* 30; Montgomery, *Memoirs,* 146.

174 that Rommel bluffed him: This was asserted in 1960 by Barnett, *Desert Generals,* 292–93.

174 17 and 23 November: QTs 6433, 6437, 6714, 6717, 6839, 6944.

174 prospect of success: A.M. 23, QT 6839, 0834/24.

174 for Montgomery's estimate: Montgomery, *Alamein to the Sangro,* 30.

174 54 on 2 December: QTs 6839, 7012, 7629, 7829. Similar figures for 4 December in OKW/KTB ii.1084.

174 Army's tank specialists: QT 6971; cf. QT 6749.

175 (. . . nonexistent for some time): QT 7041.

175 von Rintelen in Rome: QT 6756.

175	25 October and 14 December: QT 7423, 8931.
175	still far from secure: QTs 6528, 6714, 6743, 6756, 6981.
175	(. . . and Arab labor away): QTs 7832, 7865, 8049, 8553, 8583, 8655, 8758.
176	Williams to Montgomery's biographer: Hamilton ii.92–93.
176	jointly on 22 November: QTs 6839, 6944.
176	first seeking permission: QTs 7280, 7389, 7751.
176	according to Westphal,: Westphal, *Erinnerungen,* 186; Rommel, 365–69; Irving, 224–27.
176	(. . . would never be kept): QT 7782, VM 403.
177	another decrypt: QT 7517.
177	transport to do the same: QTs 7772, 7789, 7903.
177	move they might make: QT 8134; cf. 8055, 8057, 8159.
177	". . . Rommel slips away?": Gilbert vii.279.
177	British turning movement: E.g., QTs 8237, 8307, 8640, 8755, 8946.
177	ground forces on the 15th: QT 8601.
178	at the end of December: Gilbert vii.279.
178	Please reply urgently: QTs 9039, 9401. Rommel's account is in Rommel, 377.
179	several times repeated: QTs 9145, 9433.
179	for days on end: QTs 9177, 9681.
179	acute in late November: QTs 9363, 9364; VM 1609.
179	assault on Axis shipping: QT 9681.
179	". . . the Tripolitanian mousetrap": QTs 9731, 9856; VMs 111, 141, 266, 291.
179	was now "imperative": VMs 232, 233.
179	the Italians wanted: VMs 346, 379, 639.
180	met Bastico on 30 December: OKW/KTB iii.13, 120; GS iv.338; MME iv.230; Irving, 233-34.
180	immensely long signal: VM 403; cf. VMs 401, 445, 498, 539, 958.
180	as soon as possible: VMs 542, 624.
180	stand up against it: VM 1393.
181	(. . . in the recent past): E.g., VM 1030.
181	to Mareth at once: VMs 1754, 1769, 1984.

CHAPTER 8: Torch

184	British troops in North Africa: C 41.
184	under the TORCH cover plan: GS iv.138; Cruickshank, 34-49.
185	motor transport and 350 guns: QT 3750.

185	reinforcement of Panzer Army,: QT 2242.
185	"the Gibraltar situation": QT 4615.
185	Aegean on 29 October: QT 4693.
185	fourth of November: QTs 5170, 5186, 5306, 5426.
185	signal to Rommel: QT 5207.
185	(. . . to discover its destination): QTs 5377, 5382.
185	Comiso, in Sicily, to Tobruk: QTs 5270, 5306.
186	different German authorities: QTs 5399, 5400, 5402, 5408, 5425, 5448, 5459, 5490, 5494.
186	about Allied intentions: GS iv.65; OKW/KTB ii.115, 857.
186	(. . . many German aircraft): QT 4106.
186	into the Germans' arms: OKW/KTB ii.918.
186	triumph for security: Masterman, 110.
187	within a few hours: QTs 5451, 5532, 5543, 5544.
187	". . . comrades of the air": QT 5547.
187	among fighter pilots: QT 5700.
187	at El Aouina airfield: QTs 5764, 5779.
187	reported until the 10th: QTs 5777, 5796.
187	dawn on 11 November: QT 5874.
188	Early on 9 November: 0330/9, QT 5706, 1919/9.
188	the first moves of German aircraft: 1800/9, QT 5720, 2314/9.
188	in many quarters: GS iv.118.
190	(. . . water from Sicily): MME iv.419; OKW/KTB ii.112.
190	poach Rommel's supplies: QT 6148.
190	Axis in North Africa: OKW/KTB ii.118, 927, 956; GS iv.172.
190	Kampfgruppe T: 10/11, QT 5896, 1552/11.
190	Aouina next day: QTs 5864, 5924, 5952.
190	a convoy of two steamships: 12/11, QTs 5931, 5934, 0606/12.
191	(. . . tanks and motor transport): QTs 5920, 5938, 6010, 6033.
191	had also arrived: QTs 5999, 6030, 6042, 6102.
191	redirected to Tunisia: QTs 6083, 6092, 6103, 6131, 6148, 6151, 6194, 6208, 6255, 6528.
191	anything hitherto seen in Africa: See Terraine, 391.
191	tanks were due shortly: QTs 6186, 6291, 6361, 6345, 6399, 6400, 6452.
192	educational tours: NA.SRH-031.
192	into the New Year: BI ii.740–43.
192	cautiously satisfied: 2000/16, QT 6356, 0447/17.

193	with the rather less sanguine views: 1600/16, QT 6347, 0351/17.
193	Just over a week later: 2030/25, QTs 7008, 7021, 0827/26.
193	(. . . road on 17 November): QTs 6425, 6539, 6546, 6602, 6747.
193	a score of anti-tank guns: 26/11, QT 7091, 0842/27.
193	defended at all costs: QTs 7106, 7189, 7295.
193	scratch defense force: QT 7163.
194	as quickly as possible: QTs 6779, 7184.
194	to attack at dawn on 1 December: 2000/30, QT 7455, 0453/10.
194	Tunis was most acute: QT 7729.
194	the whole of Tunisia: QTs 7541, 7537.
194	(. . . and Sfax as well): E.g., QTs 7408, 7460, 7483, 7742, 7771.
194	it a tempting target: QTs 6828, 7047.
194	be sent at once,: QTs 7221, 8058.
194	losses were "intolerable": QT 7273.
195	source of the raids: QT 8583.
195	the shorter sea crossing: QT 8127.
195	traffic began at once: QTs 8291, 8306, 8312.
195	succor Panzer Army: QTs 9027, 9084, 9313.
195	to extend his bridgehead: QT 7922.
195	Fifth Panzer Army: QTs 8234, 8668; OKW/KTB ii.1076–77.
195	into immediate effect: QTs 8311, 8327, 8712, 8772, 9181, 9234.
195	(. . . massive air support): QT 9132.
196	of 1,000 a day: QTs 8761, 9662.
196	(. . . Hitler ordering it): QTs 9327, 9587, 9950; NWA 338.
196	beginning of December: QTs 7472, 7770.
196	action on Christmas Eve: QTs 8234, 8933, 8966, 9260, 9380; OKW/KTB ii.1186.
198	became available next day: VMs 1068, 1110, 1154, cf. OKW/KTB iii.35–36.
198	and the same time: VM 1288.
198	arrived on 26 January: VMs 1281, 1327, 1339, 1477, 1492, 1661, 2289, 2368, 2574, etc.
198	Gabes from the rear: VMs 147, 291.
198	out ten days later: VM 942.
199	(. . . with Rommel's command): VMs 353, 444, 478.

199	Gafsa on 3 January: VM 375.
199	". . . Rommel is to survive": VM 633.
199	a few days later: VMs 1320, 1453.
199	watched on 22 January: VM 2017.
199	were seen at Sbeitla: VM 2211.
199	launched from that direction: VM 2573.
200	review of 24 January: VM 2406.
202	such an undertaking: VM 2858.
202	counterattack through Fondouk: VMs 2978, 2995.
202	on 10 February: VM 3485.
202	(. . . independent Pichon-Fondouk plan): E.g., VM 3396.
203	his armor into Tunisia: Clark, 153.
203	at least another month: MME iv.275–76.
203	of the Axis command: VMs 3613, 3798 of 9 and 12 February; cf. Cs 93, 94 of 26 January.
204	Supremo directive of 11 February: 11/2, VMs 4001, 4003, 1865/14.
205	heavy air raid on Sbeitla: 1800/13, VMs 3939, 3953, 3968, 2101/13.
205	On 7 February, the Fifth Panzer: P.M. 7, VMs 3485, 3498, 0006/8.
205	(. . . from Faid and Gafsa): VM 3179.
205	was decrypted on 12 February: 11/2, VMs 3777, 3884, 0436/12.
205	about its location: NWA 405.
206	(. . . powerful long-barreled IVs): VMs 3396, 3790, 3856, 3868, 3962; see also VMs 3183, 4075, 4473.
206	Feriana-Kasserine-Sbeitla: MME iv.292–93.
206	This led Kesselring to deduce: 16/2, VM 4221, 0459/17.
206	likely future developments: 1930/17, VM 4299, 2133/18.
206	already on the move: VM 4133.
206	defense of Mareth: VMs 4315, 4438.
206	about the wisdom of further advance: 2200/17, VM 4390, 2123/18.
206	von Arnim's intentions: VM 4487.
206	to abandon Tunisia altogether: Rommel, 401–2.
207	(. . . Rommel later called it): Rommel, 402.
207	(. . . almost 200 tanks): VM 3573.
207	scope of the operation: VMs 4473, 4588, 4592, 4602.
207	but intensive training: Bradley, 31, 44.
208	(. . . invitation to attend it): Hamilton ii.141–43.
208	". . . teach amateurs their job": Jackson, *Africa*, 355.

208	(. . . Montgomery called him): Hamilton ii.114.
208	postwar *Crusade in Europe:* Eisenhower, 158.
208	of information, Ultra: Lewin, *Ultra,* 273–74; Hamilton ii.165.
209	the 18th Army Group: PRO.WO 208/3581.
209	Comando Supremo's order: P.M. 22, VMs 4762, 4793, 1433/23.
209	by the following evening: See also VMs 4931, 4939, 4967, and all of 25 February.
209	(. . . Fifth Panzer Army's Front): VMs 4997, 5005.
210	positively welcome an attack: Alexander, "African Campaign," 872.
210	having become unbalanced: Montgomery, *Alamein to the Sangro,* 44–45.
210	Enfidaville in northern Tunisia: OKW/KTB iii.155–56, 187–88, NWA 475–76, 510–11.
210	documented by 1 March: VMs 4907, 5028, 5050, 5068, 5095, 5111, 5182, 5189, 5197, 5207, 5244, 5262, 5273; cf. VM 5654.
210	the 6th or later: VM 5440.
210	the "known units": 3/3, VM 5605, 0331/5.
210	under orders to follow: 4/3, VM 5620, 0612/5.
210	warning was not needed: VM 5722.
210	Thus forearmed: Cf. Hamilton ii.154–55.
212	the attack in advance: VM 6021.
212	accusing finger at Messe: Kesselring, 152.
212	ships on 7 March: VMs 5860, 5865; Santoni, 226.
212	improve convoy escort: OKW/KTB iii.198.
212	were sunk nevertheless: VMs 6296, 6354, 6404.
212	". . . protect the convoys": OKW/KTB iii.236, 1603.
212	had just found, however: Rommel, 419.
212	Y Service summaries: PRO.WO 208/3581.
213	(. . . three panzer divisions): E.g., VMs 6173, 6224, 6813, 6911, 6979, 7280, 7237, 7256. For example, the tank strength of the 10th Panzer at El Guettar was 26 at 1300 hours on 23 March, and had fallen to 16 next morning. These figures were signaled at 1824/23 and 0805/25 respectively.
213	and Italian air forces: VM 6146.
213	machines of all types: VMs 6709, 6886, 6977.
213	all that was ordered: VMs 6660, 6698, 6806.
213	Early on the morning of the 19th: 1400/17, VM 6814, 0606/19.

213	a concentration of 4000 vehicles: 19/2, VM 6836,1426/19.
213	soon after Christmas: Montgomery, *Alamein to the Sangro,* 47; Shaw, 236–38.
213	". . . than I had hoped": Alexander, "African Campaign," 874; Alexander, *Alamein to the Sangro,* 50. Hamilton ii.187 implies that an original intention of secrecy was abandoned only after Freyberg's column was sighted.
213	on 19 March: 19/3, VM 6964, 2214/20.
214	(. . . divisions were hastily drafted): WO 208/3581, entry for 19 March, and VMs 6845, 7217.
214	of the fighting there: VMs 7337, 7395, 7412, 7415.
214	55 under repair: VMs 7511, 7537. The 21st Panzer had had 60 "runners" only twenty-four hours earlier (VM 7418).
214	the official history declares: MME iv.354.
215	sailing of a convoy: VM 7481.
215	(. . . in Naples harbor): VM 7817.
215	were on the way: VM 7823.
215	men a day by air: VMs 8234, 8254, 8976.
215	after it was issued: VMs 7900, 7908.
215	scarp above Enfidaville: VM 8133.
215	several tank returns: VMs 7045, 7825, 8095, 8127, 8242, 8839.
216	the Mareth-Akarit area: VMs 8534, 8556, 8569, 8572.
216	until the last minute: VMs 8729, 8776.
216	". . . not a good battle": GS iv.352.
216	without his consent: VM 8971.
216	foot for lack of it: VMs 8872, 8964.
217	bad effect on morale: Kesselring, 155.
217	to be sent in April: ML 13; cf. VMs 9801, 9814.
218	unwanted reinforcements: E.g., VMs 8837, 9514; MLs 10, 76, 86, 773, 1427.
218	days is much disputed: Compare, for instance, MME iv.416; Nicolson, *Alex,* 186; OKW/KTB iii.361, 373; Hunt, 174; Alexander, "African Campaign," 878; Clayton, 236–37.
218	surface movement impossible: VM 9921; MLs 1088, 1103, 1569, 1597, 1759, 1767; Cs 120, 124, 125, 129, 131.
218	the water they needed: MLs 490, 669, 862, 1024, 1111.

CHAPTER 9: Sicily

221	Sicily before the assault: GS iv.368–69; Gilbert vii.379–80.
221	in the near future: VM 5072.
221	". . . tune of his piping": Hamilton ii.257.
222	present the greater danger: GS iv. 465–66.
222	MINCEMEAT: Local color and interesting background have been assembled by Roger Morgan in *After the Battle* (1980), 54, 1–25.
222	to them than Italy: OKW/KTB iii/1.178; QT 2016; VMs 5487, 5672.
223	defenses to be improved: OKW/KTB iii.1429, 1432–33; GS iv.370, 463; Deakin, *Brutal Friendship,* 378–93.
223	". . . in present circumstances": OKW/KTB iii.1430–31.
223	in the Mediterranean: Cruickshank, 51, 146.
223	". . . on a large scale": VM 5072; see p. 221, above.
223	"According to a source: 12/5, ML 1955, 1551/15.
224	of extra shipping space: MLs 1942, 1983, 1995.
224	arrived on 14 June: MLs 2400, 2513, 2733, 4439.
224	increased on 13 May: MLs 1949, 1972.
224	airfields were feared: ML 2443.
224	aircraft in Sardinia: MLs 1991, 2625, 5077.
224	Sardinia by sea and air: MLs 2452, 2473, 2509, 2907, 2986, 3239, 3241, 3272, 3286, 3352, 3429, 3529, 3538, 3510, 7959, 7961, and many others.
224	strong by 2 June: ML 3668.
225	had doubled in strength: ML 6805.
225	(. . . 15th Panzergrenadier Division): ML 5781.
225	there and for Sicily: ML 4013.
225	was being arranged: MLs 4373, 5212, 5299.
225	were landed in Corsica: ML 8157.
225	Messina in a single day: ML 4818.
225	now going to Sardinia: MLs 5217, 5296.
225	established in Sicily: ML 2753.
225	(. . . in stolen lorries): ML 7927.
226	(. . . straits on 21 June): MLs 4839, 4877, 4898, 5002.
226	"two part Panzergrenadier division": ML 4055.
226	possessed 42 tanks: ML 2242.
226	available until 21 July: MME v.41; ML 8309.
227	its antimony and copper: OKW/KTB iii.1612.
227	caused, on its own: As Montagu, *Man Who Never Was,* 130, 132–34, claims. Far less information about German

strategic planning was available when Montagu published his book in 1953, of course.

228   Cassino by 21 June: MLs 2394, 2643, 2888, 5529.

228   reconstituted, for Siena: MLs 3301, 5221, 5456, 5503.

228   southern France to Foggia: MLs 4862, 5500.

228   between Florence and Rome: MLs 5456, 5499, 5799.

228   and the 29th PG: OKW/KTB iii.1771; MME v. 90; Cs 149; 150, 151; MLs 7812, 8051.

228   14th and subsequent days: MLs 7288, 7390, 7630, 7673, 7719, 7829.

228   noted on 17 July: MLs 7739, 7867, 7936, 8330.

228   was lagging behind demand: ML 4679.

229   have been about 240: MLs 4471, 6186; cf. 5081.

229   (. . . in the Mediterranean): MK 5728.

229   serviceable out of 260: ML 5088.

229   operated against the landing: MME v.46, 99; Jackson, Italy, 29.

229   to the ground troops: E.g., MLs 8501, 8689.

229   thereby made apparent: Cf. Terraine, 573–74; Clayton, 256–61.

229   week before HUSKY: MME v.46, 74–75, 99.

230   experienced panzer general: C 142; ML 5720.

230   operational control altogether: OKW/KTB iii.778; MME v.44.

230   should the Italians defect: GS iv.464; SSI 50; Irving, 264–65. OKW/KTB iii.783 gives a somewhat later date.

230   giving up his post: CX/MSS 2544/T 27, 2607/T8, C 132. The sentence was omitted from ML 2394.

231   According to von Senger: von Senger, 147.

231   Sicily nor Sardinia: OKW/KTB iii.752–53.

231   both nations by air: MLs 6581, 6810.

231   (. . . the airborne troops): MME v.9.

231   airfields in their charge: MLs 3557, 3864, 4948.

232   their base in Sicily: ML 6873.

232   coast or in Greece: ML 7159.

232   a few days later: MLs 7288, 7390, 7414, 7550, 7630, 7633, 7673, 7703, 7719, 7729, 7792.

232   "Can our left flank": A.M. 14, ML 7393, 1334/14.

233   bearing its intended fruit: MLs 7447, 7490, 7610, 7741.

233   (. . . XIV Panzer Korps): ML 7812.

233   have to evacuate Sicily: Kesselring, 164; cf. SSI 237.

233   "Sicily cannot be held": OKW/KTB iii.789–91.

233   with a future evacuation: MLs 7518, 7543, 7562, 7709, 8301.

233	success a month later: MLs 7638, 7658.
233	had set his heart: Hamilton ii.305–10.
233	not until the 21st: MLs 7989, 8001, 8302.
233	Sicily to the last: MLs 8497, 8568, 8731, 8775, 8952.
234	equipment, and transport: JPs 1024, 1027, 1111, 1370. Cf. SSI 410.
234	according to some accounts: MME v.165; SSI 376; Terraine, 579.
234	(. . . Alexander wrote afterward): Alexander, *Memoirs*, 168.
234	". . . plan," complained Montgomery: Hamilton ii.348.
235	Sicily, Sardinia, and Corsica: OKW/KTB iii.839.
235	be done in three days: MME v.122, OKW/KTB iii.855.
235	necessary if it fell: Montgomery, *Alamein to the Sangro*, 88; Hamilton ii.347.
235	". . . evacuation of Sicily": Roskill iii/1.146.
235	(. . . supply until 6 August): ML 9539, JP 200. JP 122 may have referred to traffic from Sicily to the mainland, not the opposite, as the War Office thought at the time.
235	a practice ferrying exercise: 30/7, ML 9601, 2101/1.
235	signs of withdrawal: MME v.174.
235	evacuation had started: Jackson, *Alexander,* 225; SSI 412.
235	". . . on the ferry system": JP 357.
235	guarantee complete evacuation: JPs 1019, 1022.
237	home more vigorously: JPs 1257, 1274, 2279.
237	later years by Kesselring: Kesselring, 165.

CHAPTER 10: The Italian Campaign

237	plans by 1 July: GS iv.663, 669.
240	line in the Apennines: IKW/KTB iii.1073–74.
240	the Mediterranean theater: Fraser, *Alanbrooke,* 363.
240	aircraft were available: E.g., JPs 1288, 2658.
241	Formia, north of Gaeta: JPs 1247, 1480, 1484, 2165, 2214, 2409.
241	were close at hand: JPs 2125, 2190.
241	Gaeta, Naples, and Salerno: JP 2475.
241	as early as the 10th: JP 717.
241	hours of 3 September: JPs 2851, 3127, 3134, 3145, 3192.
241	Montgomery's ponderous arrangements: Montgomery, *Alamein to the Sangro,* 100.
241	some Canadian soliders: De Guingand, *Operation Victory,* 317; Bryant ii.27.

241   the exclusion of others: JPs 1561, 2959, 3024.

241   poured into both islands: JPs 1511, 1712, 1752, 2130, 2530, 2981.

241   months was envisaged: JP 3262.

241   (. . . was known to be low): JP 1807.

241   disaffection in Croatia: JPs 1652, 3171.

242   to the Aegean islands: Cs 167, 168, 174; JPs 1037, 1390, 1425, 1521, 1800, 2273, 2359, 2427, 2494. Cf. OKW/KTB iii.841–45 and 1453, which show that large-scale changes were, in fact, already under consideration before the fall of Mussolini. Surviving traces of them, notable of the earlier intention to move Army Group B to Salonika, not surprisingly baffled the order-of-battle experts at the War Office who commented on ML 9625 and JP 1390.

243   north Italy in earnest: OKW/KTB iii.851; Rommel, 431–34.

243   (. . . loss of prestige): OKW/KTB iii.1449.

244   by force if necessary: C 157; ML 9026.

244   rather than Rommel's: MLs 7882, 9279.

244   (. . . ready for Army Group B): OKW/KTB iii.785.

244   Russian front respectively: JP 37.

244   Adolf Hitler Division in Russia: JP 635.

244   the framework of ACHSE: OKW/KTB iii.838.

244   at Verona on 14 August: JP 1388.

245   Rest and Refitting Staff: 17/8, JP 1487, 1322/19.

245   Army Group B itself: 17/8, JP 1512, 1703/19.

245   circle of recipients: JP 2261.

245   Army Group B in early September: MME v.213.

245   Ultra in central Italy: MLs 9373, 9394; JPs 1075, 2540.

246   Rome on 22 August: JP 1828.

246   (. . . south of Florence): OKW/KTB iii.1451, JP 4273.

246   ". . . reserve in Upper Italy": JP 2760.

246   penetrated beyond Lombardy: JPs 2621, 2947, 2952, 2981, 3456.

246   been at Kesselring's disposal: JPs 2911, 2952, 3080.

246   ". . . is pinning us down": OKW/KTB iii.929.

247   time to affect operations: JPs 3738, 3748, 3764, 3767, 3770, 3780, 3812, 3884.

247   warnings that reinforcements: A.M. 9, JP 3809, 1514/9.

247   beachhead would be bombed: 1630/10, JP 3955, 1958/10.

247   denuded of troops: 11/9, JP 4082, 2102/11.

247   "last reserves" to Salerno: JP 4655.

247   even on the 15th: JP 4516.

249	Trieste, Ljubljana, and Pola: JPs 3769, 3853, 3878, 3389, 3903, 4192, 4214, 4262, 4421, 4533.
249	met stiffer resistance: E.g., JPs 5642, 5752.
249	fortnight from 14 September: Rommel, 445–46; Irving, 277–78.
249	twenty-four hours later: JPs 4743, 4793, 4801.
249	"final defence line" manned: JPs 4877, 5080.
250	environs of Rome: JPs 5051, 5401.
250	to "Blocking Line B": JPs 5651, 5677.
250	Confirmation came: 1/10, JP 6048, 1419/2.
250	certainly on the 8th: P.M. 7, JP 6578, 0703/8.
250	"the final winter line": Cf. GS v.61.
250	Army Group B reported that: 3/10, JP 6915, 0534/10.
250	at Hitler's personal orders: OKW/KTB iii.1096.
251	the end of September: Irving, 279.
251	". . . other theaters of war": OKW/KTB iii.1168.
252	along the Dalmatian coast: JPs 6473, 6489, 6545, 6696, 6747, 6762, 7762.
252	northern Italy was possible: BI iii/1.114–17; MME v.332; STC 187.
253	". . . you are now deploying": Churchill v.135.
253	". . . before we reach Rome": Alexander, *Memoirs,* 117; Churchill v.194; STC 180; cf. GS v.68.
253	as for self-congratulation: GS v.69.
253	consultation with Alexander: Churchill v.216–20.
254	and Cassino in December: E.g., JPs 6812, 7839, 8431, 9028, 9165, 9971.
254	to prevailing shortages: E.g., JPs 9479, 9483, 9836, 9926; VLs 1541, 1883, 2448, 3357, 4449. An exceptional use of horses to make up for a shortage of motor transport was serious enough for Kesselring to complain to Berlin about it. The interruption of supplies by the POINT-BLANK railway-interdiction bombing program was reflected in several of these signals, for example, VLs 1541 and 3357; see also JPs 6557, 6570.
255	in Italy all told: VLs 1397, 1922, 5202, 5255.
255	in December and January: JPs 7260, 9468, 9580, 9643, 9817, 9863, 9916; VLs 94, 1369, 1377.
255	each end of the line: VLs 2051, 2055, 3006.
255	(". . . keep on building'"): OKW/KTB iii.1306.
255	Rommel on 17 October: STC 244; Irving, 280.
257	a few days later: MME v.378–79.
257	". . . still in the balance": OKW/KTB iii.1220.

257	(. . . a cable appointing Rommel): Rommel, 446.
257	". . . command in all Italy": VL 107.
257	GOC Army Group C: VL 668.
257	coast through Perugia: VL 985.
257	France in the spring: VLs 8693, 8846, 9032.
257	". . . the show," he wrote: Fraser, *Alanbrooke,* 394.
257	". . . front is becoming scandalous": Churchill v.300.
259	of the Adriatic and Greece: VLs 3053, 3624, 3771, 3774, 3805, 3855.
259	solution could be propounded: VLs 3540, 4129, 4158, 4430, 4441.
259	Rome in early November: JPs 9096, 9470.
259	a month or six weeks: OKW/KTB iv.122; STC 319.
259	to Rome in a few days: GS v.174.
260	deadlock had been found: Nicolson, 229-30; Vaughan Thomas, 21, 43; STC 354.
260	are sufficient evidence: STC 363.
260	his lack of enterprise: STC 355, 426; Richardson, 167.
260	nothing to alleviate: Conditions in the bridgehead are movingly described by Raleigh Trevelyan in *The Fortress.*
261	for 1 December 1943: VLs 1427, 1563.
261	the next similar return: VL 5398.
261	behind the 94th Division: VLs 4423, 4427.
262	the landings took place: OKW/KTB iv.124–25.
262	for another fortnight: VL 5383.
262	as Westphal later asserted: Weatphal, *German Army in the West,* 158.
262	were being set up in Rome: VL 144.
262	Fliegerkorps XI in the capital: VLs 2854, 3027, 3774, 3981.
262	somewhere near Rome: VLs 3552, 3937.
263	which von Senger feared: STC 318–19.
263	was on the way: VLs 4308, 5383.
263	In the very early hours of the 22nd: 2300/19, VL 4331, 0304/20.
263	front from the 94th division: 18/1, VL 4302, 1904/19.
263	drafted into the same area: VLs 4464, 4476.
263	down with it from Rome: 1300/21, VL 4506, 1802/22.
263	his first hours ashore: Jackson, *Italy,* 185; Verney, 46. It is not clear whether the two divisions had by then been identified on the main front through battle contact, or

whether Lucas was given Ultra information appropriately disguised. In any case, my remark in *Journal of Contemporary History* 16 (1981), 137, now needs correction.

264 ". . . further than we did": PRO.CAB 65/47 WM (44), 7 July 1944, pp. 9-10.

264 surprise had given him: Alexander, "Allied Armies in Italy," 2908–13; Alexander, *Memoirs,* 125.

265 ". . . was a stranded whale": Churchill v.432.

265 Before midday on 22 January: 1130/22, VL 4559, 0952/23.

265 mountains east of Rome: VLs 4767, 4775.

265 for the bridgehead too: VLs 4949, 4952, 4982, 5038, 5049.

265 of Kesselring's orders: 24/1, VL 5359, 538 0610/2.

265 clearly that the signal: The German text of VL 5359 is in OKW/KTB iv.131.

265 Order of the Day for 28 January: VL 5309.

265 twenty-five years later: Nicolson, *Alex,* 233.

265 (. . . premature revelation of Ultra): My suggestion in *Journal of Contemporary History* 16 (1981), 150, written before I saw VL 5309, was ingenious but wrong.

267 Hard on the heels of this: 28/1, VL 5449, 1421/3.

267 command dated 25 January: VL 5398.

267 (. . . secrecy in handling them): VL 5594.

267 reinforcements arrived late: VL 5631.

268 finally began on 16 February: P.M. 15, VL 6352, 0454/16.

268 to call FISCHFANG off: MME v.749; STC 422–23; Clark, 308; Verney, 176.

268 (. . . for the Alban Hills): Jackson, *Italy,* 199–201.

269 ". . . most important triumphs": Letter to the author, 20 July 1986.

269 from 22 February onward: VLs 6891, 7040, 7053, 7057.

269 kept "until D-Day": VLs 7088, 7117, covering the 26th and 29th PG and the Goering and 362nd divisions.

269 on the 27th: VLs 7266, 7270.

269 six miles from the shore: VL 7740, a late decrypt.

269 (. . . more under repair): VL 7771, which was not in fact available until the fighting had begun to die down.

269 figures in early February: VLs 5922, 6019.

269 Soon, heavy losses: VLs 7447, 7454; cf. MME v.753–56.

269 of comparative quiescence: VLs 7538, 7590, 7621.

269 composed a lengthy appreciation: VL 8072.

271	". . . the fighting in Italy": Fraser, *Alanbrooke*, 404.
273	". . . resistance to OVERLORD": Alexander, "Allied Armies in Italy," 2916.
274	for the summer of 1944: KVs 192, 773, decrypted and signaled on 12 April.
275	breakout at Anzio: GS v.263-64; OKW/KTB iv.478; Kesselring, 191.
275	on the west coast: VLs 7892, 8045, 8408.
275	dismissed as unlikely: KV 930.
275	of the deception planners: CTA 79; OKW/KTB iv.489.
275	little useful intelligence: KV 3172.
275	anxiety about Bari: VL 9662; KVs 670, 886, 888, 921, 971, 3168, 3172, 4008, 4302, 4313.
276	over the land battle: VLs 7194, 7427.
276	went beyond double figures: VLs 9234, 9381, 9384; KVs 54, 2025, 2130, 2455, 2557, 2640, 3027, 3109, 3391, 3574.
276	every twenty-four hours: MME v.689; CTA 41.
277	reports of serious damage: E.g., VLs 9243, 9344, 9432, 9457, 9492, 9614; KVs 2144, 2543, 2815, 3192, and many more.
277	armies on the same day: VLs 8395, 8469, 8554, 8662, 9082, 9318, 9319, 9430, 9431, 9447, 9484, 9555, 9556, 9668, 9756, 9931; KVs 217, 335, 387, 777, 819, 1298, 1460, 1697, 1912, 2007, 2052, 2217, 2400, 2485, 2528, 2669, 2684, 3412, 3223, 3343, 3544.
277	One of them: VL 9193.
278	as far as Ultra knew: VLs 9583, 9956; KV 24.
278	protection round many harbors: VL 9810; KVs 1096, 1152, 2405, 2490, 3398.
278	well monitored by Ultra: For instance, VLs 9216, 9647; KVs 63, 434, 1870, 2134, several of which are very long signals conveying in some cases quite detailed cargo manifests; many other signals were sent with high priority as potential targets.
278	". . . strained manpower situation": KV 3482.
279	over Jodl's signature: KV 2388
279	just been signaled: KVs 712, 762, 801, 863.
279	four in the last: KV 1232; cf. MME vi/1.74.
280	21 March and 12 May: VLs 9361, 9872; KVs 772, 1929, 2540, 3190, 3971.
281	to be under threat: KV 4087.
281	coast watching at Ostia: KV 1963.
282	Chief Engineer on 15 April: KVs 1578, 3097.

282	during World War II: Jackson, *Rome,* 211.
283	large sectors of it: for example, KVs 4794, 4990.
283	front on 23 May: 2300/22, KV 4999, 0421/24.
283	(. . . four days before this): KV 4777.
284	in the Liri valley: KVs 4383, 4302, 4313, 4400, 4967, 5605.
284	forty-eight hours later: KVs 4556, 4876.
284	moved south by road: KV 5401.
284	von Mackensen's bitter complaints: Kesselring, 202; Jackson, *Rome,* 146.
284	own erroneous assessment: Vaughan Thomas, 223; Verney, 235.
284	favored by both sides: KV 4588.
284	Alexander the Churchillian "cop": Churchill v.536.
285	". . . communications to Rome": Gilbert vii.751, 753.
285	(. . . for recent losses): KV 6102.
285	few antitank guns: KVs 5761, 5796.
285	stocks south of the Alps: KV 5916.
286	". . . Kesselring and Truscott": Jackson, *Alexander,* 291.
286	in the week of OVERLORD: KV 6745.
286	assessed at only 5 percent: KVs 6885, 7032. Lower figures are given under some headings in MME vi/1.250. Casualties are identical, ibid. 284.
286	of Pisa and Rimini: Alexander, *Memoirs,* 189; GS v.266–67.
286	flown by its aircraft: KVs 3291, 3391, 3514, 3715, 3854, etc.
287	eastern and western fronts: See, for instance, XL 272 of 29 June.
287	of his Army Group: OKW/KTB iv.517.
287	(. . . signaled until 9 June): KV 7169.
287	". . . prove a serious obstacle": GS v.266–67; Alexander, "Allied Armies in Italy," 2931; Jackson, *Italy,* 252; CTA 229.
288	on 12 October 1943: JP 6915. See p. 264 above.
288	should be constructed there: OKW/KTB iii.1083, 1096, 1141–44; MME v.319, 377n.
288	Pesaro on the Adriatic: VLs 5359, 5381, 5503.
288	engineer in April and May: KVs 1578, 3091, 4321, 5345.
289	by Hitler in mid-June: KV 9843. See also KV 9465 and XL 351. A slightly fuller text may be found in OkW/KTB iv. 513–23.
289	more divisions to Anvil: Bryant ii.215; GS v.346–47.

290	wrote in his diary: Bryant ii.224; Fraser, *Alanbrooke,* 430–31. Part of the signal is quoted in GS v.353, which was published eighteen years before the existence of Ultra was admitted.
290	(. . . the south of France): XLs 6753, 6919. See p. 296 below, and Bennett, 152.
291	he wrote to Churchill: Gilbert vii.829.
291	". . . to be responsible": MME vi/1.313–35; GS v.356.
291	". . . continued our advance here": Gilbert vii.899, 914.
292	supplies for themselves: KVs 7965, 4328.
292	the customary restraints: KVs 8423, 8431, 8925.
292	usual four-point scale: KVs 8546, 8570, 8691, 8867.
292	1944-pattern infantry division: KVs 7933, 9314.
292	". . . depriving other divisions": XLs 235, 294.
293	were they in numbers: XL 449.
293	its failing strength: XL 3696.
293	Tigers was recorded twice: KVs 8344, 8444, 8674.
293	bitterly to Jodl and OKW: This is one of several occasions on which an Ultra signal reproduces almost exactly the wording of an entry in the OKW War Diary. Compare XL 1688 with OKW/KTB iv.582.
296	soon after Hitler ordered them: KVs 6029, 6157, 6428, 6556, 6728, 7933, 9100; XLs 199, 270, 489.
296	the end of July: XLs 3691, 4044.
296	leaving its tanks behind: XLs 1963, 2456, 2912, 3110, 3778.
296	(. . . the west) were recorded: XLs 4756, 7280, 7479, 7506, 7720.
297	threat of imminent invasion: XL 7268.
297	On the morning of 17 August: 0940/17, XLs 6753, 6919, 1408/17.
297	Genoa against a landing: XLs 2241, 5456, 6551, 6601, 7198, 7246.
297	the end of 1943: E.g., JP 9518; VLs 3053, 5359, 7194; KVs 192, 628, 773, 3884, 7751; XLs 130, 689, 3920, 4192, 4320, 6013.
298	Flivo was attached: E.g., XLs 5094, 5951.
298	by a given date: E.g., XL 9527; HPs 658, 6182, 7849, 8144.
298	to the Gothic Line: HPs 1200, 1490, 1839, 1957, 2714, 2825, 2868, 7738, 7902, 8309, 9352.
298	than on 25 May: KV 5283; BT 821.
298	up from the Reich: HPs 1741, 7577.

299	Allies only 312,000: CTA 545.
300	time required for repairs: E.g., XLs 9256, 9960; HPs 213, 2092, 4822, 4937, 6182, 6710, 7308, 7847, 7865, 7938, 8158, 8342.
300	between Bolzano and Trent: HPs 995, 1087.
300	(". . . causes a crisis"): HP 4937.
300	at least three weeks: HP 7577.
300	beginning of September: XL 9805.
300	night ground-attack sorties: HPs 5987, 7111, 7214.
301	movements for lack of it: HPs 2282, 3600, 7355.
301	". . . at present assured": HPs 3703, 8656.
303	the war against Japan: Bryant ii.268; GS v.401, 507–9.
304	Armies West by August: 8/8, XL 5257, 0036/15.
304	Kesselring declared a first-degree alarm: 12/8, XL 6013, 1308/13.
304	pattern of Allied strategy: XLs 8575, 8610, 9527.
306	(". . . must be considered smashed"): HP 2954.
306	710th Division from Scandinavia: HPs 6182, 7308, 7867, 8144, 8966, 9255, 9367; BT 840.
307	as in the west: Bennett, 226–27.
307	tank- and gun-strength returns: BTs 5624, 6355, 7212, 8608, 8786, 8904, 9454.
308	than from the Fourteenth Army: BTs 2377, 2338, 2385, 2248, 2667, 2733, 2748, 2840, 2843, 3966, 3972, 4003, 4004, 6152, 6317, 6475, etc.
309	Yet reserves were essential: BTs 2635, 2879.
309	to be built up: BTs 2744, 3014, 3574.
310	time, instead of monthly: BT 4854.
310	made it necessary: BT 3367.
310	critical fuel situation: BT 5510.
310	out of the surplus: BT 6351.
310	". . . is approaching a climax": BT 6125.
311	decline in buffer stocks: BT 6253.
311	Army Group quartermaster: BTs 3742, 3833, 3992, 4595, 4753, 4953, etc.
311	beginning of January: BT 1882.
311	end of the month: BTs 4136, 4632, 5004, 6157, 6671.
311	less than 150 miles: BTs 5782, 6402, 6419, 6868, 7398, 7933, 8421, 8523.
312	mind when he wrote: Churchill vi.454.
312	rupture of their communications: See, for instance, BT 8695, of 26 March, and KO 1474, of 25 April.
312	to be curtailed: BT 3750.

312	were being crippled: BTs 6402, 6420, 6675.
313	3,700 out of 20,000: BT 8350.
313	(. . . sunk the same day): BTs 8527, 8528, 8573.
313	period up to 8 April: KOs 138, 363.
313	were ruled out: KOs 555, 586, 588.
313	of all his generals: BTs 2769, 3337, 5274; cf. 2017.
314	hands of the enemy: HPs 894, 993.
314	(. . . in 1962), Alexander wrote: Alexander, *Memoirs,* 137.
315	(". . . *sondern ueberhaupt*"): OKW/KTB iv. 562.
315	offensive loomed closer: CGA 438–39; OKW/KTB iv.1392.
315	in Liguria to halt it: BT 6868.
315	behind the front: BT 7463.
316	on the mainland behind: BTs 7340, 7427, 7590.
316	the same day, 12 March: BT 7445.
316	last gasp in Budapest: BT 3813.
316	as cadres to Holland: BTs 8181, 8182.
317	end of the month: BTs 8747, 9402, 9436.
317	Alexander himself: Alexander, "Allied Armies in Italy," 2959.
317	of 21 and 23 March: BTs 8241, 9014, 9094.
320	far west as Modena: BTs 9488, 9543.
320	Modena to meet it: Cf. CTA 460–62; Jackson, 306.
320	(. . . Istria) on 6 April: BTs 9676, 9742, 9974.
320	somewhere in Slovenia: KO 260.
320	(. . . along the Tagliamento): BT 9922.
320	tank return of 10 April: KO 469.
321	of armor was known: KO 469.
322	". . . decisive final battle": KOs 496, 525.
322	von Vietinghoff himself: KOs 1071, 1156.
323	line along the Po: KO 1219.
323	in precipitate flight: Jackson, *Italy,* 314; CTA 492.
323	the sanction of OKW: KO 1558.
323	". . . to strategic containment": GS vi.121.
323	". . . a magic-lantern show": Jackson, *Alexander,* 310; Smith and Agarossi, 45.
323	". . . thought to be impossible": Nicolson, *Alex,* 282.

CHAPTER 11: Yugoslavia

329	with the occupying forces: Deakin, 144; Clissold, 72; Wheeler, 105–9; Roberts, 35, 367; PRO.WO 208/2006.
330	". . . be able to revolt": GS iii.334.

331	SOE for supply-dropping: Wheeler, 166–68.
331	rising in Yugoslavia: GS iii.558, iv.386.
331	"T. E. Lawrence complex": Barker, in Auty and Clogg, 30.
331	Eden's in April 1943: Wheeler, 230.
331	the end of the war: Gilbert vii.892.
332	six or seven weeks: Barker, *British Policy,* 157; Foot, 235; Sweet-Escott, in Auty and Clogg, 9; GS v.84.
332	have gone to Tunisia: Dedijer, 220.
332	(. . . the autumn of 1942): OKW/KTB iii.139, iv.633.
332	superior to Mihajlović's: Deakin, 153; Roberts, 20.
332	enlist their cooperation: Deakin, 201; Wheeler 189–90.
332	only to reject it: GS iv.386.
333	Africa from Greek ports: OLs 1057, 1667, 1672, 1720, 1803, 2039.
333	they had appreciated: MK 9551, QT 2016; OKW/KTB ii.140.
333	both London and Cairo: BI iii/1.502.
334	two Croat divisions: VMs 1515, 1542, 1879, 2438.
334	at the highest level: PRO.FO 371/37579; Deakin, in Auty and Clogg, 103; Davidson, 118–19; Barker, *British Policy,* 162; Wheeler, 204-5.
335	". . . with the Jugoslav leaders": Churchill iv.828.
335	break with Mihajlović: BI iii/1.142.
335	be given to both: Wheeler, 208-9.
335	supplies to the Partisans: Deakin, 185-87, and in Auty and Clogg, 103-4.
335	". . . government like a bombshell": Roberts, 93.
335	be removed elsewhere: Auty and Clogg, 76; cf. Deakin, 191.
335	the middle of April: Djilas 226–36; 242–44; Wheeler, 226–27.
335	collaboration in March: Deakin, 191.
335	make representations in Rome: OKW/KTB iii.99, 168–75.
336	". . . him any effective help": Churchill iv.839–40.
336	". . . are my only support": Deakin, 192.
336	reinforcements to Crete: VMs 5672, 6386.
336	drafted into Attica: VMs 3987, 5487.
336	even before MINCEMEAT: OKW/KTB iii.116, 121, 183, etc.
336	beginning of April: VM 8393.
336	operations in Yugoslavia: Barker, *L'opzione Istriana,* 5; PRO.CAB 80/70, CCS 244/1.

336	the same direction: VMs 6142, 8574, 8955; ML 378.
336	track in Greece: VM 6142; ML 92.
336	decrypt of the fifth: ML 2012.
337	and lasted a month: OKW/KTB iii.482–87 gives full details of participating troops and their movements.
337	at Serbia from Montenegro: ML 2034.
337	from the disarming order: ML 2265.
337	formations in Yugoslavia: MLs 1956, 1970, 2014, 2176, 2277, 2400, 2442.
337	it closed round them: Deakin, 211–21; Davidson, 123; Dedijer, 319–20, Auty, 255–57.
338	against the partisans: Gilbert vii.435; MLs 1956, 1983, 2014, 2277, 2388, 2442, 3103, 3133, 3165, 3274, 3755, 3858, 3970, 4302, 4439, 4609, 4629, 5054, 5307.
338	". . . whole scene and balances": Gilbert vii.440.
339	". . . units in the field": E.g., ML 8888; JP 9464; VLs 1793, 1899; cf. BI iii/1.164n for other aspects of the same items.
339	(. . . body of partisans left): MLs 3133, 3163, 3274, 3970, 4457, 4599, 4609, 4627; OKW/KTB iii.660, 669.
340	denied help in future: GS iv.482–83; Churchill v.410; Deakin, 223–24; BI iii/1.149.
340	(. . . until 1 September): JP 3288.
340	supply line was enlarged: MLs 4774, 4787, 4836, 4970, 5178, 5970.
340	either Tito or Mihajlović: MLs 2519, 4302, 5211, 5714, 6490, 6563.
340	(. . . main Belgrade-Zagreb line): MLs 7819, 7843, 8008, 9045, 9125.
341	(. . . down on 3 September): JP 3171.
341	". . . x date to y date: Early examples are MLs 6488, 8927; JPs 39, 208, 1147, 2275, 3171, 3457.
341	the spring and summer: See BI iii/1.669-70.
342	Belgrade by 23 August: JP 1897; his presence in Greece was discovered ten days earlier, but not the reason for it.
342	were subordinate to him: JPs 2273, 2427; cf. MME v.208–9; OKW/KTB iii.1015. Both von Weichs and the Second Panzer Army had last been identified in Russia.
343	repelling an Allied landing: OKW/KTB iii.1252–55; MME v.568, in part duplicated by JP 8899; see also JP 7590.
343	from Split via Knin: JP 5584.
343	to be reckoned with: JP 6009.

343	to the Foreign Office: Personal information from Sir William Deakin.
344	at the end of November: JPs 4421, 4533, 5952, 6282, 6887, 7592, 8022, 8715.
344	in September and October: Roskill iii/1.205.
344	onward to the Aegean: JP 5317; cf. 5211.
344	Aegean in mid-October: Roskill iii/1.206–7; Pope, 155–62.
345	British coastal forces: VLs 2018, 2167, 2254, 2295, 2376, 2478, 2505, 2559; Roskill iii/1.207; Pope, 165.
345	second Panzer Army on 2 December: VL 1077.
345	it when practicable: VLs 1138, 1235, 1473, 1848, 2065, 3171, 3210, 3499, 4142, etc.
345	appreciation of 29 August: C 181, not signaled as JP 4961 until 20 September.
345	usual London recipients: PRO.WO 208/2020.
346	December to implicate him: BI iii/1.159.
346	Maclean's "blockbuster" report: PRO.FO 371/37615.
346	". . . others to do it": Churchill v.121, 411; GS v.81; Gilbert vii.505.
347	called the Sixth Offensive: VLs 544, 575, 1381, 1785, 1797, 3455.
347	indefinitely on 23 April: VLs 3064, 3471, 3640, 3729, 4173, 4209, 6271, 6397, 6446, 6457, 6464, 6691, 6729, 6800, 7094; KVs 136, 1247, 2024, 2490; OKW/KTB iv.658.
348	south of Virovitica: VL 8039.
348	Sava near Ogulin: VL 8579.
348	traced in great detail: VLs 3361, 4340, 4435, 4513, 5023, 5543, 5553, 6921, 7044.
348	clear after the event: VL 9625.
349	help of other evidence: KVs 4845, 4788, 4842, 4886, 4912, 4948, 5059, 5074, 5076, 5457, 5459.
349	". . . an independent state": Tito, *Sabrana djela* ("Collected Works") xxxiii.213. I owe this reference to Dr. Dusan Biber.
349	". . . to Stalin's armies": OKW/KTB iv.816.
349	go on to Moscow: C 255, KV 6392.
350	Fifth or Eighth armies in Italy: BTs 366, 465.
350	from the southeast: HP 3180.
350	to be implemented: HPs 2875, 2943, 3026, 3051, 3316, 3776.
350	to select bombing targets: HPs 5744, 6192.

350	assist Army Group F: HPs 9340, 9596.
350	took over in March: BT 8625.
350	brigades in January: BT 2909.
350	second half of February: BTs 4789, 4830.
350	of the general surrender: KO 2037.
351	were fighting Germans: XLs 9404, 9405.
351	against communism: C 334.
351	in the near future: HP 1204.
351	unless handled adroitly: HP 5992.
351	Chetnik-Partisan conflict: E.g., BTs 2029, 2909.
351	the former before long: OKW/KTB iii.121.
351	the Adriatic to Vienna: GS v.175; Auty and Clogg, 41.
352	mentioned than Istria: E.g., VLs 3809, 5563; KVs 4087, 9550; XLs 1907, 7807, 9505, 9701; HP 5842. There were many others.
352	preferred the latter: GS v.266–67, 345–47.
353	meeting on 7 July: PRO.CAB 65/47.
353	(. . . assault on Vienna): Bryant ii.304.
353	conference authorized this: Barker, "Opzione," 30, quoting PRO.CAB 80/88 CSS 176 16/9/44.
353	came to being realized: Ibid.
353	scheme was canceled: GS vi.56.

CHAPTER 12: Toward an Assessment

357	the Alps was improbable: NA. SRH-006 p.26; SRH-023 Tab F. p.6.
360	". . . in Montgomery's repertoire": *Dictionary of National Biography, 1971-80,* 581.
362	respect for Ultra: BI iii/1.190.
364	". . . have been our undoing": E. T. Layton, *And I Was There* (Morrow, 1985), 445.

Appendix II: The Mood of Early 1941

367	wrote Churchill: Churchill iii.152.
367	as June 1940: Churchill iii.20.
367	Simović coup: BI i.371, 451.
368	". . . forward with success": Moorehead, 149.

Appendix III: Auchinleck, Montgomery, and Rommel

370   ". . . then to fight": Rommel, 377.

Appendix IV: A Shortened War?

371   even before Alamein: GS iv.197.
372   beside his solid wisdom: Contrast Fraser, *Alanbrooke,*
             305, 333, 527–29, with Grigg, *1943: The Victory That
             Never Was,* esp. 210–14, and Hamilton ii. 70–71.

Appendix V: Axis Supplies Before Kasserine

373   notice of his trip: C 95.
373   visit the south Russian front: OKW/KTB iii.130–33.
374   ammunition, petrol, and rations: VMs 2720, 3137.
374   8,000 tons of fuel: VM 4920.
374   Gabès, Sfax, and Sousse: VM 4775.
374   all the Tunisian harbors: VM 5315.
374   illness in August 1942: MKA 2615; see p. 147, above.
374   European climate for some time: C 91.
375   Kasserine by surprise: Irving, 245; Rommel, 411.

Appendix VI: The Intelligence Aftermath of Kasserine

376   rather unconvincingly: BI ii.761-63.

Appendix VII: STRANGLE

377   . . . "reserves to the battlefront": Terraine, 594, 598.
378   controversy in miniature: BTs 6145, 6218.

Appendix VIII: Tank Returns

379   "at least 50" at the time: PRO.WO 208/3581, entry for 9
             March.
379   as 52 in Alexander's dispatch: Alexander, "African Cam-
             paign," 872.

379	from the three panzer divisions: VM 5960, 6064, 6271, 6309.
379	gave 85 runners: VM 6173.
379	evening before the battle: VM 6065.
380	return for 28 January: VL 5581.
380	15 and 12 respectively under repair: VLs 1427, 1563.
380	50 or 60 Mark Vs (Panthers): VL 7771.
380	second half of 1944: XLs 5185, 5797, 6087, 6362, 6982; BTs 518, 576.
381	a few fragmentary returns: XLs 8298, 8552; HPs 732, 6739.
381	changed several times: XL 5185; HP 6930.

Appendix IX: The Gothic Line

382	on 24 April 1944: MME vi/1.57n.
382	until 18 May: KV 4321.
382	on 15 June: OKW/KTB iv.519.
382	almost at once: KVs 9645, 9843, for example.
382	sixty-year-old kingdom: Procopius, *Gothic War* 8.xxix.1-4, xxxv.31-38.

Appendix X: Italian Defenses, or an Alpine Fortress?

387	to Gorizia and Trieste: OKW/KTB iv.591.
387	(GOC Lower Alps Security Areas): OKW/KTB iii.1137.
387	course of a *Voralpenstellung:* KV 4145. See XL 5859 of 12 August for the German.
387	Jablonica pass in Silesia: HP 166.
387	into the Udine basin: XL 5638.
388	and 3 August: Trevor-Roper, 176–81.
388	GOC Lower Alps (*Alpenvorland*): HP 1949.
388	for at least a month: XL 9264.
388	Salzburg-Klagenfurt route: HP 166; BTs 99, 890, 2799, 3454.
388	allotted offices there: BT 3776.
388	(. . . "on a large scale"): BT 5456.
388	the Drava near Lienz: BT 3776.
389	going to the Salzburg area: See Bennett, 238-40.
389	coincide with that of the *Voralpenstellung:* HPs 8539, 9035, 9422.

389	intended to be a fortress: BT 9200.
390	on 24 April: L. F. Ellis, *Victory in the West* (HMSO, 1968) ii.429.
390	its "war potential": KO 496.
390	still free from invasion: KOs 1814, 1858, 1866, 1944, 2070.
391	to have been the defensive ring: KO 1876; Jackson, 315.

Appendix XI: Operation SUNRISE

392	general strike in Turin: KO 969.
392	rather than practical value: Cs 499, 501; but KOs 1795 and 1761, embodying some of the information therein, have for some reason been withheld from the files in the PRO.

Appendix XII: Missing Links

393	later Army Group E: BI ii.663.
395	since the summer of 1942: Davidson, 115–17; Auty and Clogg, 211–24, 236; BI iii.1.502.
395	when posted to SOE: For example, Foot, 232.
396	these unquestionable facts, some: E.g., Martin, 117–20; Beloff, 88-89.
396	Partisans in Yugoslavia: Hammond, 30, 40-43, 181.

Appendix XIII: Cos and Leros

398	reinforcements were steadily brought in: E.g., MLs 7944, 8209, 9563; JPs 2153, 2617, 3376, 5573, 6482, 6819, 7852, 7932, 8030.
398	early on 5 October: JP 6292.
398	few hours by another: JP 6352.
398	now in German hands: JPs 6503, 6504, 6505.
398	details about it provided: JPs 8975, 9114, 9121, 9155, 9197, 9229, 9264, 9341.
398	yet another postponement: JPs 9391, 9502, 9503.
398	tough British resistance: JPs 9645, 9799.

PERSONALITIES

NOTE: Ranks and titles listed are in most cases the last held.

British

Airey, Lt. Gen. Sir Terence — Chief Intelligence Officer, 15th Army Group and Allied Armies in Italy

Alanbrooke, Field Marshal Viscount — Chief of the Imperial General Staff, 1941–46

Alexander of Tunis, Field Marshal Viscount — Successively, C-in-C Middle East, 1942–43, and of Allied Armies in Italy (15th Army Group), 1943–44; Supreme Allied Commander, Mediterranean, 1944–45

Anderson, Lt. Gen. Sir Kenneth — Comdr. First Army 1942–43

Auchinleck, Field Marshal Sir Claude — C-in-C Middle East, 1941–42

Broadhurst, Air Vice-Marshal Sir Harry — Comdr. Desert Air Force, 1943–44

Brooke: See Alanbrooke

Clarke, Brig. Dudley — Head of "A" Force (Deception), 1941–45

Coningham, Air Marshal Sir Arthur — Comdr. Desert Air Force, July 1941–January 1943; Comdr.

	Northwest African Tactical Air Force, 1943–44
Cripps, Sir Stafford	British Ambassador to Russia, 1940–42; Minister of Aircraft Production, 1942–45
Cunningham, Lt. Gen. Sir Alan	Comdr. Eighth Army, 1941
Cunningham of Hyndhope, Admiral of the Fleet Viscount	Naval C-in-C Mediterranean, 1939–42
Deakin, Lt. Col. Sir William	First British liaison officer with Tito, May 1943
Dill, Field Marshal Sir John	Chief of the Imperial General Staff, 1940–41; head of British Mission in Washington, 1941–44
Dorman-Smith, Maj. Gen. Eric	Deputy Chief of Staff, GHQ Middle East, 1942
Eden, Anthony	Foreign Secretary, 1940–45
Freyberg, Lt. Gen. Sir Bernard	Comdr. New Zealand Division, 1940–45
Gott, Lt. Gen. W.H.E.	Comdr. XIII Corps, 1942
Harding, Field Marshal Lord	Chief of Staff, successively, Cyrenaica Command and XIII Corps, 1940–41; Director of Military Training Cairo, 1942; Comdr. 7th Armored Division, 1942–43; Chief of Staff, Allied Armies in Italy, 1944; Comdr. XIII Corps, 1945
Harwood, Admiral Sir Henry	Naval C-in-C Mediterranean, May 1942–February 1943
Horrocks, Lt. Gen. Sir Brian	Comdr. XIII Corps, later X Corps, 1942–43
Hunt, Lt. Col. Sir David	Second-in-command to Airey (q.v.)
Leese, Lt. Gen. Sir Oliver	Comdr. XXX Corps, 1942–43, Eighth Army, 1944–45
McCreery, Lt. Gen. Sir Richard	Chief of Staff 18th Army Group, 1943; Comdr. X Corps, 1943

Montgomery of Alamein, Field Marshal Viscount	Comdr. Eighth Army, 1942–43
O'Connor, Lt. Gen. Sir Richard	Comdr. Western Desert Force, 1940–41
Ritchie, Lt. Gen. Sir Neil	Comdr. Eighth Army, 1941–42
Tedder, Air Chief Marshal Lord	AOC-in-C Middle East, 1941–43; Comdr. Allied Middle East Air Force, 1943
Wavell, Field Marshal Earl	C-in-C Middle East, 1939–41
Williams, Brig. Sir Edgar	Chief Intelligence Officer, Eighth Army, 1942–43; 21
Wilson, Field Marshal Sir Henry Maitland	C-in-C Middle East, 1943–44; Allied Supreme Commander Mediterranean, 1943–44

American

Bradley, Gen. Omar	Comdr. II Corps, 1943
Clark, Gen. Mark	Comdr. Fifth Army, 1943–44, 15th Army Group, 1944–45,
Eisenhower, Gen. Dwight D.	Allied Supreme Commander Mediterranean, 1943–44
Fredendall, Lt. Gen. Lloyd	Comdr. II Corps, 1942–43
Hodges, Lt. Gen. Courtney	Comdr. First Army, 1944
Lucas, Maj. Gen. John	Comdr. VI Corps, 1943
Patton, Gen. George	Comdr. II Corps, 1943; Seventh Army, 1943
Truscott, Gen. Lucian	Comdr. VI Corps, 1943–44; Fifth Army, 1944–45

German

Arnim, Generaloberst Juergen von	Comdr. Fifth Panzer Army, September 1942; Comdr. Army Group Africa, March 1943
Baade, Oberst Ernst-Guenther	Comdr. Messina Straits Defense Area, July 1943

Bayerlein, Generalleutnant Fritz	Chief of Staff Afrika Korps, then, successively, of Panzergruppe Afrika, Panzer Army Africa, and First Italian Panzer Army
Canaris, Admiral Wilhelm	Chef Amt Ausland/Abwehr until February 1944
Cruewell, Gen. Ludwig	Comdr. Afrika Korps until captured May 1942
Doenitz, Grossadmiral Karl	C-in-C of the German navy from January 1943
Froehlich, General der Flieger Stefan	Fliegerfuehrer Afrika, March 1941–April 1942
Geissler, General der Flieger Hans	Comdr. Fliegerkorps X until August 1942
Goering, Reichsmarschall Hermann	C-in-C of the Luftwaffe
Guderian, Generaloberst Heinz	Comdr. Second Panzer Army in Russia until dismissed December 1941; later Inspector of Armored Troops, then Chief of the General Staff of the Army, July 1944–March 1945
Halder, Generaloberst Franz	Chief of the General Staff of the Army until dismissed September 1942
Hube, Gen. Hans	Comdr. XIV Panzer Korps, July–October 1943
Jodl, Generaloberst Alfred	Chef Wehrmachtfuehrungsstab (Head of Operations Staff), OKW
Keitel, Generalfeldmarschall Wilhelm	Head of OKW
Kesselring, Generalfeldmarschall Albert	OB South, November 1941–November 1943, then OB Southwest until March 1945
Lemelsen, Gen. Joachim	Comdr. XIV Panzer Korps, October 1943; then Acting Comdr. tenth Army; Comdr. fourteenth Army, until February 1945

Loehr, Generaloberst Alexander	OB Southeast, January–August 1943, then Comdr. Army Group E
Mackensen, Generaloberst Eberhard von	Comdr. Fourteenth Army, 1944
Nehring, Gen. Walter	Chief of Staff Afrika Korps, June–August 1942; Comdr. XC Corps, November–December 1942
Paulus, Generalfeldmarschall Friedrich	Deputy Chief of Staff of the Army, later Comdr. Sixth Army in Russia
Raeder, Grossadmiral Erich	C-in-C of the navy until January 1943
Richthofen, Generalfeldmarschall Wolfgang Freiherr von	Comdr. Luftflotte 2 from June 1943
Rintelen, Gen. Enno von	Military Attaché, Rome, and German General at HQ Italian Armed Forces
Rommel, Generalfeldmarschall Erwin	Comdr., successively, Afrika Korps, Panzergruppe Afrika, Panzer Army Africa, and Army Group Africa
Rundstedt, Generalfeldmarschall Gerd von	OB West from March 1942
Seebohm, Hauptmann	Comdr. Wireless Listening Company Africa
Senger und Etterlin, Generalleutnant Frido von	Liaison Officer with Italian 6th Korps in Sicily; later Comdr. XIV Panzer Korps
Student, Gen. Kurt	Comdr. Fliegerkorps XI (Airborne Troops)
Stumme, Gen. Georg	Comdr. Panzer Army Africa September–October 1942
Thoma, Gen. Wilhelm Ritter von	Comdr. Afrika Korps, October 1942
Vietinghoff, Generaloberst Gottfried von	Comdr. Tenth Army from August 1943; OB Southwest, March–May 1945

Warlimont, Gen. Walter — Deputy Head of Wehrmachtfuehrungsstab (Operations Staff), OKW

Weichs, Generalfeldmarschall Maximilian Freiherr von — OB Southeast from August 1943

Westphal, Generalmajor Siegfried — Successively Operations Officer and Chief of Staff Panzer Army Africa, then Chief of Staff OB Southwest

Witthoefft, Gen. — Comdr. Venetian Coast Defense Area, October 1943–September 1944, then Comdr. Korps Witthoefft

Zangen, Gen. Gustav-Adolf von — Comdr. Army Group von Zangen from January 1944

Italian

Ambrosio, Gen. Vittorio — Chief of Staff Italian Armed Forces from February 1943

Bastico, Marshal Ettore — C-in-C, North Africa, July 1941–February 1943

Cavallero, Marshal, Count Ugo — Chief of Staff Italian Armed Forces until February 1943

Ciano, Count — Italian Foreign Secretary

Guzzoni, Gen. Alfredo — Comdr. Sixth Army

Graziani, Marshal Rodolfo — C-in-C North Africa until March 1941

Messe, Marshal Giovanni — Comdr. 1 Army, February–May 1943

Roatta, Gen. Mario — Chief of Staff Italian Army, February 1942–December 1943

COVER NAMES

Allied

ANIMALS	Following MINCEMEAT, to distract German attention from Sicily by suggesting an invasion of southern Greece
ANVIL	Landing in southern France, August 1944. Later renamed DRAGOON
AVALANCHE	Landing at Salerno, September 1943
BATTLEAXE	British attack in Egypt, June 1941
BAYTOWN	Landing in the heel of Italy, September 1943
BREVITY	British attack in Egypt, May 1941
CRUSADER	British attack in Cyrenaica, November 1941
DIADEM	Allied attack at Cassino and in the Liri valley, May 1944
DRAGOON	See ANVIL
GYMNAST	Proposed British occupation of French North Africa, November 1941
HUSKY	Landing in Sicily, July 1943
JAEL	Original OVERLORD cover plan, suggesting a landing in Istria
LIGHTFOOT	The Alamein battle plan
LUSTRE	British expedition to Greece, 1941

MINCEMEAT	Deception plan to disguise HUSKY
OLIVE	Allied attack in Italy, August 1944
OVERLORD	The landing in France, June 1944
POINTBLANK	Strategic bombing of Germany
RATWEEK	Harassment of German retreat from the Balkans, September 1944
ROUNDUP	Proposed invasion of western Europe, 1943
SHINGLE	The Anzio landing, January 1944
STRANGLE	Interruption of German communications in Italy by bombing, summer 1944
STRIKE	Final assault on Tunis, May 1943
TORCH	The landing in Northwest Africa, November 1942
WHIPCORD	Proposed invasion of Sicily, 1942

German

ACHSE	Action to be taken in the Balkans and Italy in the event of an Italian surrender in the Balkans and Italy, September 1943
ALARICH	Earlier version of ACHSE, Italy only
BARBAROSSA	Invasion of Russia, June 1941
FREISCHUETZ	Attack on Vis, spring 1944
HERBSTNEBEL	Withdrawal across river Po, September 1944
HERKULES	Airborne attack on Malta, summer 1942
KONSTANTIN	Earlier version of ACHSE, Balkans only
KUGELBLITZ	Anti-Partisan operation, December 1943
MERKUR	Airborne attack on Crete, May 1941
ROESSELSPRUNG	Raid on Tito's HQ at Drvar, May 1944
SCHLUESSELBLUME	Anti-Partisan operation, March 1943
SCHWARZ	Anti-Partisan operation, May–June 1943
SOMMERNACHTSTRAUM	Desert operation by Rommel, September 1941

VENEZIA	Rommel's Gazala attack, May 1942
WEISS	Anti-Partisan operation, March 1943
ZITADELLE	Offensive of south Russian front, July 1944

MAIN EVENTS 1939–1945

1939

1 September	Germans invade Poland
3 September	Britain declares war on Germany

1940

10 May	Germans invade France, Belgium, and Holland
10 June	Italy declares war on Britain
23 June	Capitulation of France
August–September	Battle of Britain
13 September	Italians invade Egypt
7 December	British advance against Italians begins
Winter 1940–41	Night raids on Britain: "The Blitz"

1941

21 January	British capture Tobruk
6 February	Italians annihilated at Beda Fomm
12 February	Rommel arrives in Tripoli
7 March	British troops land in Greece
28 March	Battle of Cape Matapan: British defeat Italian fleet
30 March	Rommel attacks in Cyrenaica
6 April	Germans invade Yugoslavia and Greece

12 April	Tobruk invested
29 April	British evacuate Greece
20 May	Germans attack Crete
31 May	British evacuate Crete
8 June	British and Free French invade Syria
22 June	Germans invade Russia
1 July	Auchinleck replaces Wavell as C-in-C Middle East
11 July	Vichy French surrender in Syria
14 August	Atlantic Charter signed
2 September	Eighth Army established
16 September	British and Russians occupy Persia
18 November	CRUSADER: British offensive in Cyrenaica
26 November	Ritchie replaces Cunningham in command of Eighth Army
7 December	Japanese raid on Pearl Harbor; Germany declares war on United States
8 December	German offensive halted outside Moscow

1942

21 January	Rommel's counterattack in Cyrenaica begins
15 February	Fall of Singapore
26 May	Rommel's attack at Gazala begins
4 June	Battle of Midway
21 June	Fall of Tobruk
25 June	Auchinleck takes over direct command of Eighth Army
30 June	Rommel halted at Alamein
8 August	Churchill in Cairo; Alexander and Montgomery appointed C-in-C Middle East and commander of Eighth Army, respectively
19 August	Dieppe raid
31 August	Battle of Alam Halfa
September	Russian offensives at Moscow and Leningrad
25 September	Hitler dismisses Halder as Chief of Staff, OKH
23 October	Battle of Alamein begins
3 November	Rommel's retreat from Alamein begins
8 November	TORCH: Allied landings in North Africa
23 November	Eighth Army reaches Agheila
13 December	Rommel evacuates Agheila

1943

14 January	Casablanca conference
23 January	Eighth Army captures Tripoli
30 January	Doenitz replaces Raeder as C-in-C German navy
31 January	German surrender at Stalingrad
19 February	German attack at Kasserine
6 March	Battle of Medenine
20 March	Eighth Army attacks the Mareth Line
6 April	Battle of Wadi Akarit
11 May	Second Washington conference (Trident)
13 May	German surrender in Tunisia
23 May	First British liaison officer parachuted to Tito; Doenitz withdraws U-boats from the Atlantic
10 July	HUSKY: Allied landing in Sicily
12 July	ZITADELLE: German offensive at Kursk, abandoned; Russian offensive at Orel begins
25 July	Mussolini arrested
17 August	Quebec conference (Quadrant); Axis resistance in Sicily ends
3 September	BAYTOWN: British landing at Reggio
9 September	AVALANCHE: Allied landing at Salerno; surrender of Italy
15 September	British occupy Cos and Leros
25 September	Russians capture Smolensk
1 October	Allies enter Naples
4 October	Germans recapture Cos
6 November	Russians capture Kiev
16 November	Germans recapture Leros
22 November	Cairo conference, first stage (Sextant)
1 December	Tehran conference (Eureka)
3 December	Cairo conference, second stage

1944

22 January	SHINGLE: Allied landing at Anzio
6 March	Russian offensive in Ukraine begins
18 March	Germans occupy Hungary
11 May	DIADEM: Allied offensive in Italy
23 May	Anzio bridgehead and main front join up
25 May	ROESSELSPRUNG: German raid on Tito's HQ at Drvar

3 June	Tito flown to Vis
4 June	Fall of Rome
6 June	OVERLORD: Allied landing in Normandy
20 July	Attempt on Hitler's life
4 August	Allies enter Florence
5 August	Russians outside Warsaw
13–20 August	Battle of the Falaise pocket
20 August	Paris freed
25 August	OLIVE: Allied assault on the Gothic Line
4 September	Antwerp captured
17 September	MARKET GARDEN: the Arnhem attack
20 October	Russians and Partisans enter Belgrade
16 December	German attack in Ardennes

1945

4 February	Yalta conference (Argonaut)
13 February	Russians capture Budapest
23 March	Allies cross the Rhine
9 April	Allied offensive in Italy
12 April	Death of Roosevelt
13 April	Russians capture Vienna
25 April	Russians and Americans meet at Torgau
29 April	German surrender in Italy
30 April	Hitler commits suicide
7 May	German surrender in northern Europe
17 July	Potsdam conference
6 and 9 August	Atomic bombs dropped on Japan
14 August	Surrender of Japan

GLOSSARY

Abbreviations

AFHQ	Allied Forces Headquarters
AOC; AOC-in-C	Air Officer Commanding; Air Officer Commanding-in-Chief
"C"	Commonly used title of the head of the British secret service
CGS	Chief of the General Staff (of an army or army group)
CIGS	Chief of the Imperial General Staff (in effect, head of the British army)
C-in-C	Commander-in-Chief
CoS	Chief of Staff
DCGS	Deputy CGS
DMI	Director of Military Intelligence
ELAS	Greek Popular Liberation Army (Communist-led)
GAF	German Air Force
GAFSE	German Air Force Command Southeast
GHQ	General Headquarters
GOC	General Officer Commanding (commanding general)
GSO 1	General Staff Officer, Grade 1
JG	Jagdgeschwader (fighter)
JIC	Joint Intelligence Committee
KG	Kampfgeschwader (bombers)
LRDG	Long Range Desert Group
M/T	Motor transport
NA	National Archives (Washington)

OB S	*Oberbefehlshaber* (commander-in-chief), South
OB SE	*Oberbefehlshaber* (commander-in-chief), Southeast
OB SW	*Oberbefehlshaber* (commander-in-chief), Southwest
OKH	Supreme Command of the Army
OKL	Supreme Command of the Air Force
OKM	Supreme Command of the Navy
OKW	Supreme Command of the Armed Forces
PG	Panzergrenadier (lorried infantry)
PRO	Public Record Office (London)
RAF	Royal Air Force
RN	Royal Navy
SD	Sicherheitsdienst
SLU	Special Liaison Unit (handling Ultra)
SOE	Special Operations Executive
W/T	Wireless telegraphy

Miscellaneous Terms

Abteilung	Detachment
Abwehr	Secret Service
Afrika Korps	Rommel's armored force, consisting of 15th and 21st Panzer divisions
Fifth Army	U.S. army in Italy
Eighth Army	British army in North Africa and Italy
Army Group C	Army component of OB Southwest's command
Army Groups E, F	Army components of OB Southeast's command
Bombe	The computer-like machine which, given a "menu" by the cryptographers, sought solutions to Enigma keys
Comando Supremo	Italian Supreme Command
Flak	Antiaircraft artillery (from *Fl*ieger*a*bwehr*k*anonen)
Fliegerfuehrer Afrika	Head of the GAF in Africa
Fliegerkorps	Air Korps; component of a Luftflotte
Flivo (Flieger-verbindung-soffizier)	Air liaison officer attached to an army command
Foreign Armies West	Intelligence section of OKH charged with gathering information about the British and American armies

Fuehrer-   Hitler's headquarters
    hauptquartier

Geschwader   Basic organizational unit of the Luftwaffe, corresponding approximately to the British group and the American wing. Subdivided normally into three Gruppen of 30 aircraft each; each Gruppe subdivided into three Staffeln.

Gruppe: See Geschwader

Heeres-   Army Signals branch
    nachrichten-
    wesen

Luftflotte   Air Fleet (GAF battle command, consisting of 2 or more Fliegerkorps)

Luftgaustab   GAF administrative ground command

Matilda   British infantry tank

Organisation   Nazi construction corps
    Todt

Panther   See German Tank Types

Panzergrenadier Lorried infantry

Ratzeburg   Hitler's headquarters in Poland

Tiger   See German Tank Types

Via Balbia   The Italian-built coastal road in Cyrenaica

Wehrkreis, -e   Territorial base and recruitment areas in Germany

Wehrmacht   Armed Forces

Y Service   Organization to study external features of undecoded radio traffic and to decode lower-grade coded transmissions

German Tank Types

Type	Main gun	Maximum speed	Weight
III	50 mm	12 mph	22 tons
IV	75 mm (short-barrel)	25 mph	25 tons
IV Special	75 mm (long-barrel)	25 mph	25 tons
V (Panther)	75 mm (long-barrel)	34 mph	45 tons
VI (Tiger)	88 mm	25 mph	54 or 68 tons

BIBLIOGRAPHY

Public Record Office

Ultra signals to commands abroad. See Appendix I.

Printed Sources

A. *Official histories, cited by abbreviated titles*

British

BFP	E. L. Woodward. *British Foreign Policy.* 5 vols. HMSO, 1970–76.
BI i	F. H. Hinsley et al. *British Intelligence in the Second World War.* Vol. i. 1979.
BI ii	F. H. Hinsley et al. *British Intelligence in the Second World War.* Vol. ii. 1979.
BI iii/1	F. H. Hinsley et al. *British Intelligence in the Second World War.* Vol. iii, part 1. 1979.
GS iii	J.M.A. Gwyer. *Grand Strategy.* Vol. iii, Part 1. *1941–2.* HMSO, 1964.
	J.R.M. Butler. *Grand Strategy.* Vol. iii, Part 2. *1941–2.* HMSO, 1964.
GS iv	M. Howard. *Grand Strategy.* Vol. iv, *1942–3.* HMSO, 1972.
GS v	J. Ehrman. *Grand Strategy.* Vol. v, *1943–4.* HMSO, 1956.

GS vi   J. Ehrman. *Grand Strategy*. Vol. vi, *1944–5*. HMSO, 1956.

MME ii   I.S.O. Playfair. *The Mediterranean and Middle East*. Vol. ii. HMSO, 1956.

MME iii   I.S.O. Playfair. *The Mediterranean and Middle East*. Vol. iii. HMSO, 1960.

MME iv   I.S.O. Playfair. *The Mediterranean and Middle East*. Vol. iv. HMSO, 1966.

MME v   C.J.C. Molony. *The Mediterranean and Middle East*. Vol. v. HMSO, 1973.

MME vi/1   W.G.F. Jackson. *The Mediterranean and Middle East*. Vol. vi, Part 1. HMSO, 1984.

American
NWA   G. F. Howe. *Northwest Africa*. Washington, 1957.
SSI   A. N. Garland and H. M. Smyth. *Sicily and the Surrender of Italy*. Washington, 1968.
STC   M. Blumenson. *Salerno to Cassino*. Washington, 1968.
CTA   E. F. Fisher. *Cassino to the Alps*. Washington, 1977.

German
OKW/KTB   *Kriegstagebuch des Oberkommandos der Wehrmacht*. Frankfurt am Main: Bernard & Graefer, 1961-65. vol. i, ed. H. A. Jacobsen. 1965. vol, ii, ed. A. Hillgruber. 1963. vol. iii, ed. W. Hubatsch. 1963. vol. iv, ed. P.- E. Schramm. 1961.

B. *Other printed sources*

Alexander, H.R.L.G. *The Alexander Memoirs*. Ed. John North Cassell, 1962.
———, "The African Campaign from El Alamein to Tunis." Supplement to *The London Gazette*, 5 February 1948.
———, "The Allied Armies in Italy from 3 September 1943 to 12 December 1944." Supplement to *The London Gazette*, 12 June 1950.
Andrew, C.M. *Secret Service*. Heinemann, 1985.
———, and D. Dilks. *The Missing Dimension*. Macmillan, 1984.
Auchinleck, C. "Operations in the Middle East from 1 November 1941 to 15 August 1942." Supplement to *The London Gazette*, 15 January 1948.

Auty, P., and R. Clogg. *British Policy Towards Wartime Resistance in Yugoslavia and Greece*. Macmillan, 1975.

Barker, E. *British Policy Towards South-eastern Europe in the Second World War*. Macmillan, 1976.

——, "L'Opzione Istriana: obiettivi politici e militari della Gran Bretagna in Adriatico 1943–4." *Qualestoria* N.S. 10 (febbraio 1982).

Barnett, C. *The Desert Generals*. Allen & Unwin, 1960; 2nd ed. 1983.

——, *The Audit of War*. Macmillan, 1986.

Beesly, P. *Very Special Intelligence*. Hamish Hamilton, 1977.

——, *Room 40*. Hamish Hamilton, 1982.

Behrendt, H.O. *Rommels Kenntnis vom Feind im Afrikafeldzug*. Freiburg: Verlag Romback, 1980. Eng. trans. as *Rommel's Intelligence in the Desert Campaign*. Kimber, 1985.

Beloff, N. *Tito's Flawed Legacy*. Gollancz, 1975.

Bennett, R. F. *Ultra in the West*. Hutchinson, 1979.

Blumenson, M. *Patton*. Cape, 1986.

Bond, B. *British Military Policy Between Two World Wars*. Oxford, 1980.

Bradley, O. N. *A Soldier's Story*. Eyre & Spottiswoode, 1951.

Bryant, A. *The Turn of the Tide*. Collins, 1957. Cited as Bryant i.

——, *Triumph in the West*. Collins, 1957. Cited as Bryant ii.

Calvocoressi, P. *Top Secret Ultra*. Cassell, 1980.

Carlton, D. *Anthony Eden*. Allen Lane, 1981.

Carver, M. *El Alamein*. Batsford, 1962.

——, *Tobruk*. Batsford, 1964.

——, *The War Lords*. Weidenfeld & Nicolson, 1976.

——, *Harding of Petherton*. Weidenfeld & Nicolson, 1978.

——, *Dilemmas of the Desert War*. Batsford, 1986.

Churchill, R. S. *Winston S. Churchill*. Vol. iii, *1914–1916*. Heinemann, 1971.

Churchill, W. S. *The Second World War*. 6 vols. Cassell, 1948–54.

Clark, Mark. *Calculated Risk*. Harper, 1951.

Clayton, A. *The Enemy Is Listening*. Hutchinson, 1980.

Clissold, S. R. *Whirlwind*. (Gresset, 1949).

Colville, J. *The Fringes of Power*. Hodder & Stoughton, 1985.

Connell, J. *Auchinleck*. Cassell, 1959.

——, *Wavell*. Cassell, 1964.

Cowles, V. *The Phantom Major*. Collins, 1958.

Creveld, M. van. "Rommel's Supply Problem 1941–2." *Royal United Services Journal*, September 1974.

Cruickshank, C. *Deception in World War II*. Oxford, 1979.

Davidson, B. *Special Operations Europe*. Gollancz, 1980.

Davin, D. M. *Crete.* Oxford, 1953.
Deakin, F.W.D. *The Embattled Mountain.* Oxford, 1971.
———, The Brutal Friendship. Weidenfeld and Nicolson, 1962.
Dedijer, V. *With Tito Through the War.* Alexander Hamilton, 1951.
de Guingand, F. *Operation Victory.* (Hodder and Stoughton, 1947).
———, *Generals at War.* Hodder & Stoughton, 1964.
Djilas, M. *Wartime.* Harcourt Brace Jovanovich, 1977.
Eisenhower, D. *Crusade in Europe.* Heinemann, 1949.
Foot, M.R.D. *S.O.E. 1940–1946.* BBC, 1984.
Fraser, D. *Alanbrooke.* Collins, 1982.
———, *And We Shall Shock Them.* Hodder & Stoughton, 1983.
Garlinski, J. *Intercept.* Dent, 1979.
Gilbert, M. *Winston S. Churchill: Finest Hour.* Heinemann, 1983.
    Cited as Gilbert vi.
———, *Winston S. Churchill: Road to Victory.* Heinemann, 1986.
    Cited as Gilbert vii.
Graham, D., and S. Bidwell. *The Battle for Italy, 1943–5.* Hodder and
    Stoughton, 1986.
Grigg, J. *1943: The Victory That Never Was.* Eyre Methuen, 1980.
Halder, F. *Kriegstagebuch.* Ed. H. A. Jakobsen, 3 vols. Kohlhammer,
    1962–64.
Hamilton, N. *Monty: The Making of a General.* Hamish Hamilton,
    1981. Cited as Hamilton i.
———, *Monty: Master of the Battlefield.* Hamish Hamilton, 1983.
    Cited as Hamilton ii.
———, *Monty: The Field Marshal.* Hamish Hamilton, 1986. Cited as
    Hamilton iii.
Hammond, N.G.L. *Venture into Greece.* Kimber, 1983.
Horne, A. *To Lose a Battle.* Macmillan, 1969.
Horrocks, B. *A Full Life.* Collins, 1960.
Howarth, P. *Intelligence Chief Extraordinary.* Bodley Head, 1986.
Hunt, D. *A Don at War.* Kimber, 1966.
Irving, D. *The Trail of the Fox.* Weidenfeld & Nicolson, 1977.
Jackson, W.G.F. *The North African Campaign.* Batsford, 1975.
———, *The Battle for Italy.* Batsford, 1967.
———, *The Battle for Rome.* Batsford, 1969.
———, *Alexander of Tunis as Military Commander.* Batsford, 1971.
Jenner, R., and D. List. *The Long Range Desert Group.* Osprey, 1983.
Jones, R. V. *Most Secret War.* Hamish Hamilton, 1978.
Kahn, D. *The Codebreakers.* Macmillan, 1967.
Kennedy, J. *The Business of War.* Hutchinson, 1957.
Kesselring, A. *Memoirs.* Kimber, 1974.
Kitson, F. *Warfare as a Whole.* Faber & Faber, 1987.

Lees, M. *Special Operations Executed*. Kimber, 1986.

Lewin, R. *The Life and Death of the Afrika Korps*. Batsford, 1977.

————, *Ultra Goes to War*. Hutchinson, 1978.

————, *The Chief*. Hutchinson, 1980.

————, *Hitler's Mistakes*. Cooper, 1984.

Liddell Hart, B.H. *Memoirs*. 2 vols. Cassell, 1965.

————, *The Other Side of the Hill*. Collins, 1981.

MacLachlan, O. *Room 39: Naval Intelligence in Action, 1939–1945*. Weidenfeld, 1965.

Macksey, K. *Kesselring and the Making of the Luftwaffe*. Batsford, 1978.

Maclean, Fitzroy. *Eastern Approaches*. Cape, 1949.

Martin, D. *Patriot or Traitor? The Case of General Mihailovich*. Hoover Institution, 1979.

Masterman, J. M. *The Double Cross System*. Yale, 1972.

Mellenthin, F. W. von. *Panzer Battles*. Cassell, 1955.

Montgomery, B. L. *El Alamein to the River Sangro*. Hutchinson, 1948.

————, *Memoirs*. Collins, 1958.

Montagu, E. *The Man Who Never Was*. Evans, 1955.

————, *Beyond Top Secret U*. Peter Davies, 1977.

Moorehead, A. *African Trilogy*. Hamish Hamilton, 1944.

Mure, D. *Master of Deception*. Kimber, 1980.

Nicolson, N. *Alex*. Weidenfeld & Nicolson, 1973.

Overy, R. J. *The Air War 1939–1945*. Europa Publishers, 1980.

Parrish, T. *The Ultra Americans*. Stein & Day, 1986.

Pope, D. *Flag 4*. Kimber, 1954.

Richardson, C. *Flashback*. Kimber, 1985.

Roberts, W. R. *Tito, Mihajlović and the Allies*. Rutgers, 1973.

Rhodes, James, R. *Anthony Eden*. Weidenfeld & Nicolson, 1986.

Rohwer, J., and E. Jaeckel, eds. *Die Funkaufklaerung und ihre Rolle im Zweiten Weltkrieg*. Stuttgart: Motorbuch, 1979.

Rommel, E. *The Rommel Papers*. Ed. B. H. Liddell Hart. Harcourt Brace, 1953.

Roskill, S. W. *The War at Sea*. 3 vols. HMSO, 1954–61.

Santoni, A. *Il vero traditore*. Mursia, 1981.

Schmidt, H. W. *With Rommel in the Desert*. Harrap, 1951.

Senger und Etterlin, F. von. *Neither Fear Nor Hope*. Macdonald, 1963.

Shaw, W. B. Kennedy. *The Long Range Desert Group*. Collins, 1945.

Smith, B. F., and E. Agarossi. *Operation Sunrise*. Deutsch, 1979.

Stafford, D. *Britain and European Resistance*. Macmillan, 1980.

Strong, K.W.D. *Intelligence at the Top*. Cassell, 1968.

Sweet-Escott, B. *Baker Street Irregular*. Methuen, 1965.

Tedder, A. R. *With Prejudice*. Cassell, 1966.

Terraine, J. *The Right of the Line: The RAF 1939–1945*. Hodder & Stoughton, 1985.

Trevelyan, R. *The Fortress*. Cooper, 1956.

——, *Rome '44*. Secker & Warburg, 1981.

Trevor-Roper, H. R. *Hitler's War Directives*. Sidgwick & Jackson, 1964.

Vaughan Thomas, W. *Anzio*. Longman, 1961.

Verney, P. *Anzio*. Batsford, 1978.

Wark, W. K. *The Ultimate Enemy*. Cornell, 1985.

Wavell, A. P. "Operations in the Middle East from 7 February 1941 to 15 July 1941." Supplement to *The London Gazette*, 3 July 1946.

Welchman, G. *The Hut Six Story*. McGraw-Hill, 1982.

——, "From Polish Bomba to British Bombe: The Birth of Ultra." *Intelligence and National Security* 1, 71–110.

Westphal, S. *The German Army in the West*. Cassell, 1951.

——, *Erinnerungen*. Von Hase und Koehler, 1975.

Wheeler, M. C. *Britain and the War for Jugoslavia 1940–43*. Columbia, 1980.

Wilson, D. *Tito's Jugoslavia*. Cambridge, 1979.

Winterbotham, F. W. *The Ultra Secret*. Weidenfeld & Nicolson, 1974.

Young, D. *Rommel*. Collins, 1950.

Zuckerman, S. *From Apes to Warlords*. Hamish Hamilton, 1978.

INDEX